D1239318

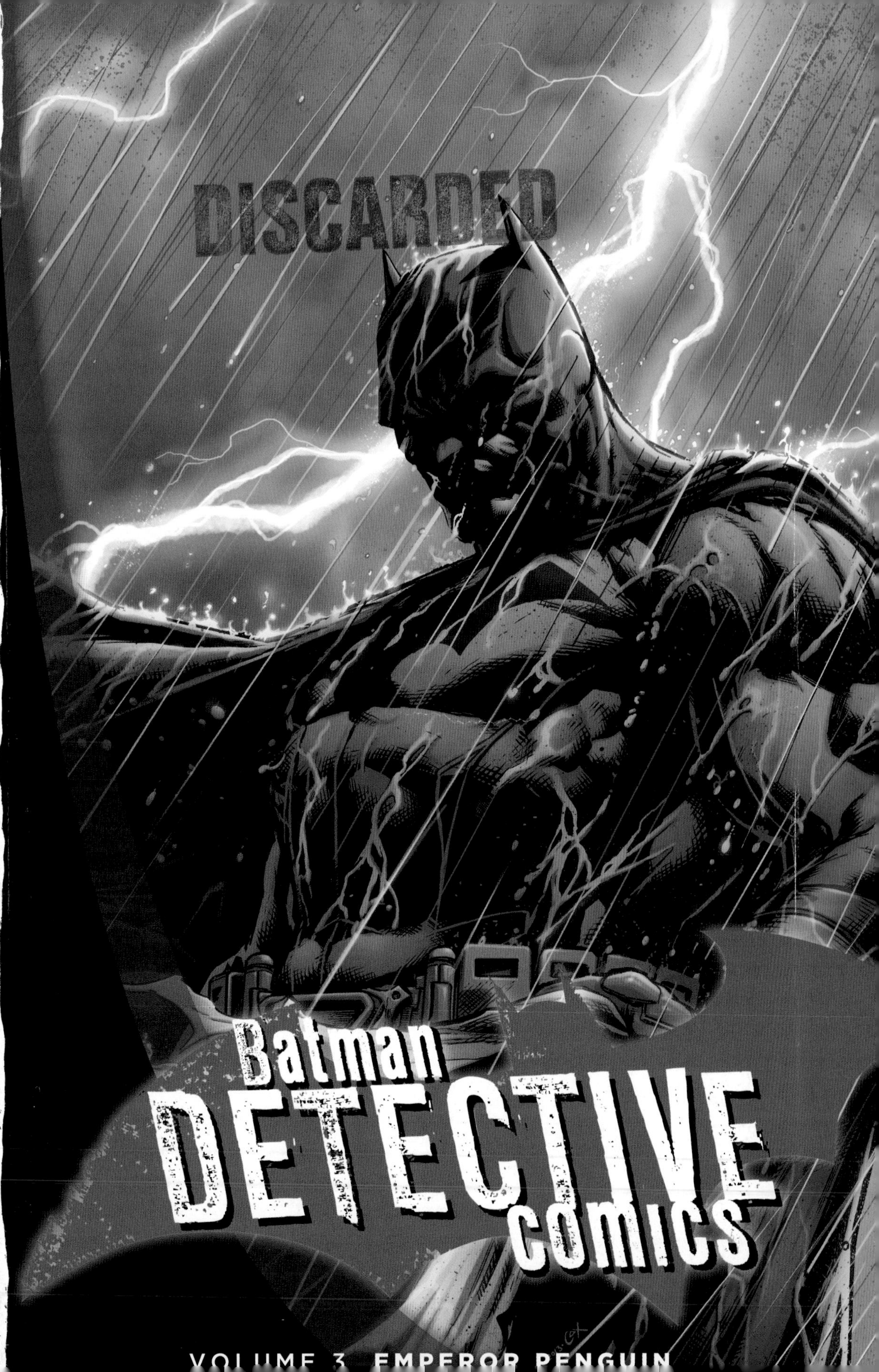
Batman
DETECTIVE
comics
VOLUME 3 EMPEROR PENGUIN

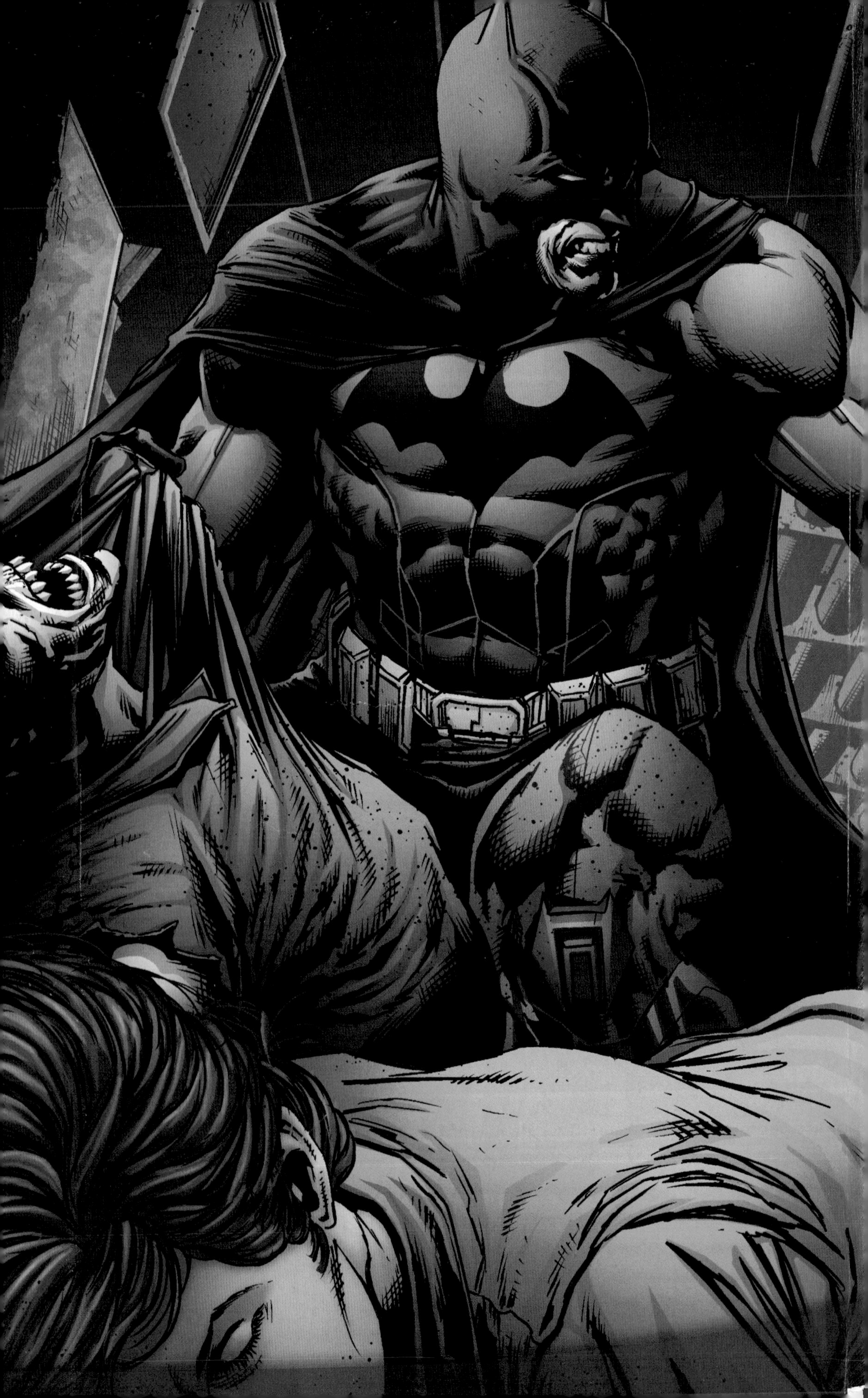

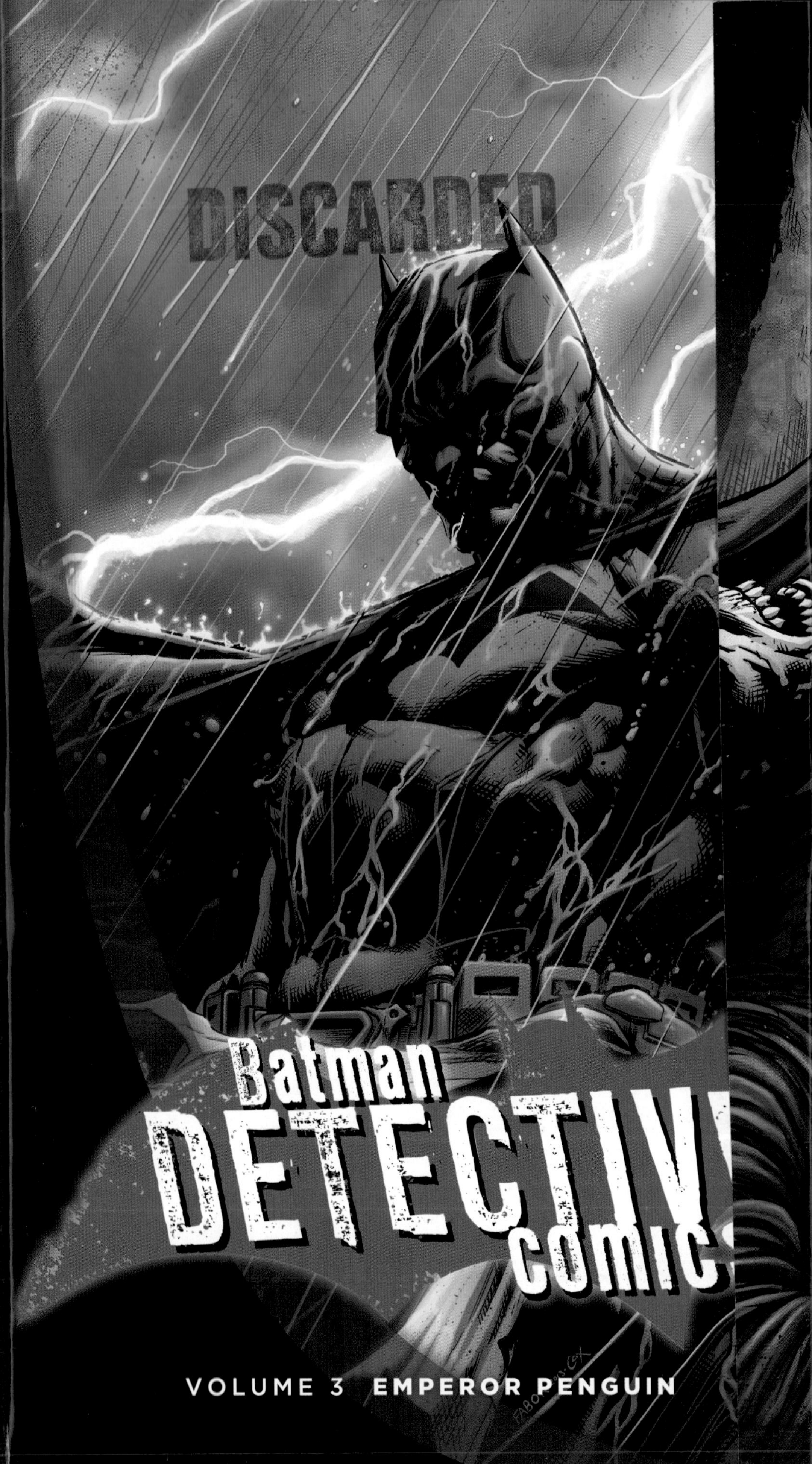
DISCARDED
Batman
DETECTIV
COMIC
VOLUME 3 EMPEROR PENGUIN

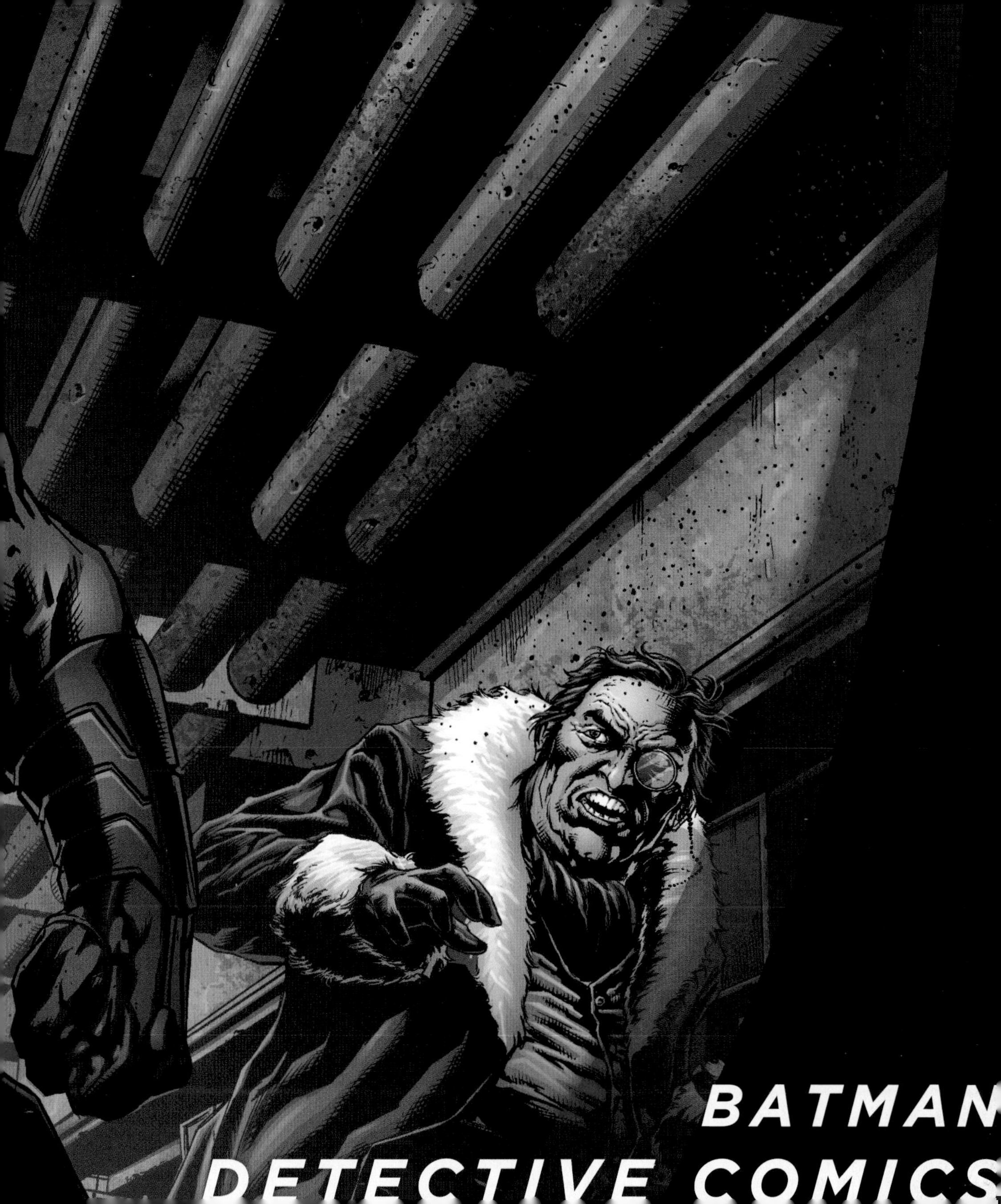
BATMAN
DETECTIVE COMICS

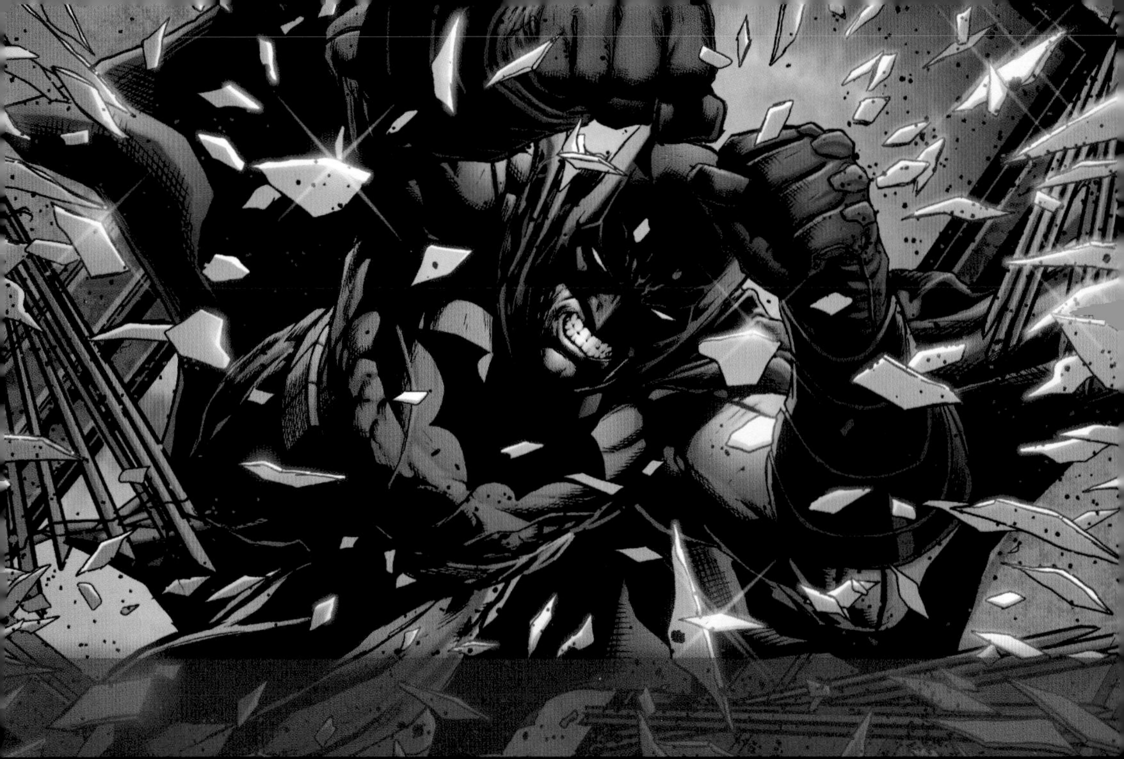

MIKE MARTS Editor - Original Series KATIE KUBERT HARVEY RICHARDS Associate Editors - Original Series
RACHEL PINNELAS Editor ROBBIN BROSTERMAN Design Director - Books
ROBBIE BIEDERMAN Publication Design

BOB HARRAS Senior VP - Editor-in-Chief, DC Comics

DIANE NELSON President DAN DIDIO and JIM LEE Co-Publishers
GEOFF JOHNS Chief Creative Officer
JOHN ROOD Executive VP - Sales, Marketing and Business Development
AMY GENKINS Senior VP - Business and Legal Affairs NAIRI GARDINER Senior VP - Finance
JEFF BOISON VP - Publishing Planning MARK CHIARELLO VP - Art Direction and Design
JOHN CUNNINGHAM VP - Marketing TERRI CUNNINGHAM VP - Editorial Administration
ALISON GILL Senior VP - Manufacturing and Operations HANK KANALZ Senior VP - Vertigo & Integrated Publishing
JAY KOGAN VP - Business and Legal Affairs, Publishing JACK MAHAN VP - Business Affairs, Talent
NICK NAPOLITANO VP - Manufacturing Administration SUE POHJA VP - Book Sales
COURTNEY SIMMONS Senior VP - Publicity BOB WAYNE Senior VP - Sales

BATMAN - DETECTIVE COMICS VOLUME 3: EMPEROR PENGUIN

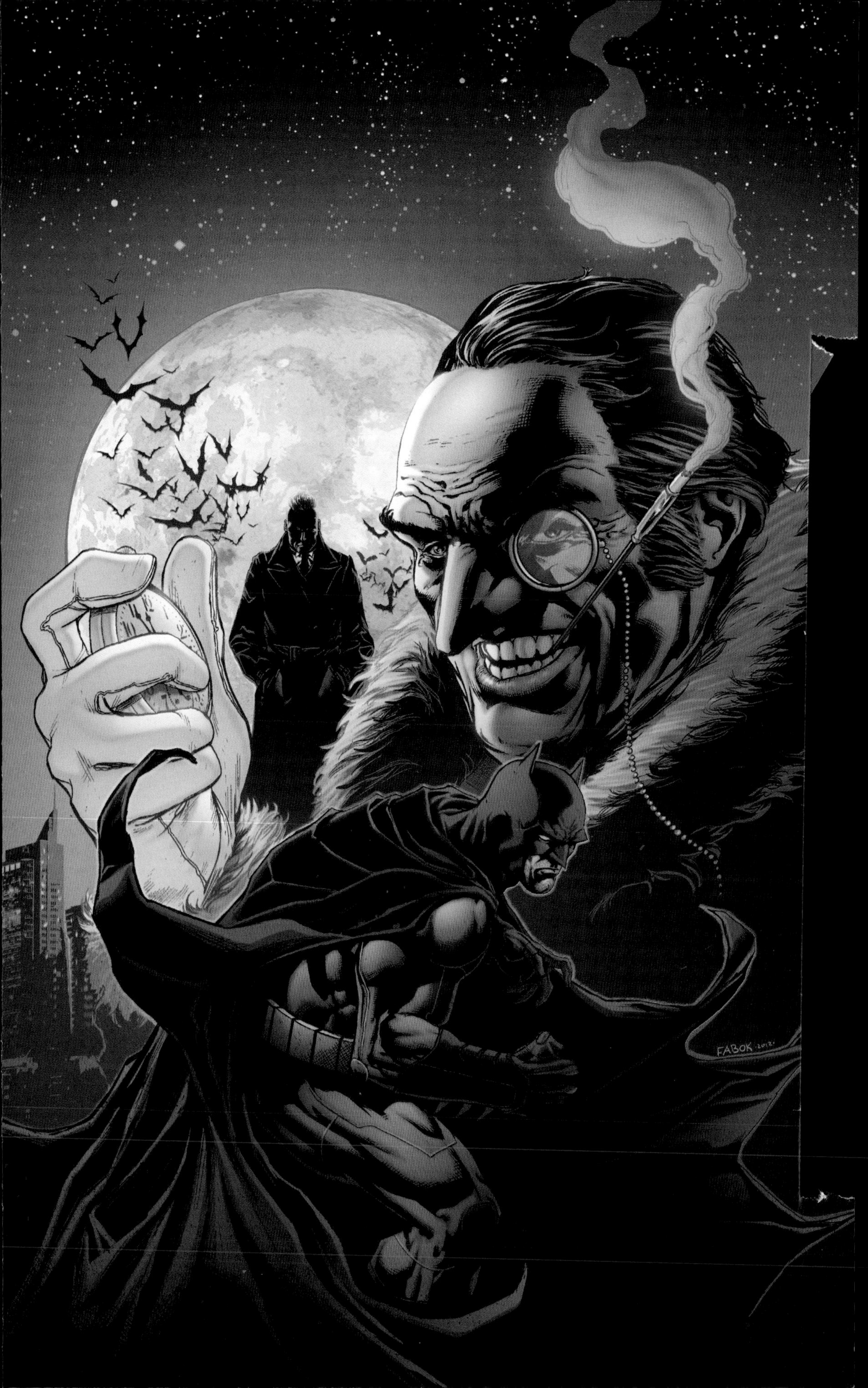
FABOK 2012

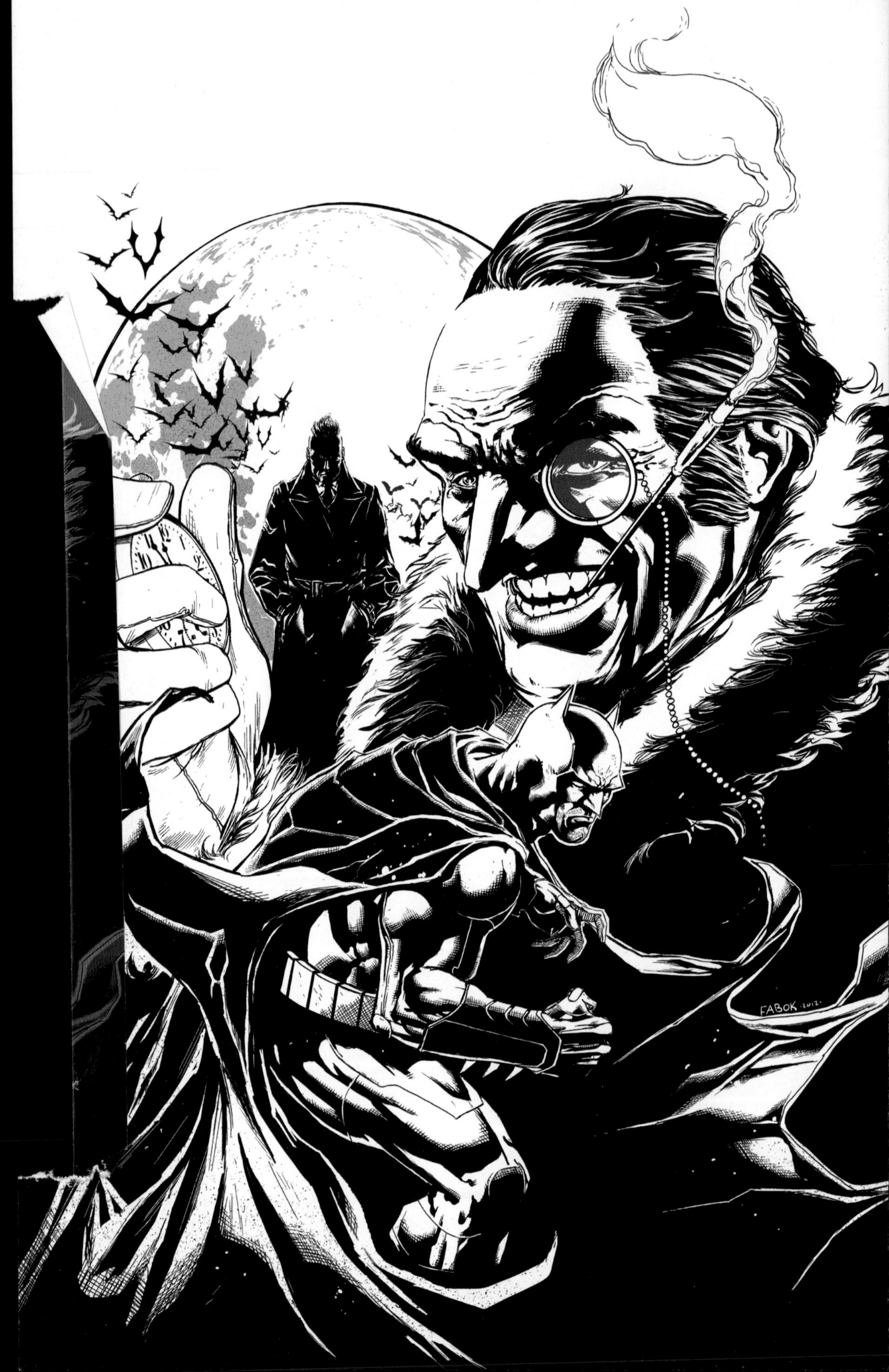
FABOK 2012

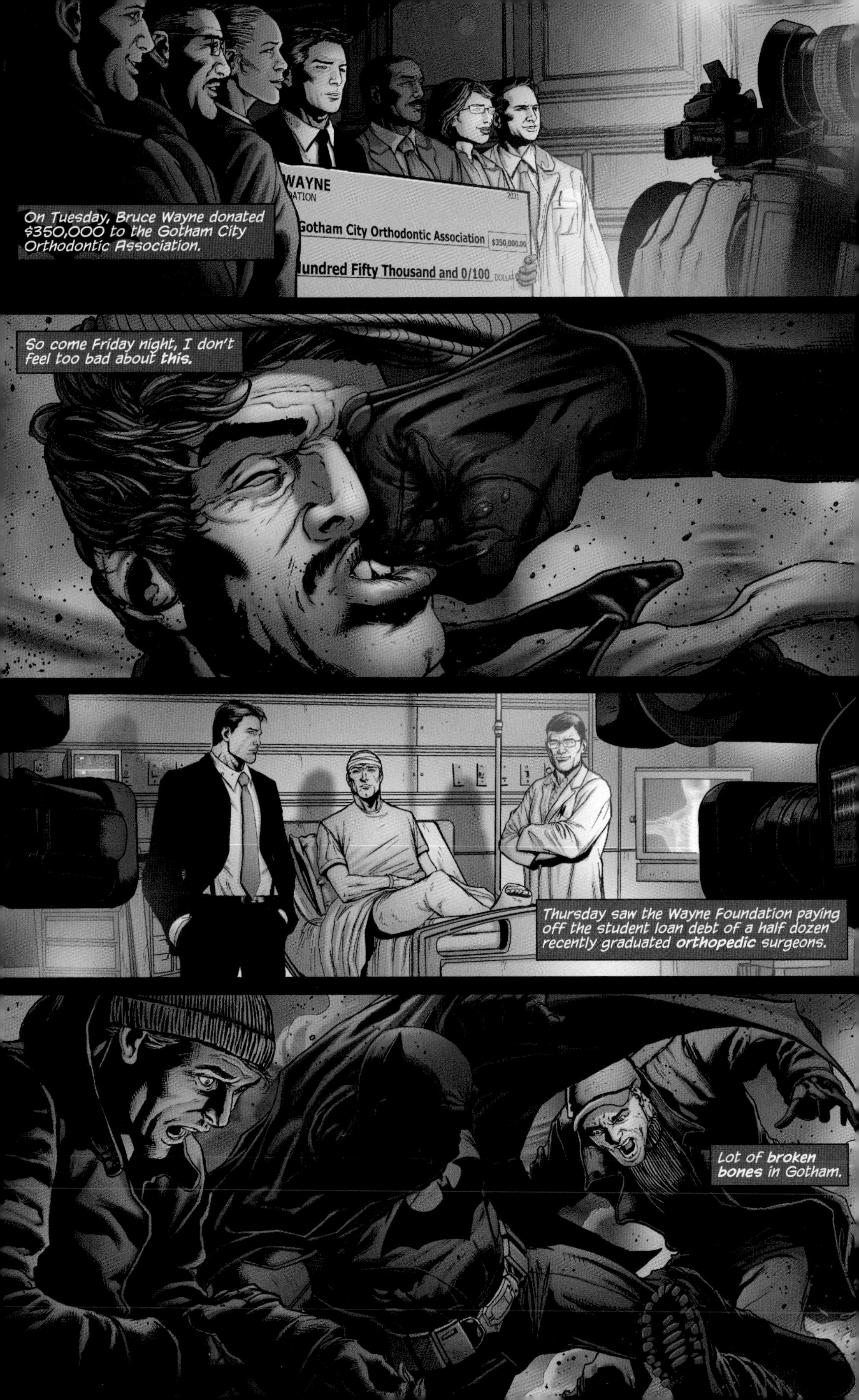
WAYNE
DATION
2031
Gotham City Orthodontic Association
$350,000.00
Hundred Fifty Thousand and 0/100
On Tuesday, Bruce Wayne donated $350,000 to the Gotham City Orthodontic Association.
So come Friday night, I don't feel too bad about this.
Thursday saw the Wayne Foundation paying off the student loan debt of a half dozen recently graduated orthopedic surgeons.
Lot of broken bones in Gotham.

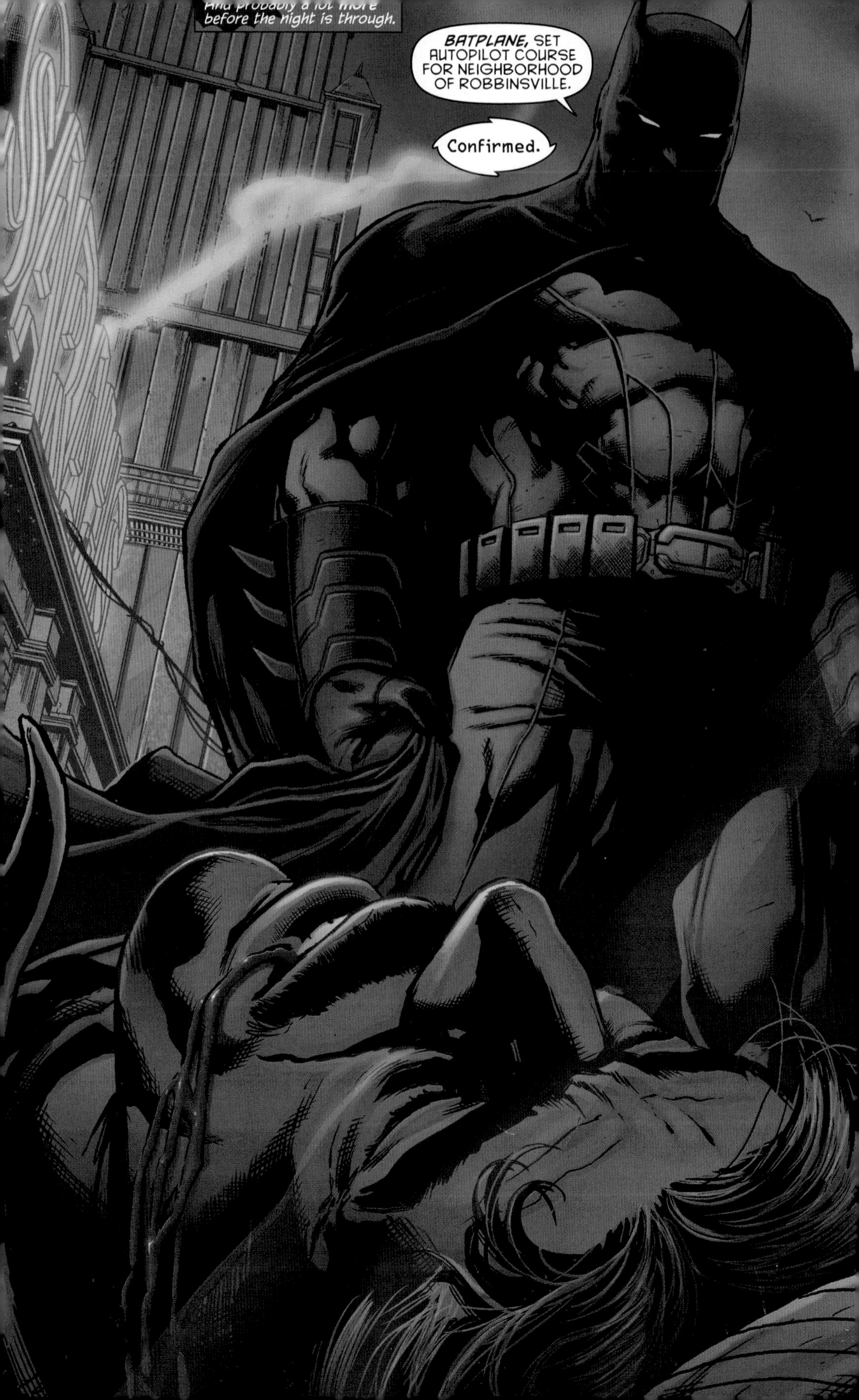
And probably a lot more
before the night is through.
BATPLANE, SET AUTOPILOT COURSE FOR NEIGHBORHOOD OF ROBBINSVILLE.
Confirmed.

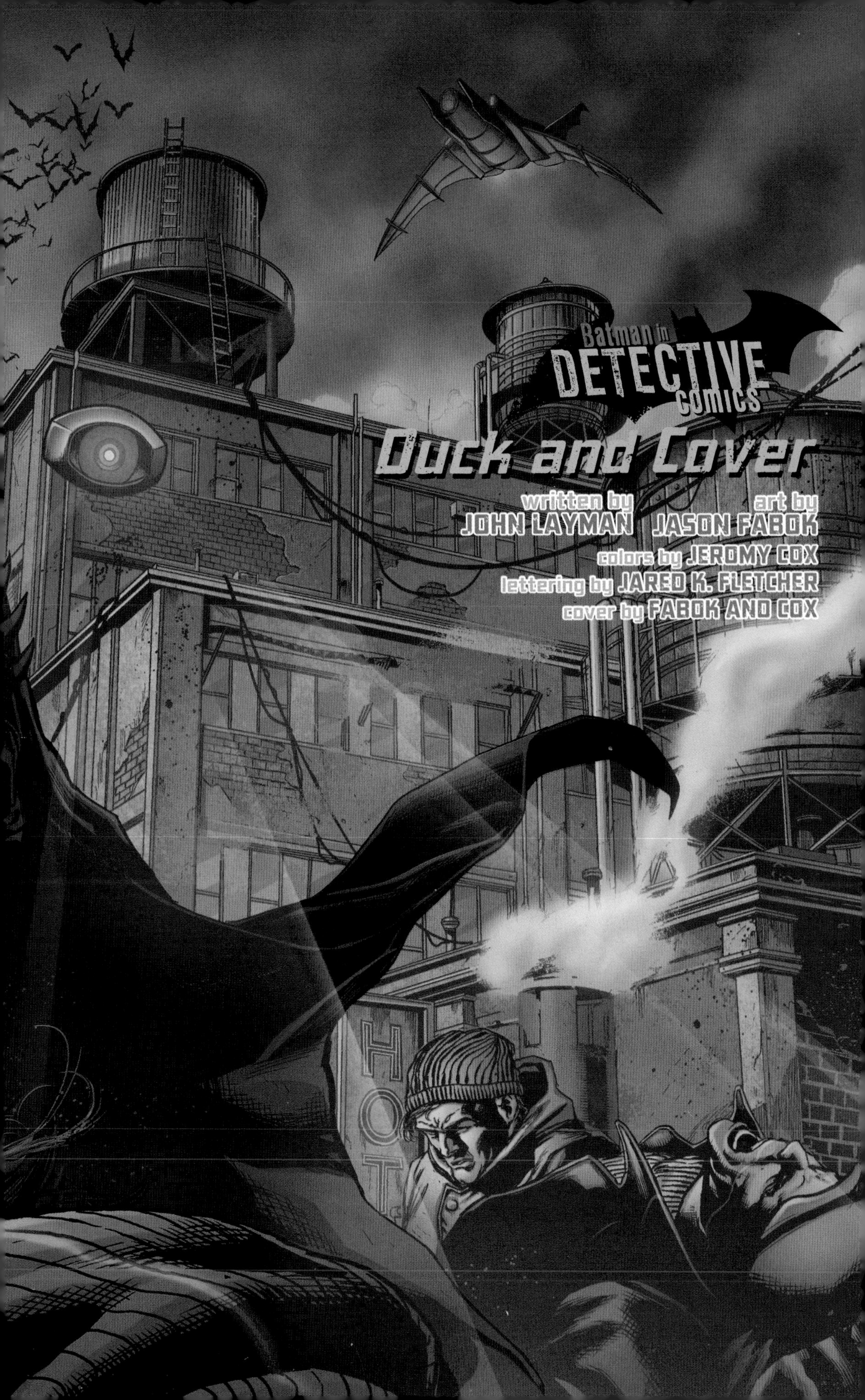
Batman in DETECTIVE COMICS
Duck and Cover
written by JOHN LAYMAN
art by JASON FABOK
colors by JEROMY COX
lettering by JARED K. FLETCHER
cover by FABOK AND COX
HOT

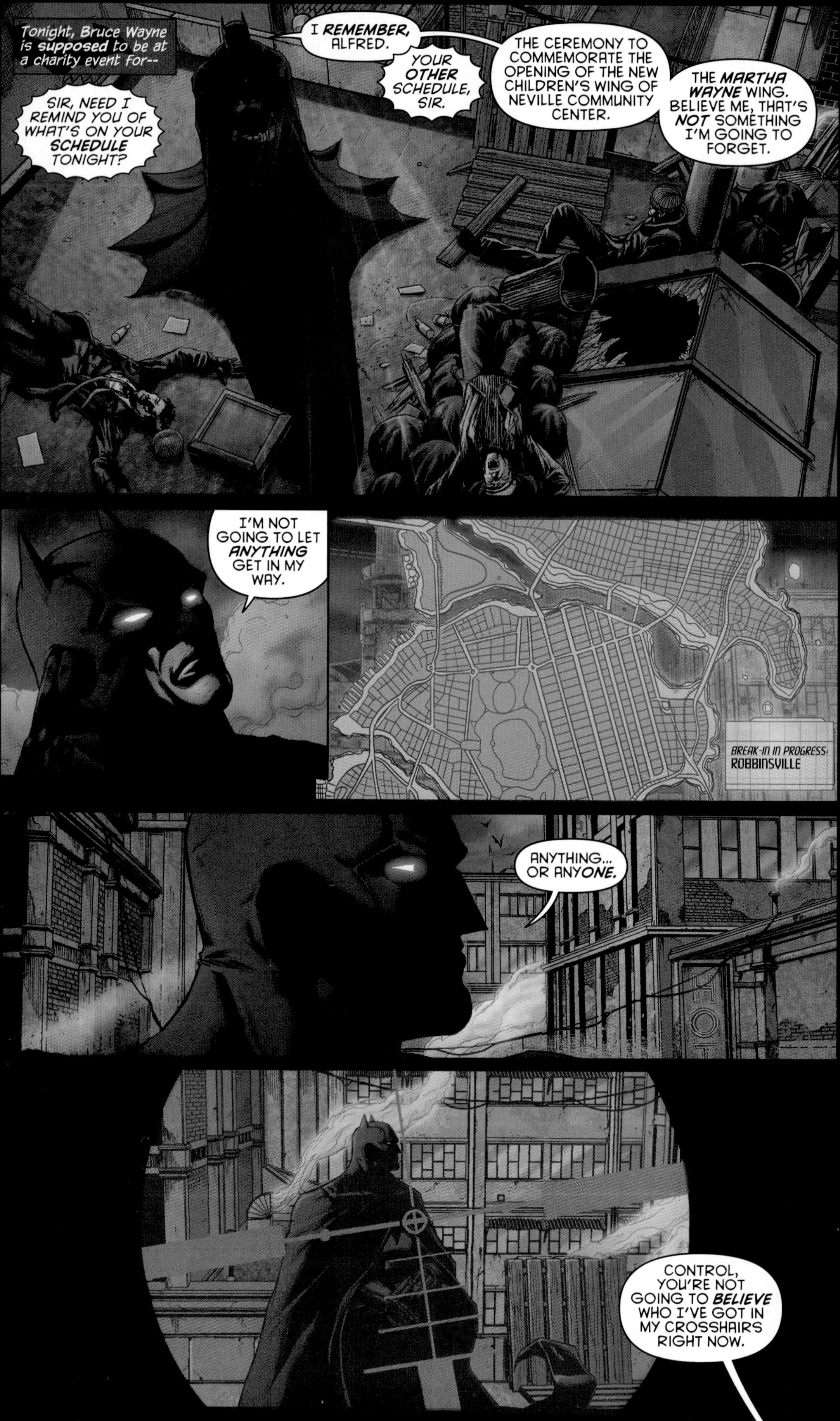
Tonight, Bruce Wayne is supposed to be at a charity event for--
SIR, NEED I REMIND YOU OF WHAT'S ON YOUR SCHEDULE TONIGHT?
I REMEMBER, ALFRED.
YOUR OTHER SCHEDULE, SIR.
THE CEREMONY TO COMMEMORATE THE OPENING OF THE NEW CHILDREN'S WING OF NEVILLE COMMUNITY CENTER.
THE MARTHA WAYNE WING. BELIEVE ME, THAT'S NOT SOMETHING I'M GOING TO FORGET.
I'M NOT GOING TO LET ANYTHING GET IN MY WAY.
BREAK-IN IN PROGRESS:
ROBBINSVILLE
ANYTHING... OR ANYONE.
CONTROL, YOU'RE NOT GOING TO BELIEVE WHO I'VE GOT IN MY CROSSHAIRS RIGHT NOW.

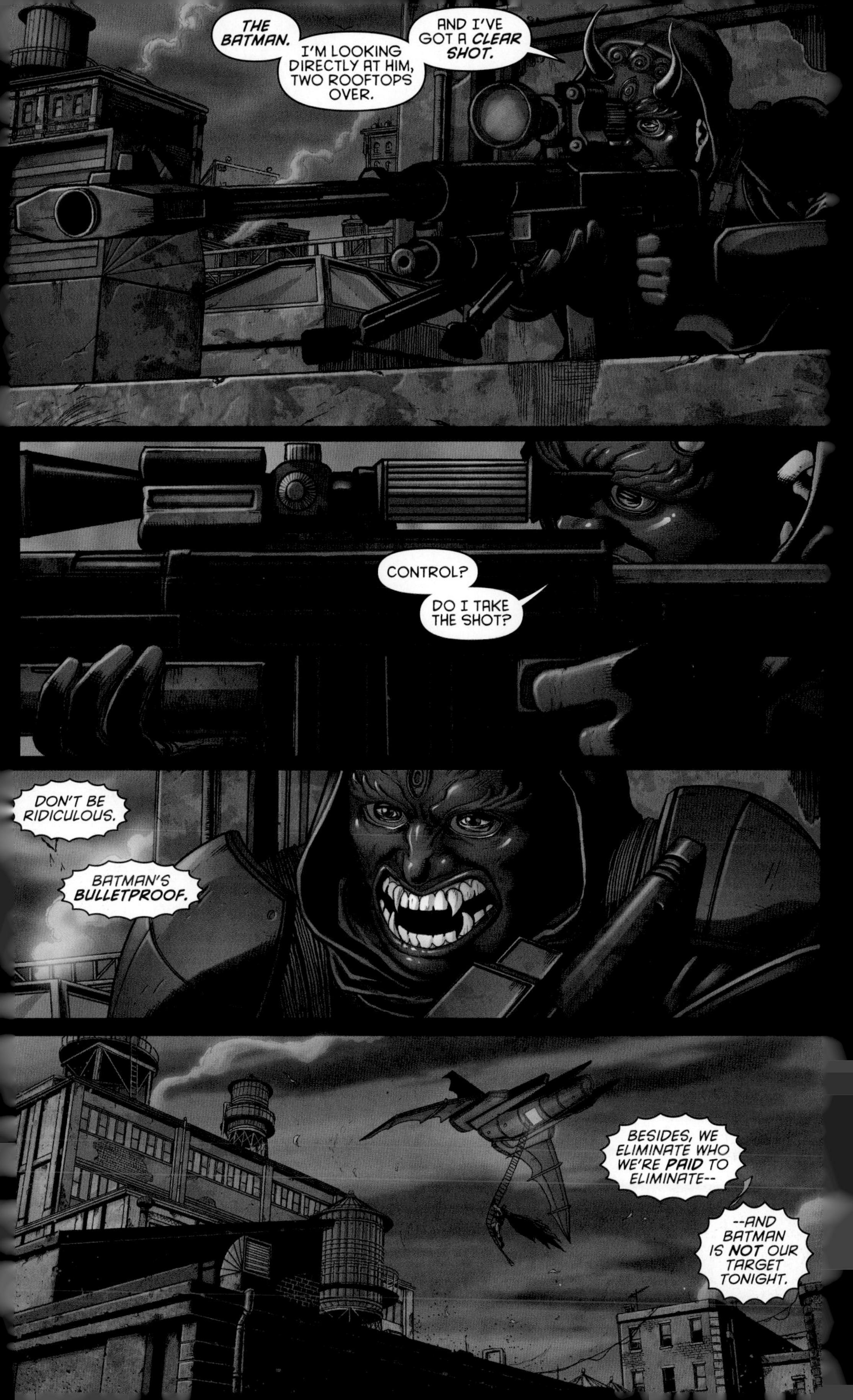
THE BATMAN.
I'M LOOKING DIRECTLY AT HIM, TWO ROOFTOPS OVER.
AND I'VE GOT A CLEAR SHOT.
CONTROL?
DO I TAKE THE SHOT?
DON'T BE RIDICULOUS.
BATMAN'S BULLETPROOF.
BESIDES, WE ELIMINATE WHO WE'RE PAID TO ELIMINATE--
--AND BATMAN IS NOT OUR TARGET TONIGHT.

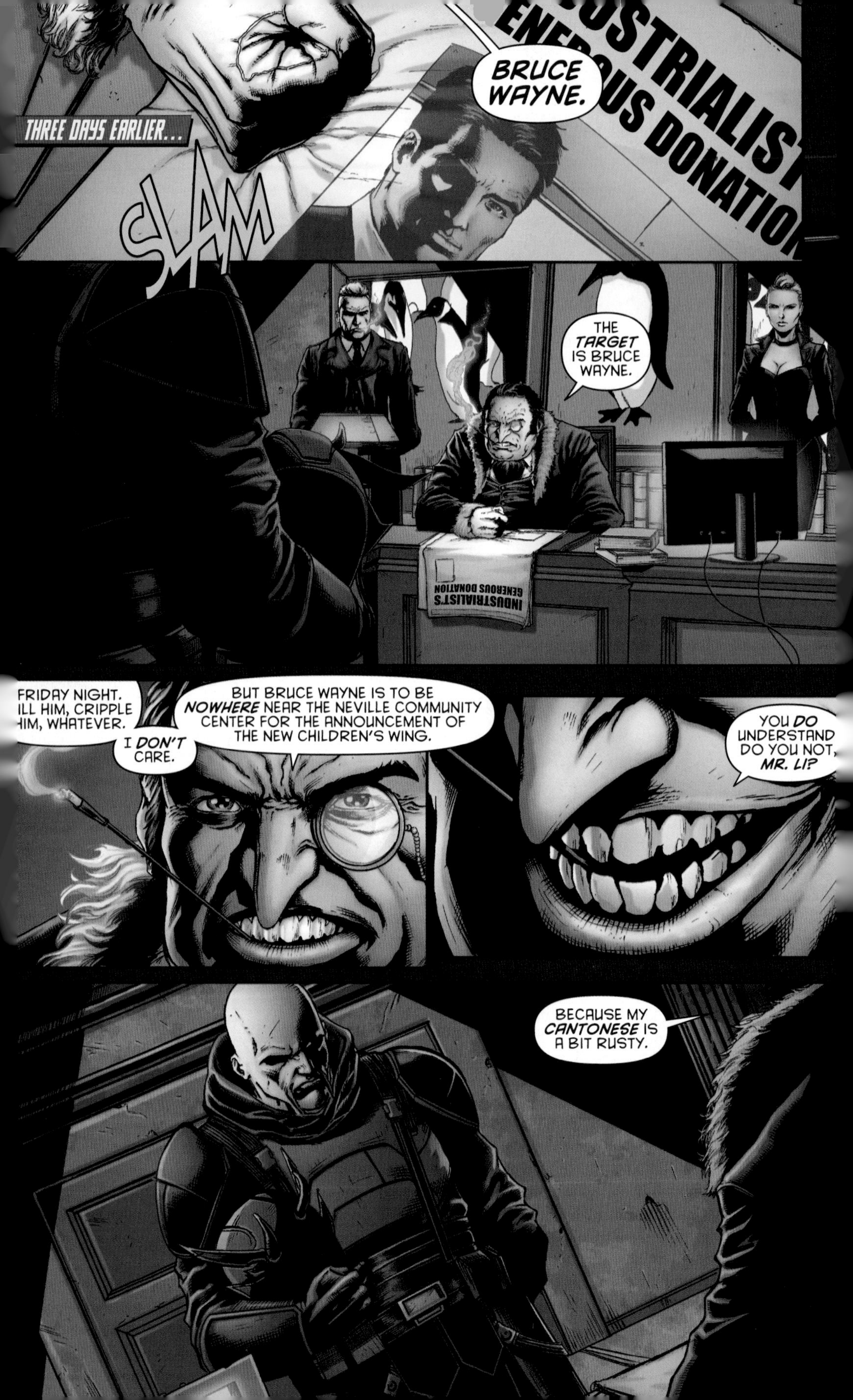
BRUCE WAYNE.
THREE DAYS EARLIER...
SLAM
INDUSTRIALIST'S GENEROUS DONATION
THE TARGET IS BRUCE WAYNE.
FRIDAY NIGHT. ILL HIM, CRIPPLE HIM, WHATEVER.
I DON'T CARE.
BUT BRUCE WAYNE IS TO BE NOWHERE NEAR THE NEVILLE COMMUNITY CENTER FOR THE ANNOUNCEMENT OF THE NEW CHILDREN'S WING.
YOU DO UNDERSTAND DO YOU NOT, MR. LI?
BECAUSE MY CANTONESE IS A BIT RUSTY.

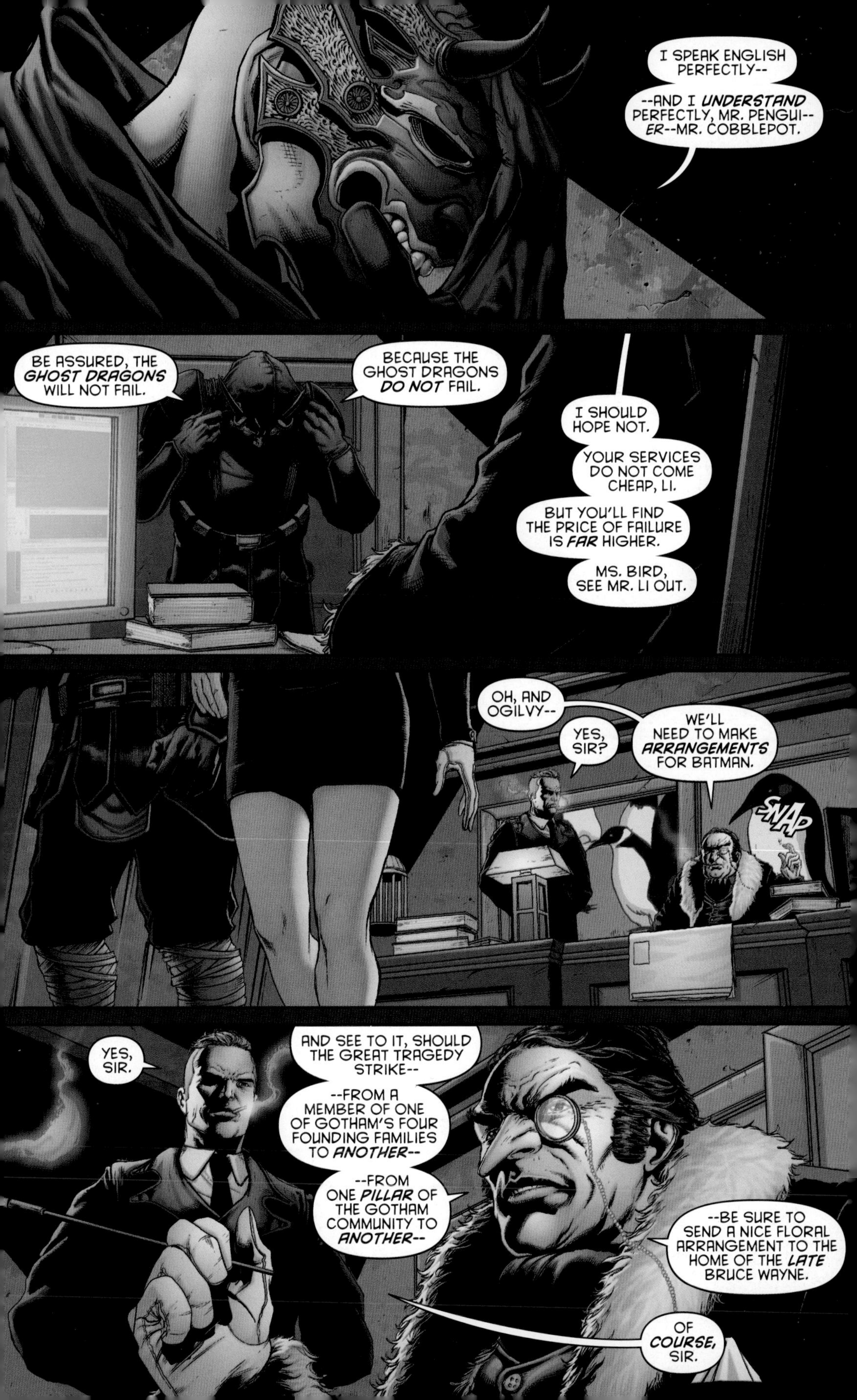

I SPEAK ENGLISH PERFECTLY--
--AND I *UNDERSTAND* PERFECTLY, MR. PENGUI-- *ER*--MR. COBBLEPOT.
BE ASSURED, THE *GHOST DRAGONS* WILL NOT FAIL.
BECAUSE THE GHOST DRAGONS *DO NOT* FAIL.
I SHOULD HOPE NOT.
YOUR SERVICES DO NOT COME CHEAP, LI.
BUT YOU'LL FIND THE PRICE OF FAILURE IS *FAR* HIGHER.
MS. BIRD, SEE MR. LI OUT.
OH, AND OGILVY--
YES, SIR?
WE'LL NEED TO MAKE *ARRANGEMENTS* FOR BATMAN.
SNAP
YES, SIR.
AND SEE TO IT, SHOULD THE GREAT TRAGEDY STRIKE--
--FROM A MEMBER OF ONE OF GOTHAM'S FOUR FOUNDING FAMILIES TO *ANOTHER*--
--FROM ONE *PILLAR* OF THE GOTHAM COMMUNITY TO *ANOTHER*--
--BE SURE TO SEND A NICE FLORAL ARRANGEMENT TO THE HOME OF THE *LATE* BRUCE WAYNE.
OF *COURSE,* SIR.

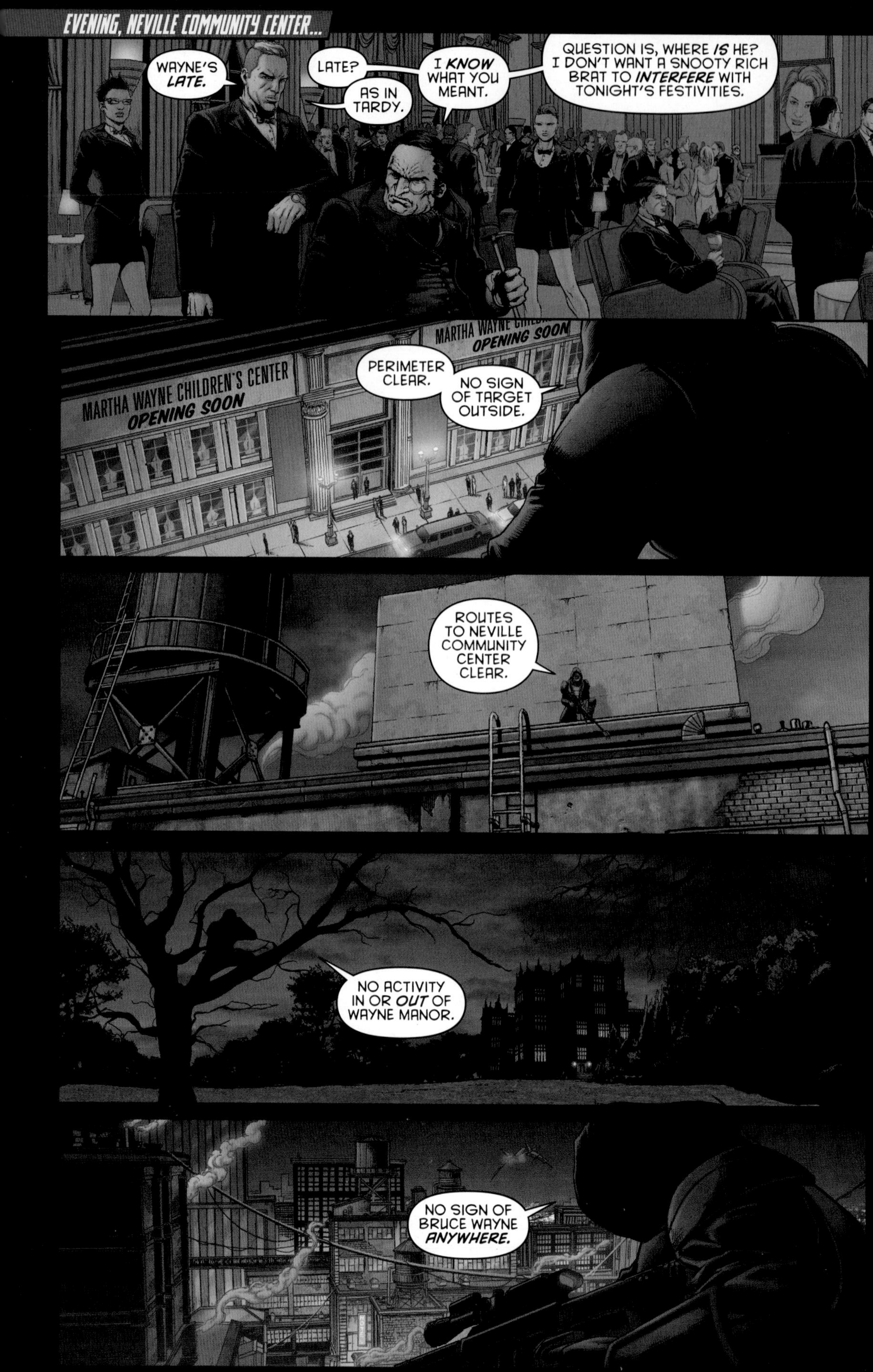
EVENING, NEVILLE COMMUNITY CENTER...
WAYNE'S LATE.
LATE?
AS IN TARDY.
I KNOW WHAT YOU MEANT.
QUESTION IS, WHERE IS HE? I DON'T WANT A SNOOTY RICH BRAT TO INTERFERE WITH TONIGHT'S FESTIVITIES.
MARTHA WAYNE CHILDREN'S CENTER OPENING SOON
PERIMETER CLEAR.
NO SIGN OF TARGET OUTSIDE.
ROUTES TO NEVILLE COMMUNITY CENTER CLEAR.
NO ACTIVITY IN OR OUT OF WAYNE MANOR.
NO SIGN OF BRUCE WAYNE ANYWHERE.

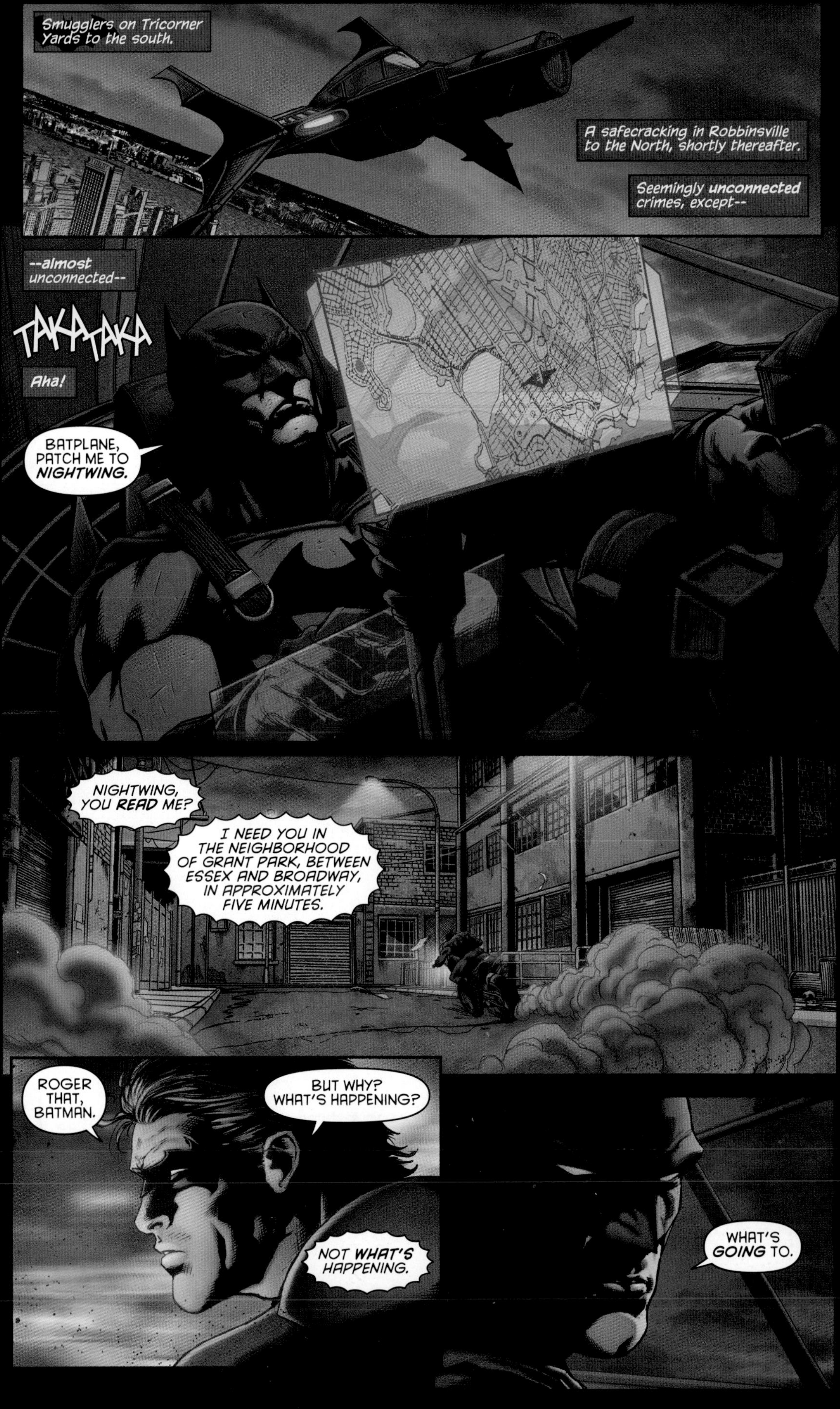

Smugglers on Tricorner Yards to the south.
A safecracking in Robbinsville to the North, shortly thereafter.
Seemingly unconnected crimes, except--
--almost unconnected--
TAKATAKA
Aha!
BATPLANE, PATCH ME TO NIGHTWING.
NIGHTWING, YOU READ ME?
I NEED YOU IN THE NEIGHBORHOOD OF GRANT PARK, BETWEEN ESSEX AND BROADWAY, IN APPROXIMATELY FIVE MINUTES.
ROGER THAT, BATMAN.
BUT WHY? WHAT'S HAPPENING?
NOT WHAT'S HAPPENING.
WHAT'S GOING TO.

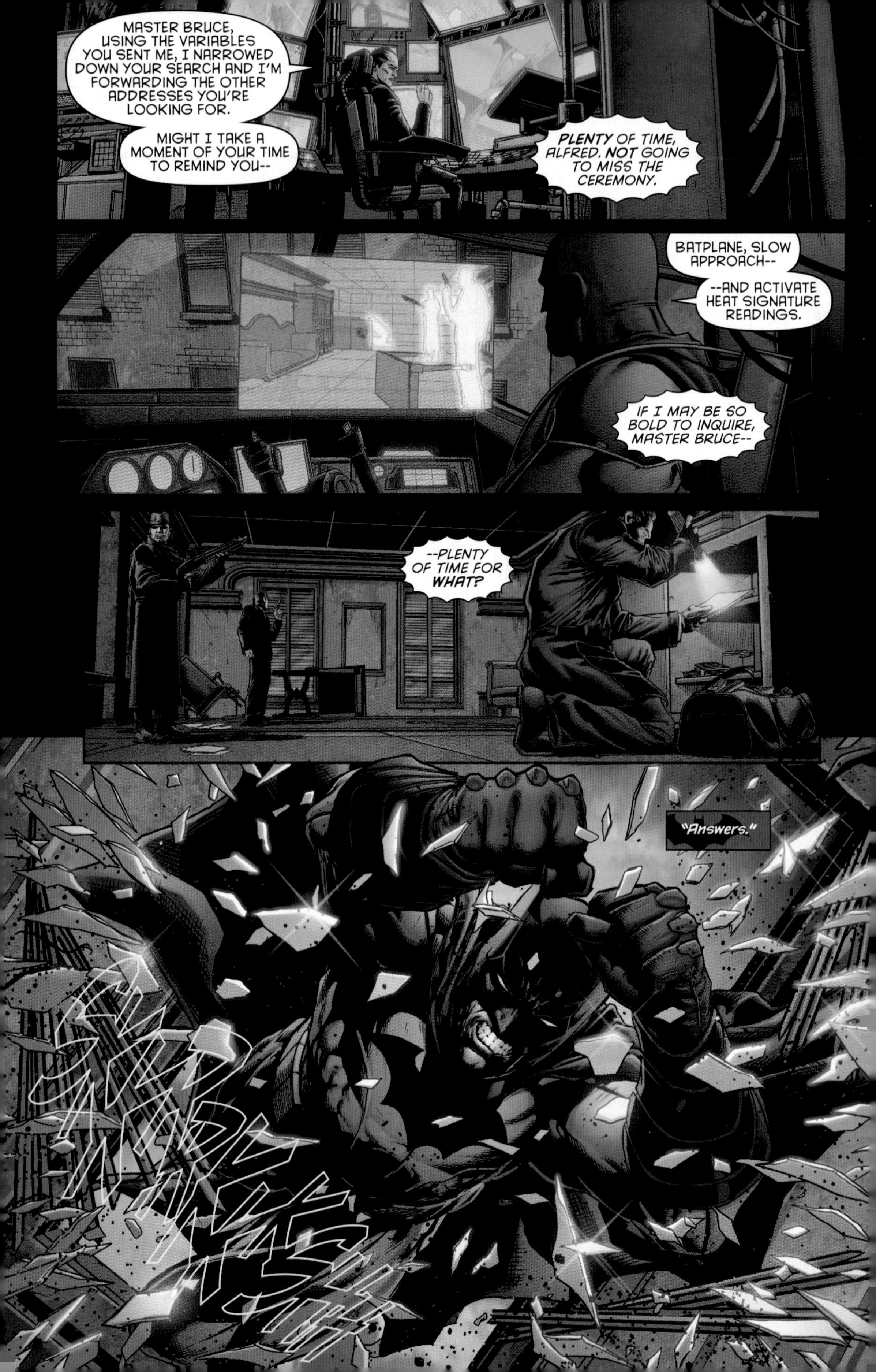
MASTER BRUCE, USING THE VARIABLES YOU SENT ME, I NARROWED DOWN YOUR SEARCH AND I'M FORWARDING THE OTHER ADDRESSES YOU'RE LOOKING FOR.
MIGHT I TAKE A MOMENT OF YOUR TIME TO REMIND YOU--
PLENTY OF TIME, ALFRED. *NOT* GOING TO MISS THE CEREMONY.
BATPLANE, SLOW APPROACH--
--AND ACTIVATE HEAT SIGNATURE READINGS.
IF I MAY BE SO BOLD TO INQUIRE, MASTER BRUCE--
--PLENTY OF TIME FOR *WHAT?*
"Answers."

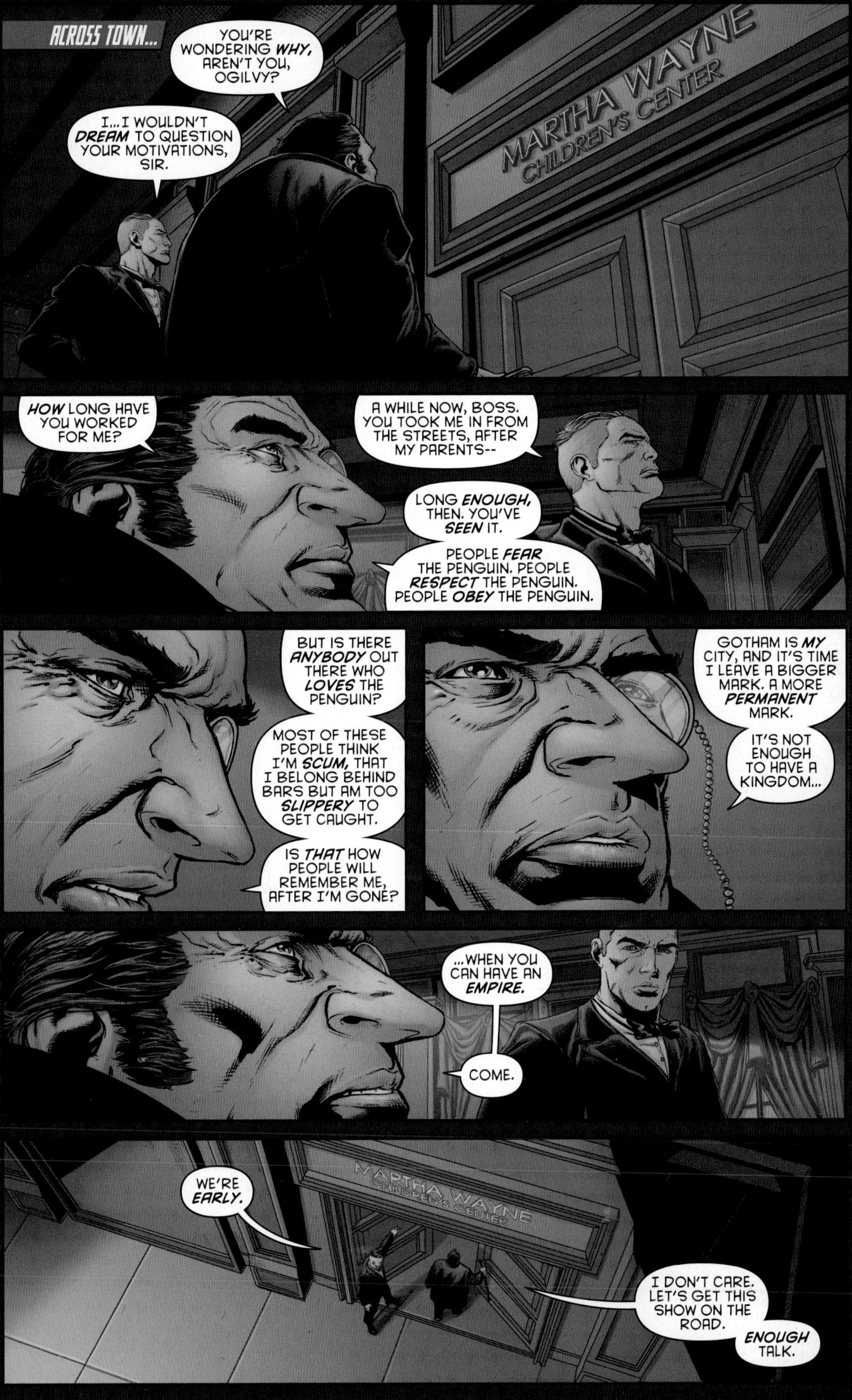
ACROSS TOWN...
YOU'RE WONDERING WHY, AREN'T YOU, OGILVY?
I...I WOULDN'T DREAM TO QUESTION YOUR MOTIVATIONS, SIR.
MARTHA WAYNE CHILDREN'S CENTER
HOW LONG HAVE YOU WORKED FOR ME?
A WHILE NOW, BOSS. YOU TOOK ME IN FROM THE STREETS, AFTER MY PARENTS--
LONG ENOUGH, THEN. YOU'VE SEEN IT.
PEOPLE FEAR THE PENGUIN. PEOPLE RESPECT THE PENGUIN. PEOPLE OBEY THE PENGUIN.
BUT IS THERE ANYBODY OUT THERE WHO LOVES THE PENGUIN?
MOST OF THESE PEOPLE THINK I'M SCUM, THAT I BELONG BEHIND BARS BUT AM TOO SLIPPERY TO GET CAUGHT.
IS THAT HOW PEOPLE WILL REMEMBER ME, AFTER I'M GONE?
GOTHAM IS MY CITY, AND IT'S TIME I LEAVE A BIGGER MARK. A MORE PERMANENT MARK.
IT'S NOT ENOUGH TO HAVE A KINGDOM...
...WHEN YOU CAN HAVE AN EMPIRE.
COME.
MARTHA WAYNE CHILDREN'S CENTER
WE'RE EARLY.
I DON'T CARE. LET'S GET THIS SHOW ON THE ROAD.
ENOUGH TALK.

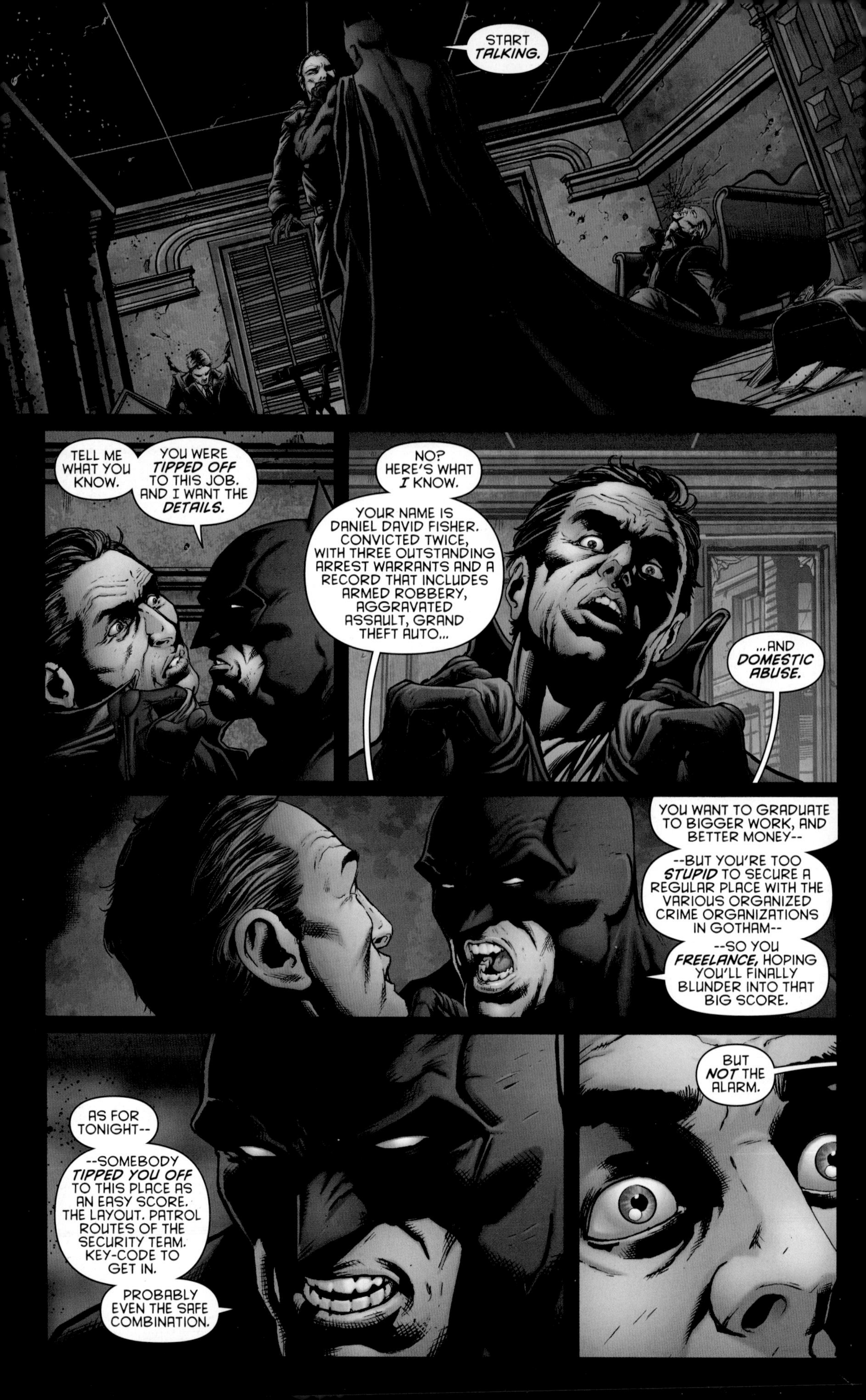
START TALKING.
TELL ME WHAT YOU KNOW.
YOU WERE TIPPED OFF TO THIS JOB. AND I WANT THE DETAILS.
NO? HERE'S WHAT I KNOW.
YOUR NAME IS DANIEL DAVID FISHER. CONVICTED TWICE, WITH THREE OUTSTANDING ARREST WARRANTS AND A RECORD THAT INCLUDES ARMED ROBBERY, AGGRAVATED ASSAULT, GRAND THEFT AUTO...
...AND DOMESTIC ABUSE.
YOU WANT TO GRADUATE TO BIGGER WORK, AND BETTER MONEY--
--BUT YOU'RE TOO STUPID TO SECURE A REGULAR PLACE WITH THE VARIOUS ORGANIZED CRIME ORGANIZATIONS IN GOTHAM--
--SO YOU FREELANCE, HOPING YOU'LL FINALLY BLUNDER INTO THAT BIG SCORE.
AS FOR TONIGHT--
--SOMEBODY TIPPED YOU OFF TO THIS PLACE AS AN EASY SCORE. THE LAYOUT. PATROL ROUTES OF THE SECURITY TEAM. KEY-CODE TO GET IN.
PROBABLY EVEN THE SAFE COMBINATION.
BUT NOT THE ALARM.

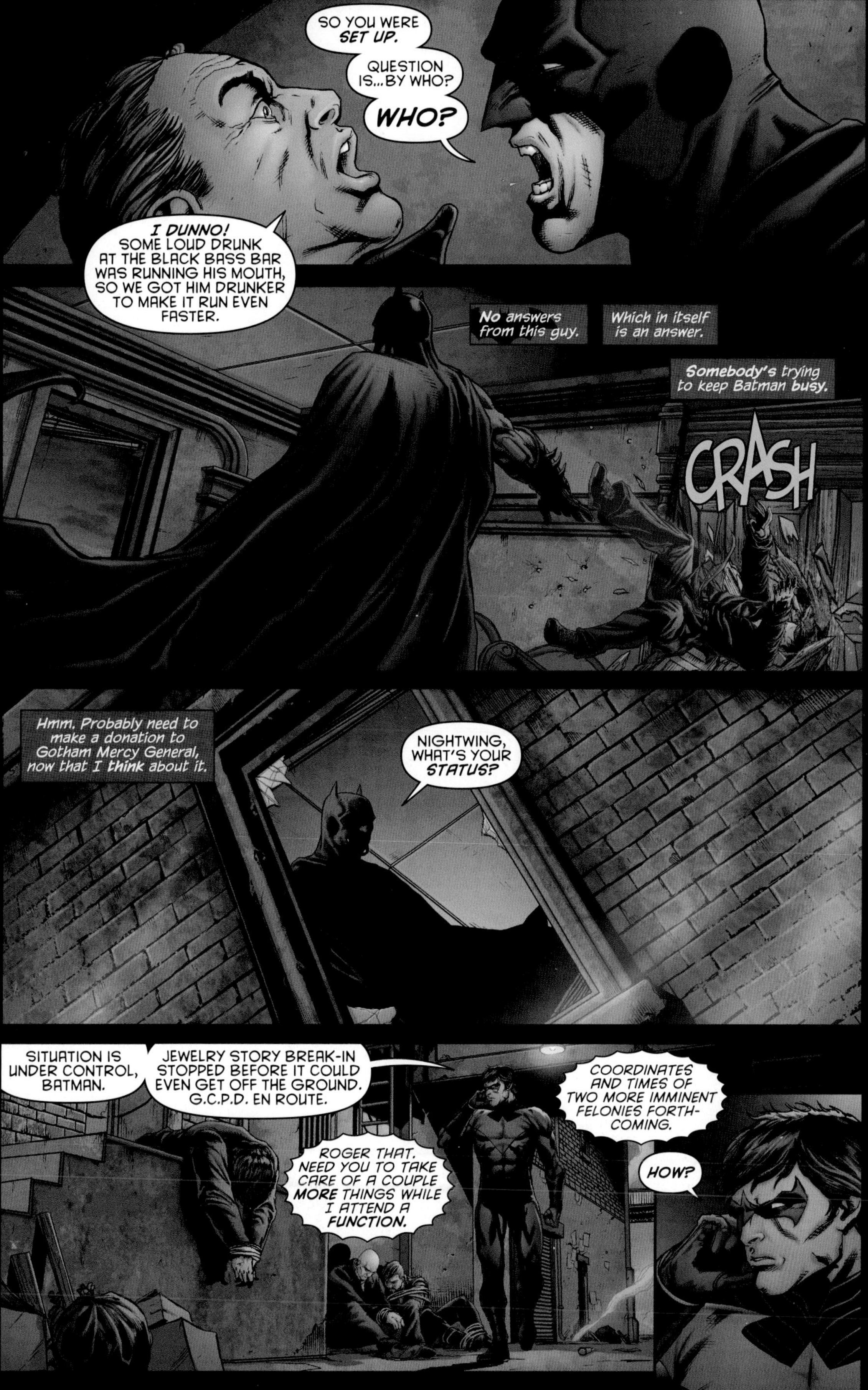

SO YOU WERE SET UP.
QUESTION IS...BY WHO?
WHO?
I DUNNO! SOME LOUD DRUNK AT THE BLACK BASS BAR WAS RUNNING HIS MOUTH, SO WE GOT HIM DRUNKER TO MAKE IT RUN EVEN FASTER.
No answers from this guy.
Which in itself is an answer.
Somebody's trying to keep Batman busy.
CRASH
Hmm. Probably need to make a donation to Gotham Mercy General, now that I think about it.
NIGHTWING, WHAT'S YOUR STATUS?
SITUATION IS UNDER CONTROL, BATMAN.
JEWELRY STORY BREAK-IN STOPPED BEFORE IT COULD EVEN GET OFF THE GROUND. G.C.P.D. EN ROUTE.
ROGER THAT. NEED YOU TO TAKE CARE OF A COUPLE MORE THINGS WHILE I ATTEND A FUNCTION.
COORDINATES AND TIMES OF TWO MORE IMMINENT FELONIES FORTH-COMING.
HOW?

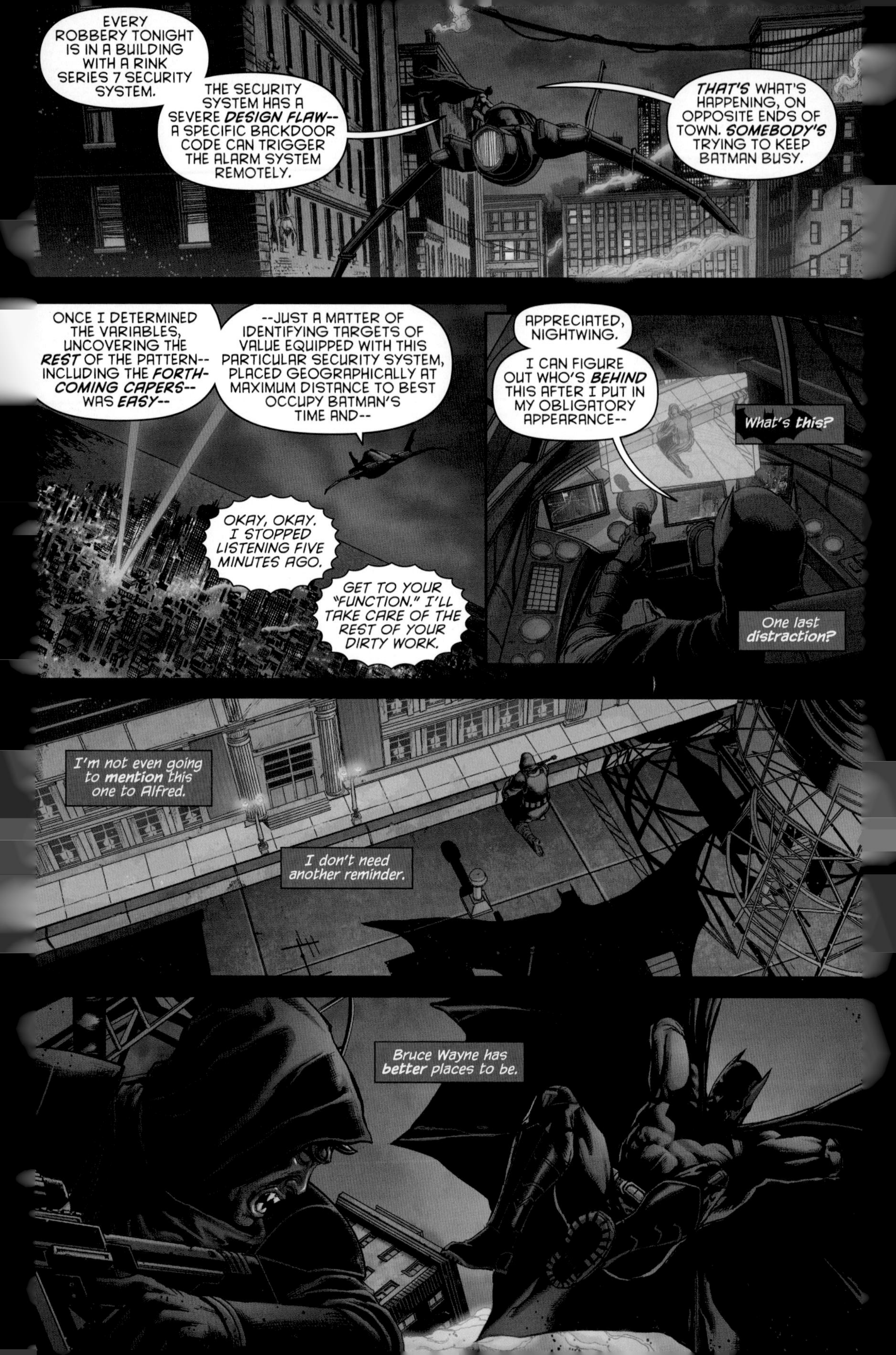
EVERY ROBBERY TONIGHT IS IN A BUILDING WITH A RINK SERIES 7 SECURITY SYSTEM.
THE SECURITY SYSTEM HAS A SEVERE DESIGN FLAW-- A SPECIFIC BACKDOOR CODE CAN TRIGGER THE ALARM SYSTEM REMOTELY.
THAT'S WHAT'S HAPPENING, ON OPPOSITE ENDS OF TOWN. SOMEBODY'S TRYING TO KEEP BATMAN BUSY.
ONCE I DETERMINED THE VARIABLES, UNCOVERING THE REST OF THE PATTERN-- INCLUDING THE FORTH-COMING CAPERS-- WAS EASY--
--JUST A MATTER OF IDENTIFYING TARGETS OF VALUE EQUIPPED WITH THIS PARTICULAR SECURITY SYSTEM, PLACED GEOGRAPHICALLY AT MAXIMUM DISTANCE TO BEST OCCUPY BATMAN'S TIME AND--
OKAY, OKAY. I STOPPED LISTENING FIVE MINUTES AGO.
GET TO YOUR "FUNCTION." I'LL TAKE CARE OF THE REST OF YOUR DIRTY WORK.
APPRECIATED, NIGHTWING.
I CAN FIGURE OUT WHO'S BEHIND THIS AFTER I PUT IN MY OBLIGATORY APPEARANCE--
What's this?
One last distraction?
I'm not even going to mention this one to Alfred.
I don't need another reminder.
Bruce Wayne has better places to be.

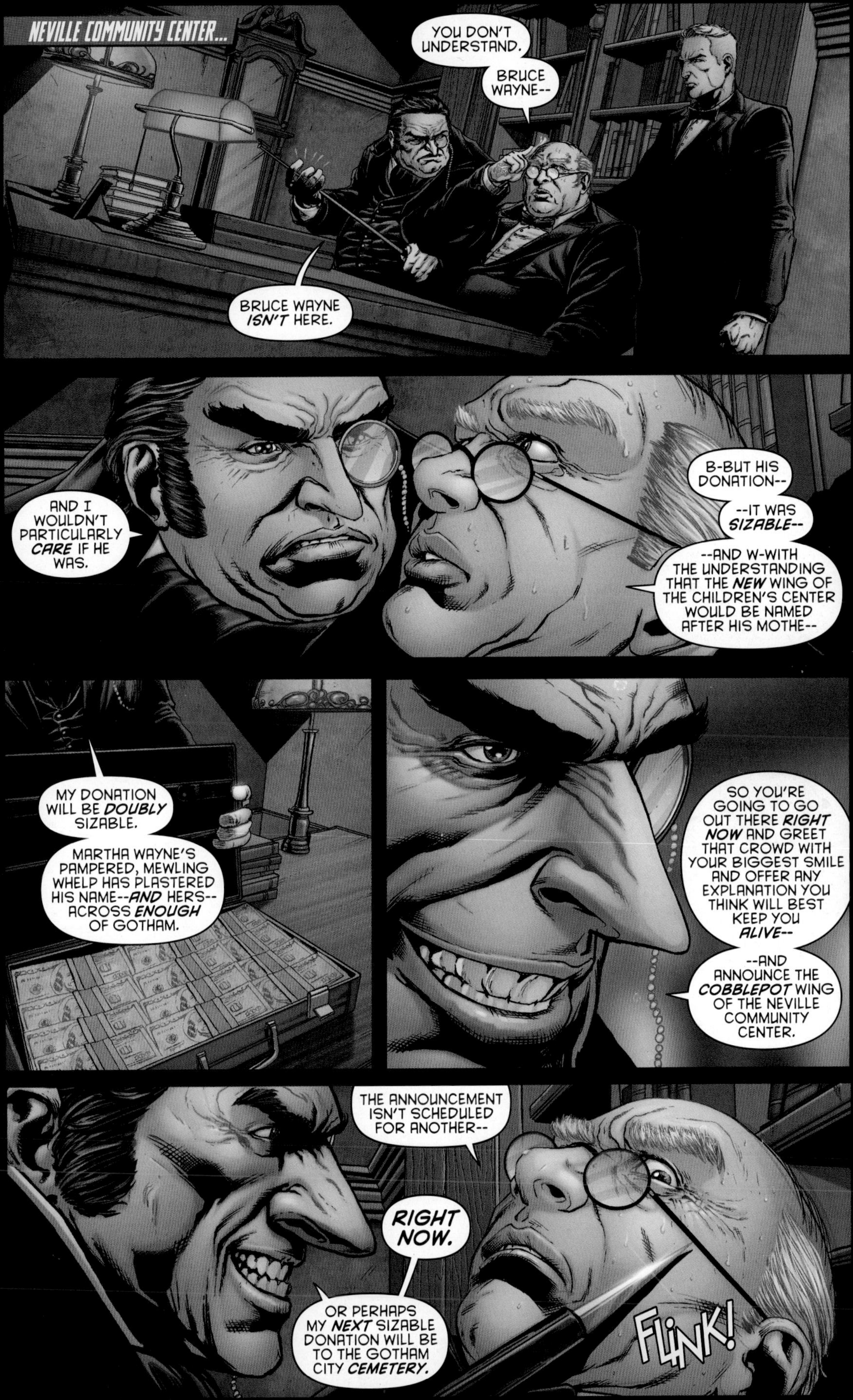
NEVILLE COMMUNITY CENTER...
YOU DON'T UNDERSTAND.
BRUCE WAYNE--
BRUCE WAYNE ISN'T HERE.
AND I WOULDN'T PARTICULARLY CARE IF HE WAS.
B-BUT HIS DONATION--
--IT WAS SIZABLE--
--AND W-WITH THE UNDERSTANDING THAT THE NEW WING OF THE CHILDREN'S CENTER WOULD BE NAMED AFTER HIS MOTHE--
MY DONATION WILL BE DOUBLY SIZABLE.
MARTHA WAYNE'S PAMPERED, MEWLING WHELP HAS PLASTERED HIS NAME--AND HERS--ACROSS ENOUGH OF GOTHAM.
SO YOU'RE GOING TO GO OUT THERE RIGHT NOW AND GREET THAT CROWD WITH YOUR BIGGEST SMILE AND OFFER ANY EXPLANATION YOU THINK WILL BEST KEEP YOU ALIVE--
--AND ANNOUNCE THE COBBLEPOT WING OF THE NEVILLE COMMUNITY CENTER.
THE ANNOUNCEMENT ISN'T SCHEDULED FOR ANOTHER--
RIGHT NOW.
OR PERHAPS MY NEXT SIZABLE DONATION WILL BE TO THE GOTHAM CITY CEMETERY.
FLINK!

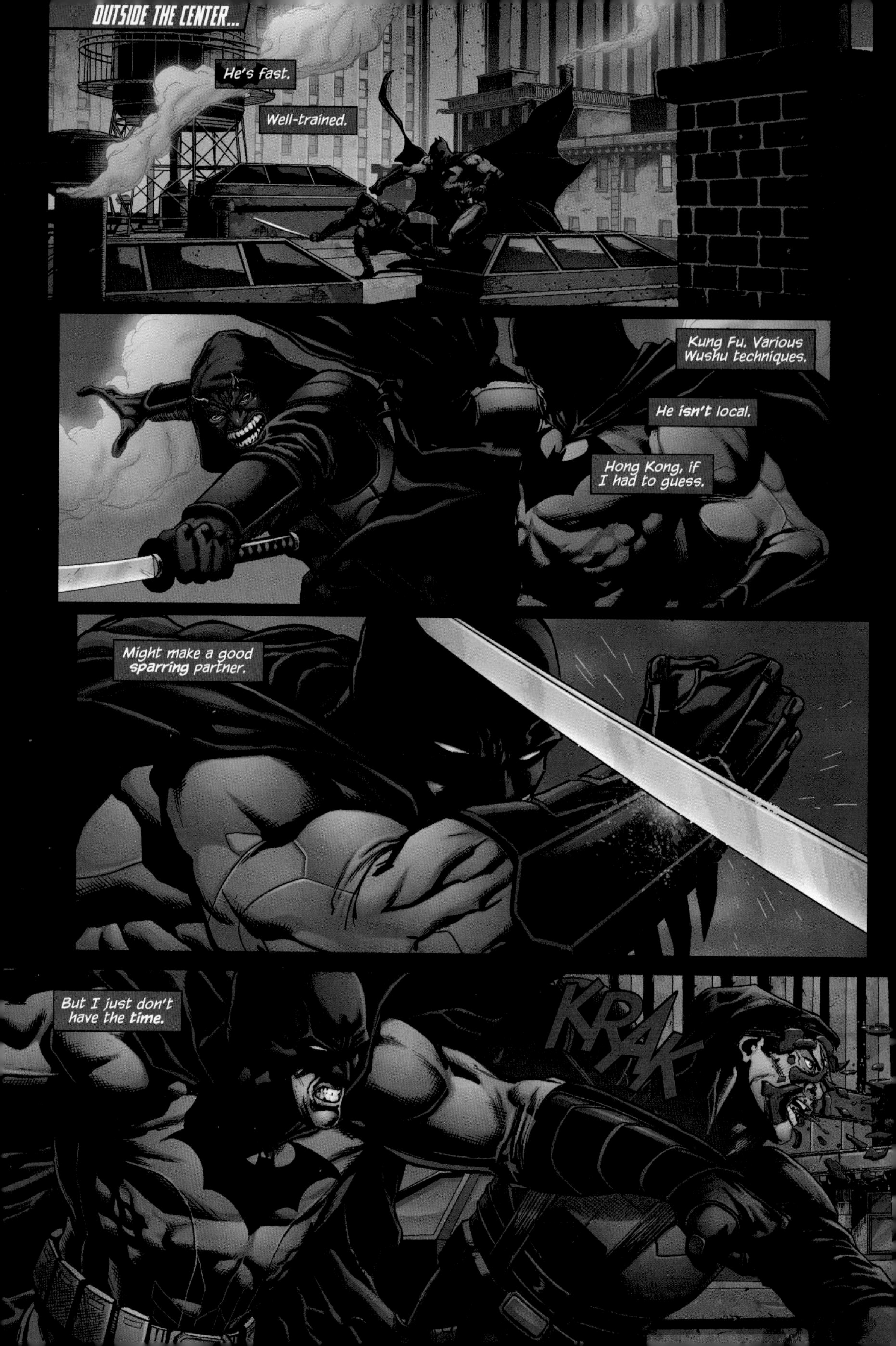
OUTSIDE THE CENTER...
He's fast.
Well-trained.
Kung Fu. Various Wushu techniques.
He isn't local.
Hong Kong, if I had to guess.
Might make a good sparring partner.
But I just don't have the time.
KRAK

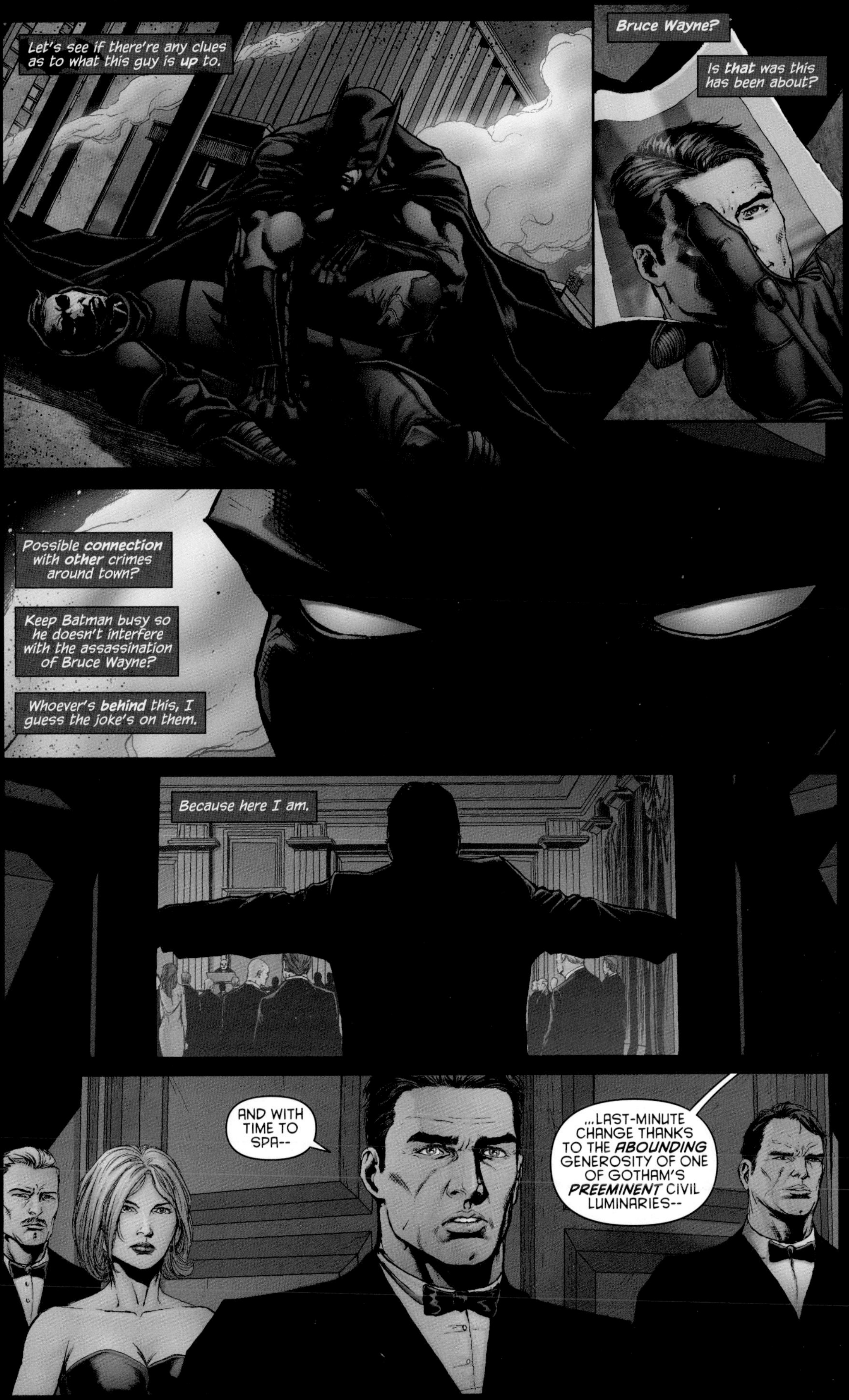
Let's see if there're any clues as to what this guy is up to.
Bruce Wayne?
Is that was this has been about?
Possible connection with other crimes around town?
Keep Batman busy so he doesn't interfere with the assassination of Bruce Wayne?
Whoever's behind this, I guess the joke's on them.
Because here I am.
AND WITH TIME TO SPA--
...LAST-MINUTE CHANGE THANKS TO THE ABOUNDING GENEROSITY OF ONE OF GOTHAM'S PREEMINENT CIVIL LUMINARIES--

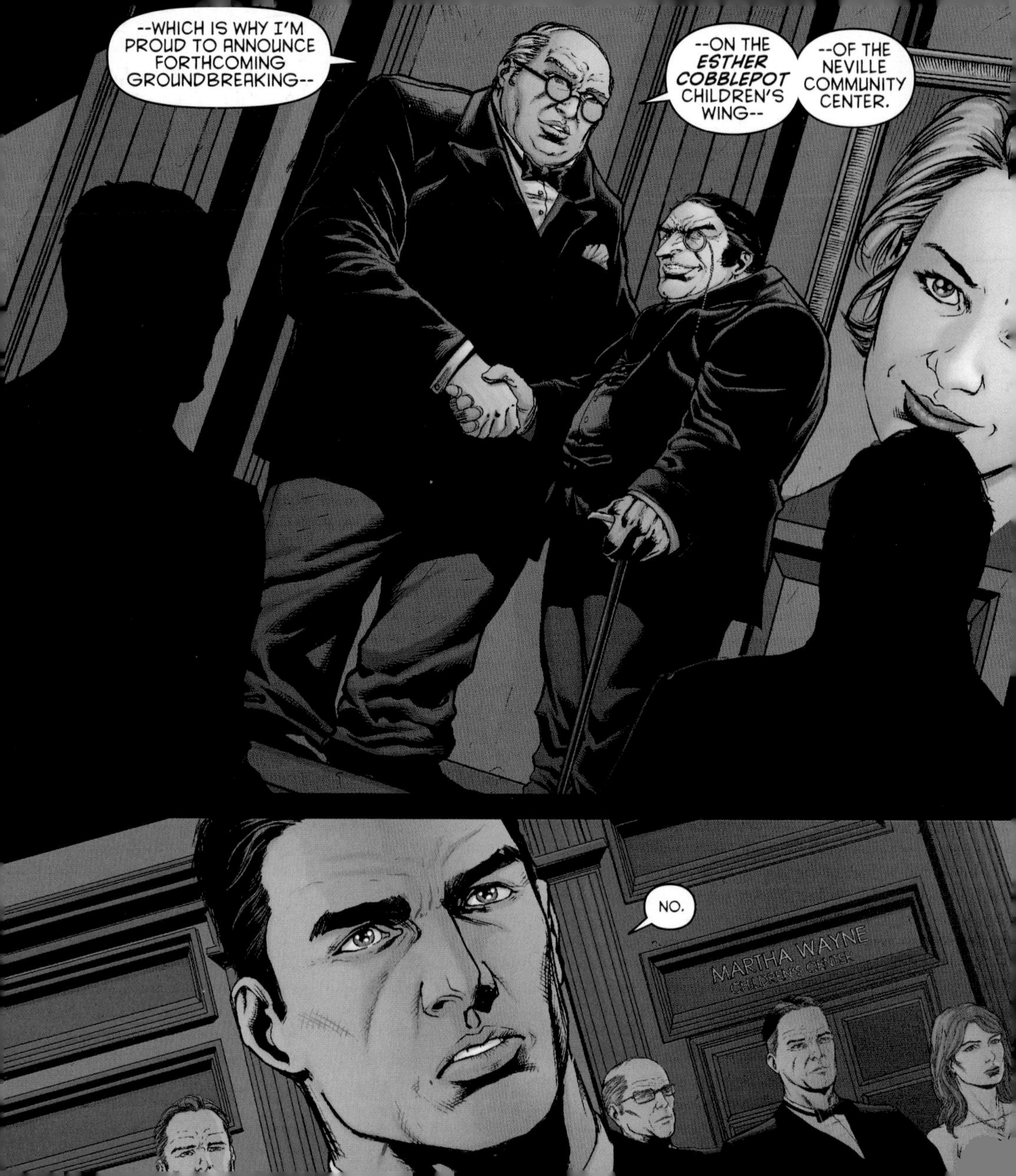
--WHICH IS WHY I'M PROUD TO ANNOUNCE FORTHCOMING GROUNDBREAKING--
--ON THE ESTHER COBBLEPOT CHILDREN'S WING--
--OF THE NEVILLE COMMUNITY CENTER.
NO.
MARTHA WAYNE CHILDREN'S CENTER

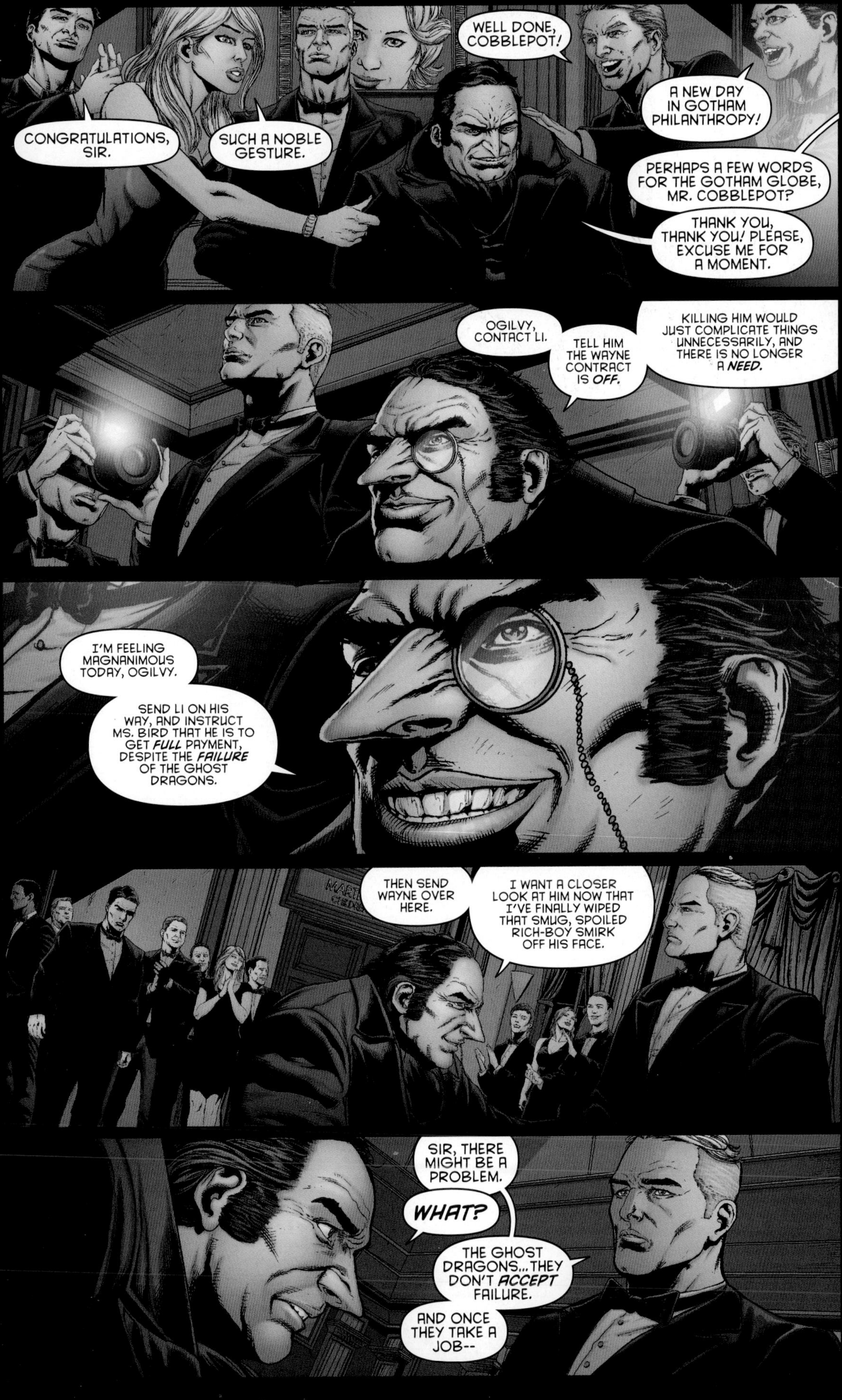
CONGRATULATIONS, SIR.
SUCH A NOBLE GESTURE.
WELL DONE, COBBLEPOT!
A NEW DAY IN GOTHAM PHILANTHROPY!
PERHAPS A FEW WORDS FOR THE GOTHAM GLOBE, MR. COBBLEPOT?
THANK YOU, THANK YOU! PLEASE, EXCUSE ME FOR A MOMENT.
OGILVY, CONTACT LI.
TELL HIM THE WAYNE CONTRACT IS OFF.
KILLING HIM WOULD JUST COMPLICATE THINGS UNNECESSARILY, AND THERE IS NO LONGER A NEED.
I'M FEELING MAGNANIMOUS TODAY, OGILVY.
SEND LI ON HIS WAY, AND INSTRUCT MS. BIRD THAT HE IS TO GET FULL PAYMENT, DESPITE THE FAILURE OF THE GHOST DRAGONS.
THEN SEND WAYNE OVER HERE.
I WANT A CLOSER LOOK AT HIM NOW THAT I'VE FINALLY WIPED THAT SMUG, SPOILED RICH-BOY SMIRK OFF HIS FACE.
SIR, THERE MIGHT BE A PROBLEM.
WHAT?
THE GHOST DRAGONS...THEY DON'T ACCEPT FAILURE.
AND ONCE THEY TAKE A JOB--

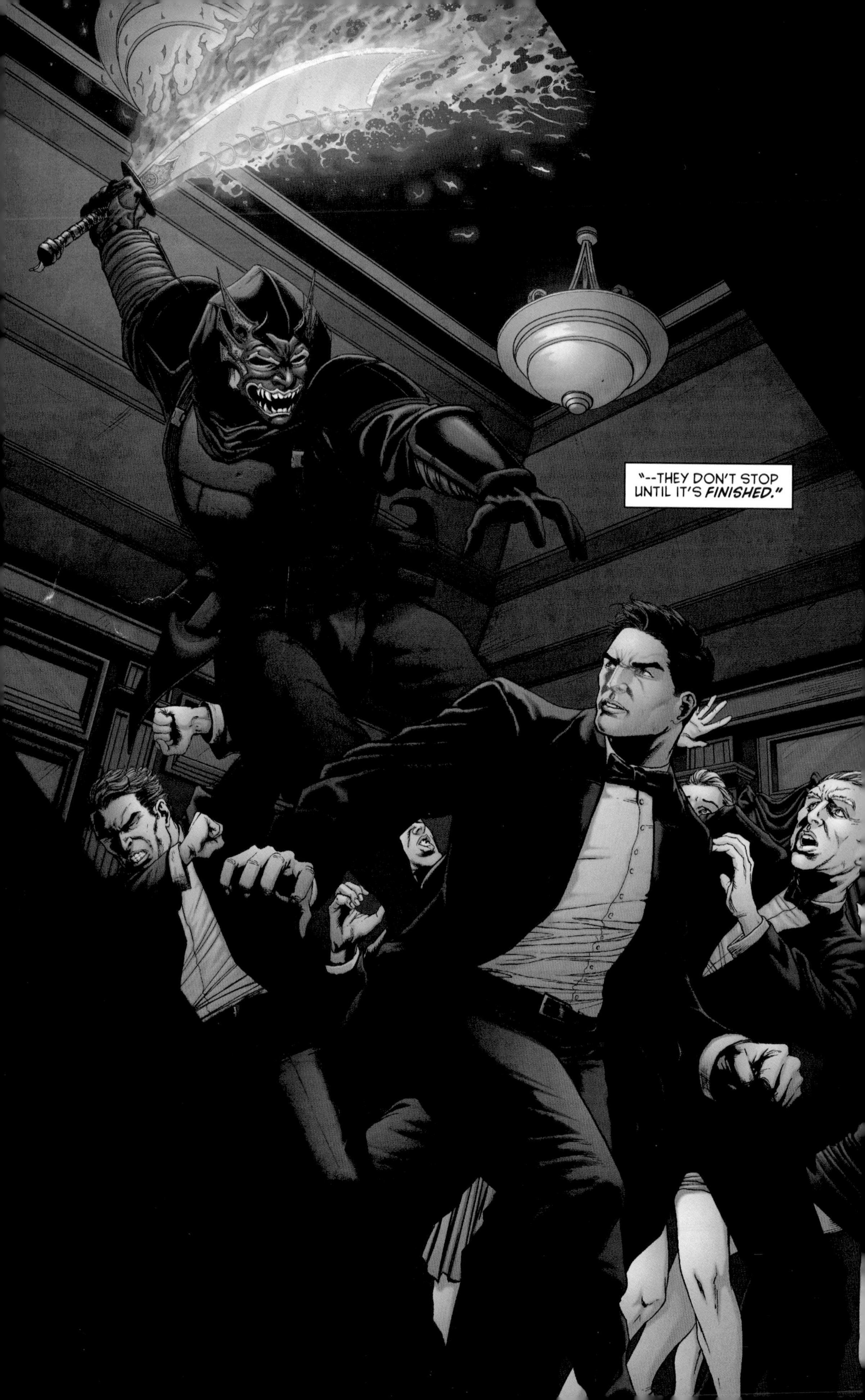
"--THEY DON'T STOP UNTIL IT'S FINISHED."

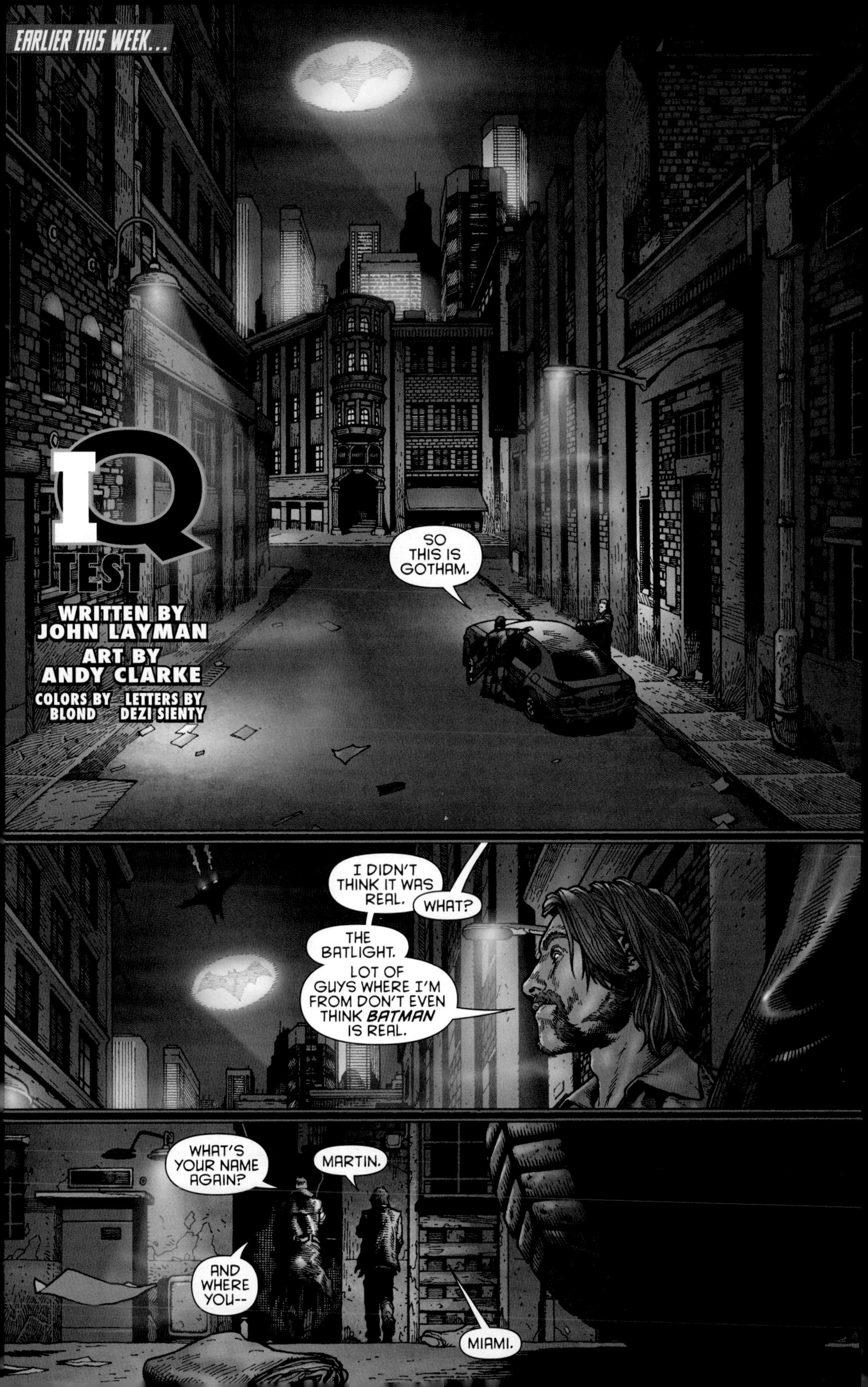
EARLIER THIS WEEK...
IQ TEST
WRITTEN BY JOHN LAYMAN
ART BY ANDY CLARKE
COLORS BY BLOND
LETTERS BY DEZI SIENTY
SO THIS IS GOTHAM.
I DIDN'T THINK IT WAS REAL.
WHAT?
THE BATLIGHT.
LOT OF GUYS WHERE I'M FROM DON'T EVEN THINK *BATMAN* IS REAL.
WHAT'S YOUR NAME AGAIN?
MARTIN.
AND WHERE YOU--
MIAMI.

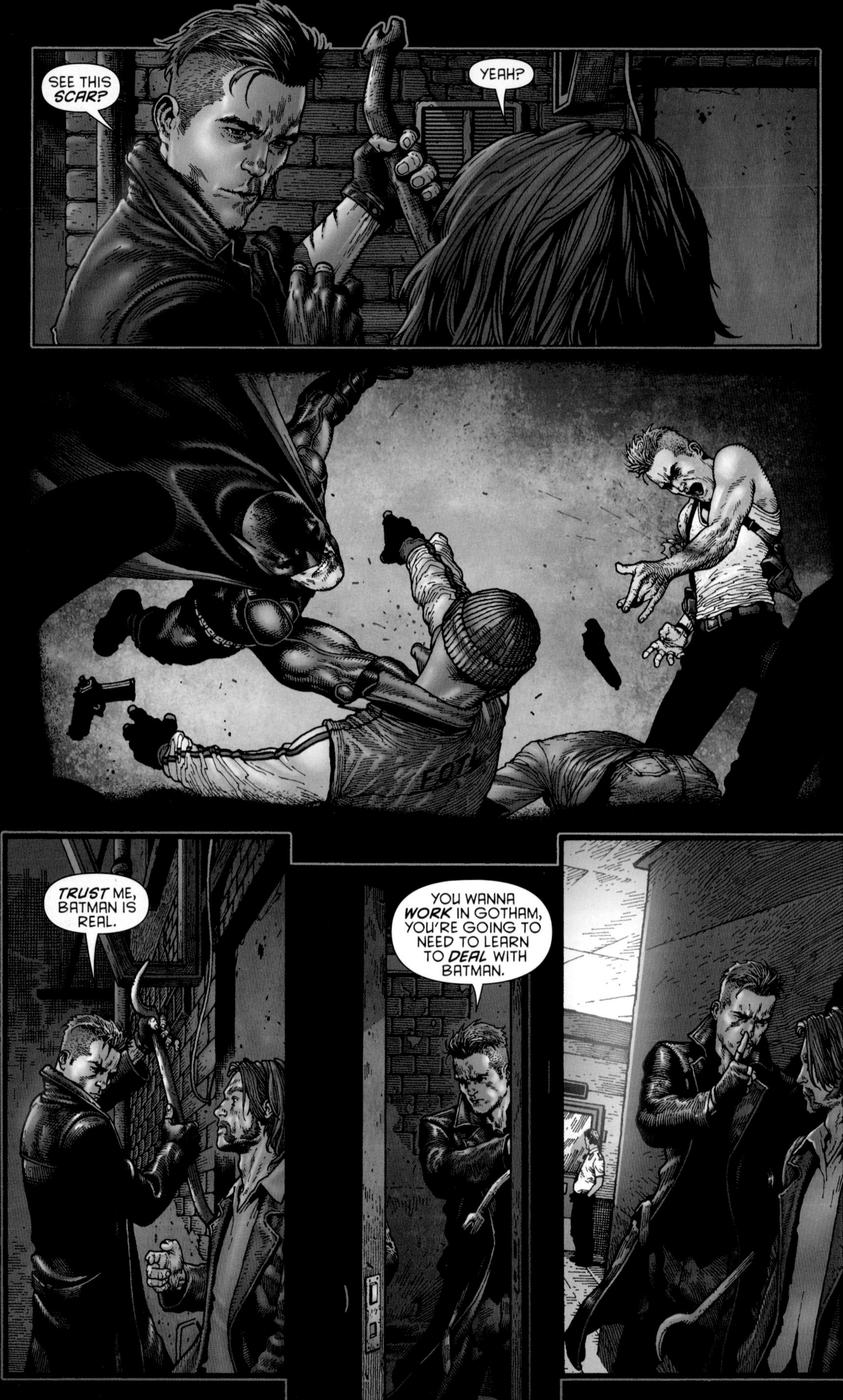
SEE THIS *SCAR?*
YEAH?
TRUST ME, BATMAN IS REAL.
YOU WANNA *WORK* IN GOTHAM, YOU'RE GOING TO NEED TO LEARN TO *DEAL* WITH BATMAN.

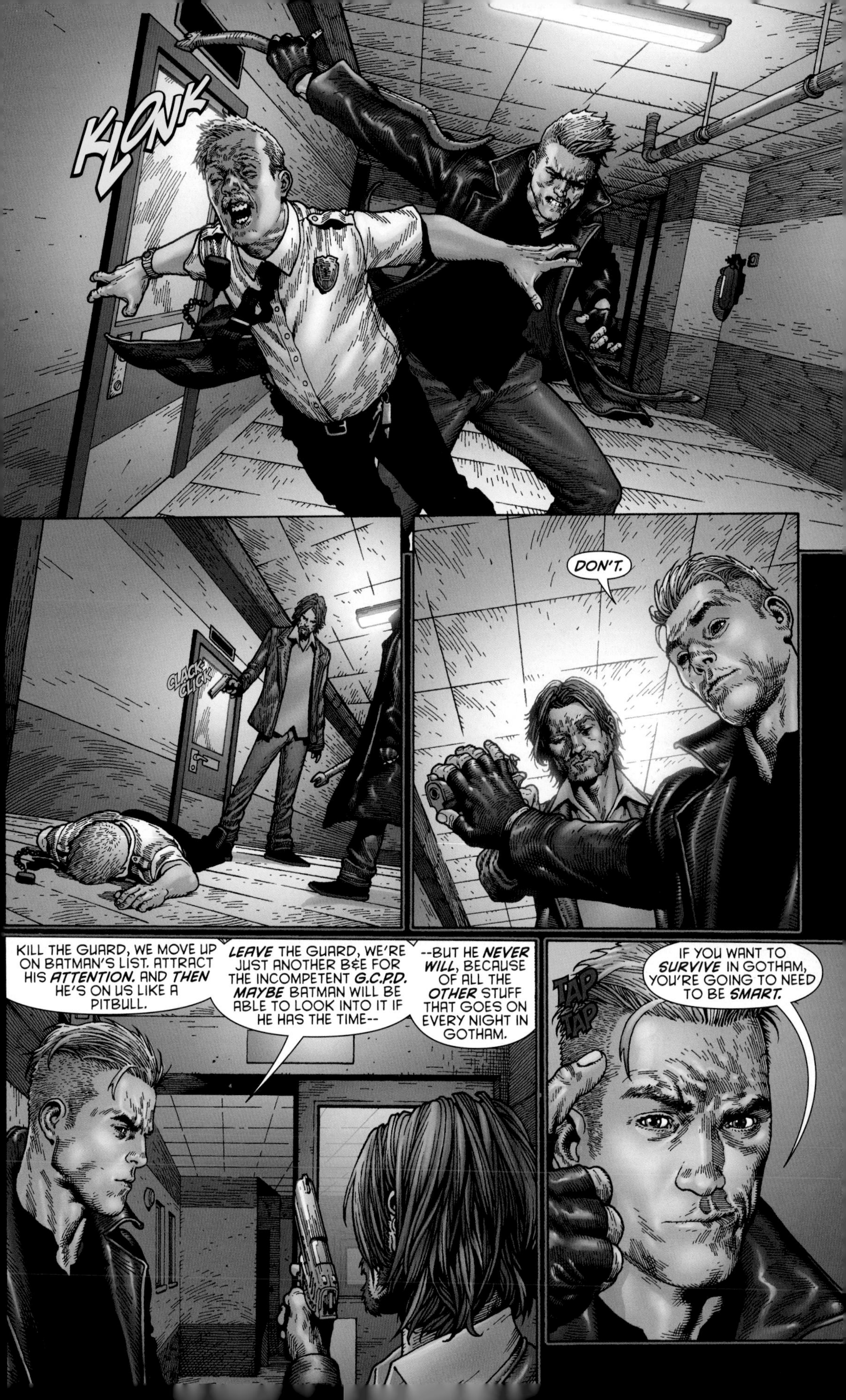
KLONK
CLACK CLICK
DON'T.
KILL THE GUARD, WE MOVE UP ON BATMAN'S LIST. ATTRACT HIS ATTENTION. AND THEN HE'S ON US LIKE A PITBULL.
LEAVE THE GUARD, WE'RE JUST ANOTHER B&E FOR THE INCOMPETENT G.C.P.D. MAYBE BATMAN WILL BE ABLE TO LOOK INTO IT IF HE HAS THE TIME--
--BUT HE NEVER WILL, BECAUSE OF ALL THE OTHER STUFF THAT GOES ON EVERY NIGHT IN GOTHAM.
TAP TAP
IF YOU WANT TO SURVIVE IN GOTHAM, YOU'RE GOING TO NEED TO BE SMART.

YOU DON'T HAVE TO WORRY 'BOUT *THAT.* YOU HEAR 'BOUT THE GRAPELAND HEIGHTS DIAMOND JOB?

THAT WAS ME, PLANNED AND EXECUTED. THE WHOLE CAPER, TOP TO BOTTOM. *THAT'S* WHAT FIRST GOT ME THE PENGUIN'S ATTENTION.

LIKE I SAID, SMART IS WHAT YOU *NEED* IN GOTHAM.

SO, UH, YOU'VE *MET* BATMAN?

ARE YOU EVEN LISTENING? IN OUR LINE OF WORK, IT'S NOT A QUESTION OF *IF* YOU'LL MEET BATMAN.

IT'S A QUESTION OF *WHEN*--

"--AND *HOW HARD.*"

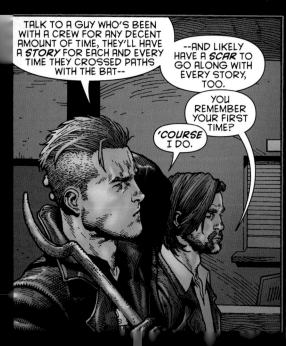

TALK TO A GUY WHO'S BEEN WITH A CREW FOR ANY DECENT AMOUNT OF TIME, THEY'LL HAVE A *STORY* FOR EACH AND EVERY TIME THEY CROSSED PATHS WITH THE BAT--

--AND LIKELY HAVE A *SCAR* TO GO ALONG WITH EVERY STORY, TOO.

YOU REMEMBER YOUR FIRST TIME?

'COURSE I DO.

EVERYBODY REMEMBERS THEIR FIRST.

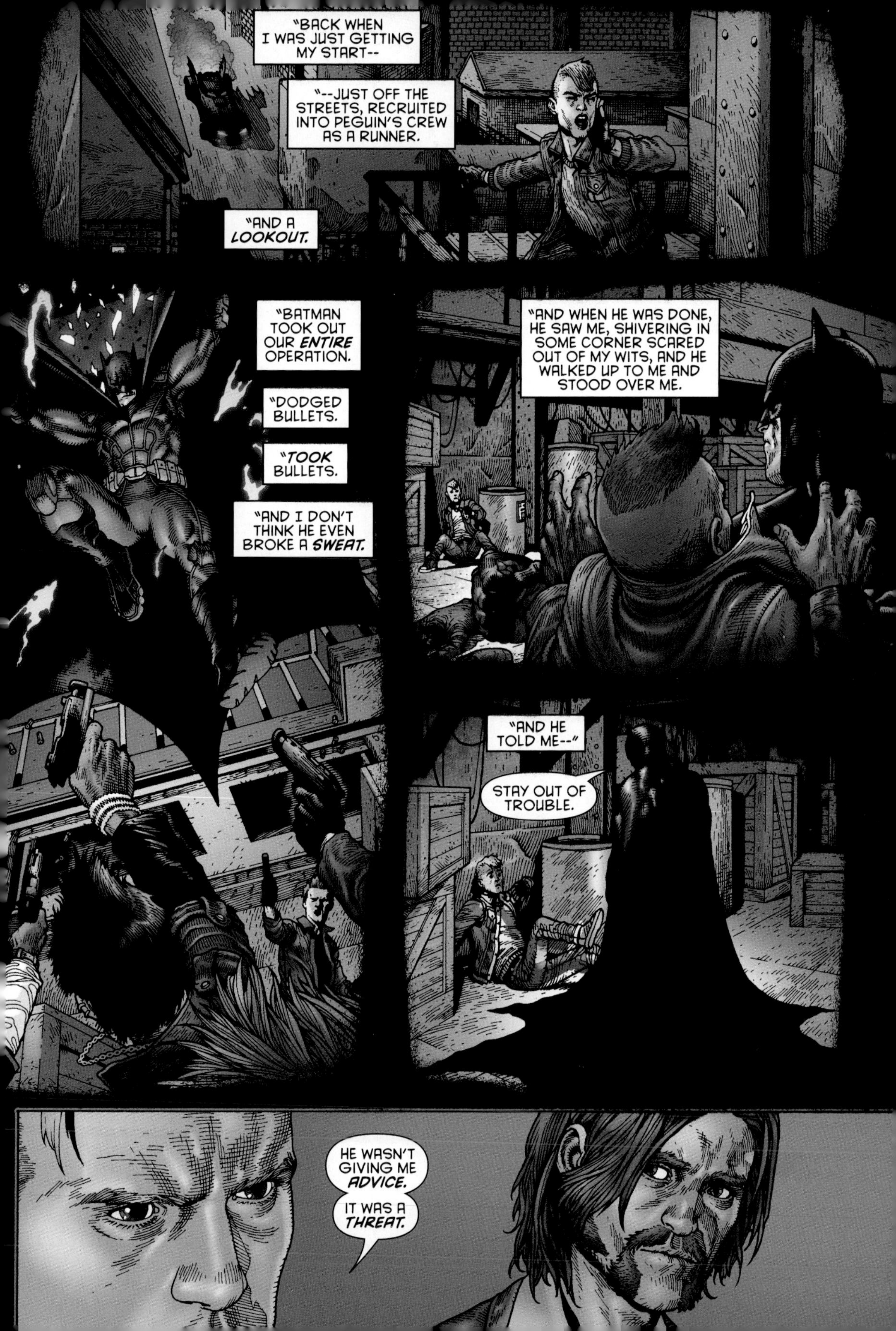
"BACK WHEN I WAS JUST GETTING MY START--
"--JUST OFF THE STREETS, RECRUITED INTO PEGUIN'S CREW AS A RUNNER.
"AND A LOOKOUT.
"BATMAN TOOK OUT OUR ENTIRE OPERATION.
"DODGED BULLETS.
"TOOK BULLETS.
"AND I DON'T THINK HE EVEN BROKE A SWEAT.
"AND WHEN HE WAS DONE, HE SAW ME, SHIVERING IN SOME CORNER SCARED OUT OF MY WITS, AND HE WALKED UP TO ME AND STOOD OVER ME.
"AND HE TOLD ME--"
STAY OUT OF TROUBLE.
HE WASN'T GIVING ME ADVICE.
IT WAS A THREAT.

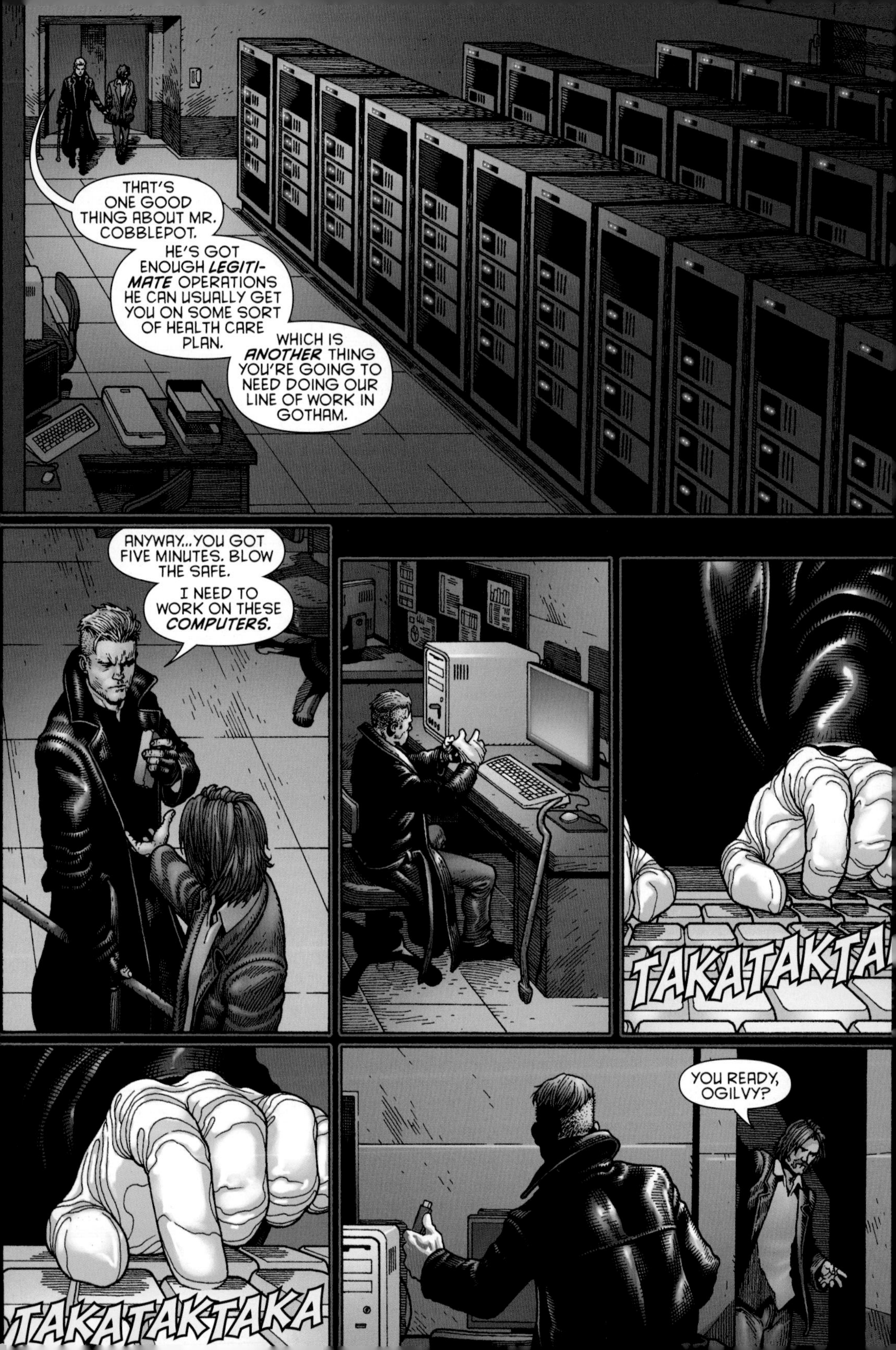
THAT'S ONE GOOD THING ABOUT MR. COBBLEPOT.
HE'S GOT ENOUGH *LEGITIMATE* OPERATIONS HE CAN USUALLY GET YOU ON SOME SORT OF HEALTH CARE PLAN.
WHICH IS *ANOTHER* THING YOU'RE GOING TO NEED DOING OUR LINE OF WORK IN GOTHAM.
ANYWAY... YOU GOT FIVE MINUTES. BLOW THE SAFE.
I NEED TO WORK ON THESE *COMPUTERS.*
TAKATAKTA
TAKATAKTAKA
YOU READY, OGILVY?

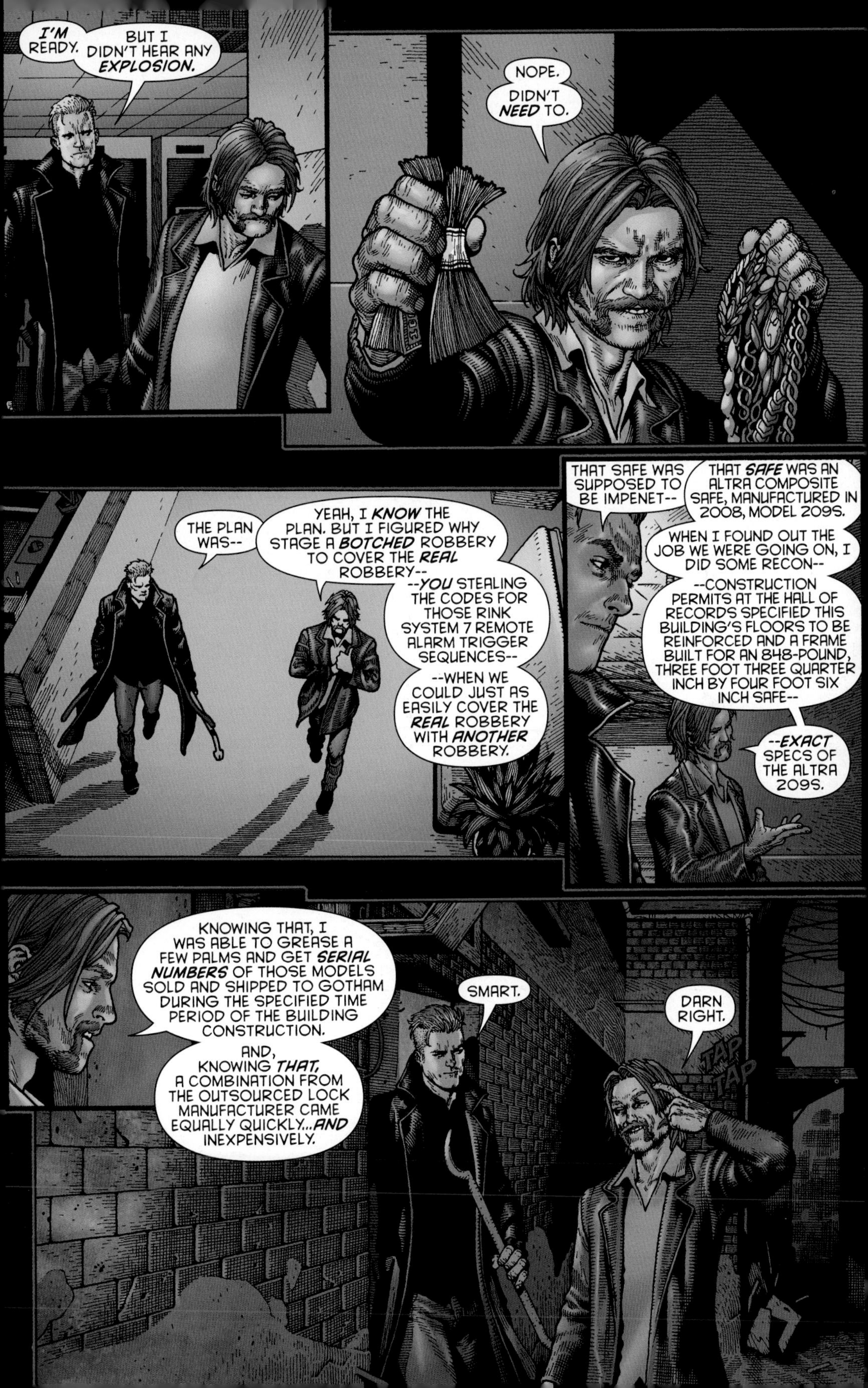
I'M READY.
BUT I DIDN'T HEAR ANY EXPLOSION.
NOPE. DIDN'T NEED TO.
THE PLAN WAS--
YEAH, I KNOW THE PLAN. BUT I FIGURED WHY STAGE A BOTCHED ROBBERY TO COVER THE REAL ROBBERY--
--YOU STEALING THE CODES FOR THOSE RINK SYSTEM 7 REMOTE ALARM TRIGGER SEQUENCES--
--WHEN WE COULD JUST AS EASILY COVER THE REAL ROBBERY WITH ANOTHER ROBBERY.
THAT SAFE WAS SUPPOSED TO BE IMPENET--
THAT SAFE WAS AN ALTRA COMPOSITE SAFE, MANUFACTURED IN 2008, MODEL 209S.
WHEN I FOUND OUT THE JOB WE WERE GOING ON, I DID SOME RECON--
--CONSTRUCTION PERMITS AT THE HALL OF RECORDS SPECIFIED THIS BUILDING'S FLOORS TO BE REINFORCED AND A FRAME BUILT FOR AN 848-POUND, THREE FOOT THREE QUARTER INCH BY FOUR FOOT SIX INCH SAFE--
--EXACT SPECS OF THE ALTRA 209S.
KNOWING THAT, I WAS ABLE TO GREASE A FEW PALMS AND GET SERIAL NUMBERS OF THOSE MODELS SOLD AND SHIPPED TO GOTHAM DURING THE SPECIFIED TIME PERIOD OF THE BUILDING CONSTRUCTION.
AND, KNOWING THAT, A COMBINATION FROM THE OUTSOURCED LOCK MANUFACTURER CAME EQUALLY QUICKLY...AND INEXPENSIVELY.
SMART.
DARN RIGHT.
TAP TAP

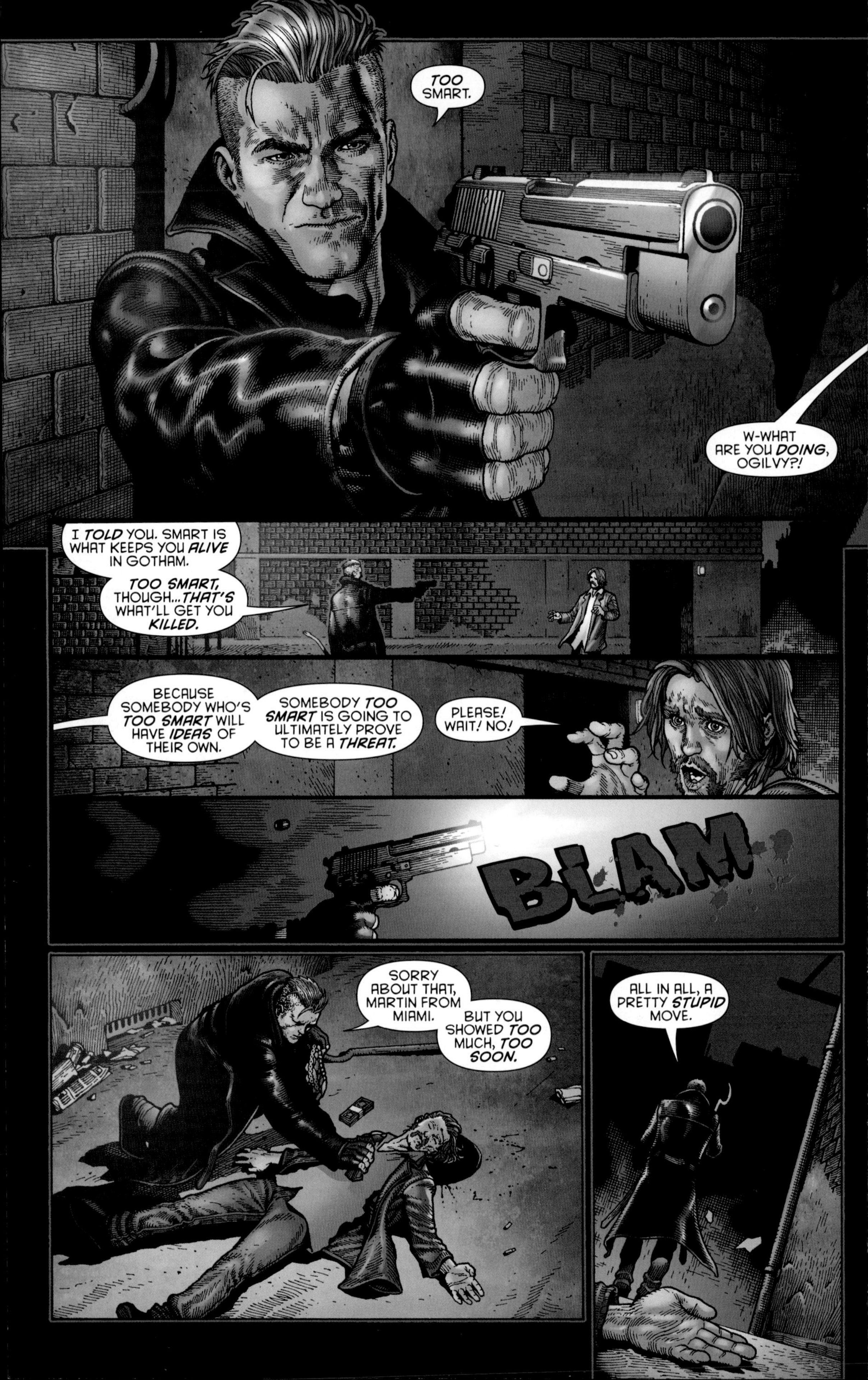
TOO SMART.
W-WHAT ARE YOU DOING, OGILVY?!
I TOLD YOU. SMART IS WHAT KEEPS YOU ALIVE IN GOTHAM.
TOO SMART, THOUGH...THAT'S WHAT'LL GET YOU KILLED.
BECAUSE SOMEBODY WHO'S TOO SMART WILL HAVE IDEAS OF THEIR OWN.
SOMEBODY TOO SMART IS GOING TO ULTIMATELY PROVE TO BE A THREAT.
PLEASE! WAIT! NO!
BLAM
SORRY ABOUT THAT, MARTIN FROM MIAMI.
BUT YOU SHOWED TOO MUCH, TOO SOON.
ALL IN ALL, A PRETTY STUPID MOVE.

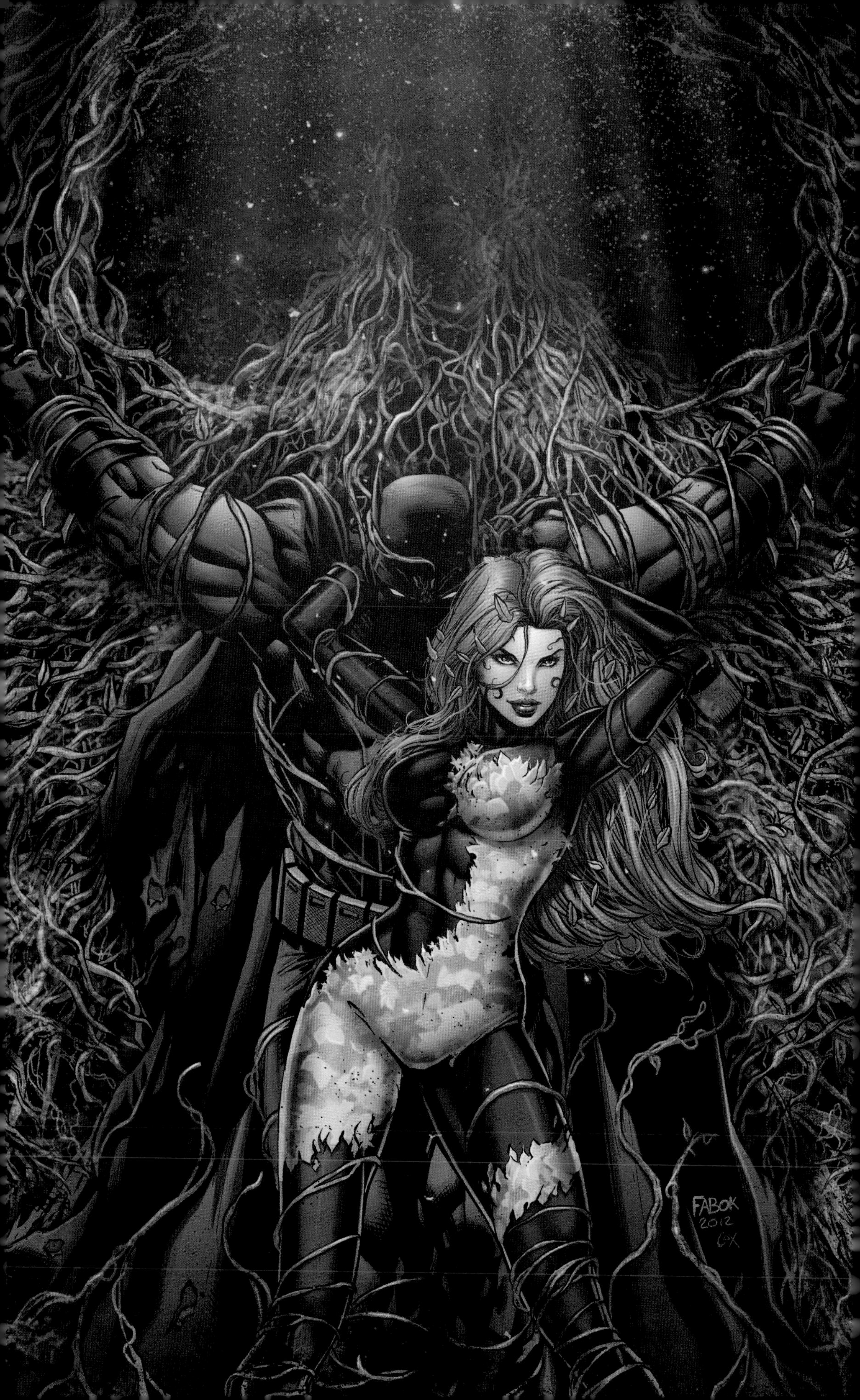
FABOK
2012
COX

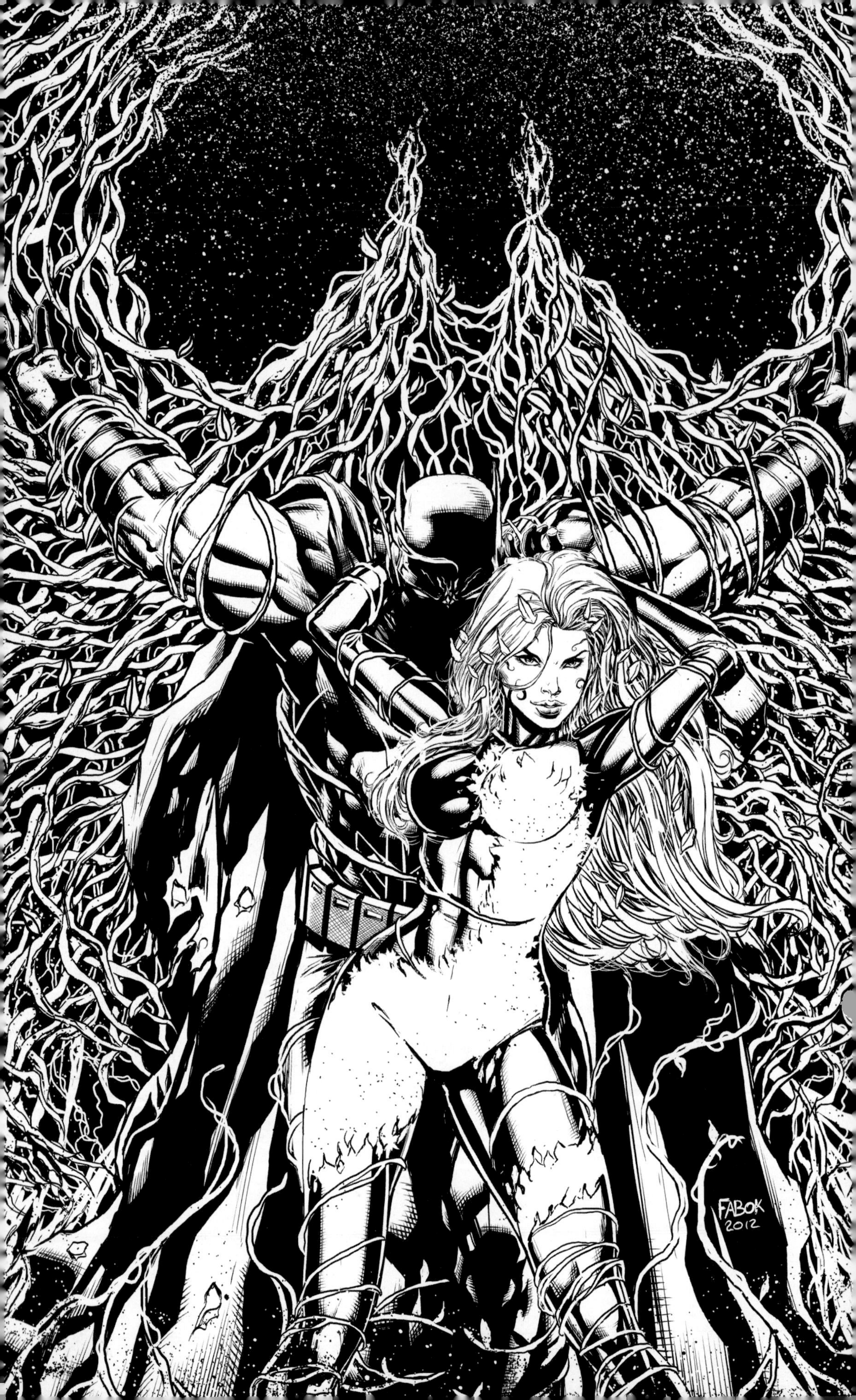
FABOK
2012

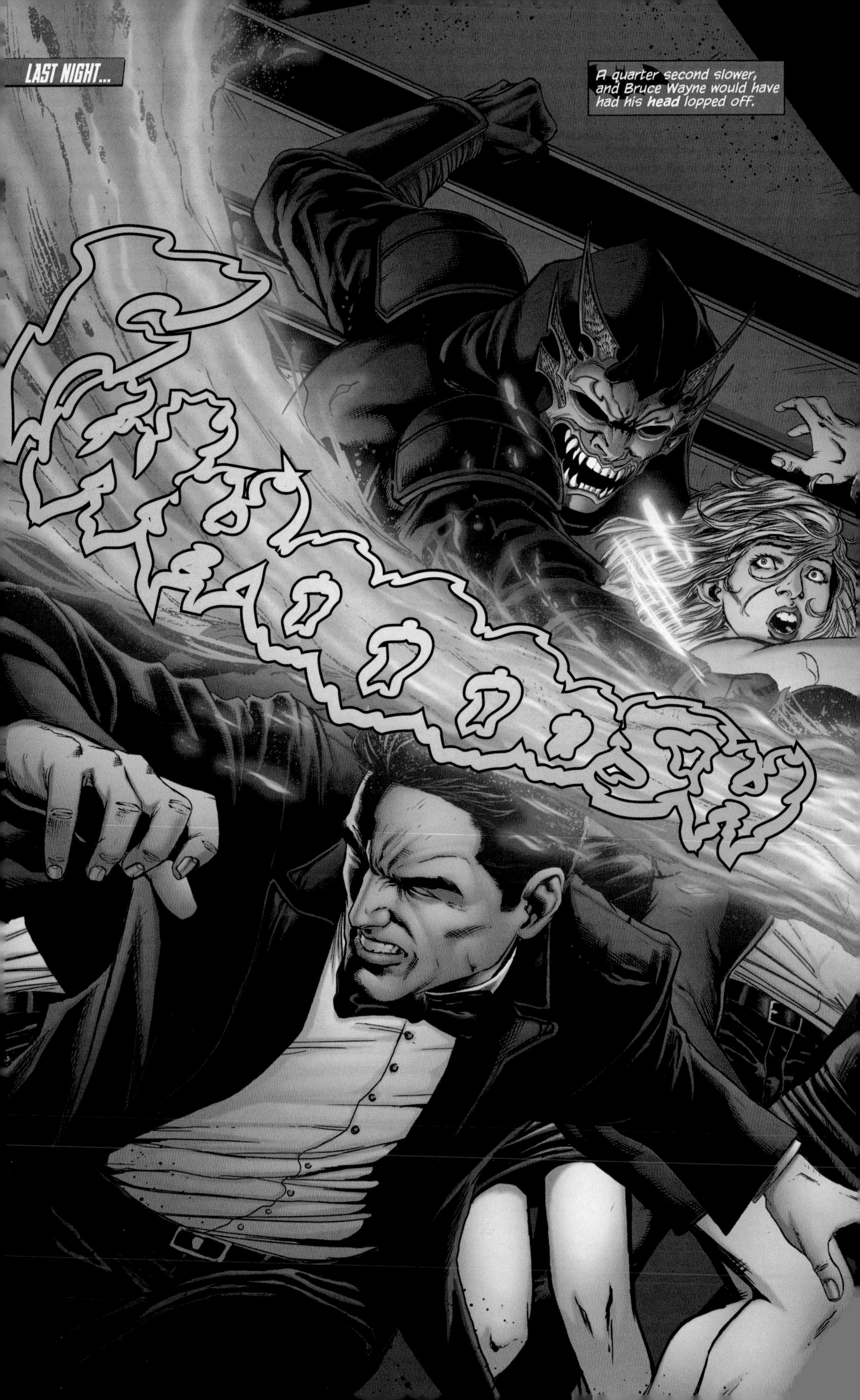
LAST NIGHT...
A quarter second slower, and Bruce Wayne would have had his **head** lopped off.

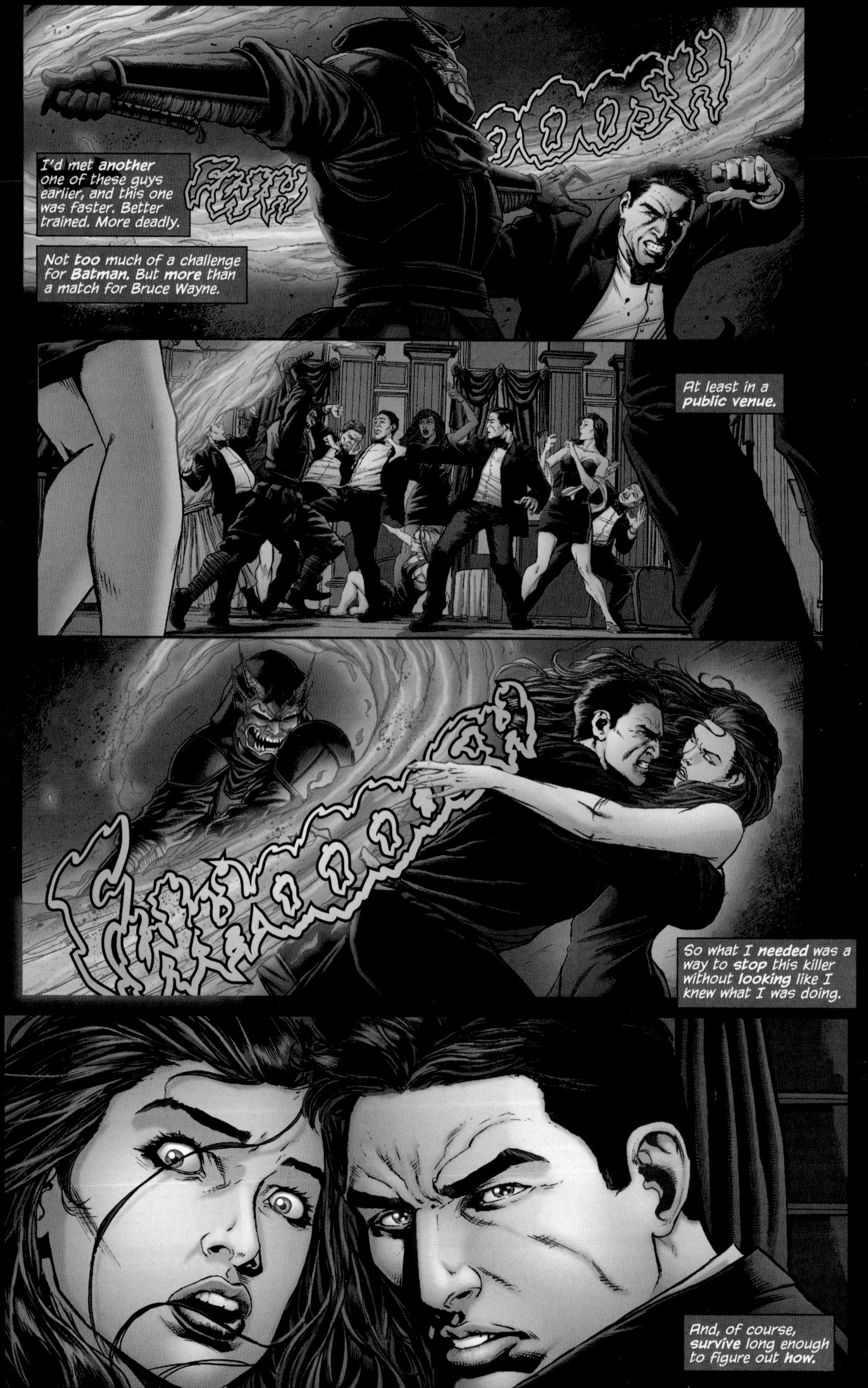
I'd met another one of these guys earlier, and this one was faster. Better trained. More deadly.
Not too much of a challenge for Batman. But more than a match for Bruce Wayne.
At least in a public venue.
So what I needed was a way to stop this killer without looking like I knew what I was doing.
And, of course, survive long enough to figure out how.

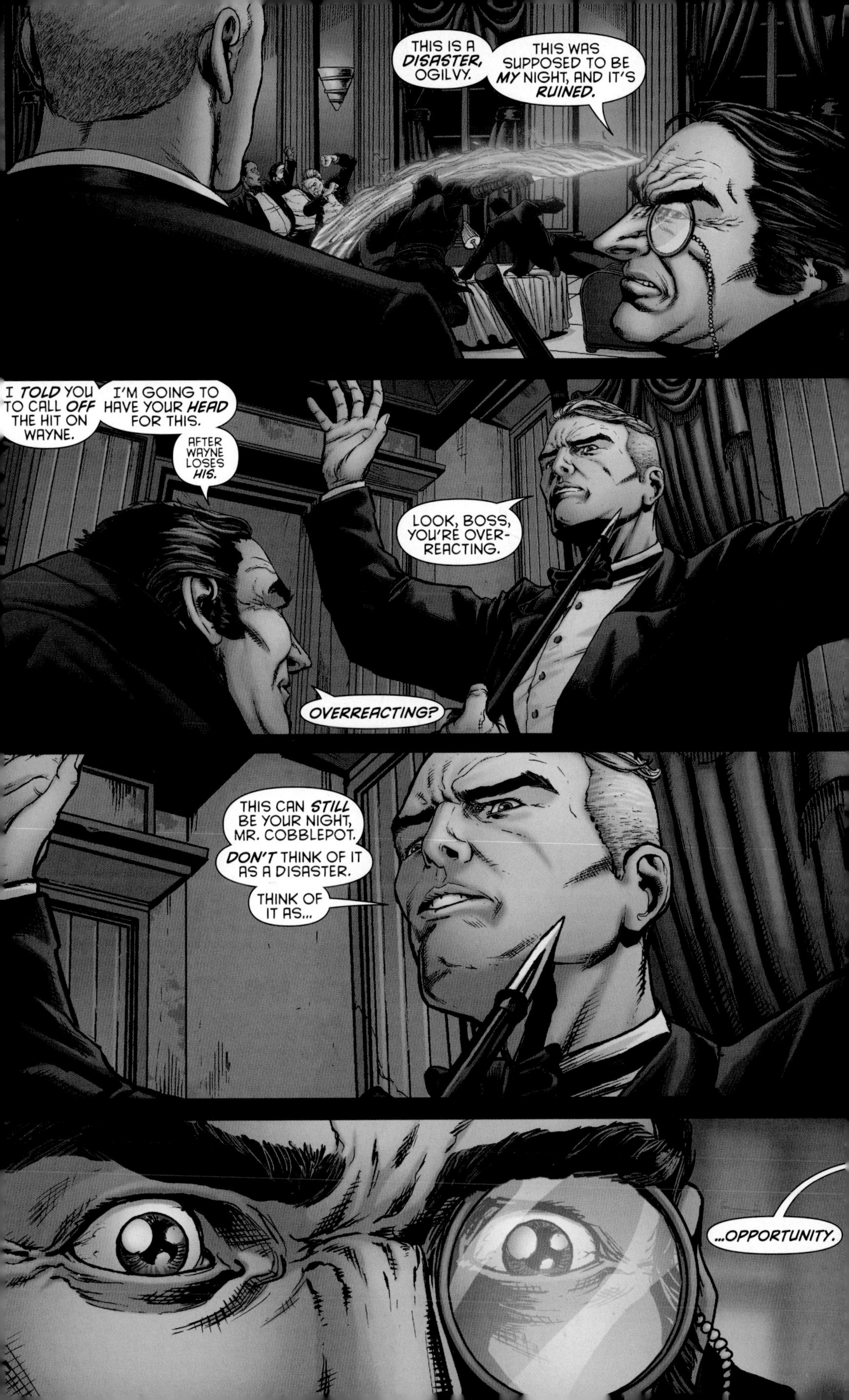
THIS IS A *DISASTER,* OGILVY.
THIS WAS SUPPOSED TO BE *MY* NIGHT, AND IT'S *RUINED.*
I *TOLD* YOU TO CALL *OFF* THE HIT ON WAYNE.
I'M GOING TO HAVE YOUR *HEAD* FOR THIS.
AFTER WAYNE LOSES *HIS.*
LOOK, BOSS, YOU'RE OVER-REACTING.
OVERREACTING?
THIS CAN *STILL* BE YOUR NIGHT, MR. COBBLEPOT.
DON'T THINK OF IT AS A DISASTER.
THINK OF IT AS...
...OPPORTUNITY.

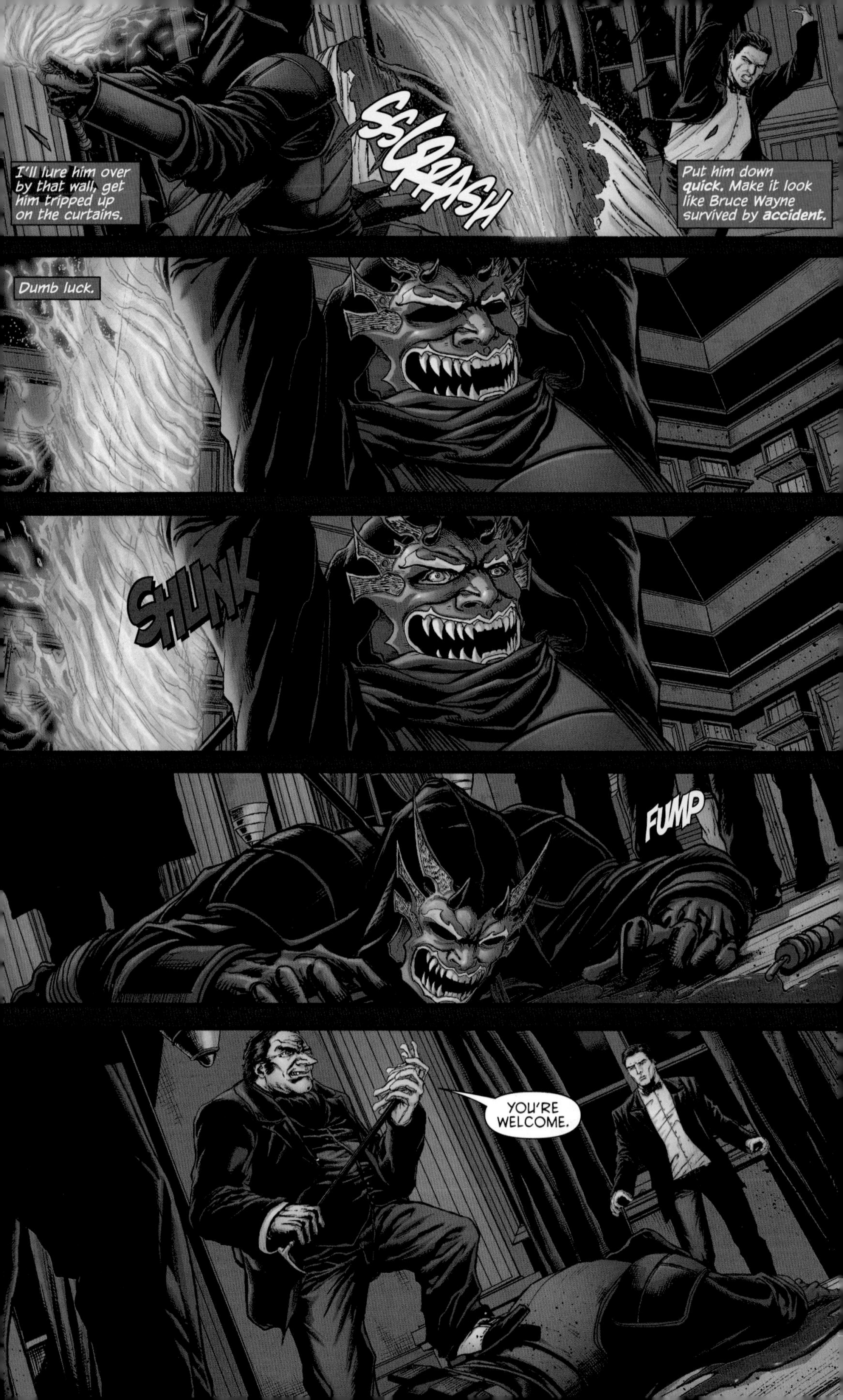

I'll lure him over by that wall, get him tripped up on the curtains.
SSCRASH
Put him down quick. Make it look like Bruce Wayne survived by accident.
Dumb luck.
SHUNK
FUMP
YOU'RE WELCOME.

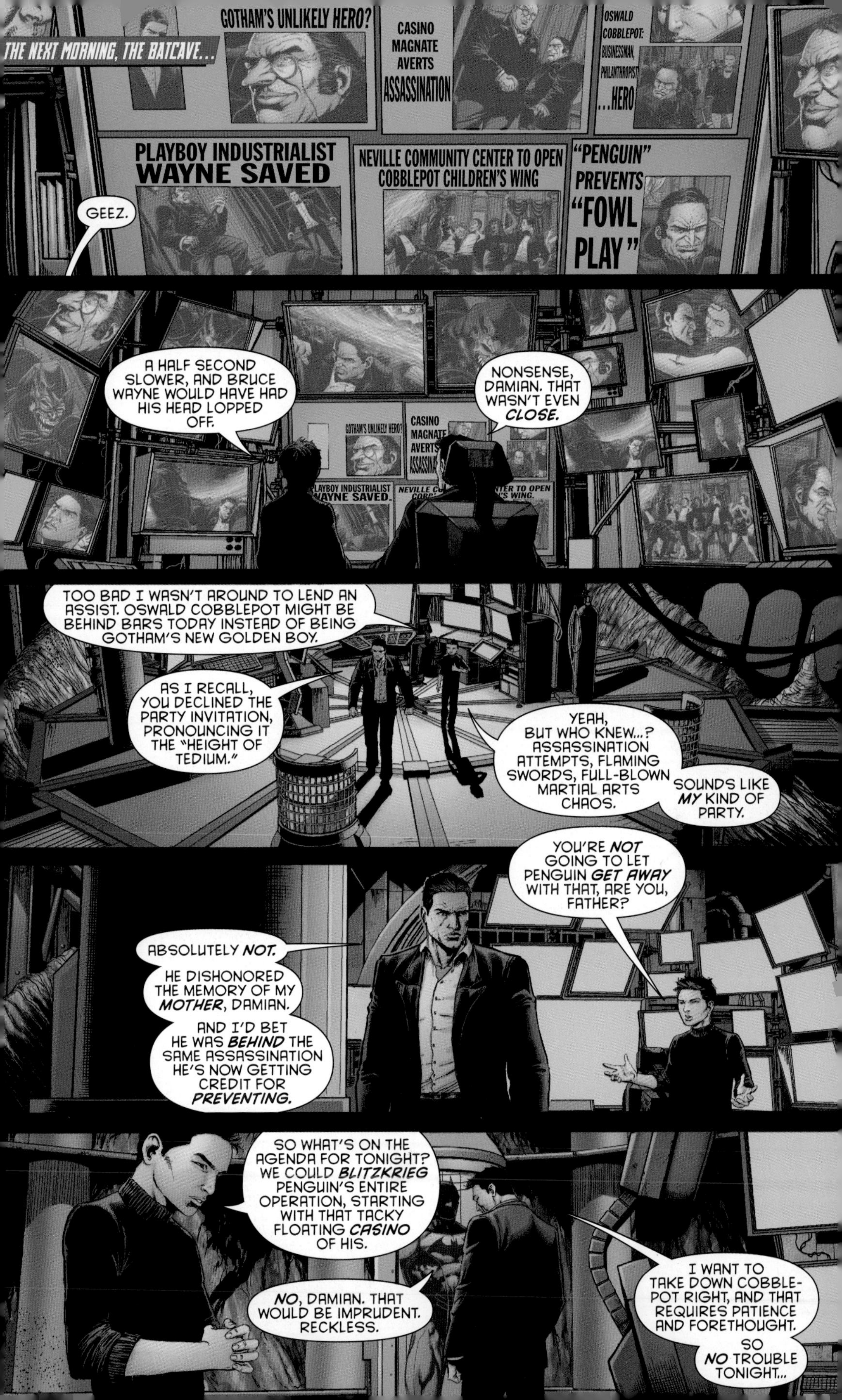
THE NEXT MORNING, THE BATCAVE...
GOTHAM'S UNLIKELY HERO?
CASINO MAGNATE AVERTS ASSASSINATION
OSWALD COBBLEPOT: BUSINESSMAN, PHILANTHROPIST ...HERO
PLAYBOY INDUSTRIALIST WAYNE SAVED
NEVILLE COMMUNITY CENTER TO OPEN COBBLEPOT CHILDREN'S WING
"PENGUIN" PREVENTS "FOWL PLAY"
GEEZ.
A HALF SECOND SLOWER, AND BRUCE WAYNE WOULD HAVE HAD HIS HEAD LOPPED OFF.
NONSENSE, DAMIAN. THAT WASN'T EVEN *CLOSE.*
TOO BAD I WASN'T AROUND TO LEND AN ASSIST. OSWALD COBBLEPOT MIGHT BE BEHIND BARS TODAY INSTEAD OF BEING GOTHAM'S NEW GOLDEN BOY.
AS I RECALL, YOU DECLINED THE PARTY INVITATION, PRONOUNCING IT THE "HEIGHT OF TEDIUM."
YEAH, BUT WHO KNEW...? ASSASSINATION ATTEMPTS, FLAMING SWORDS, FULL-BLOWN MARTIAL ARTS CHAOS.
SOUNDS LIKE *MY* KIND OF PARTY.
YOU'RE *NOT* GOING TO LET PENGUIN *GET AWAY* WITH THAT, ARE YOU, FATHER?
ABSOLUTELY *NOT.*
HE DISHONORED THE MEMORY OF MY *MOTHER*, DAMIAN.
AND I'D BET HE WAS *BEHIND* THE SAME ASSASSINATION HE'S NOW GETTING CREDIT FOR *PREVENTING.*
SO WHAT'S ON THE AGENDA FOR TONIGHT? WE COULD *BLITZKRIEG* PENGUIN'S ENTIRE OPERATION, STARTING WITH THAT TACKY FLOATING *CASINO* OF HIS.
NO, DAMIAN. THAT WOULD BE IMPRUDENT. RECKLESS.
I WANT TO TAKE DOWN COBBLE-POT RIGHT, AND THAT REQUIRES PATIENCE AND FORETHOUGHT.
SO *NO* TROUBLE TONIGHT...

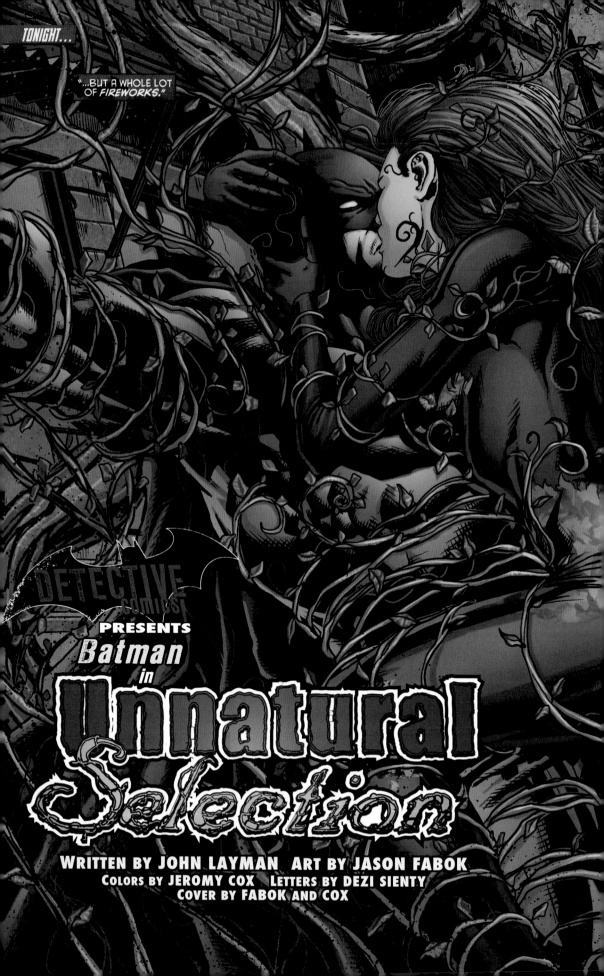

TONIGHT...

"...BUT A WHOLE LOT OF *FIREWORKS*."

DETECTIVE COMICS
PRESENTS
Batman
in
Unnatural Selection

WRITTEN BY JOHN LAYMAN ART BY JASON FABOK
COLORS BY JEROMY COX LETTERS BY DEZI SIENTY
COVER BY FABOK AND COX

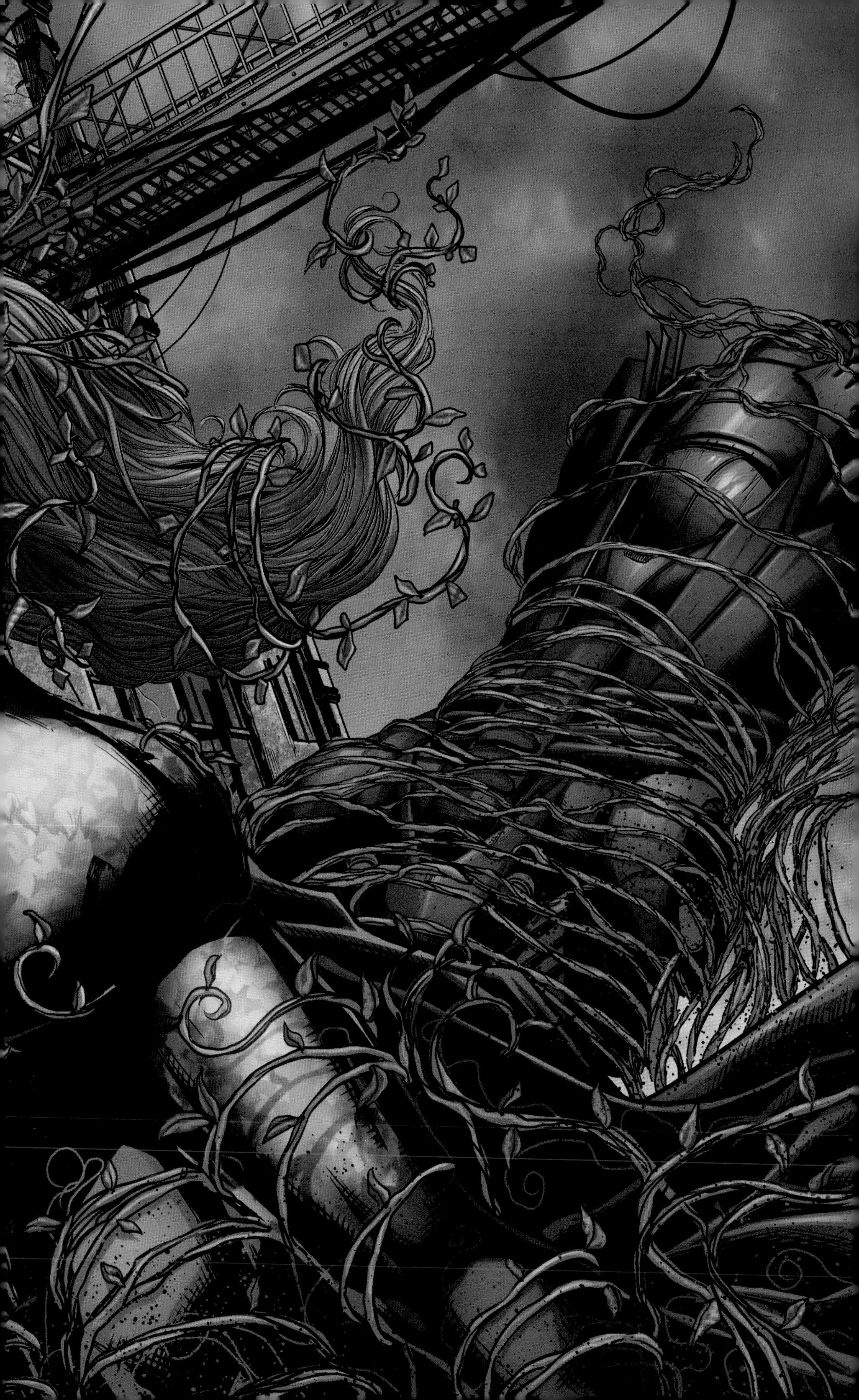

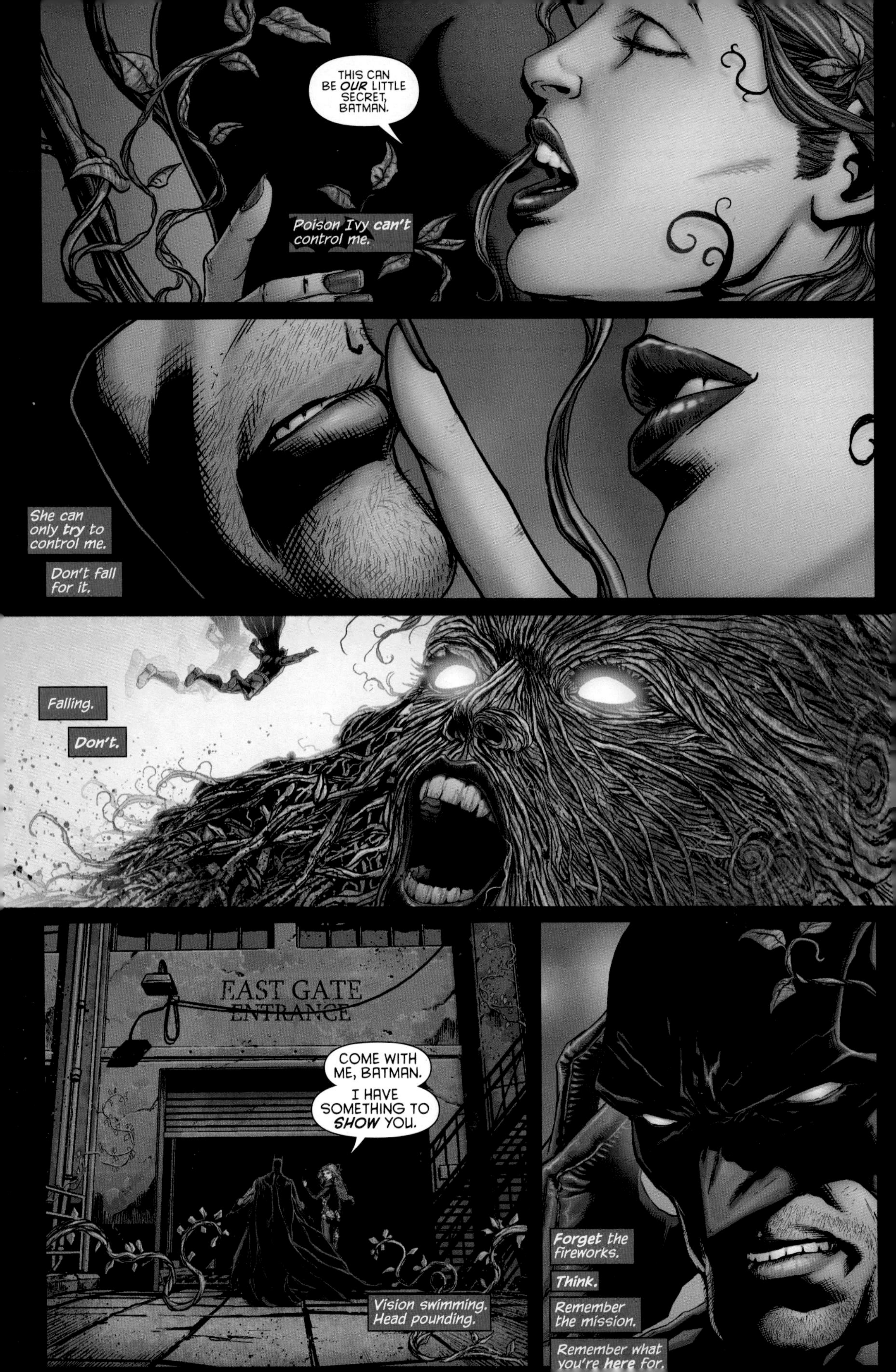
THIS CAN BE OUR LITTLE SECRET, BATMAN.
Poison Ivy can't control me.
She can only try to control me.
Don't fall for it.
Falling.
Don't.
EAST GATE ENTRANCE
COME WITH ME, BATMAN.
I HAVE SOMETHING TO SHOW YOU.
Vision swimming. Head pounding.
Forget the fireworks.
Think.
Remember the mission.
Remember what you're here for.

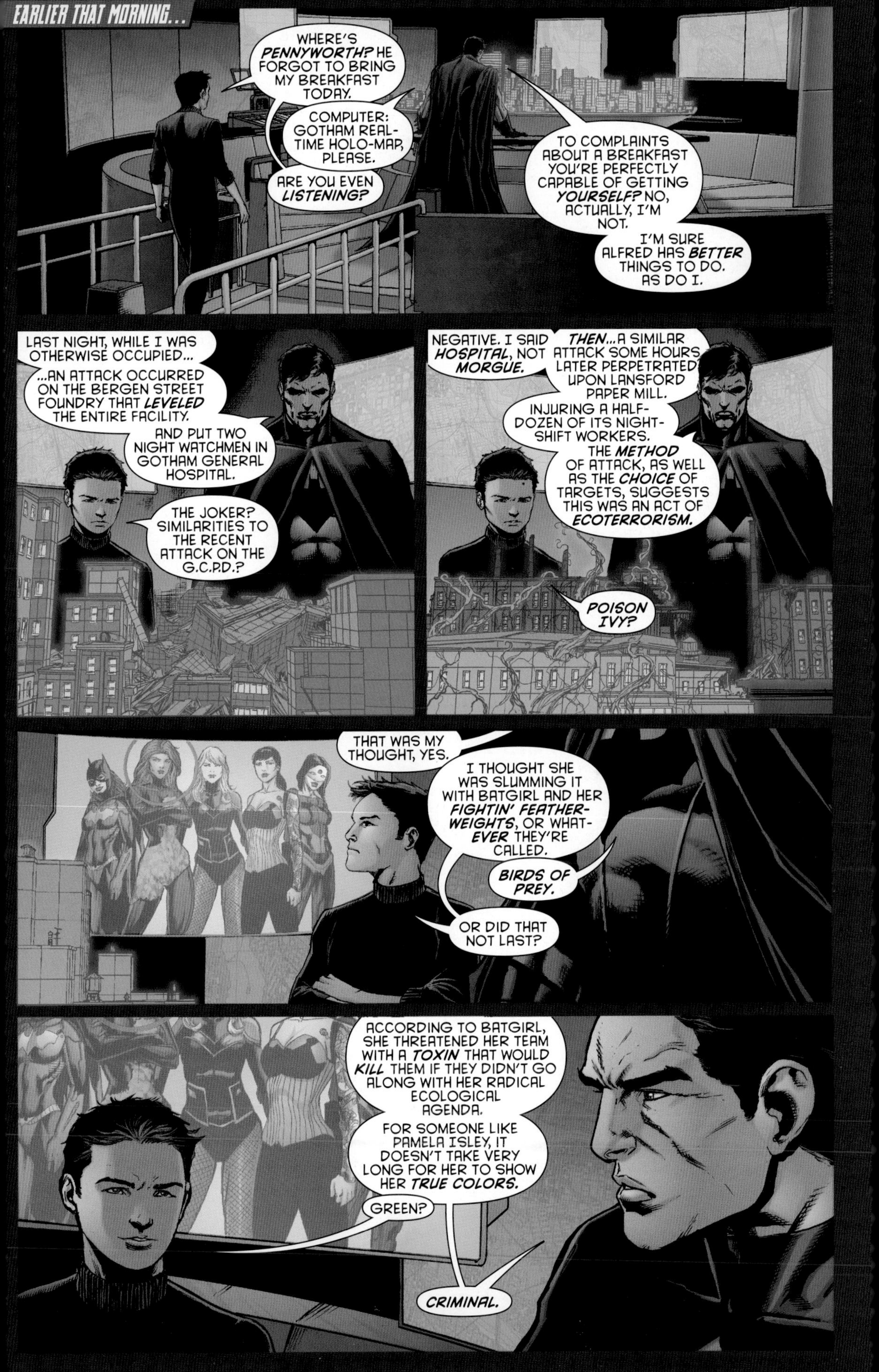

EARLIER THAT MORNING...
WHERE'S PENNYWORTH? HE FORGOT TO BRING MY BREAKFAST TODAY.
COMPUTER: GOTHAM REAL-TIME HOLO-MAP, PLEASE.
ARE YOU EVEN LISTENING?
TO COMPLAINTS ABOUT A BREAKFAST YOU'RE PERFECTLY CAPABLE OF GETTING YOURSELF? NO, ACTUALLY, I'M NOT.
I'M SURE ALFRED HAS BETTER THINGS TO DO. AS DO I.
LAST NIGHT, WHILE I WAS OTHERWISE OCCUPIED...
...AN ATTACK OCCURRED ON THE BERGEN STREET FOUNDRY THAT LEVELED THE ENTIRE FACILITY.
AND PUT TWO NIGHT WATCHMEN IN GOTHAM GENERAL HOSPITAL.
THE JOKER? SIMILARITIES TO THE RECENT ATTACK ON THE G.C.P.D.?
NEGATIVE. I SAID HOSPITAL, NOT MORGUE.
THEN...A SIMILAR ATTACK SOME HOURS LATER PERPETRATED UPON LANSFORD PAPER MILL.
INJURING A HALF-DOZEN OF ITS NIGHT-SHIFT WORKERS.
THE METHOD OF ATTACK, AS WELL AS THE CHOICE OF TARGETS, SUGGESTS THIS WAS AN ACT OF ECOTERRORISM.
POISON IVY?
THAT WAS MY THOUGHT, YES.
I THOUGHT SHE WAS SLUMMING IT WITH BATGIRL AND HER FIGHTIN' FEATHER-WEIGHTS, OR WHAT-EVER THEY'RE CALLED.
BIRDS OF PREY.
OR DID THAT NOT LAST?
ACCORDING TO BATGIRL, SHE THREATENED HER TEAM WITH A TOXIN THAT WOULD KILL THEM IF THEY DIDN'T GO ALONG WITH HER RADICAL ECOLOGICAL AGENDA.
FOR SOMEONE LIKE PAMELA ISLEY, IT DOESN'T TAKE VERY LONG FOR HER TO SHOW HER TRUE COLORS.
GREEN?
CRIMINAL.

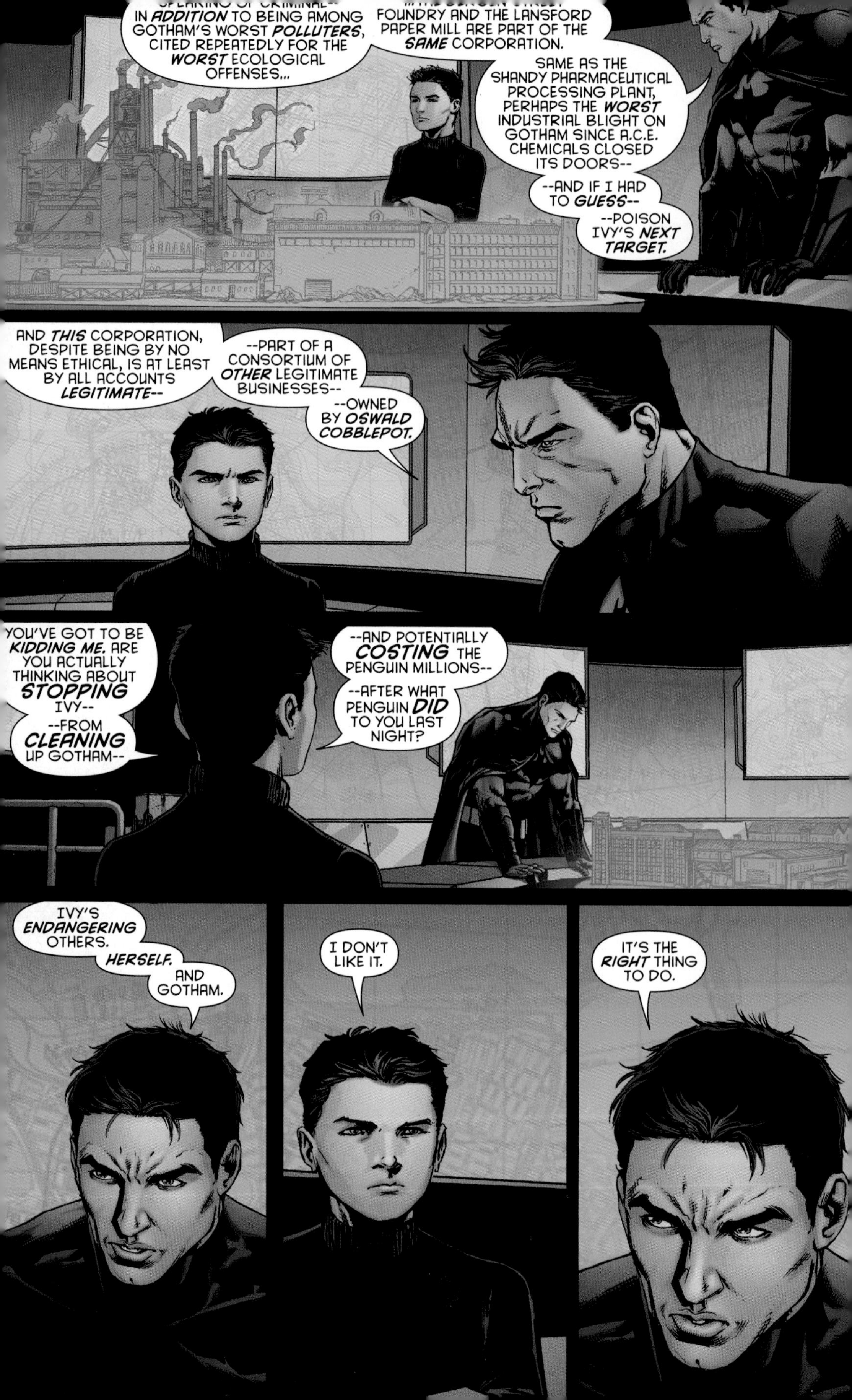
IN ADDITION TO BEING AMONG GOTHAM'S WORST POLLUTERS, CITED REPEATEDLY FOR THE WORST ECOLOGICAL OFFENSES...
FOUNDRY AND THE LANSFORD PAPER MILL ARE PART OF THE SAME CORPORATION.
SAME AS THE SHANDY PHARMACEUTICAL PROCESSING PLANT, PERHAPS THE WORST INDUSTRIAL BLIGHT ON GOTHAM SINCE A.C.E. CHEMICALS CLOSED ITS DOORS--
--AND IF I HAD TO GUESS--
--POISON IVY'S NEXT TARGET.
AND THIS CORPORATION, DESPITE BEING BY NO MEANS ETHICAL, IS AT LEAST BY ALL ACCOUNTS LEGITIMATE--
--PART OF A CONSORTIUM OF OTHER LEGITIMATE BUSINESSES--
--OWNED BY OSWALD COBBLEPOT.
YOU'VE GOT TO BE KIDDING ME. ARE YOU ACTUALLY THINKING ABOUT STOPPING IVY--
--FROM CLEANING UP GOTHAM--
--AND POTENTIALLY COSTING THE PENGUIN MILLIONS--
--AFTER WHAT PENGUIN DID TO YOU LAST NIGHT?
IVY'S ENDANGERING OTHERS.
HERSELF.
AND GOTHAM.
I DON'T LIKE IT.
IT'S THE RIGHT THING TO DO.

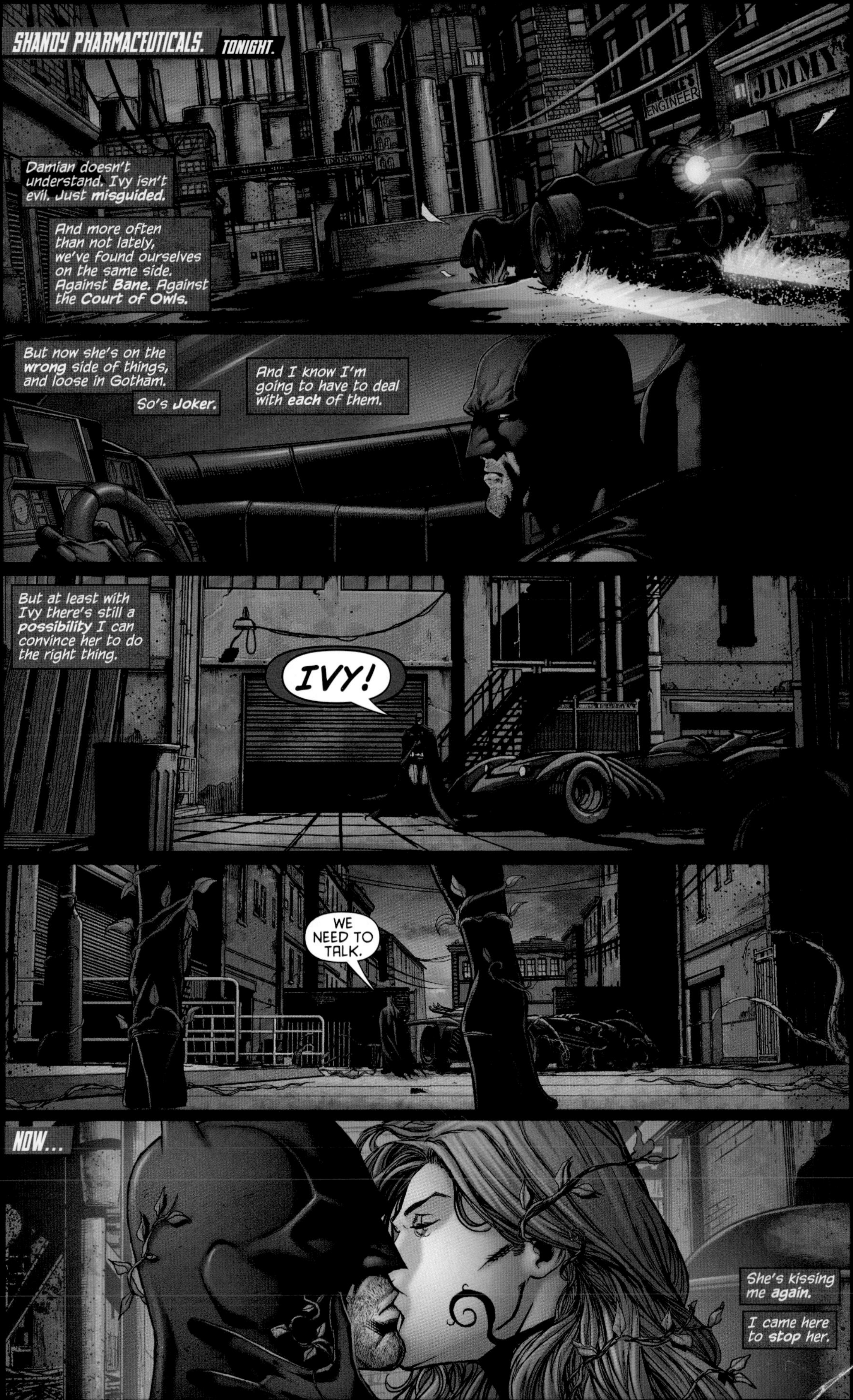
SHANDY PHARMACEUTICALS.
TONIGHT.
JIMMY
ENGINEER
Damian doesn't understand. Ivy isn't evil. Just misguided.
And more often than not lately, we've found ourselves on the same side. Against Bane. Against the Court of Owls.
But now she's on the wrong side of things, and loose in Gotham.
So's Joker.
And I know I'm going to have to deal with each of them.
But at least with Ivy there's still a possibility I can convince her to do the right thing.
IVY!
WE NEED TO TALK.
NOW...
She's kissing me again.
I came here to stop her.

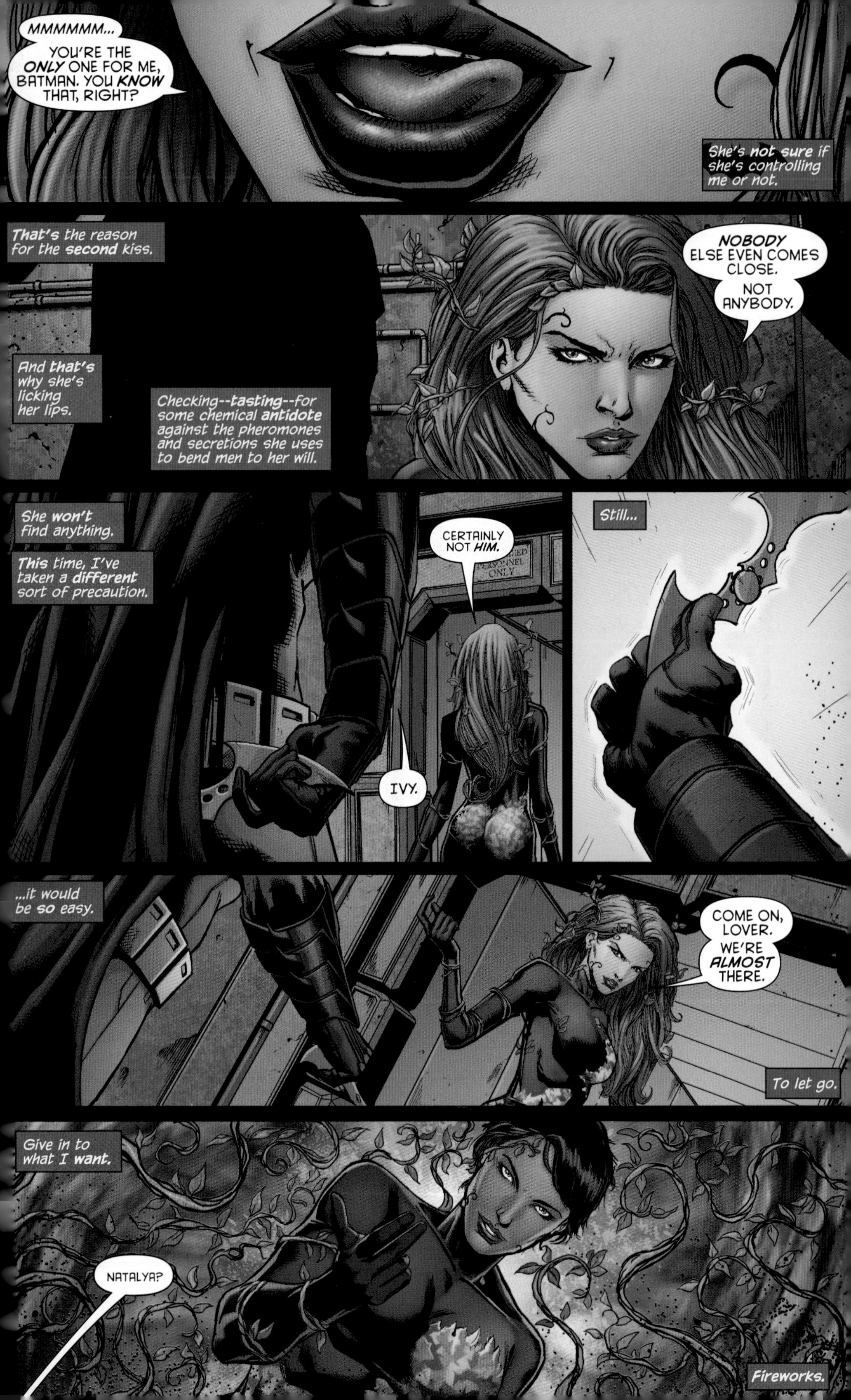

MMMMMMM...
YOU'RE THE ONLY ONE FOR ME, BATMAN. YOU KNOW THAT, RIGHT?
She's not sure if she's controlling me or not.
That's the reason for the second kiss.
NOBODY ELSE EVEN COMES CLOSE.
NOT ANYBODY.
And that's why she's licking her lips.
Checking--tasting--for some chemical antidote against the pheromones and secretions she uses to bend men to her will.
She won't find anything.
This time, I've taken a different sort of precaution.
CERTAINLY NOT HIM.
IVY.
Still...
...it would be so easy.
COME ON, LOVER.
WE'RE ALMOST THERE.
To let go.
Give in to what I want.
NATALYA?
Fireworks.

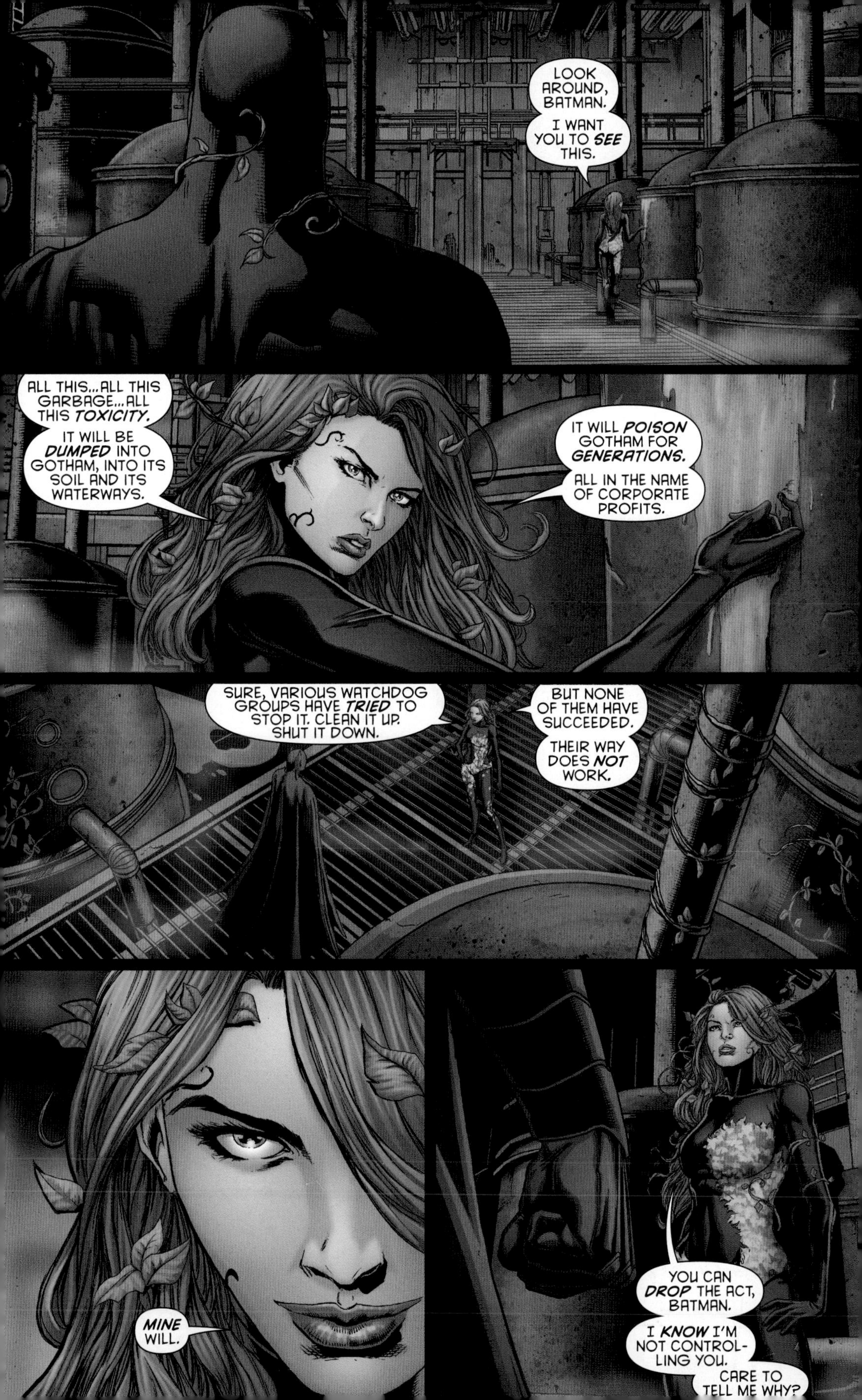
LOOK AROUND, BATMAN.
I WANT YOU TO SEE THIS.
ALL THIS...ALL THIS GARBAGE...ALL THIS TOXICITY.
IT WILL BE DUMPED INTO GOTHAM, INTO ITS SOIL AND ITS WATERWAYS.
IT WILL POISON GOTHAM FOR GENERATIONS.
ALL IN THE NAME OF CORPORATE PROFITS.
SURE, VARIOUS WATCHDOG GROUPS HAVE TRIED TO STOP IT. CLEAN IT UP. SHUT IT DOWN.
BUT NONE OF THEM HAVE SUCCEEDED.
THEIR WAY DOES NOT WORK.
MINE WILL.
YOU CAN DROP THE ACT, BATMAN.
I KNOW I'M NOT CONTROL-LING YOU.
CARE TO TELL ME WHY?

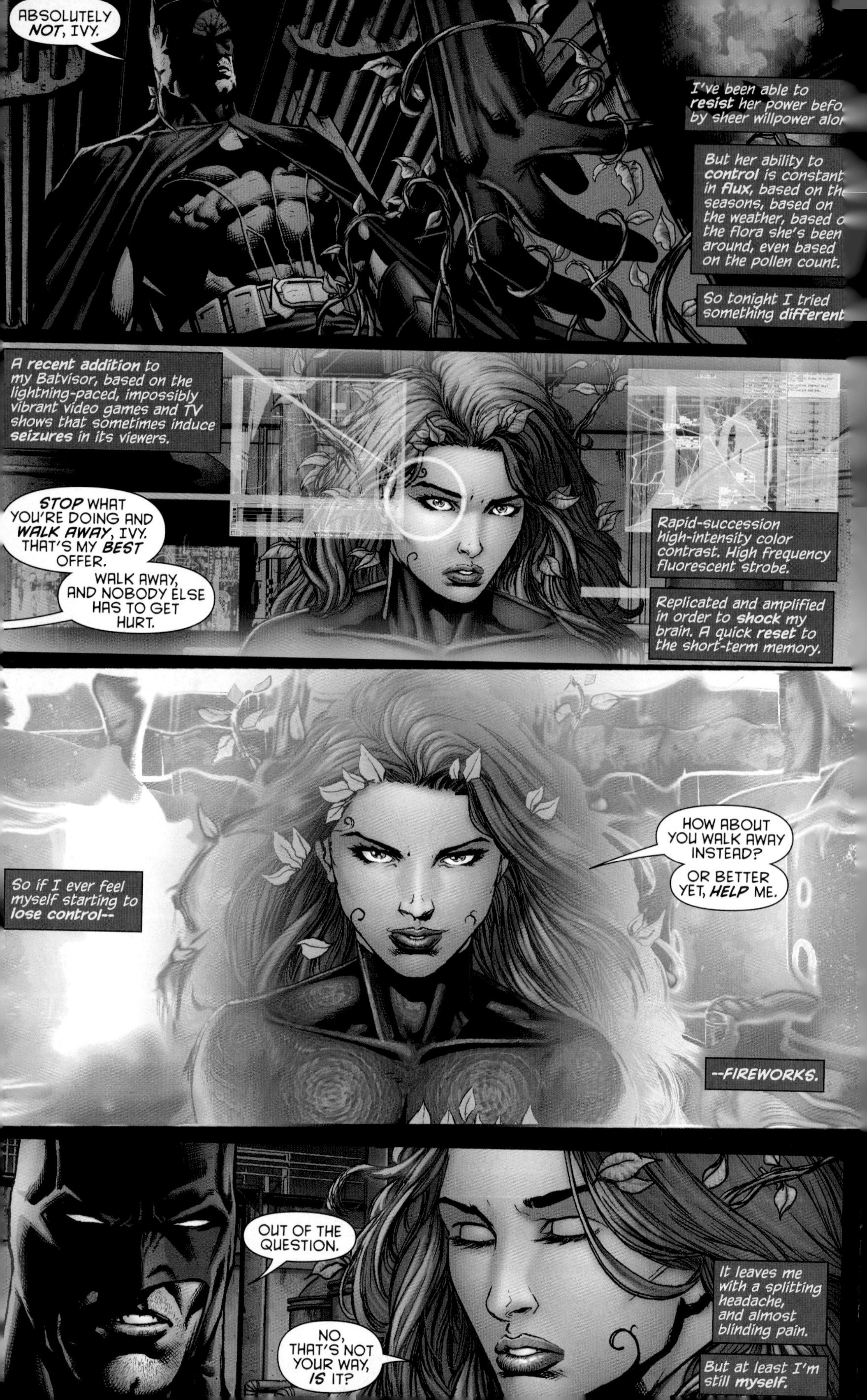
ABSOLUTELY NOT, IVY.
I've been able to resist her power befo by sheer willpower alo
But her ability to control is constant in flux, based on th seasons, based on the weather, based o the flora she's been around, even based on the pollen count.
So tonight I tried something different
A recent addition to my Batvisor, based on the lightning-paced, impossibly vibrant video games and TV shows that sometimes induce seizures in its viewers.
STOP WHAT YOU'RE DOING AND WALK AWAY, IVY. THAT'S MY BEST OFFER.
WALK AWAY, AND NOBODY ELSE HAS TO GET HURT.
Rapid-succession high-intensity color contrast. High frequency fluorescent strobe.
Replicated and amplified in order to shock my brain. A quick reset to the short-term memory.
So if I ever feel myself starting to lose control--
HOW ABOUT YOU WALK AWAY INSTEAD?
OR BETTER YET, HELP ME.
--FIREWORKS.
OUT OF THE QUESTION.
NO, THAT'S NOT YOUR WAY, IS IT?
It leaves me with a splitting headache, and almost blinding pain.
But at least I'm still myself.

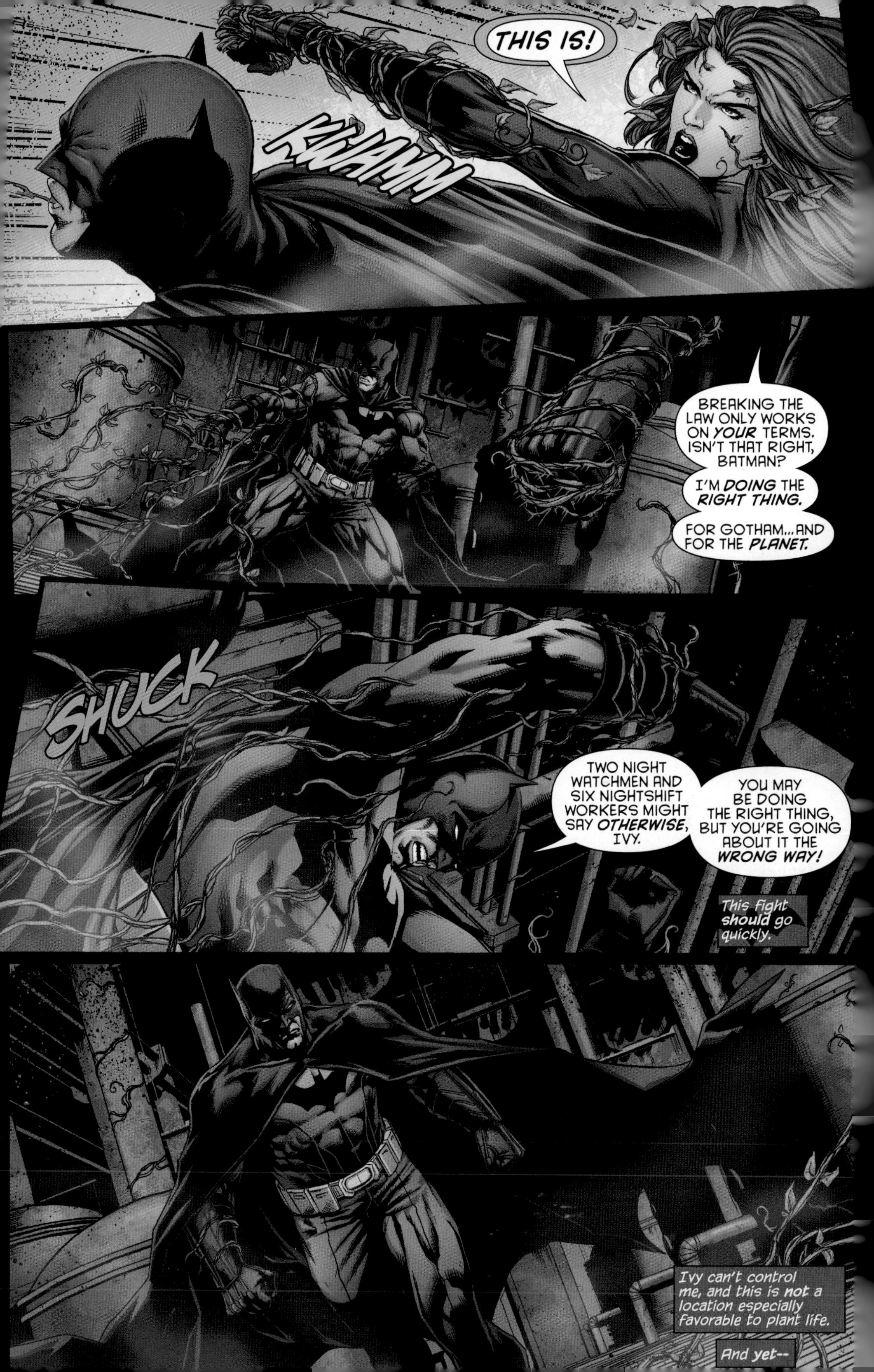
THIS IS!
KWAMM
BREAKING THE LAW ONLY WORKS ON YOUR TERMS. ISN'T THAT RIGHT, BATMAN?
I'M DOING THE RIGHT THING.
FOR GOTHAM...AND FOR THE PLANET.
SHUCK
TWO NIGHT WATCHMEN AND SIX NIGHTSHIFT WORKERS MIGHT SAY OTHERWISE, IVY.
YOU MAY BE DOING THE RIGHT THING, BUT YOU'RE GOING ABOUT IT THE WRONG WAY!
This fight should go quickly.
Ivy can't control me, and this is not a location especially favorable to plant life.
And yet--

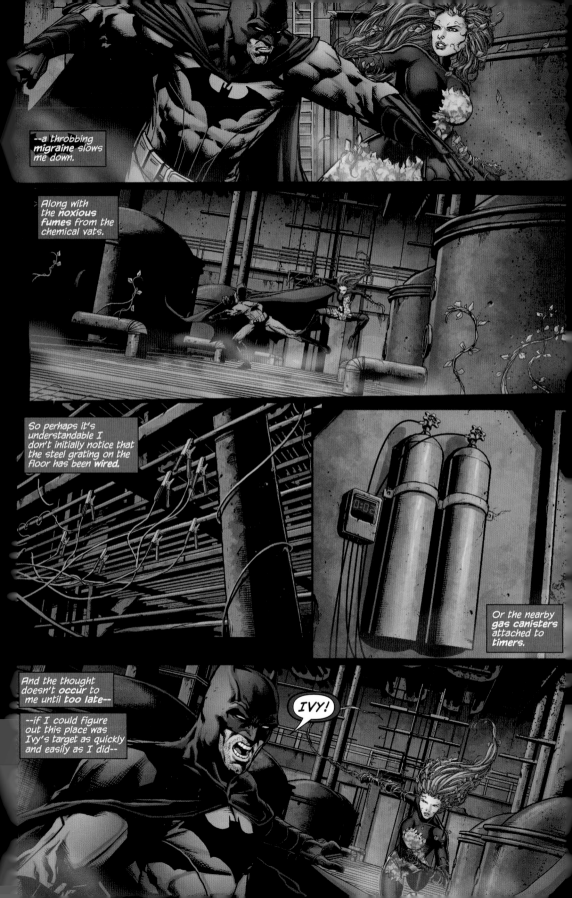

--a throbbing **migraine** slows me down.

Along with the **noxious fumes** from the chemical vats.

So perhaps it's understandable I don't initially notice that the steel grating on the floor has been **wired.**

Or the nearby **gas** canisters attached to **timers.**

And the thought doesn't **occur** to me until **too late**--

--if I could figure out this place was Ivy's target as quickly and easily as I did--

IVY!

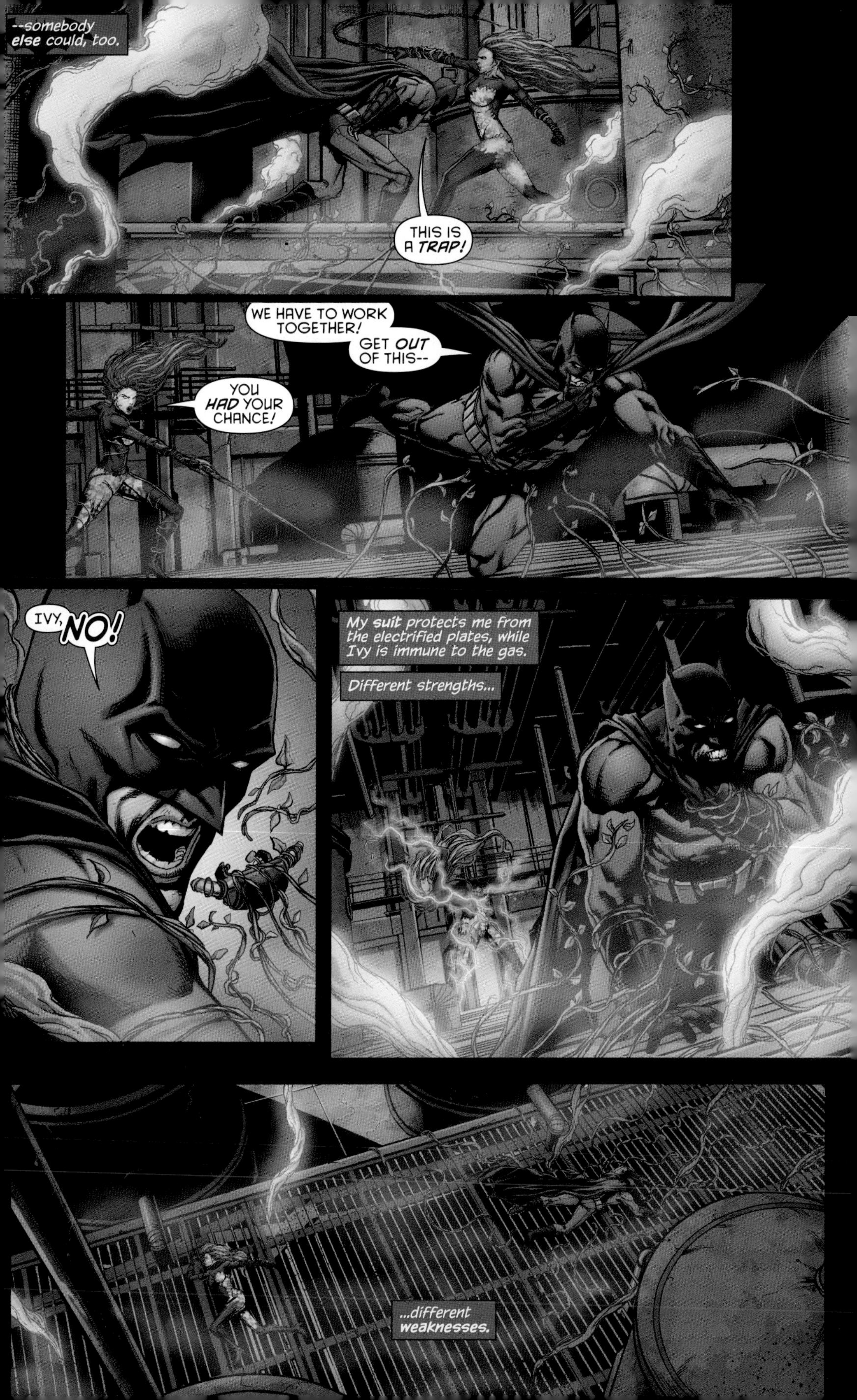
--somebody else could, too.
THIS IS A TRAP!
WE HAVE TO WORK TOGETHER!
GET OUT OF THIS--
YOU HAD YOUR CHANCE!
IVY, NO!
My suit protects me from the electrified plates, while Ivy is immune to the gas.
Different strengths...
...different weaknesses.

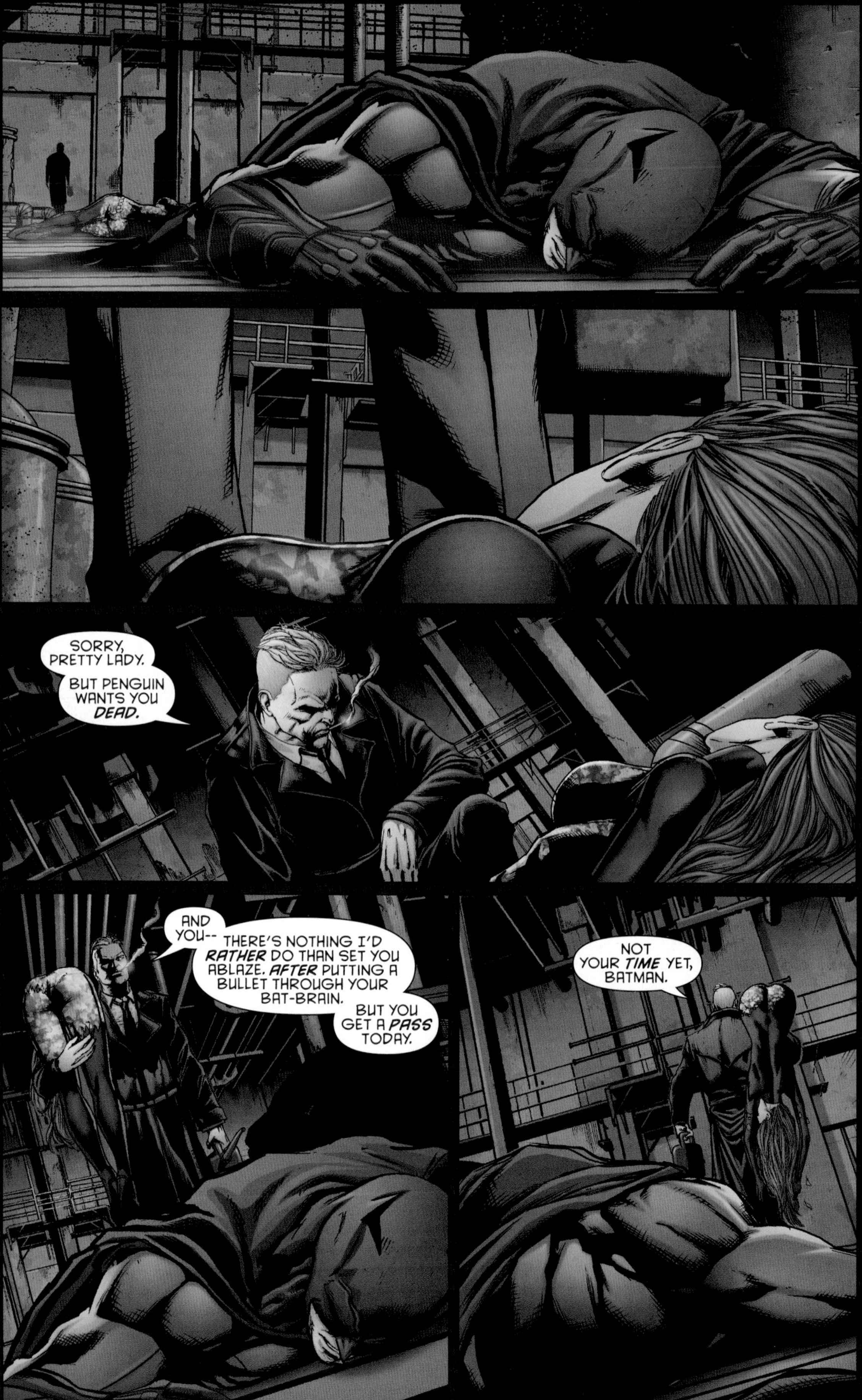
SORRY, PRETTY LADY.
BUT PENGUIN WANTS YOU DEAD.
AND YOU--
THERE'S NOTHING I'D RATHER DO THAN SET YOU ABLAZE. AFTER PUTTING A BULLET THROUGH YOUR BAT-BRAIN.
BUT YOU GET A PASS TODAY.
NOT YOUR TIME YET, BATMAN.

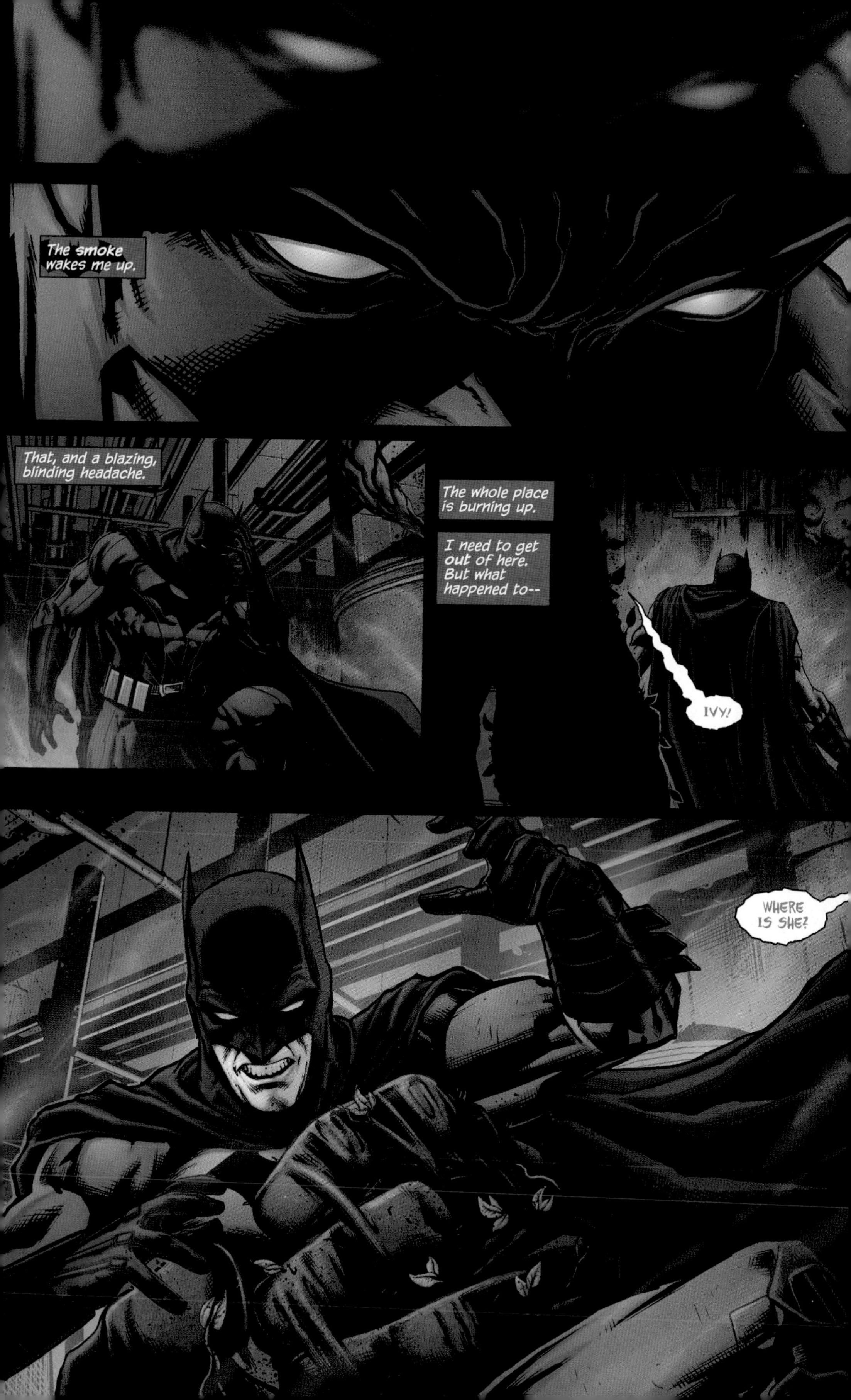
The smoke wakes me up.
That, and a blazing, blinding headache.
The whole place is burning up.
I need to get out of here. But what happened to--
IVY!
WHERE IS SHE?

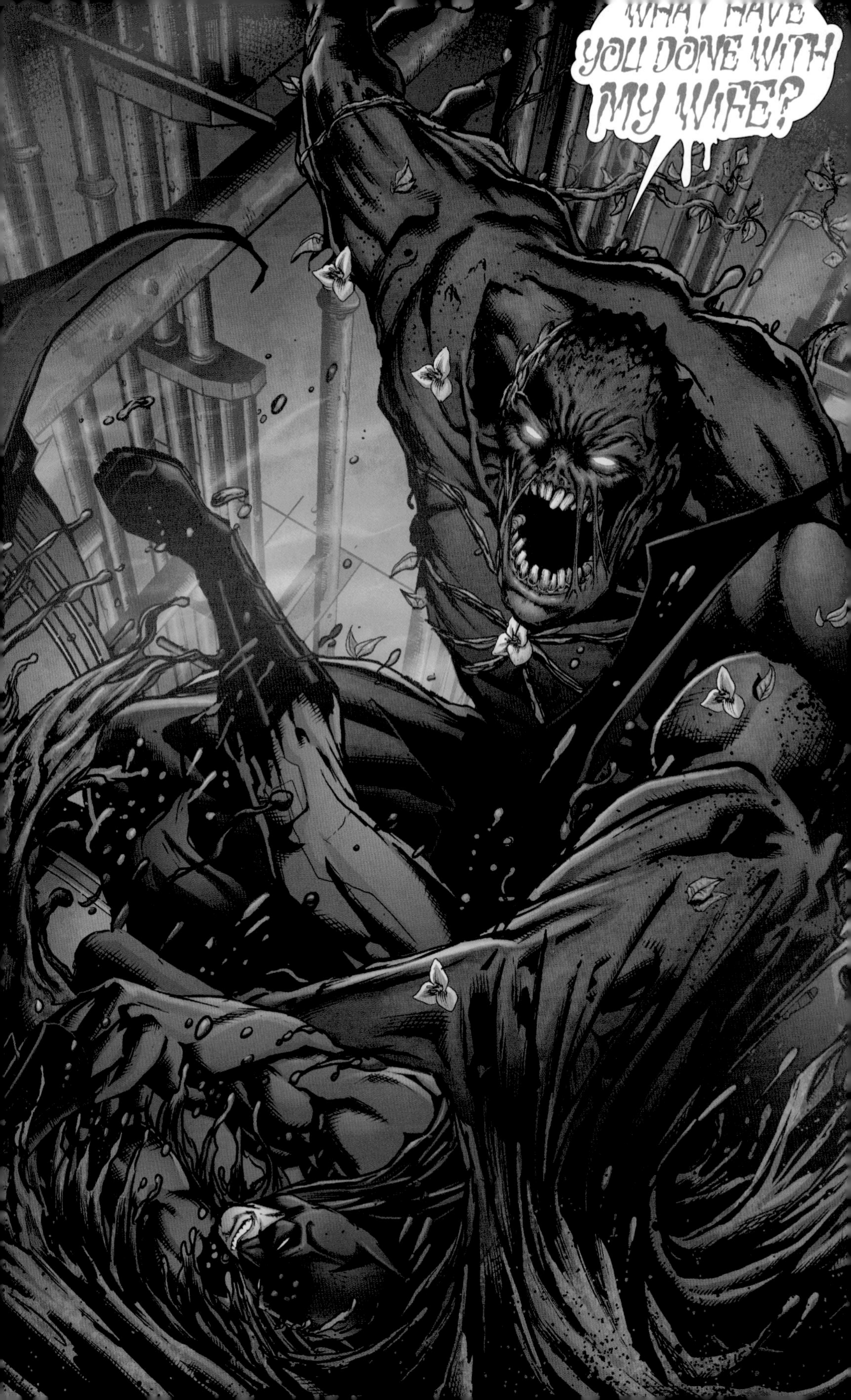
WHAT HAVE YOU DONE WITH MY WIFE?

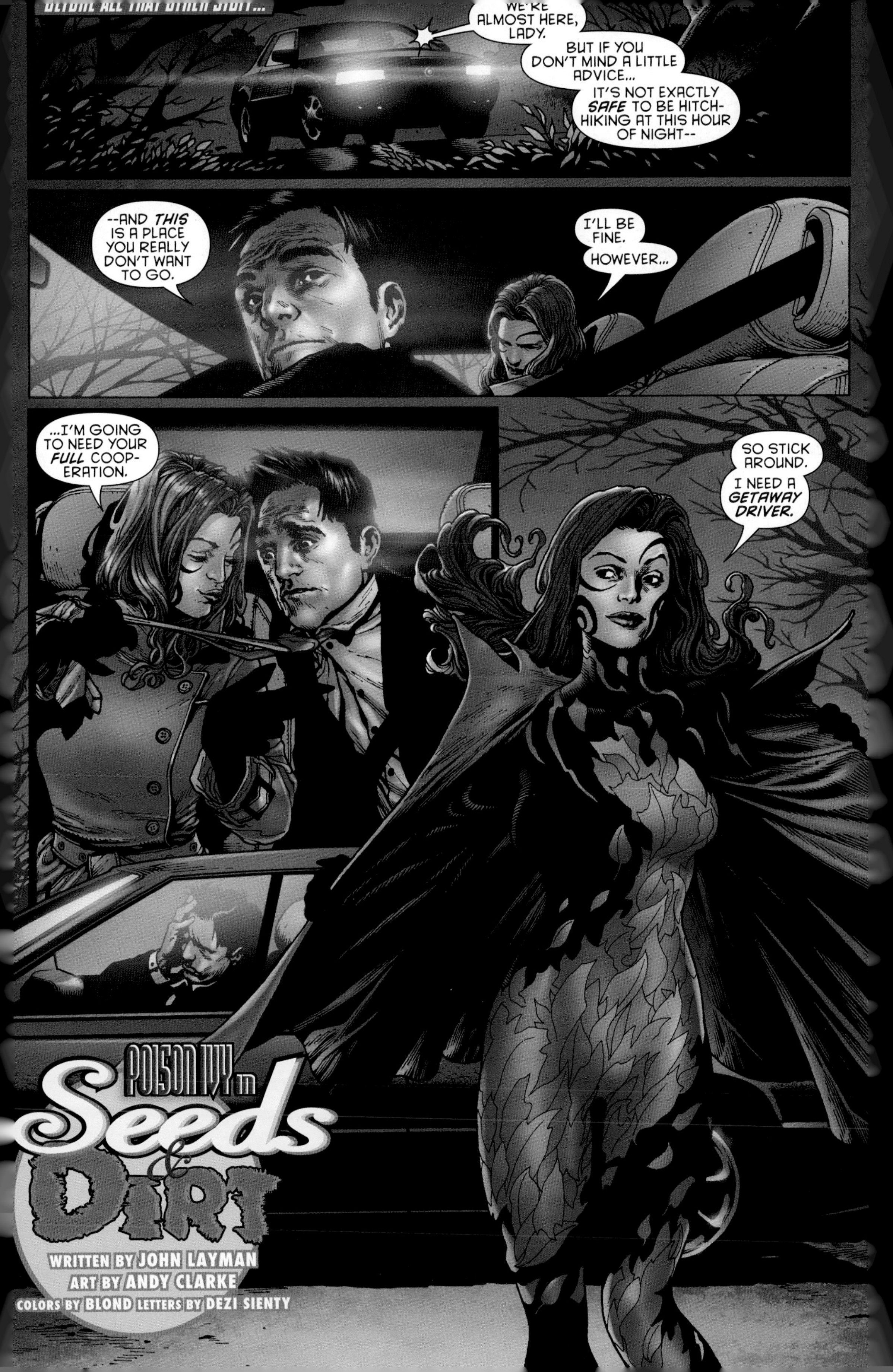

WE'RE ALMOST HERE, LADY.
BUT IF YOU DON'T MIND A LITTLE ADVICE...
IT'S NOT EXACTLY SAFE TO BE HITCH-HIKING AT THIS HOUR OF NIGHT--
--AND THIS IS A PLACE YOU REALLY DON'T WANT TO GO.
I'LL BE FINE.
HOWEVER...
...I'M GOING TO NEED YOUR FULL COOP-ERATION.
SO STICK AROUND.
I NEED A GETAWAY DRIVER.
POISON IVY in
Seeds & Dirt
WRITTEN BY JOHN LAYMAN
ART BY ANDY CLARKE
COLORS BY BLOND LETTERS BY DEZI SIENTY

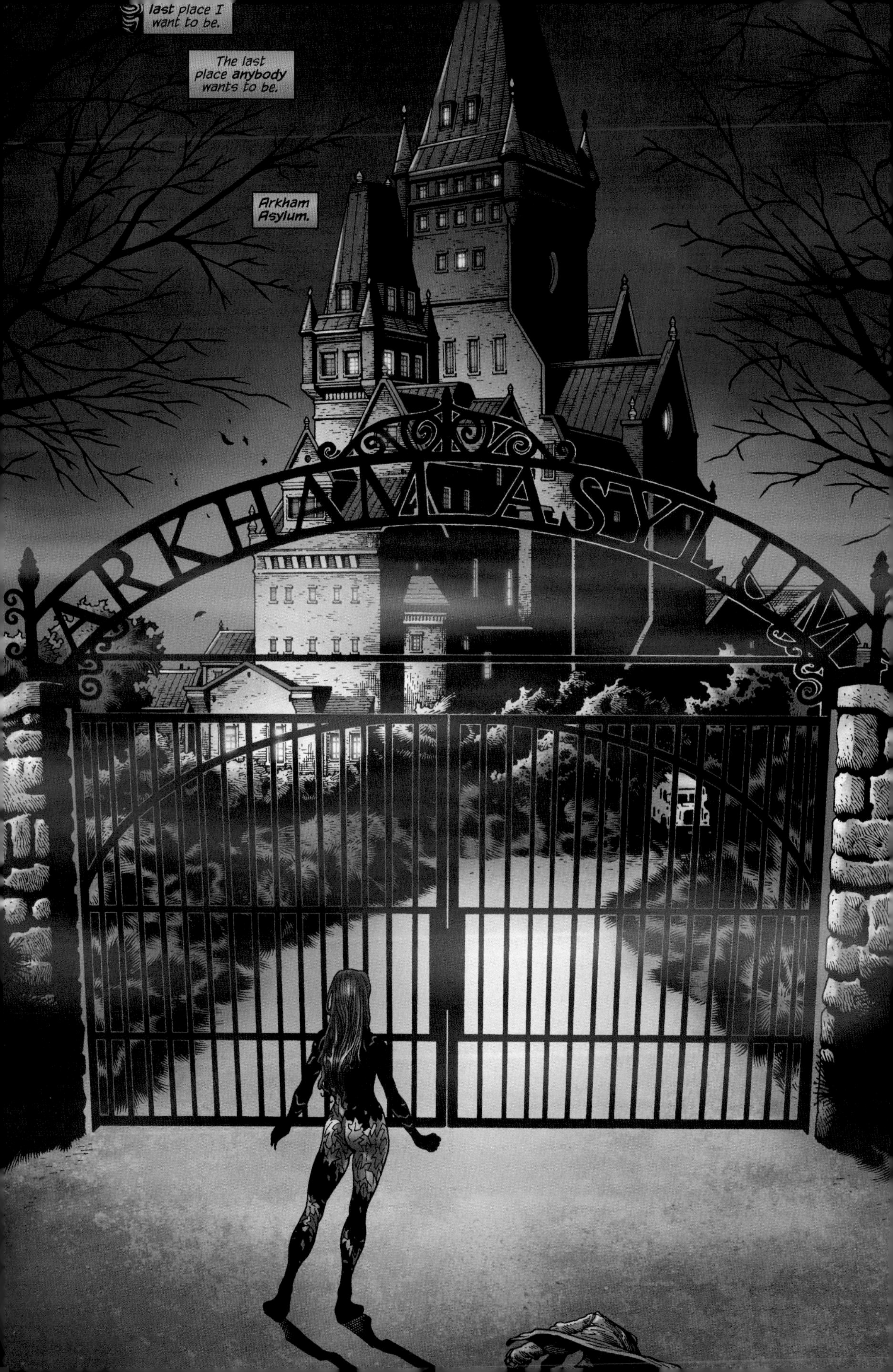

last place I want to be.
The last place anybody wants to be.
Arkham Asylum.
ARKHAM ASYLUM

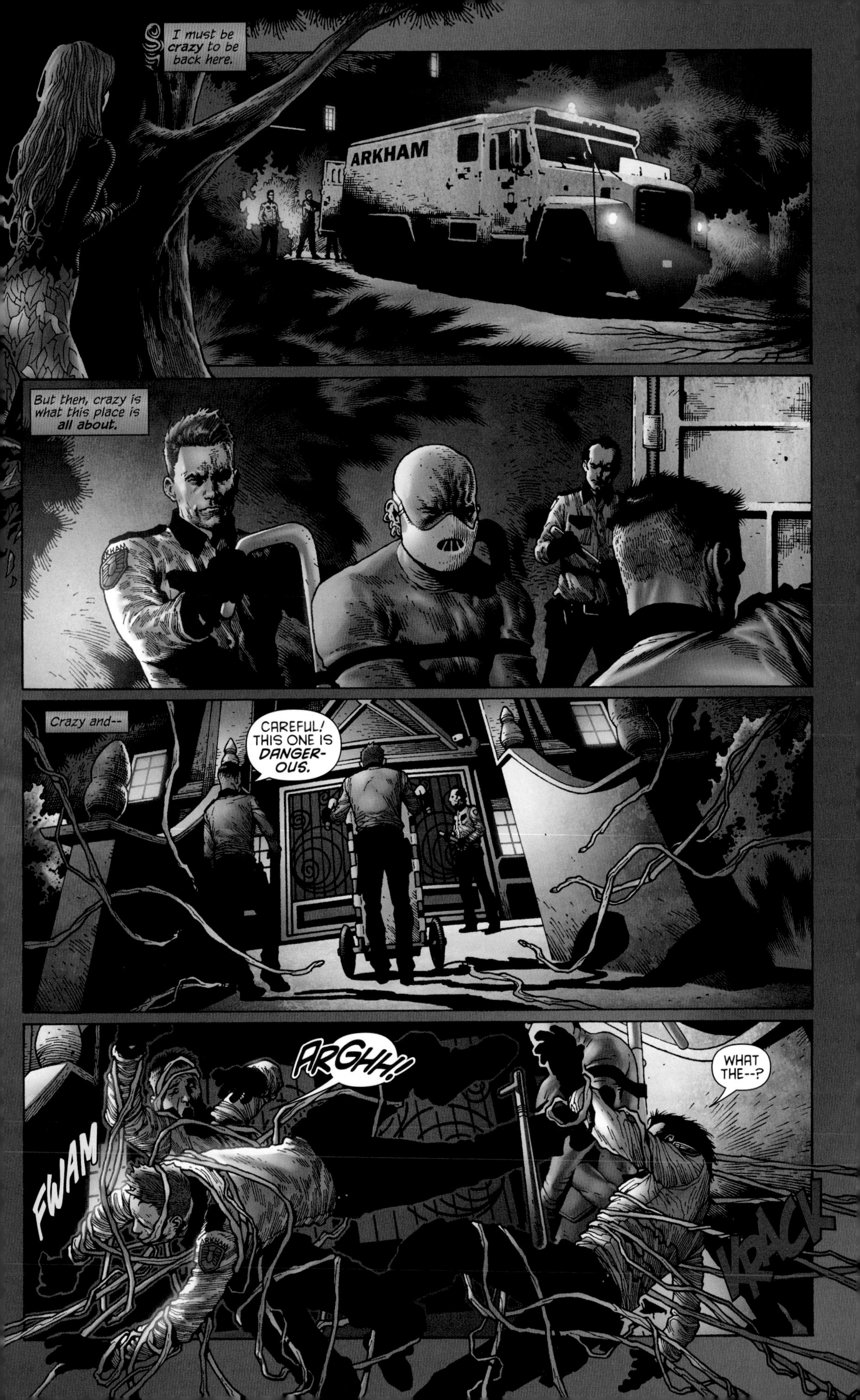
I must be crazy to be back here.
ARKHAM
But then, crazy is what this place is all about.
Crazy and--
CAREFUL! THIS ONE IS DANGER-OUS.
ARGHH!!
WHAT THE--?
FWAM

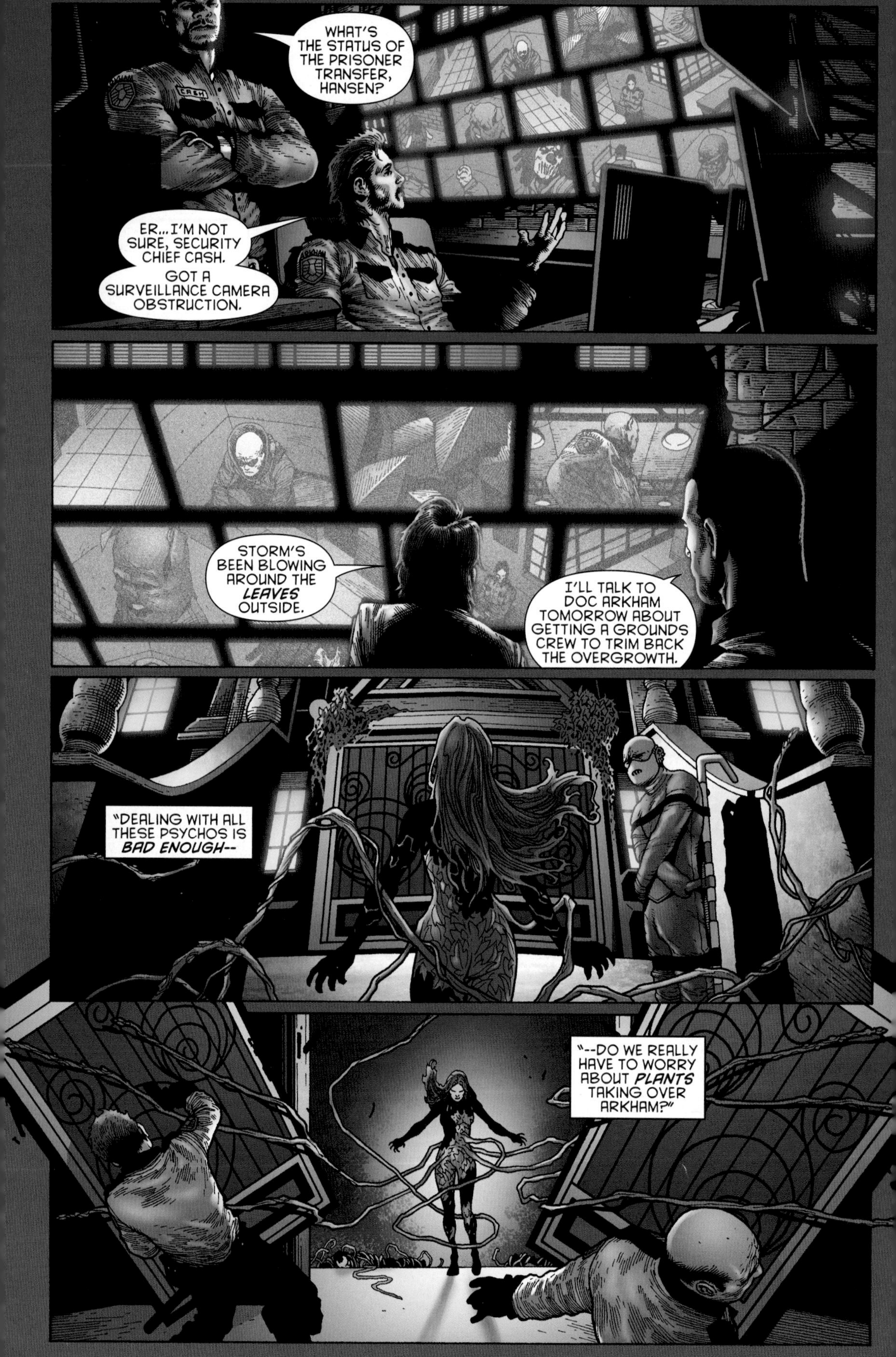
WHAT'S THE STATUS OF THE PRISONER TRANSFER, HANSEN?
ER...I'M NOT SURE, SECURITY CHIEF CASH.
GOT A SURVEILLANCE CAMERA OBSTRUCTION.
STORM'S BEEN BLOWING AROUND THE *LEAVES* OUTSIDE.
I'LL TALK TO DOC ARKHAM TOMORROW ABOUT GETTING A GROUNDS CREW TO TRIM BACK THE OVERGROWTH.
"DEALING WITH ALL THESE PSYCHOS IS *BAD ENOUGH*--
"--DO WE REALLY HAVE TO WORRY ABOUT *PLANTS* TAKING OVER ARKHAM?"

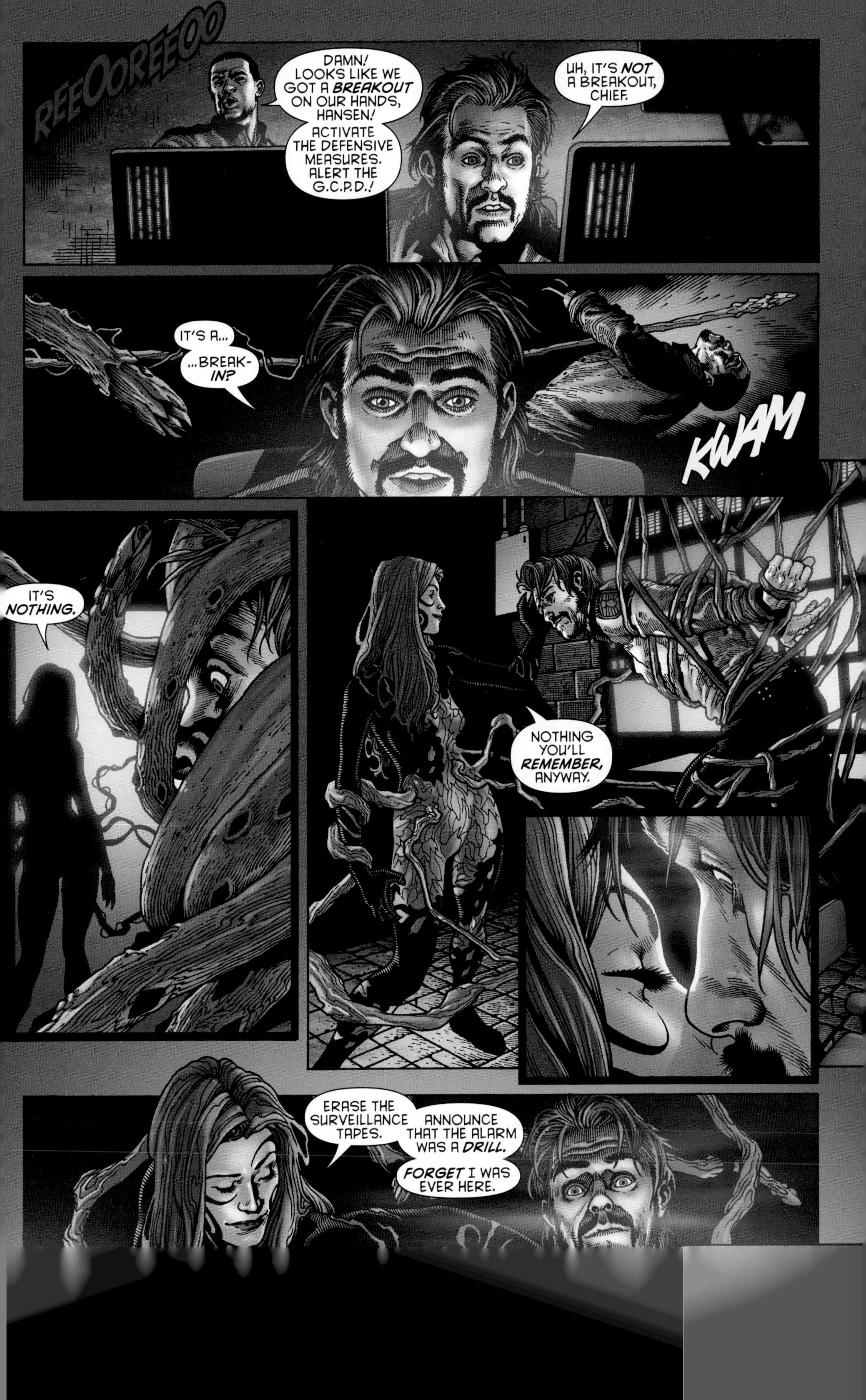
REEOOREEEOO
DAMN! LOOKS LIKE WE GOT A BREAKOUT ON OUR HANDS, HANSEN! ACTIVATE THE DEFENSIVE MEASURES. ALERT THE G.C.P.D.!
UH, IT'S NOT A BREAKOUT, CHIEF.
IT'S A...
...BREAK-IN?
KWAM
IT'S NOTHING.
NOTHING YOU'LL REMEMBER, ANYWAY.
ERASE THE SURVEILLANCE TAPES.
ANNOUNCE THAT THE ALARM WAS A DRILL.
FORGET I WAS EVER HERE.

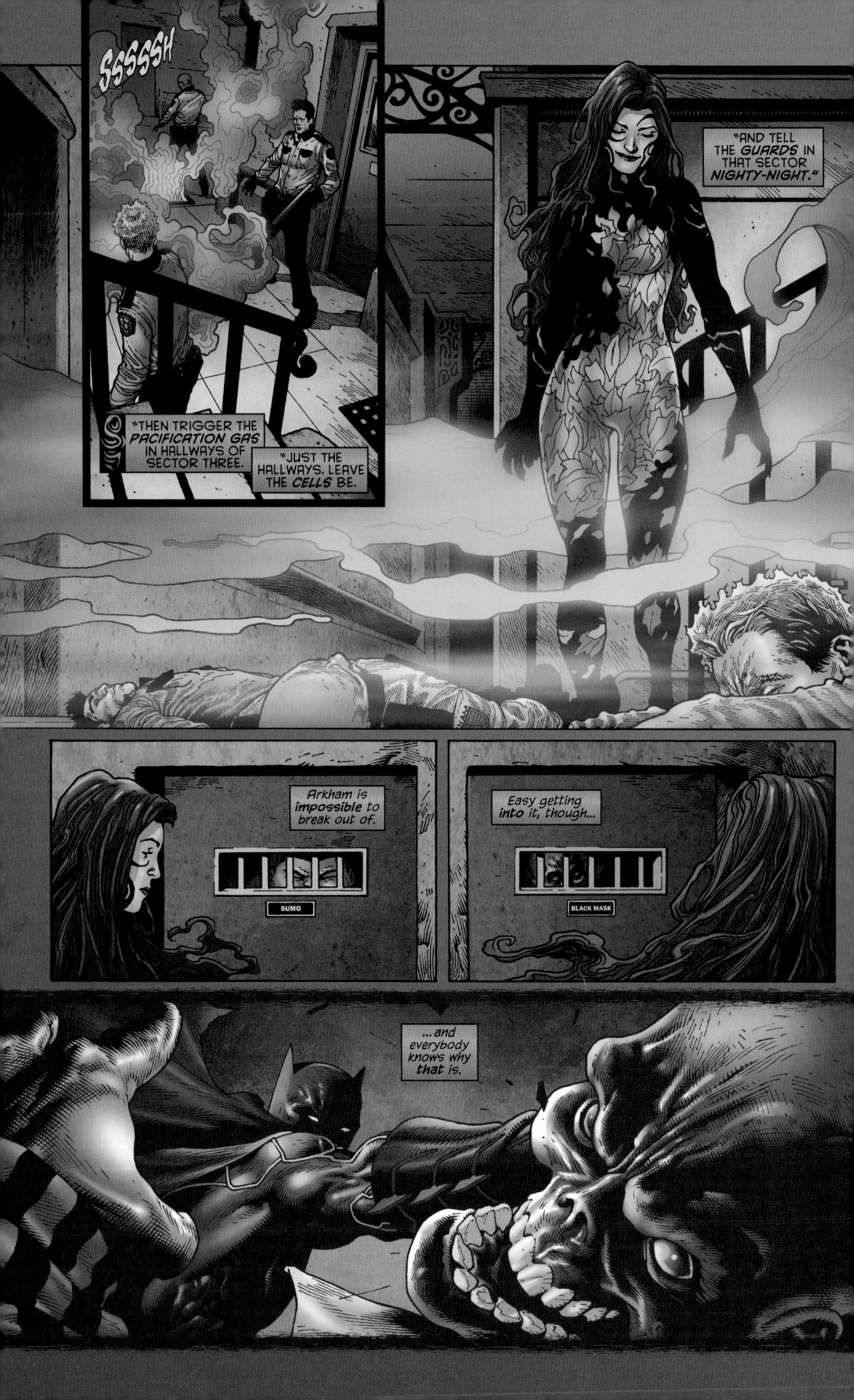
SSSSSH
"THEN TRIGGER THE PACIFICATION GAS IN HALLWAYS OF SECTOR THREE.
"JUST THE HALLWAYS. LEAVE THE CELLS BE.
"AND TELL THE GUARDS IN THAT SECTOR NIGHTY-NIGHT."
Arkham is impossible to break out of.
SUMO
Easy getting into it, though...
BLACK MASK
...and everybody knows why that is.

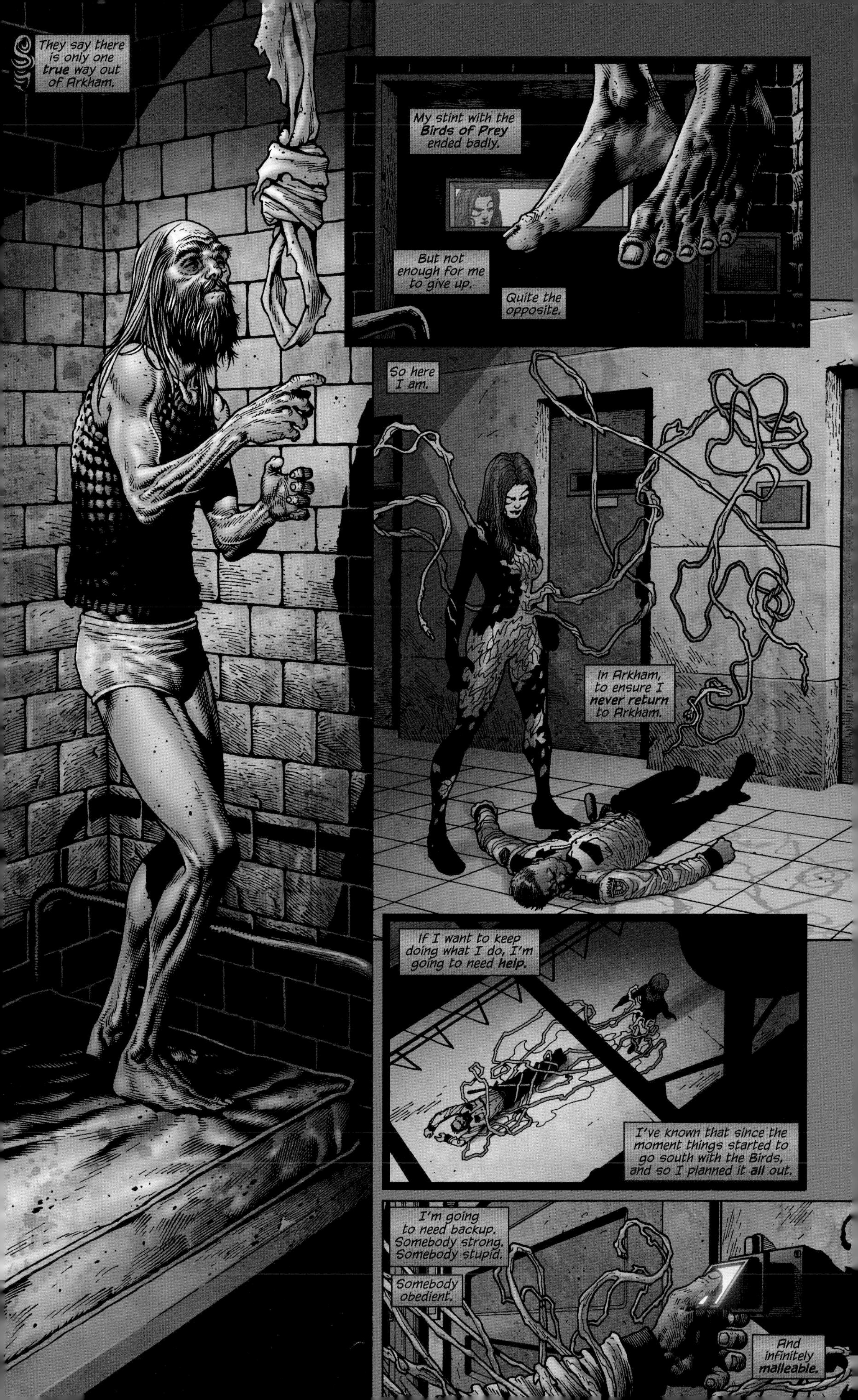
They say there is only one true way out of Arkham.
My stint with the Birds of Prey ended badly.
But not enough for me to give up.
Quite the opposite.
So here I am.
In Arkham, to ensure I never return to Arkham.
If I want to keep doing what I do, I'm going to need help.
I've known that since the moment things started to go south with the Birds, and so I planned it all out.
I'm going to need backup. Somebody strong. Somebody stupid.
Somebody obedient.
And infinitely malleable.

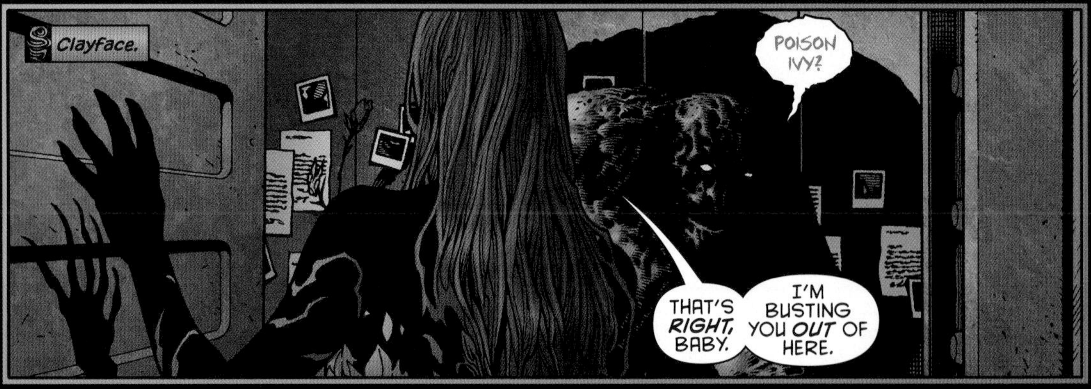
Clayface.
POISON IVY?
THAT'S *RIGHT,* BABY.
I'M BUSTING YOU *OUT* OF HERE.

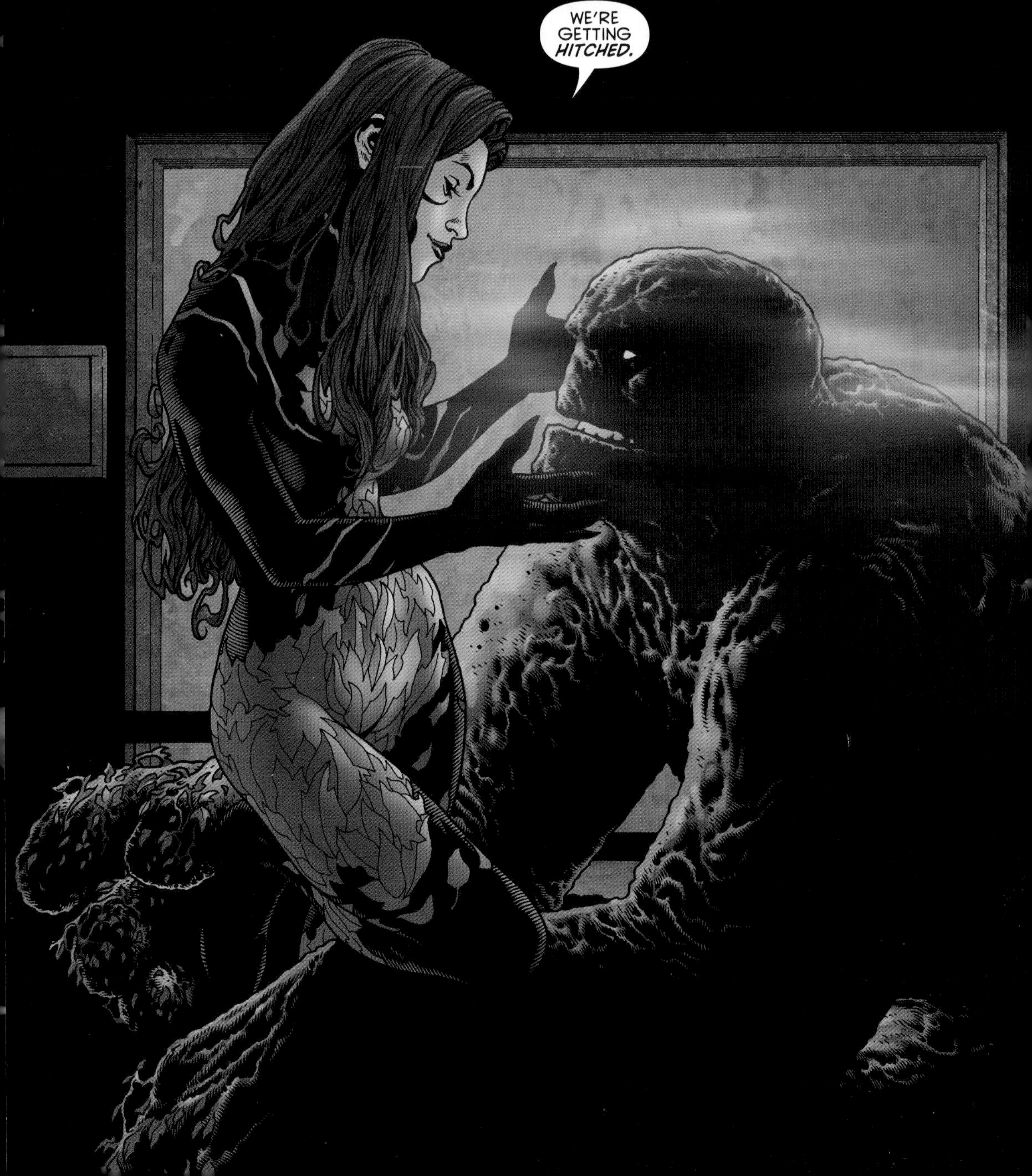
WE'RE GETTING *HITCHED.*

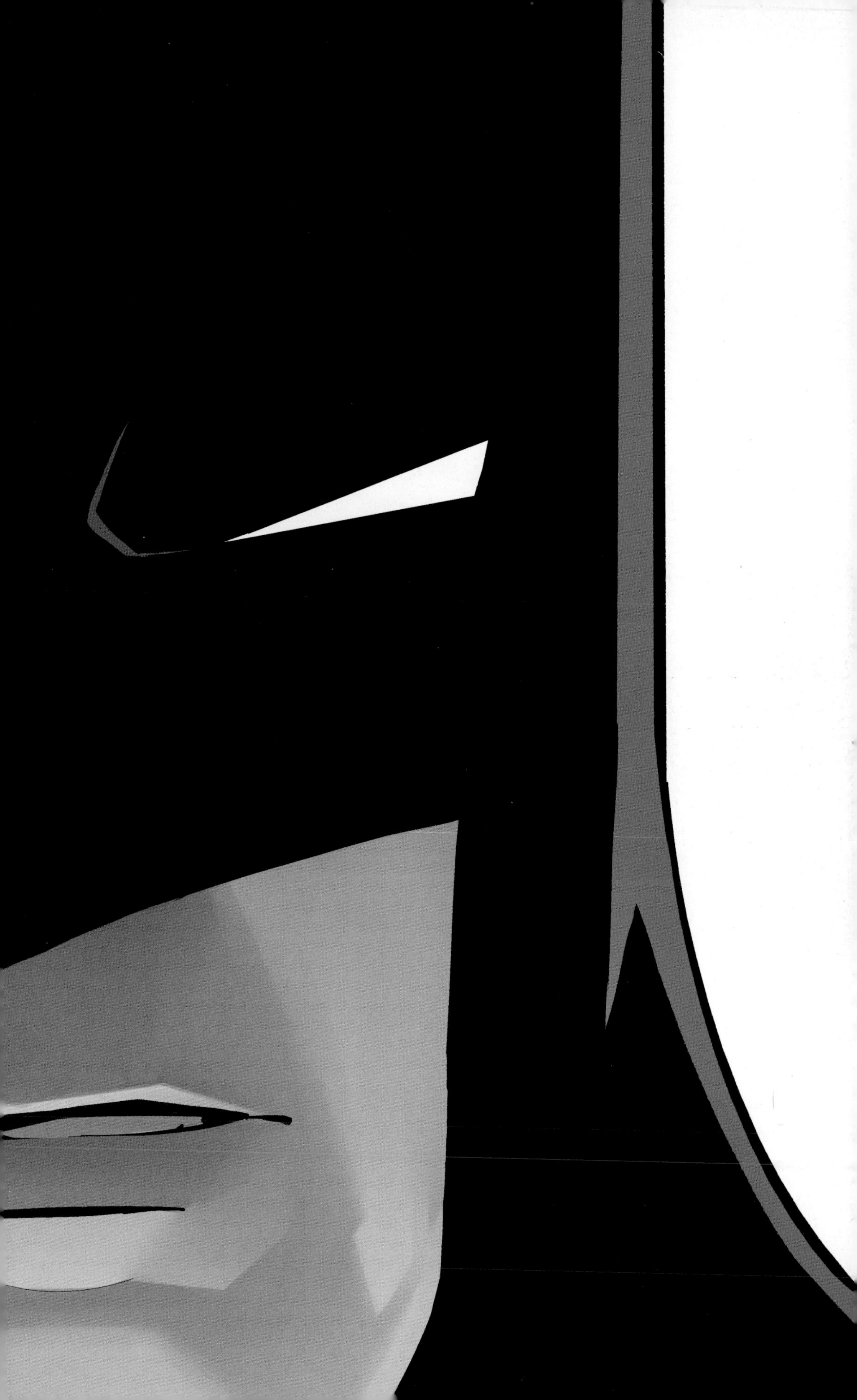

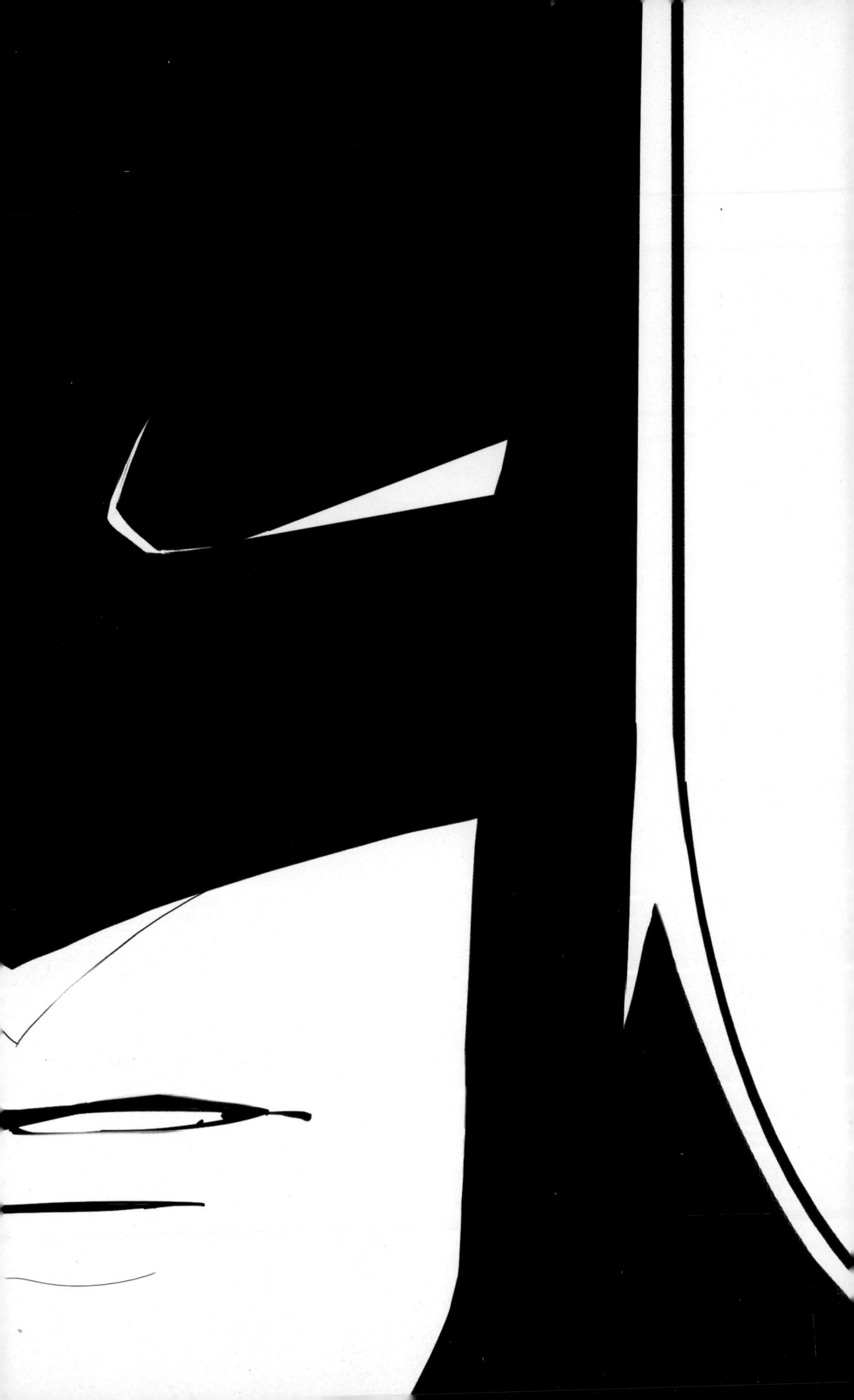

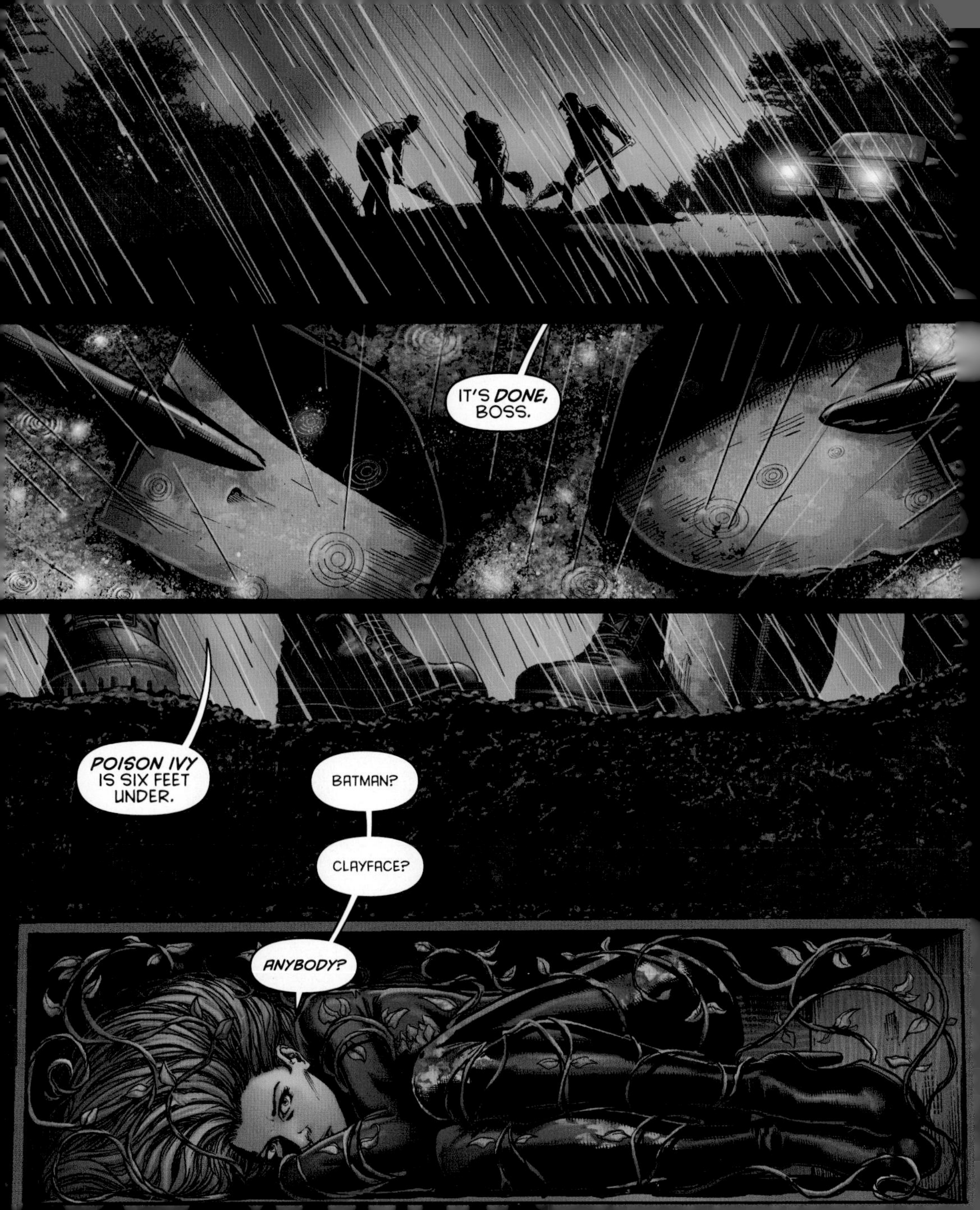
IT'S DONE, BOSS.
POISON IVY IS SIX FEET UNDER.
BATMAN?
CLAYFACE?
ANYBODY?

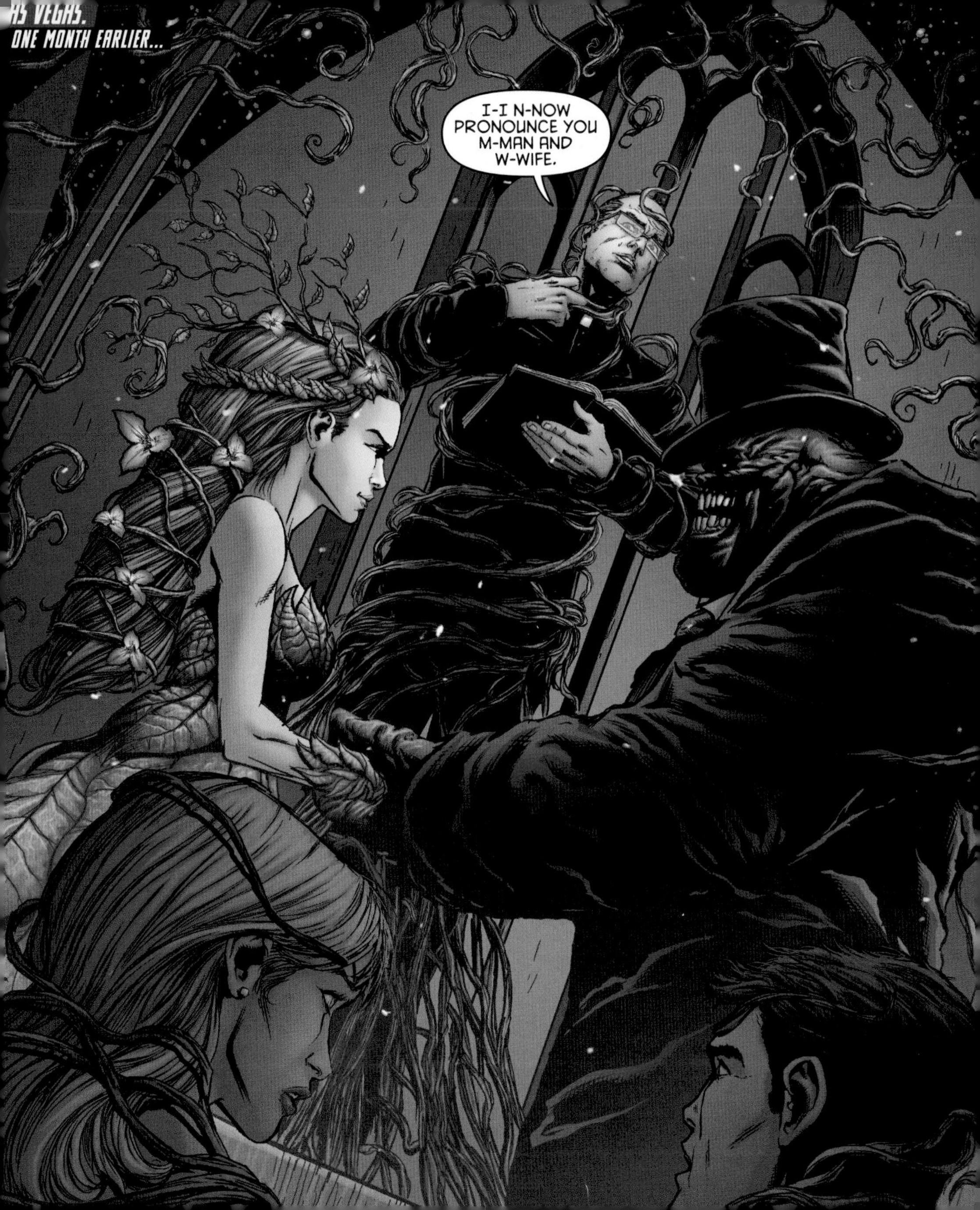
AS VEGAS.
ONE MONTH EARLIER...
I-I N-NOW PRONOUNCE YOU M-MAN AND W-WIFE.

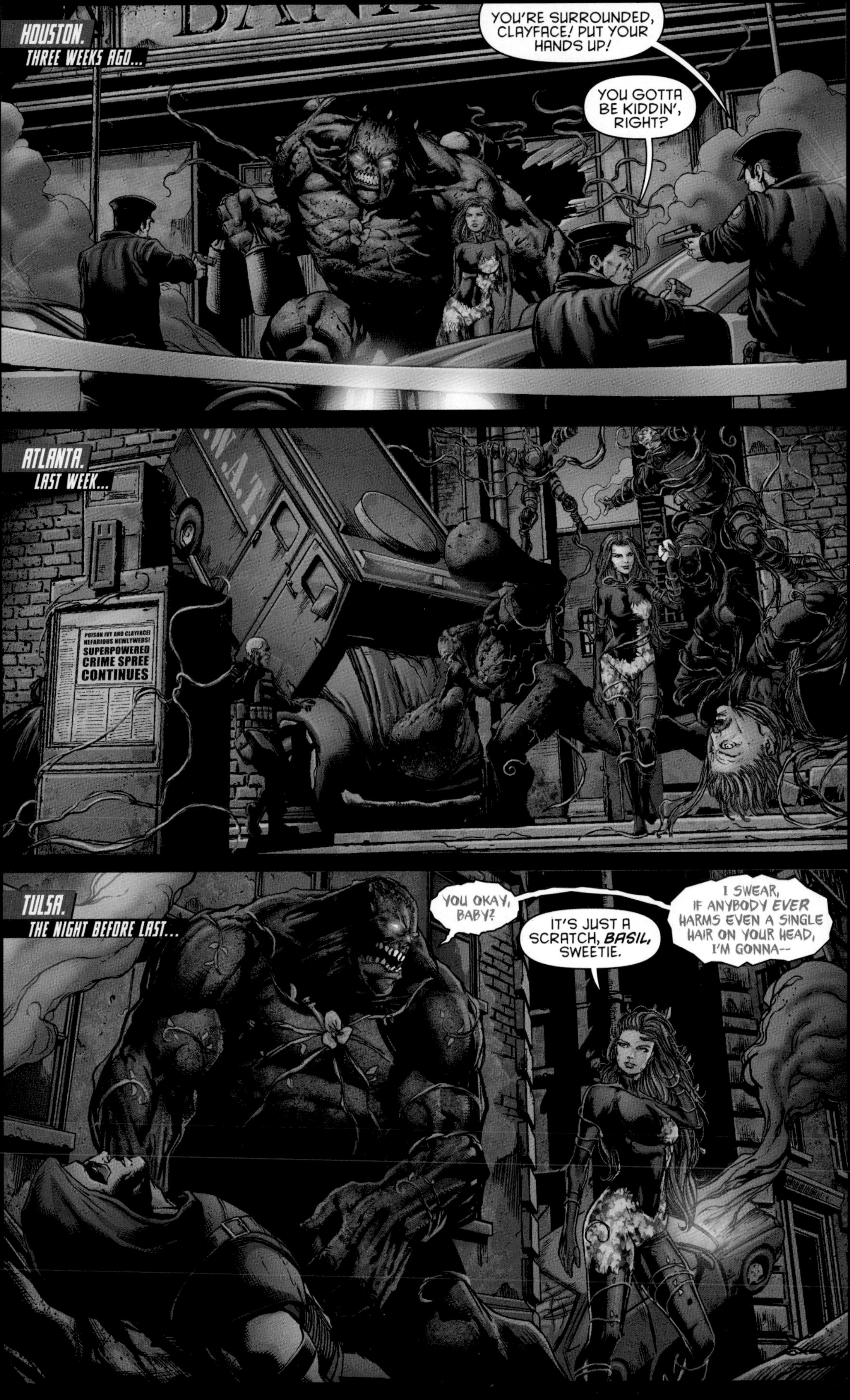
HOUSTON.
THREE WEEKS AGO...
YOU'RE SURROUNDED, CLAYFACE! PUT YOUR HANDS UP!
YOU GOTTA BE KIDDIN', RIGHT?
ATLANTA.
LAST WEEK...
POISON IVY AND CLAYFACE! NEFARIOUS NEWLYWEDS!
SUPERPOWERED CRIME SPREE CONTINUES
TULSA.
THE NIGHT BEFORE LAST...
YOU OKAY, BABY?
IT'S JUST A SCRATCH, BASIL, SWEETIE.
I SWEAR, IF ANYBODY EVER HARMS EVEN A SINGLE HAIR ON YOUR HEAD, I'M GONNA--

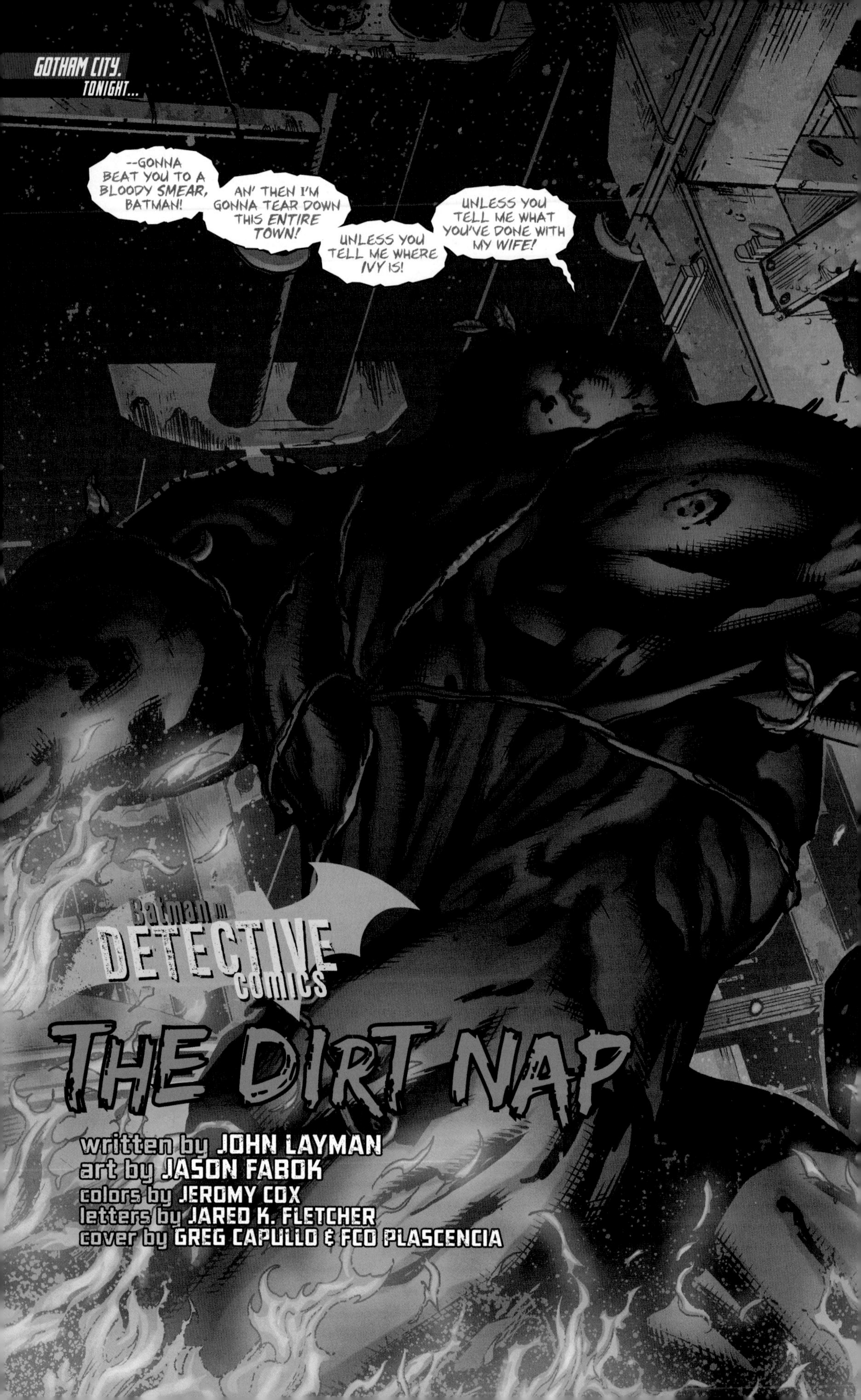
GOTHAM CITY.
TONIGHT...
--GONNA BEAT YOU TO A BLOODY SMEAR, BATMAN!
AN' THEN I'M GONNA TEAR DOWN THIS ENTIRE TOWN!
UNLESS YOU TELL ME WHERE IVY IS!
UNLESS YOU TELL ME WHAT YOU'VE DONE WITH MY WIFE!
Batman in DETECTIVE comics
THE DIRT NAP
written by JOHN LAYMAN
art by JASON FABOK
colors by JEROMY COX
letters by JARED K. FLETCHER
cover by GREG CAPULLO & FCO PLASCENCIA

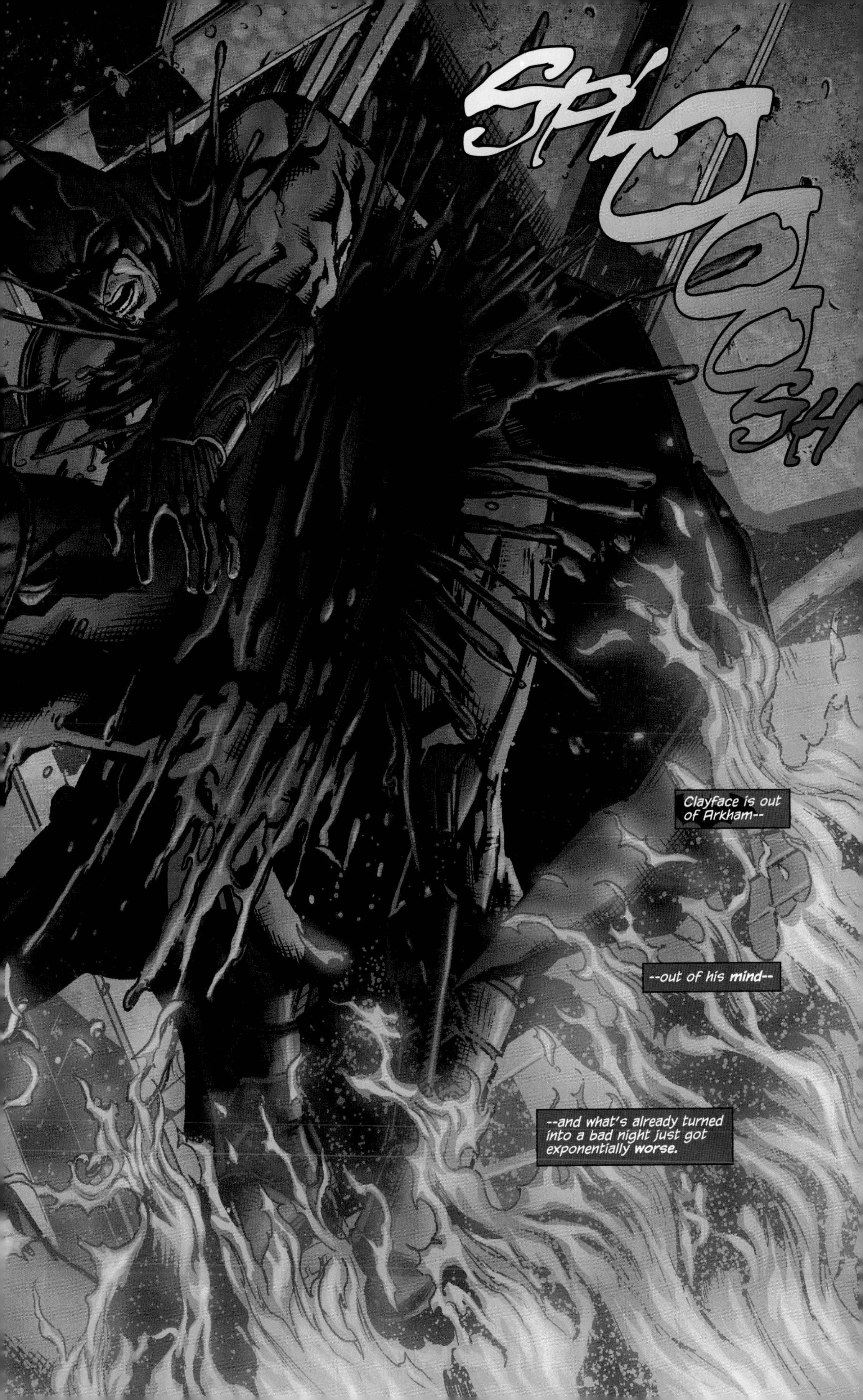
SPLOOOSH
Clayface is out of Arkham--
--out of his mind--
--and what's already turned into a bad night just got exponentially worse.

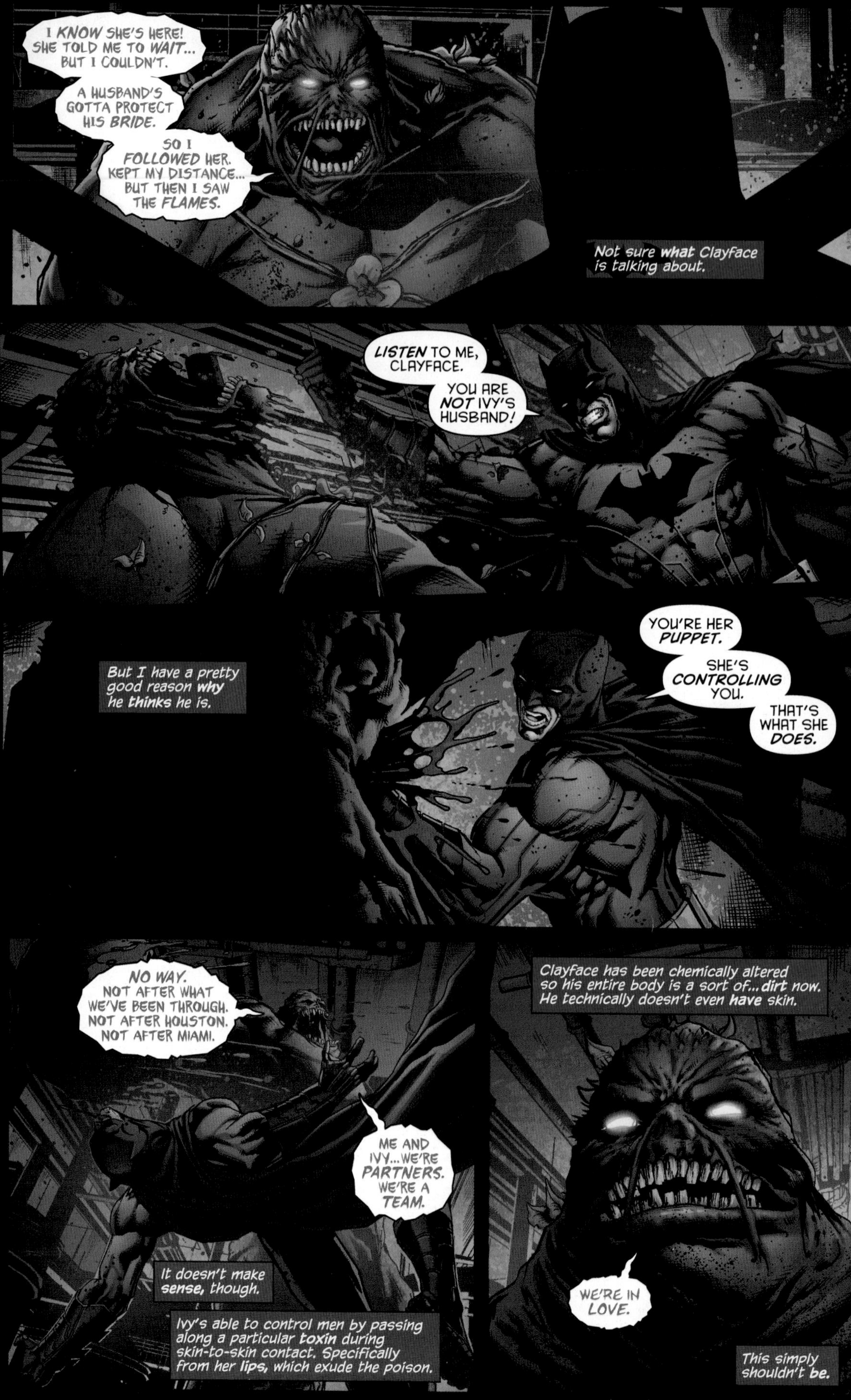
I KNOW SHE'S HERE! SHE TOLD ME TO WAIT... BUT I COULDN'T.
A HUSBAND'S GOTTA PROTECT HIS BRIDE.
SO I FOLLOWED HER. KEPT MY DISTANCE... BUT THEN I SAW THE FLAMES.
Not sure what Clayface is talking about.
LISTEN TO ME, CLAYFACE.
YOU ARE NOT IVY'S HUSBAND!
But I have a pretty good reason why he thinks he is.
YOU'RE HER PUPPET.
SHE'S CONTROLLING YOU.
THAT'S WHAT SHE DOES.
NO WAY. NOT AFTER WHAT WE'VE BEEN THROUGH. NOT AFTER HOUSTON. NOT AFTER MIAMI.
ME AND IVY... WE'RE PARTNERS. WE'RE A TEAM.
It doesn't make sense, though.
Ivy's able to control men by passing along a particular toxin during skin-to-skin contact. Specifically from her lips, which exude the poison.
Clayface has been chemically altered so his entire body is a sort of... dirt now. He technically doesn't even have skin.
WE'RE IN LOVE.
This simply shouldn't be.

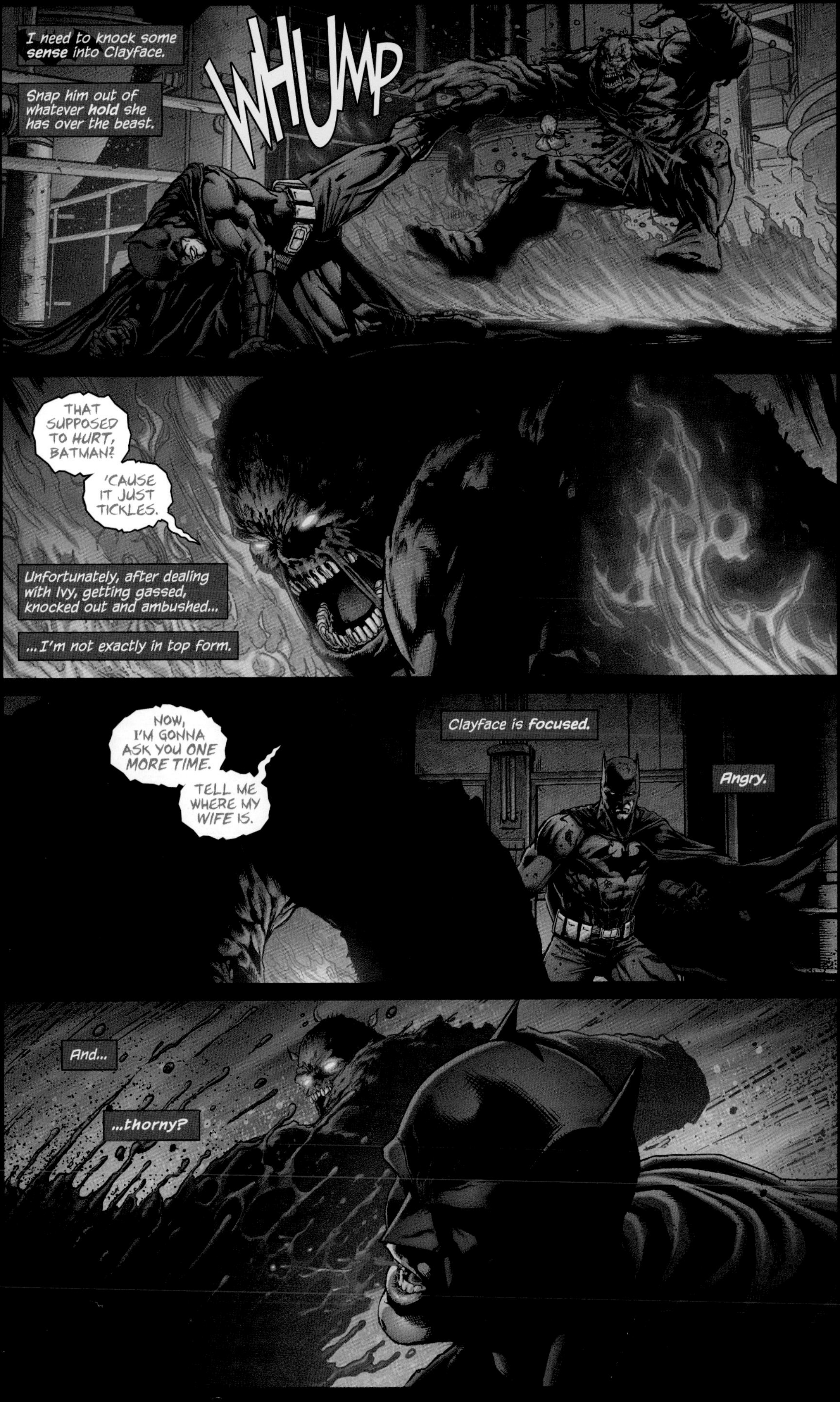
I need to knock some sense into Clayface.
WHUMP
Snap him out of whatever hold she has over the beast.
THAT SUPPOSED TO HURT, BATMAN?
'CAUSE IT JUST TICKLES.
Unfortunately, after dealing with Ivy, getting gassed, knocked out and ambushed...
...I'm not exactly in top form.
NOW, I'M GONNA ASK YOU ONE MORE TIME.
TELL ME WHERE MY WIFE IS.
Clayface is focused.
Angry.
And...
...thorny?

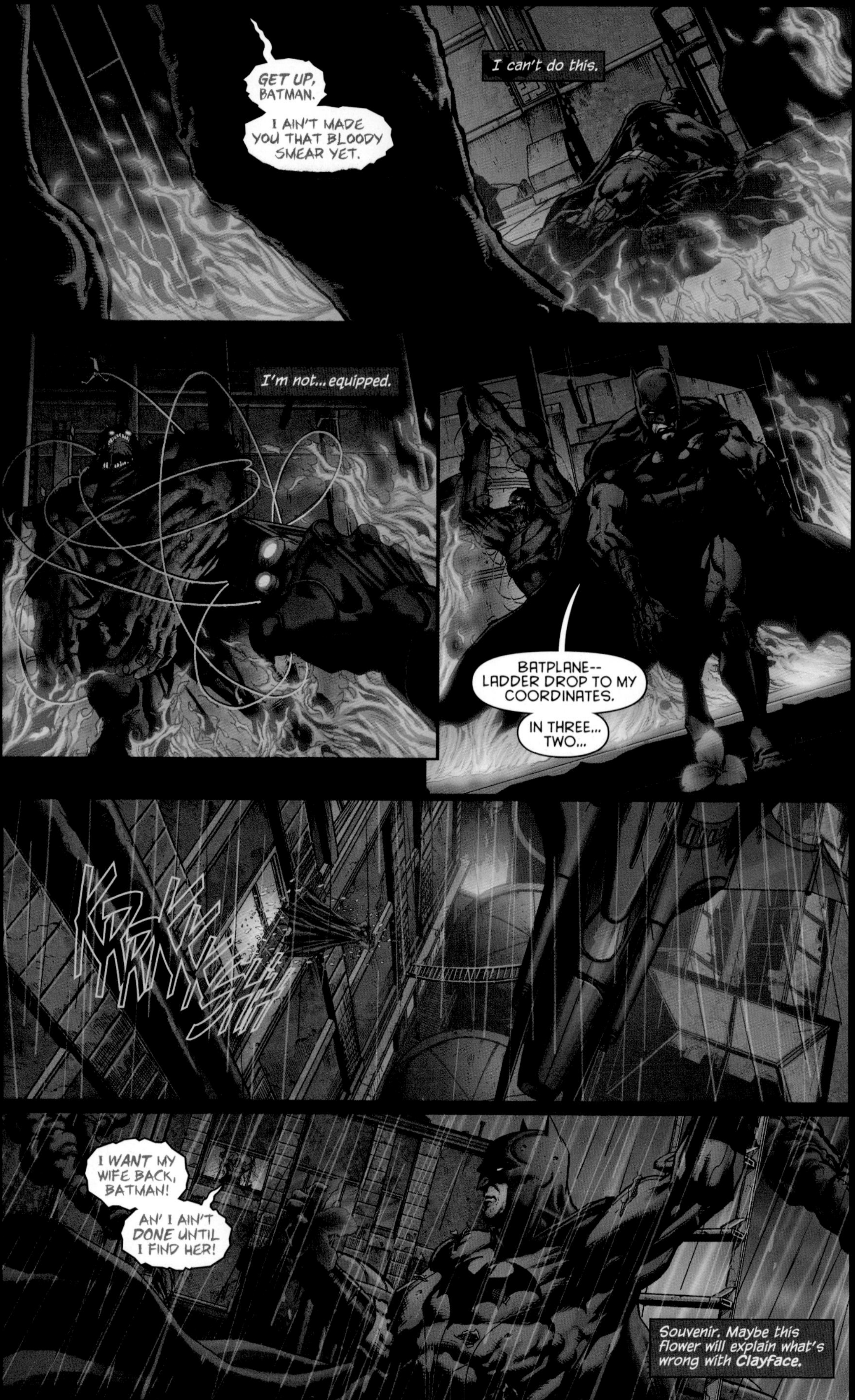
GET UP, BATMAN.
I AIN'T MADE YOU THAT BLOODY SMEAR YET.
I can't do this.
I'm not... equipped.
BATPLANE-- LADDER DROP TO MY COORDINATES.
IN THREE... TWO...
I WANT MY WIFE BACK, BATMAN!
AN' I AIN'T DONE UNTIL I FIND HER!
Souvenir. Maybe this flower will explain what's wrong with Clayface.

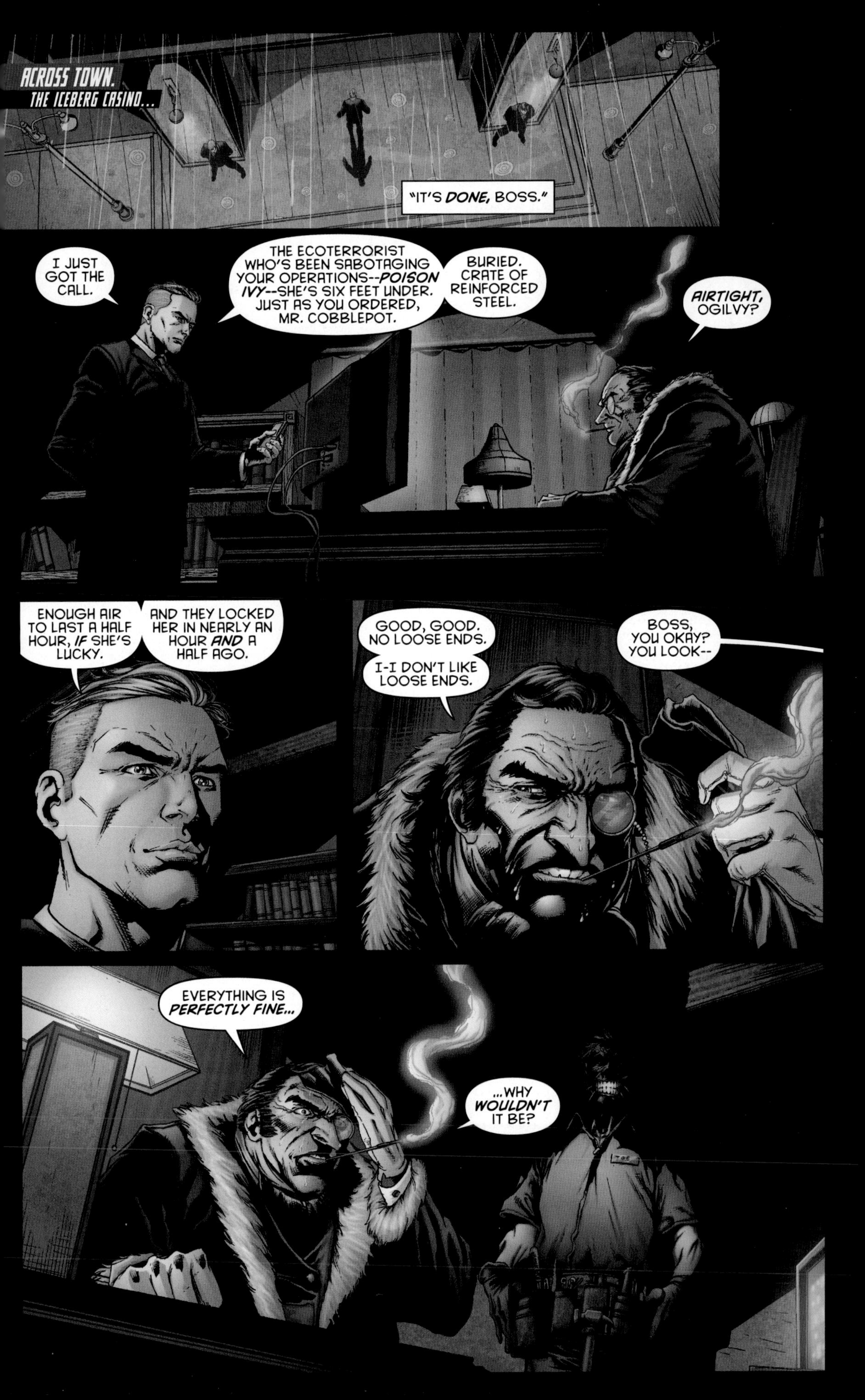
ACROSS TOWN.
THE ICEBERG CASINO...
"IT'S DONE, BOSS."
I JUST GOT THE CALL.
THE ECOTERRORIST WHO'S BEEN SABOTAGING YOUR OPERATIONS--POISON IVY--SHE'S SIX FEET UNDER. JUST AS YOU ORDERED, MR. COBBLEPOT.
BURIED. CRATE OF REINFORCED STEEL.
AIRTIGHT, OGILVY?
ENOUGH AIR TO LAST A HALF HOUR, IF SHE'S LUCKY.
AND THEY LOCKED HER IN NEARLY AN HOUR AND A HALF AGO.
GOOD, GOOD. NO LOOSE ENDS.
I-I DON'T LIKE LOOSE ENDS.
BOSS, YOU OKAY? YOU LOOK--
EVERYTHING IS PERFECTLY FINE...
...WHY WOULDN'T IT BE?

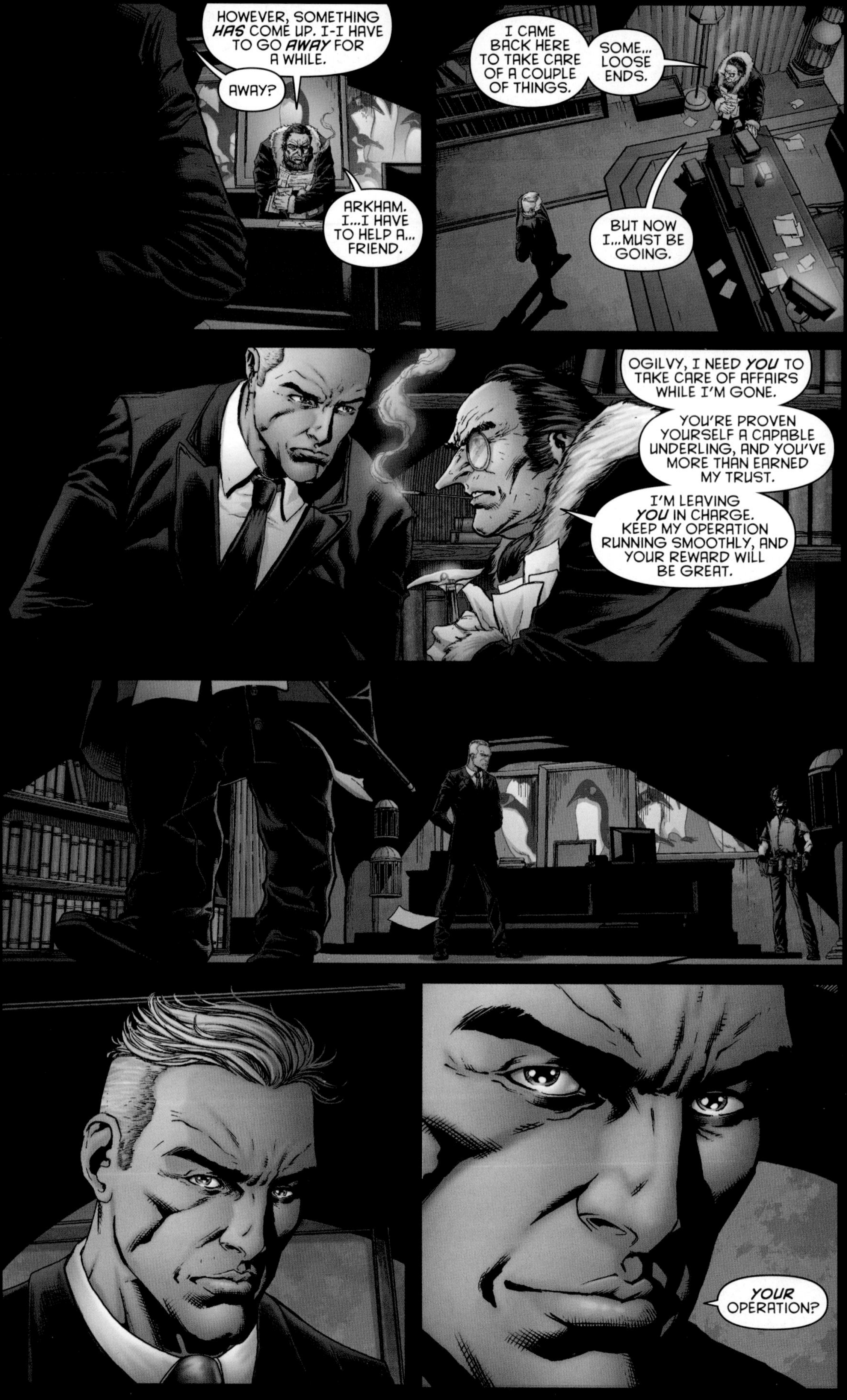
HOWEVER, SOMETHING *HAS* COME UP. I-I HAVE TO GO *AWAY* FOR A WHILE.
AWAY?
ARKHAM. I...I HAVE TO HELP A... FRIEND.
I CAME BACK HERE TO TAKE CARE OF A COUPLE OF THINGS.
SOME... LOOSE ENDS.
BUT NOW I...MUST BE GOING.
OGILVY, I NEED *YOU* TO TAKE CARE OF AFFAIRS WHILE I'M GONE.
YOU'RE PROVEN YOURSELF A CAPABLE UNDERLING, AND YOU'VE MORE THAN EARNED MY TRUST.
I'M LEAVING *YOU* IN CHARGE. KEEP MY OPERATION RUNNING SMOOTHLY, AND YOUR REWARD WILL BE GREAT.
YOUR OPERATION?

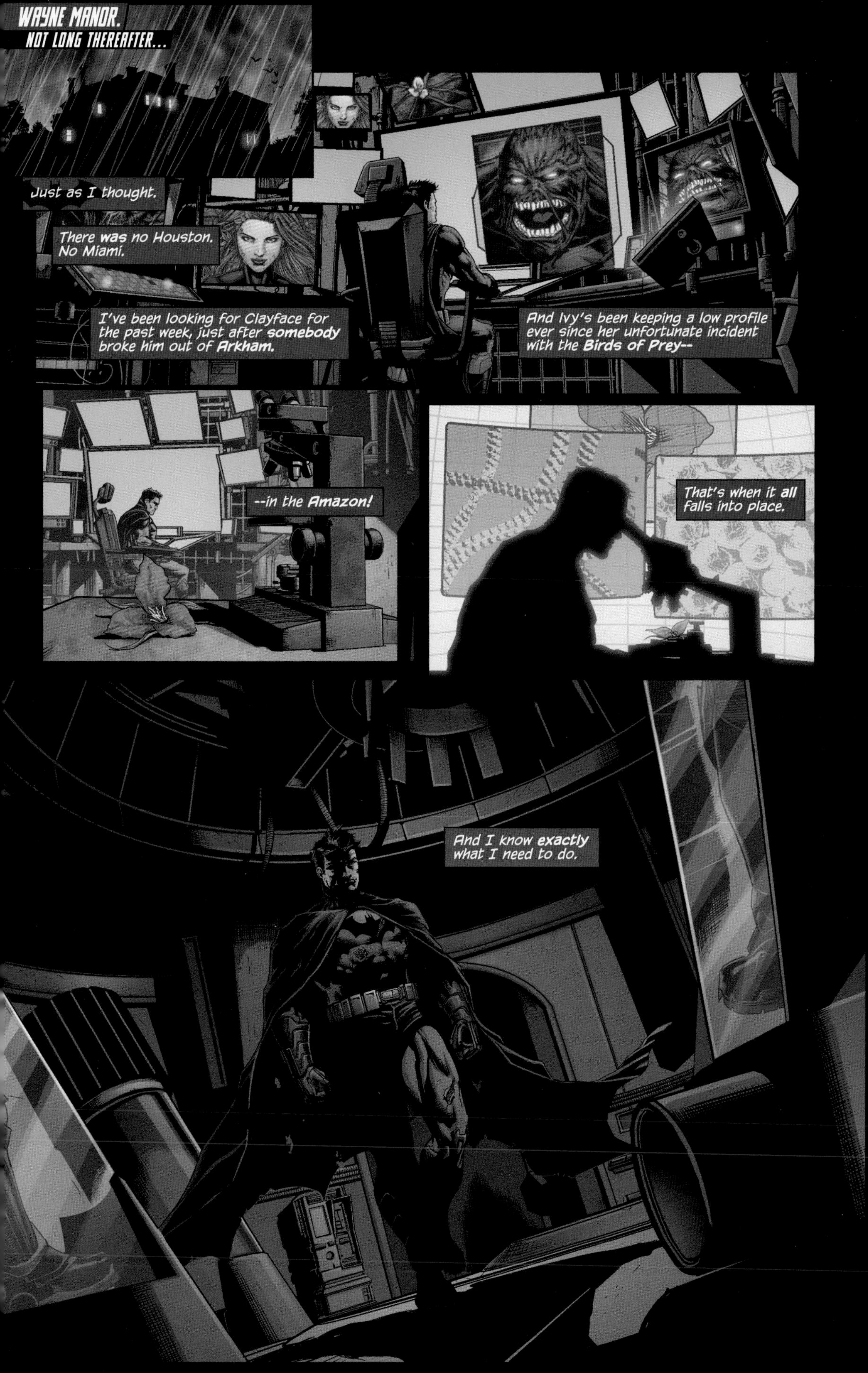
WAYNE MANOR.
NOT LONG THEREAFTER...
Just as I thought.
There was no Houston. No Miami.
I've been looking for Clayface for the past week, just after somebody broke him out of Arkham.
And Ivy's been keeping a low profile ever since her unfortunate incident with the Birds of Prey--
--in the Amazon!
That's when it all falls into place.
And I know exactly what I need to do.

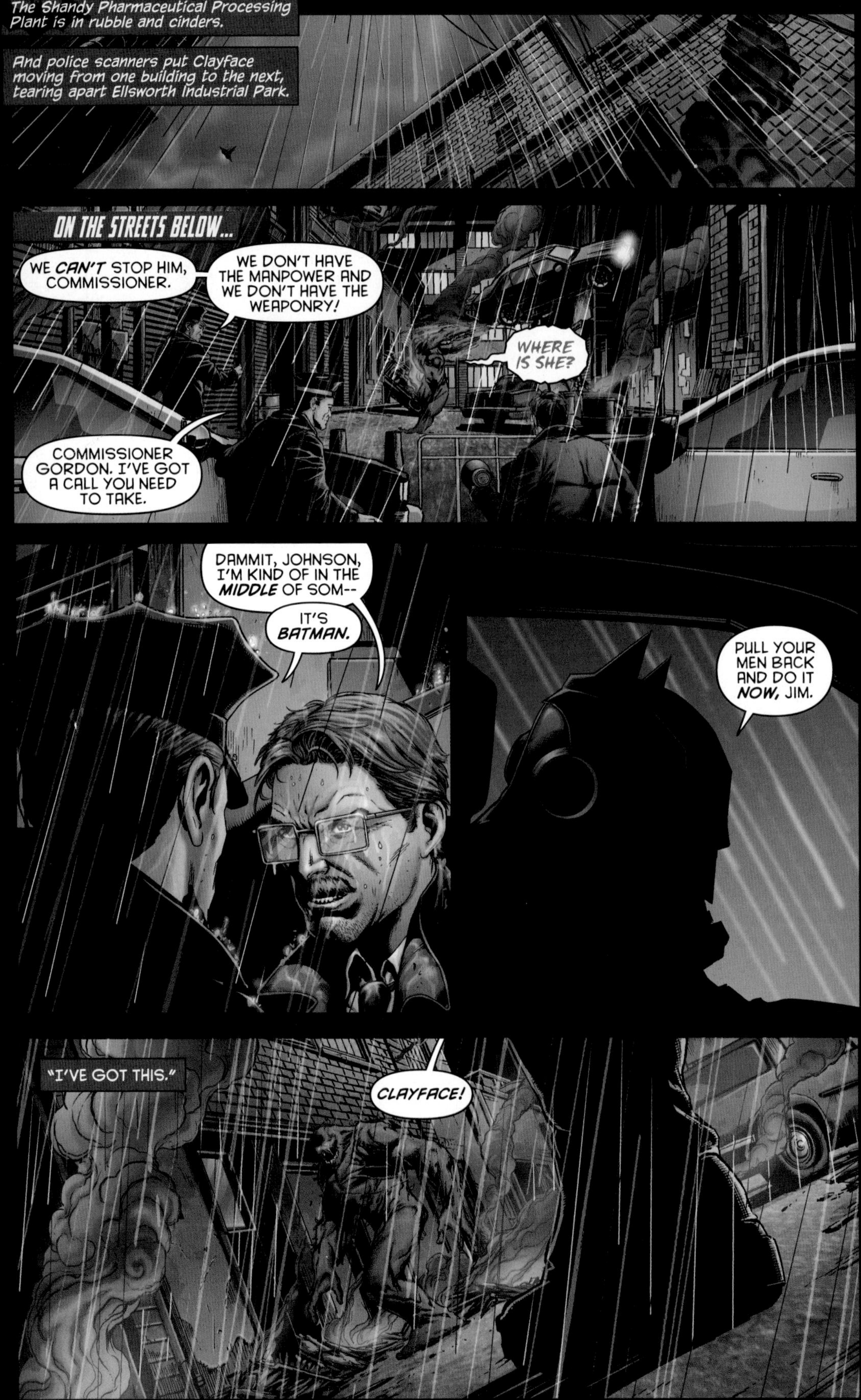
The Shandy Pharmaceutical Processing Plant is in rubble and cinders.
And police scanners put Clayface moving from one building to the next, tearing apart Ellsworth Industrial Park.
ON THE STREETS BELOW...
WE CAN'T STOP HIM, COMMISSIONER.
WE DON'T HAVE THE MANPOWER AND WE DON'T HAVE THE WEAPONRY!
WHERE IS SHE?
COMMISSIONER GORDON. I'VE GOT A CALL YOU NEED TO TAKE.
DAMMIT, JOHNSON, I'M KIND OF IN THE MIDDLE OF SOM--
IT'S BATMAN.
PULL YOUR MEN BACK AND DO IT NOW, JIM.
"I'VE GOT THIS."
CLAYFACE!

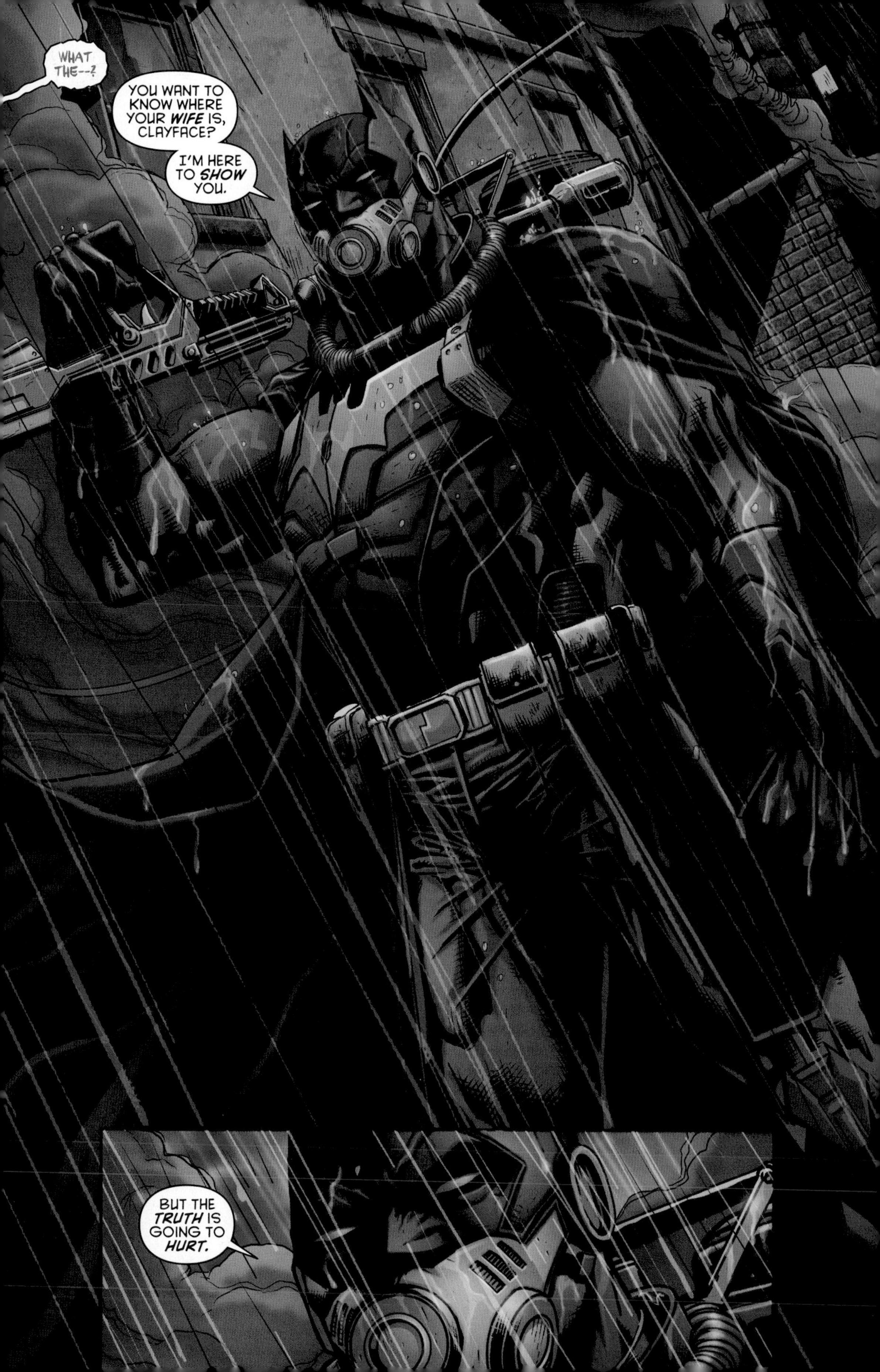
WHAT THE--?
YOU WANT TO KNOW WHERE YOUR *WIFE* IS, CLAYFACE?
I'M HERE TO *SHOW* YOU.
BUT THE *TRUTH* IS GOING TO *HURT.*

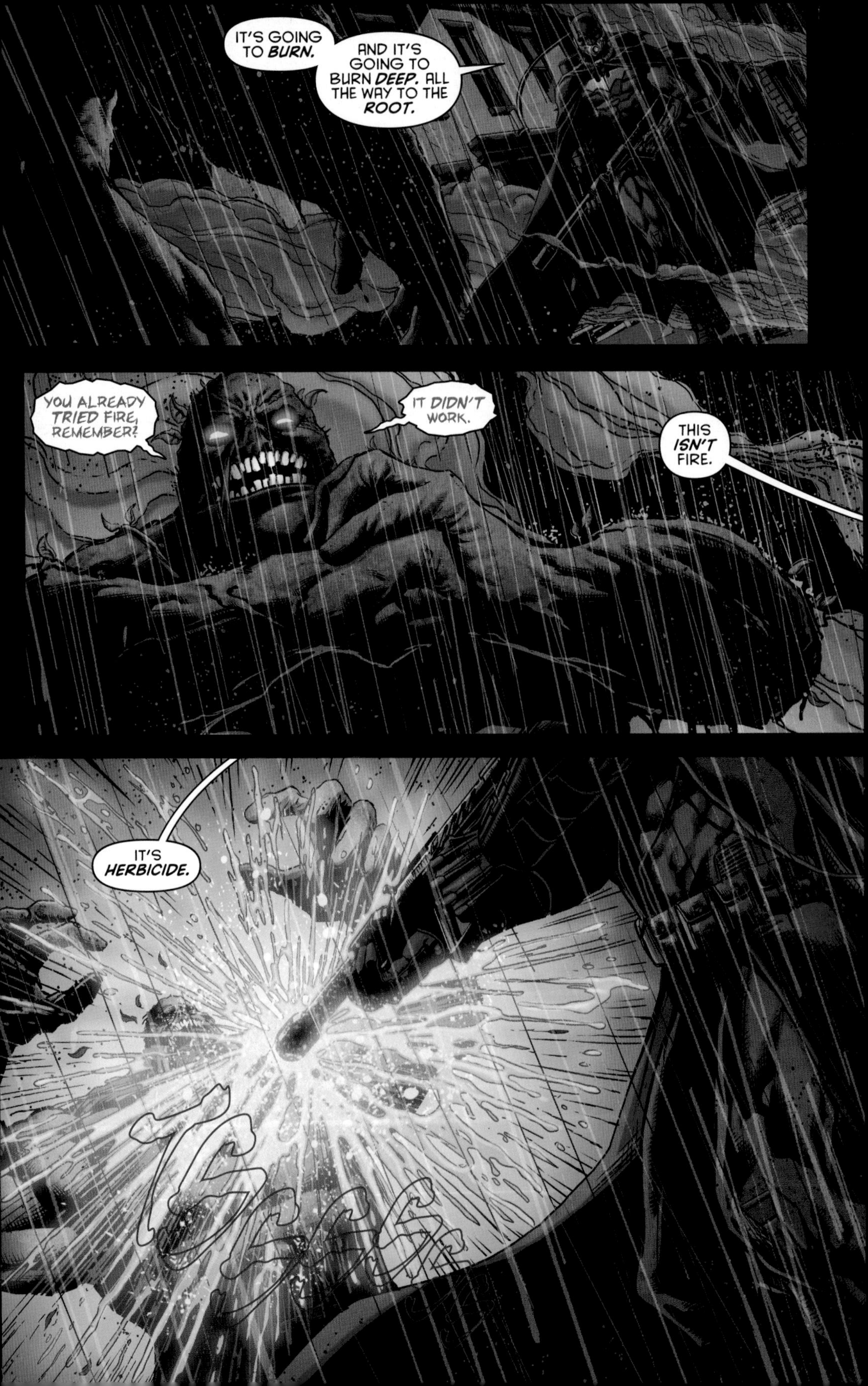
IT'S GOING TO BURN.
AND IT'S GOING TO BURN DEEP. ALL THE WAY TO THE ROOT.
YOU ALREADY TRIED FIRE, REMEMBER?
IT DIDN'T WORK.
THIS ISN'T FIRE.
IT'S HERBICIDE.

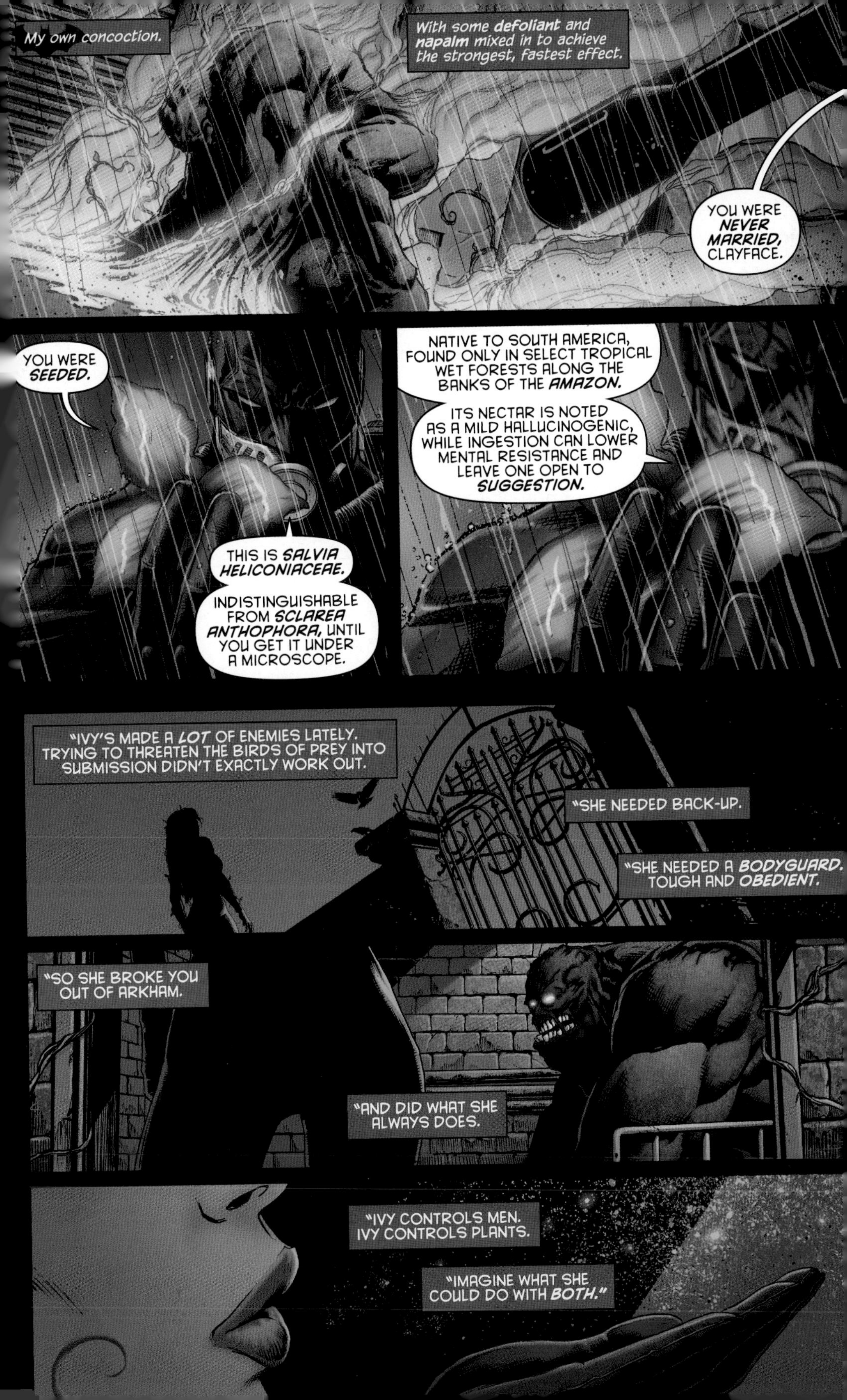
My own concoction.
With some defoliant and napalm mixed in to achieve the strongest, fastest effect.
YOU WERE NEVER MARRIED, CLAYFACE.
YOU WERE SEEDED.
THIS IS SALVIA HELICONIACEAE.
INDISTINGUISHABLE FROM SCLAREA ANTHOPHORA, UNTIL YOU GET IT UNDER A MICROSCOPE.
NATIVE TO SOUTH AMERICA, FOUND ONLY IN SELECT TROPICAL WET FORESTS ALONG THE BANKS OF THE AMAZON.
ITS NECTAR IS NOTED AS A MILD HALLUCINOGENIC, WHILE INGESTION CAN LOWER MENTAL RESISTANCE AND LEAVE ONE OPEN TO SUGGESTION.
"IVY'S MADE A LOT OF ENEMIES LATELY. TRYING TO THREATEN THE BIRDS OF PREY INTO SUBMISSION DIDN'T EXACTLY WORK OUT.
"SHE NEEDED BACK-UP.
"SHE NEEDED A BODYGUARD. TOUGH AND OBEDIENT.
"SO SHE BROKE YOU OUT OF ARKHAM.
"AND DID WHAT SHE ALWAYS DOES.
"IVY CONTROLS MEN. IVY CONTROLS PLANTS.
"IMAGINE WHAT SHE COULD DO WITH BOTH."

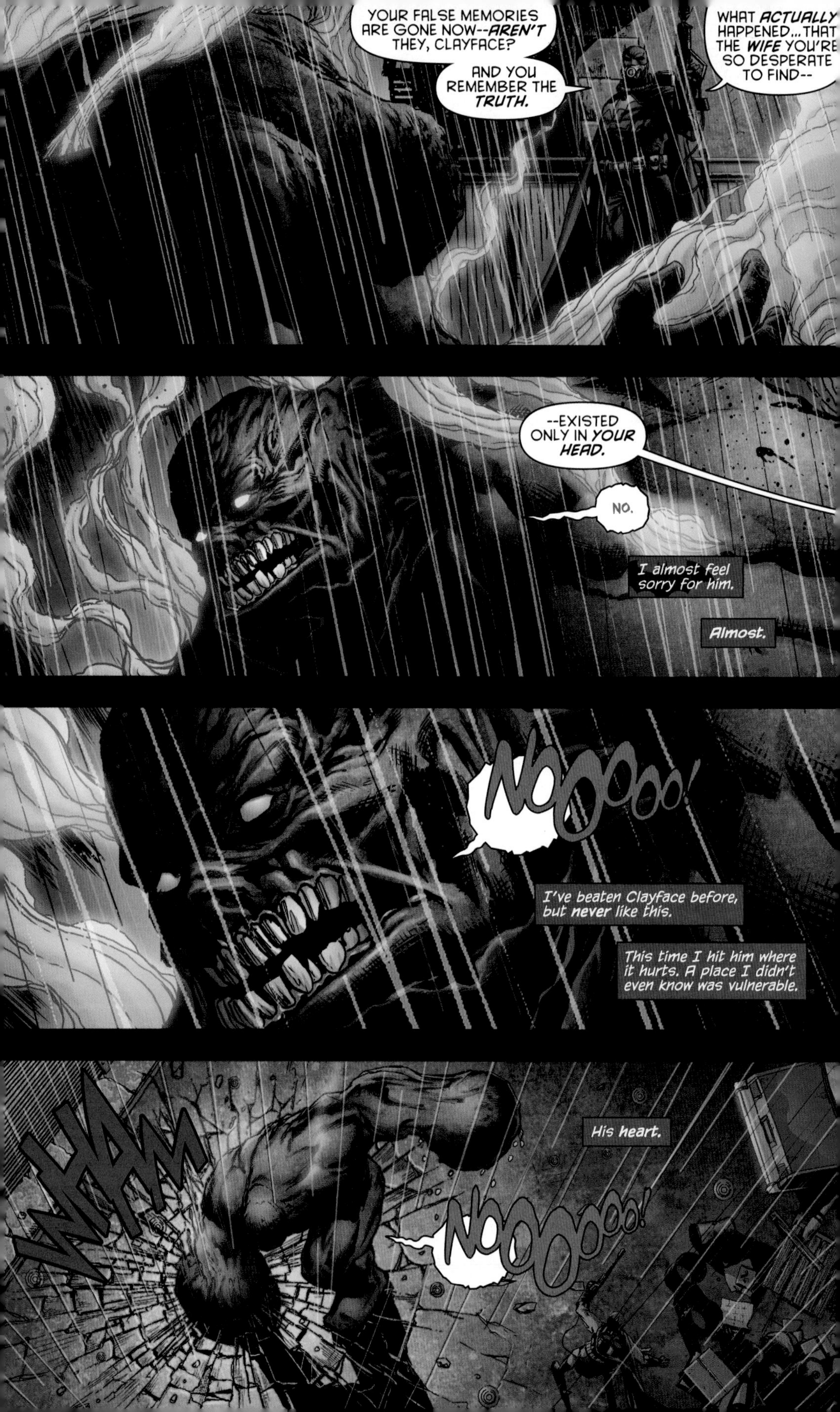

YOUR FALSE MEMORIES ARE GONE NOW--AREN'T THEY, CLAYFACE?
AND YOU REMEMBER THE TRUTH.
WHAT ACTUALLY HAPPENED...THAT THE WIFE YOU'RE SO DESPERATE TO FIND--
--EXISTED ONLY IN YOUR HEAD.
NO.
I almost feel sorry for him.
Almost.
NOOooo!
I've beaten Clayface before, but never like this.
This time I hit him where it hurts. A place I didn't even know was vulnerable.
WHAM
His heart.
NOOOoooo!

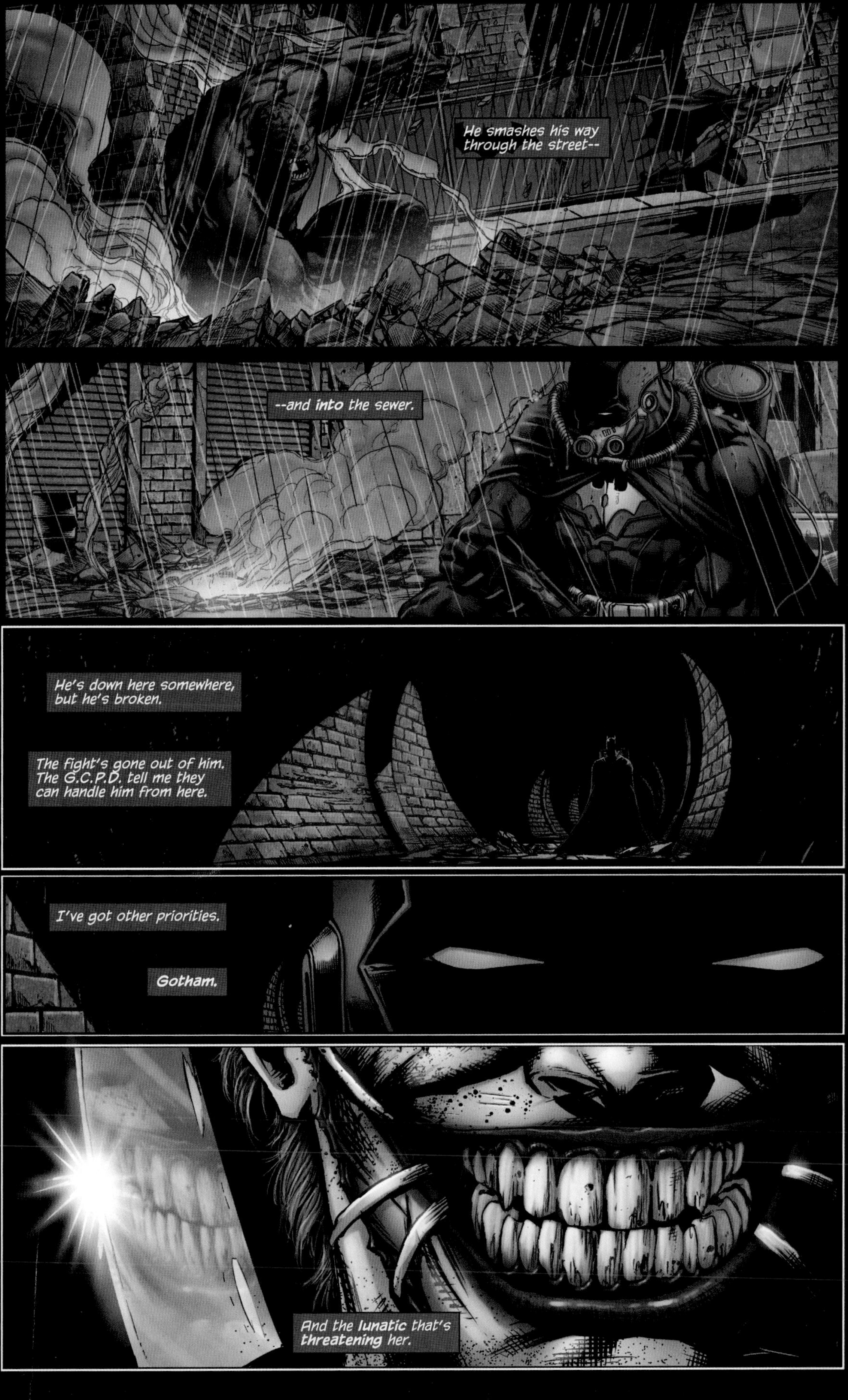

He smashes his way through the street--
--and **into** the sewer.
He's down here somewhere, but he's broken.
The fight's gone out of him. The G.C.P.D. tell me they can handle him from here.
I've got other priorities.
Gotham.
And the **lunatic** that's **threatening** her.

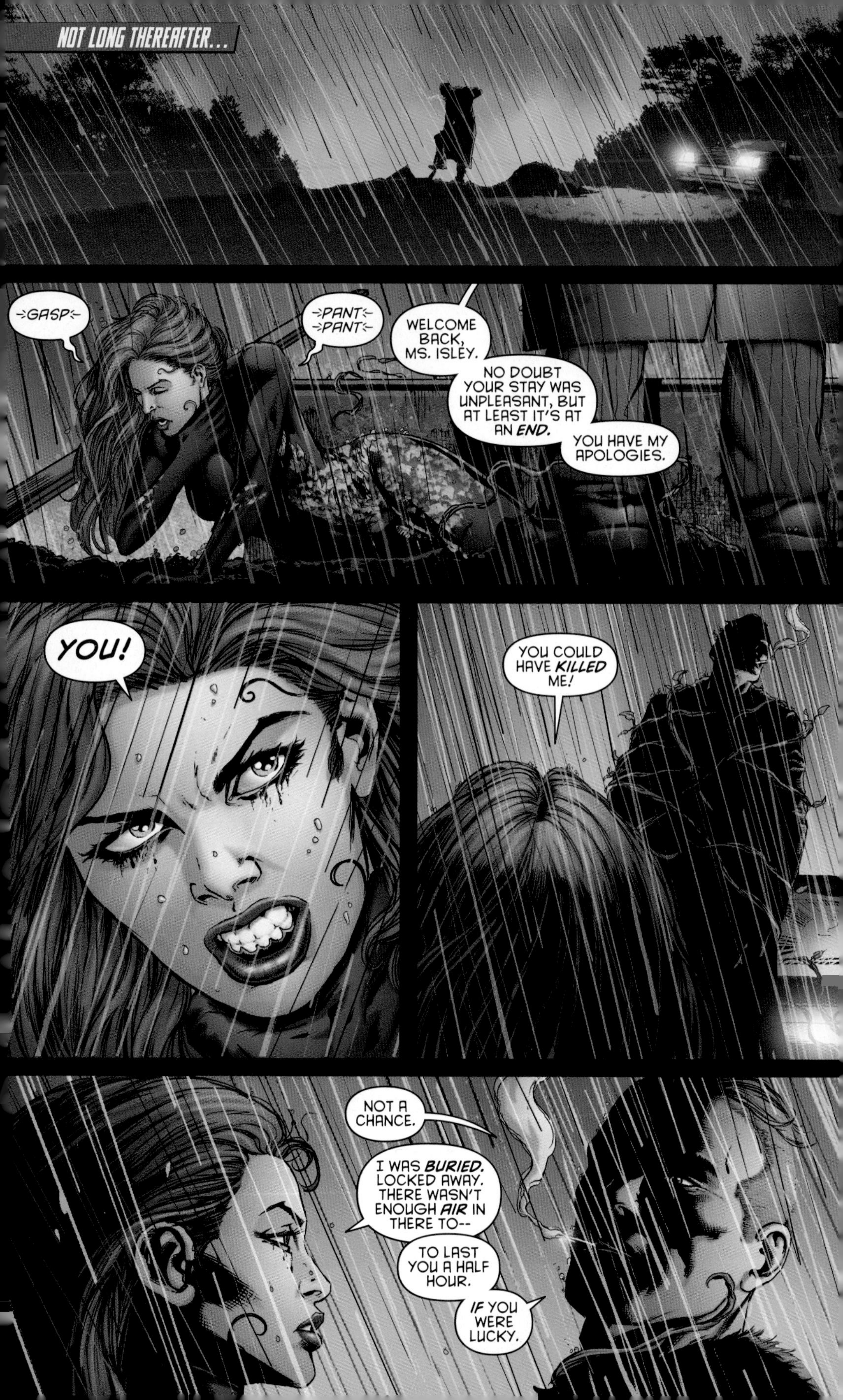
NOT LONG THEREAFTER...
-GASP-
-PANT- -PANT-
WELCOME BACK, MS. ISLEY.
NO DOUBT YOUR STAY WAS UNPLEASANT, BUT AT LEAST IT'S AT AN END.
YOU HAVE MY APOLOGIES.
YOU!
YOU COULD HAVE KILLED ME!
NOT A CHANCE.
I WAS BURIED. LOCKED AWAY. THERE WASN'T ENOUGH AIR IN THERE TO--
TO LAST YOU A HALF HOUR.
IF YOU WERE LUCKY.

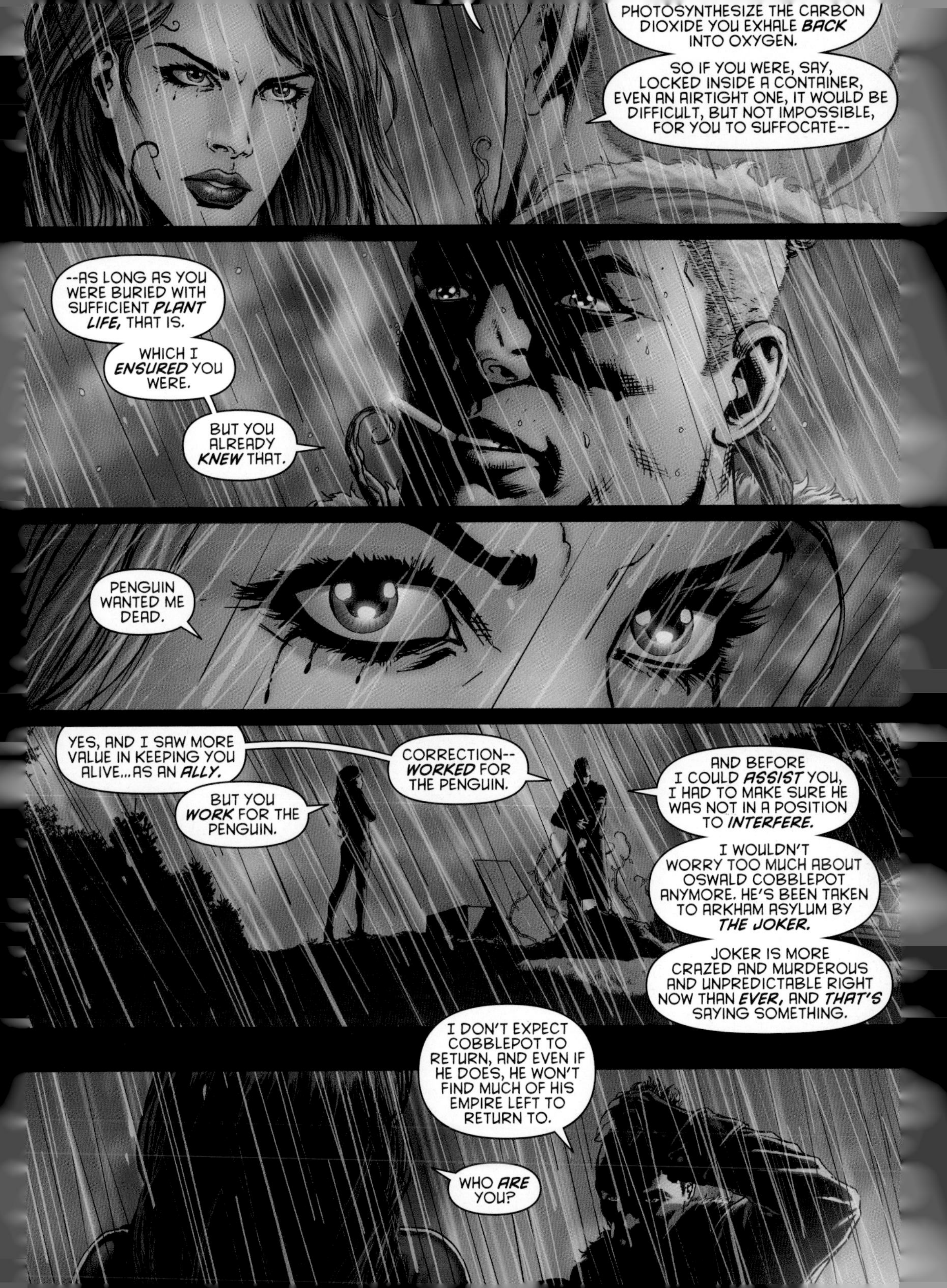
PHOTOSYNTHESIZE THE CARBON DIOXIDE YOU EXHALE BACK INTO OXYGEN.
SO IF YOU WERE, SAY, LOCKED INSIDE A CONTAINER, EVEN AN AIRTIGHT ONE, IT WOULD BE DIFFICULT, BUT NOT IMPOSSIBLE, FOR YOU TO SUFFOCATE--
--AS LONG AS YOU WERE BURIED WITH SUFFICIENT PLANT LIFE, THAT IS.
WHICH I ENSURED YOU WERE.
BUT YOU ALREADY KNEW THAT.
PENGUIN WANTED ME DEAD.
YES, AND I SAW MORE VALUE IN KEEPING YOU ALIVE...AS AN ALLY.
BUT YOU WORK FOR THE PENGUIN.
CORRECTION-- WORKED FOR THE PENGUIN.
AND BEFORE I COULD ASSIST YOU, I HAD TO MAKE SURE HE WAS NOT IN A POSITION TO INTERFERE.
I WOULDN'T WORRY TOO MUCH ABOUT OSWALD COBBLEPOT ANYMORE. HE'S BEEN TAKEN TO ARKHAM ASYLUM BY THE JOKER.
JOKER IS MORE CRAZED AND MURDEROUS AND UNPREDICTABLE RIGHT NOW THAN EVER, AND THAT'S SAYING SOMETHING.
I DON'T EXPECT COBBLEPOT TO RETURN, AND EVEN IF HE DOES, HE WON'T FIND MUCH OF HIS EMPIRE LEFT TO RETURN TO.
WHO ARE YOU?

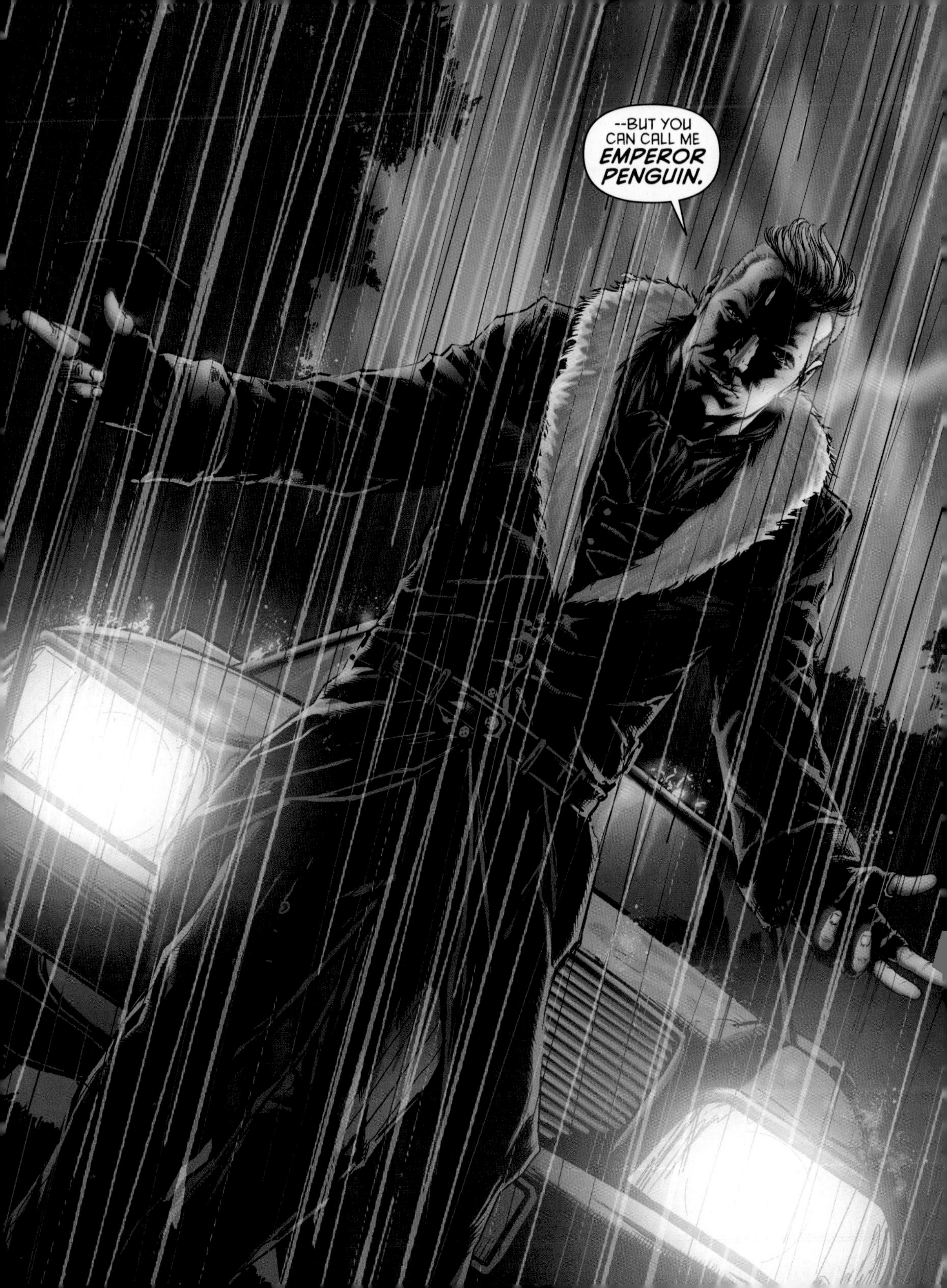
--BUT YOU CAN CALL ME EMPEROR PENGUIN.

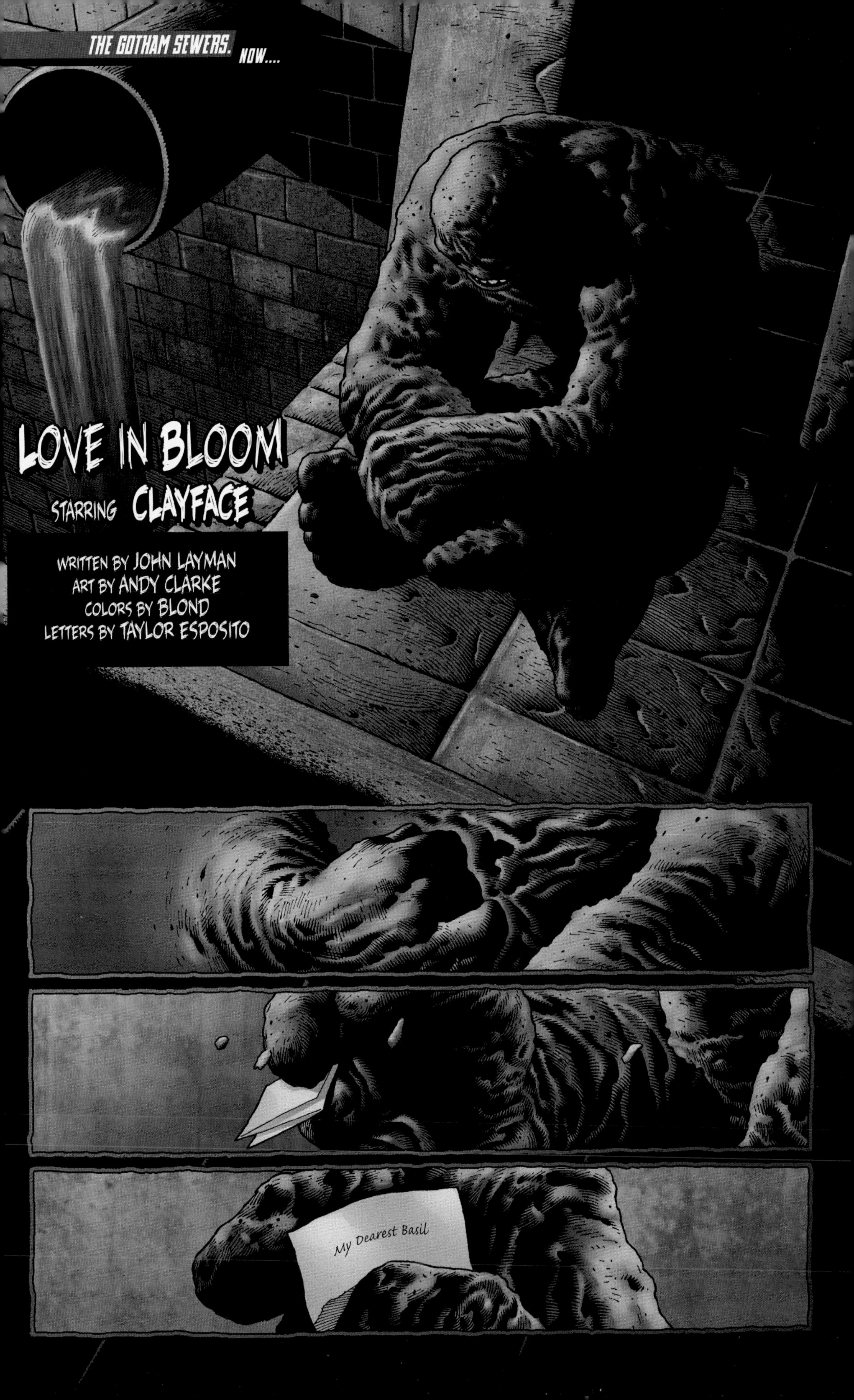
THE GOTHAM SEWERS. NOW....
LOVE IN BLOOM
STARRING CLAYFACE
WRITTEN BY JOHN LAYMAN
ART BY ANDY CLARKE
COLORS BY BLOND
LETTERS BY TAYLOR ESPOSITO
My Dearest Basil

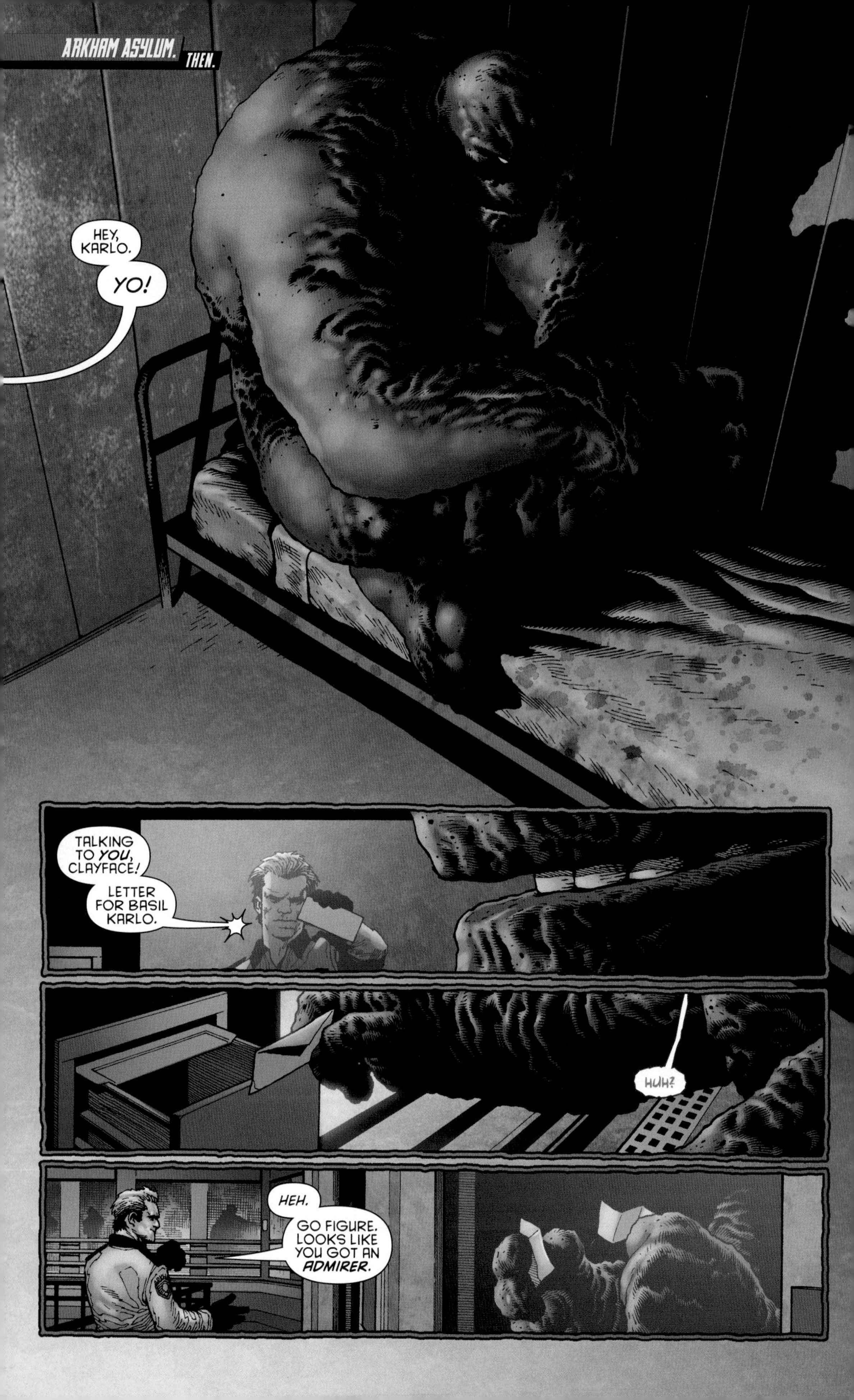
ARKHAM ASYLUM.
THEN.
HEY, KARLO.
YO!
TALKING TO YOU, CLAYFACE!
LETTER FOR BASIL KARLO.
HUH?
HEH.
GO FIGURE. LOOKS LIKE YOU GOT AN ADMIRER.

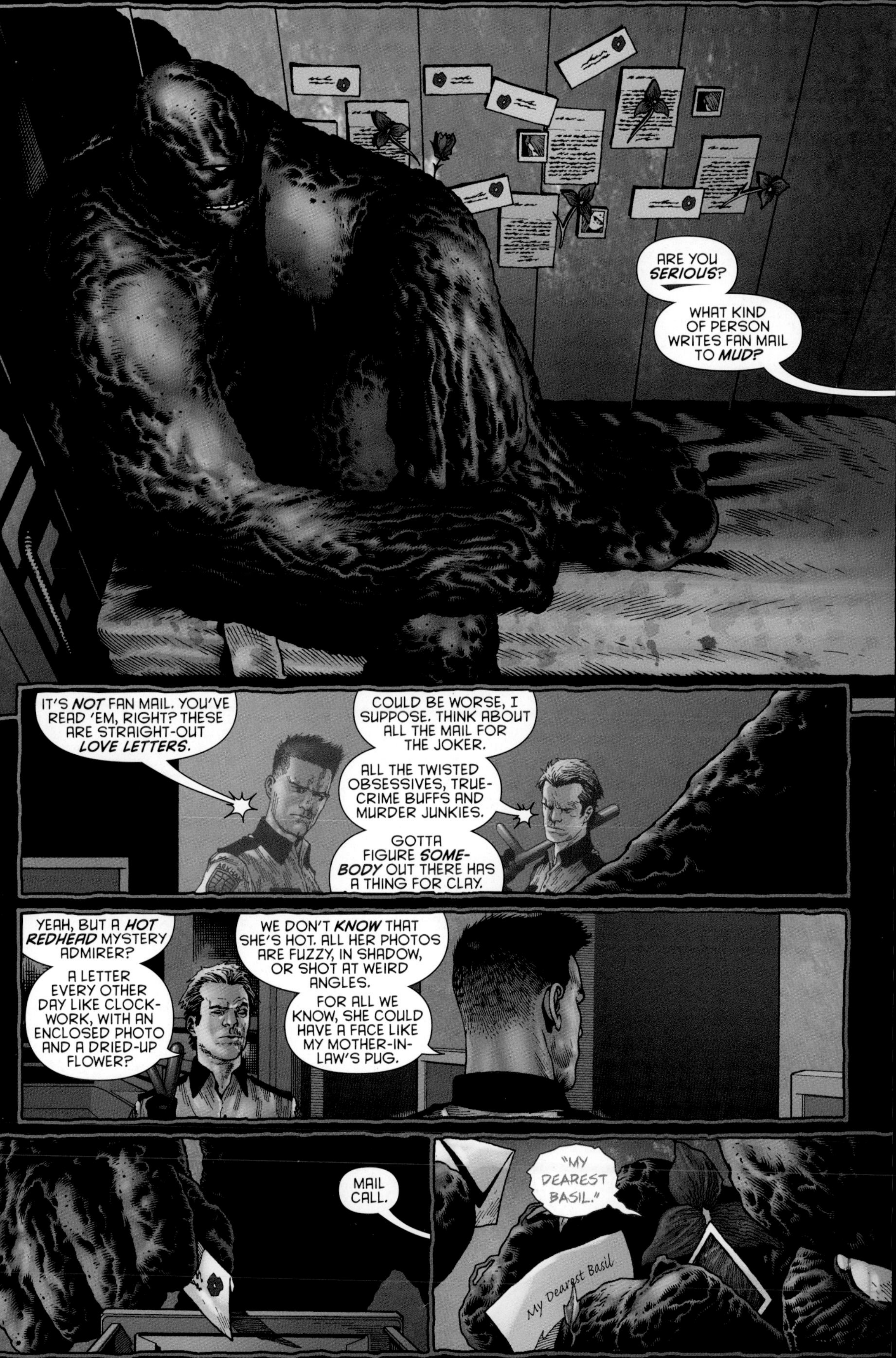

ARE YOU SERIOUS?
WHAT KIND OF PERSON WRITES FAN MAIL TO MUD?
IT'S NOT FAN MAIL. YOU'VE READ 'EM, RIGHT? THESE ARE STRAIGHT-OUT LOVE LETTERS.
COULD BE WORSE, I SUPPOSE. THINK ABOUT ALL THE MAIL FOR THE JOKER.
ALL THE TWISTED OBSESSIVES, TRUE-CRIME BUFFS AND MURDER JUNKIES.
GOTTA FIGURE SOMEBODY OUT THERE HAS A THING FOR CLAY.
YEAH, BUT A HOT REDHEAD MYSTERY ADMIRER?
A LETTER EVERY OTHER DAY LIKE CLOCKWORK, WITH AN ENCLOSED PHOTO AND A DRIED-UP FLOWER?
WE DON'T KNOW THAT SHE'S HOT. ALL HER PHOTOS ARE FUZZY, IN SHADOW, OR SHOT AT WEIRD ANGLES.
FOR ALL WE KNOW, SHE COULD HAVE A FACE LIKE MY MOTHER-IN-LAW'S PUG.
MAIL CALL.
"MY DEAREST BASIL."
My Dearest Basil

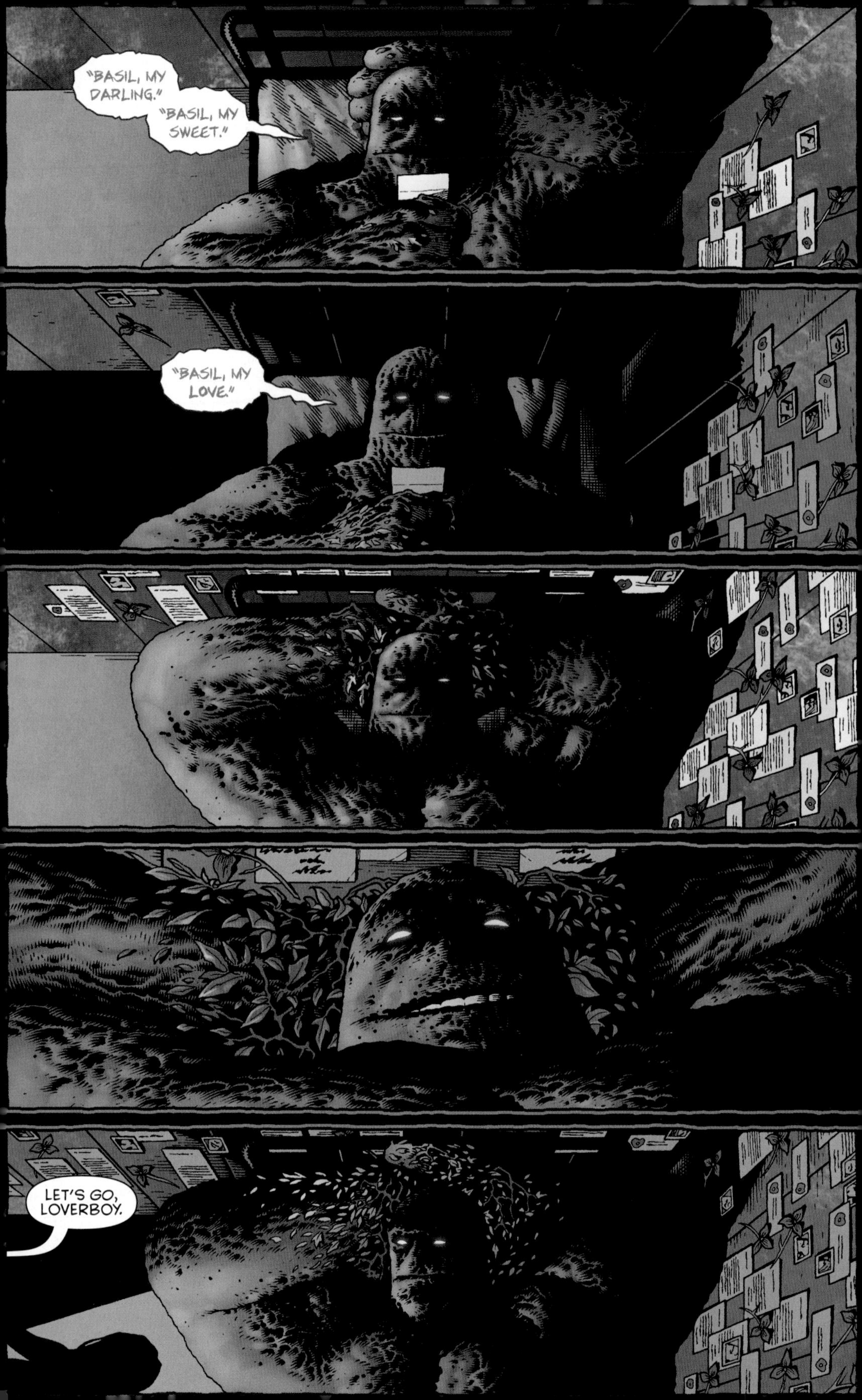
"BASIL, MY DARLING."
"BASIL, MY SWEET."
"BASIL, MY LOVE."
LET'S GO, LOVERBOY.

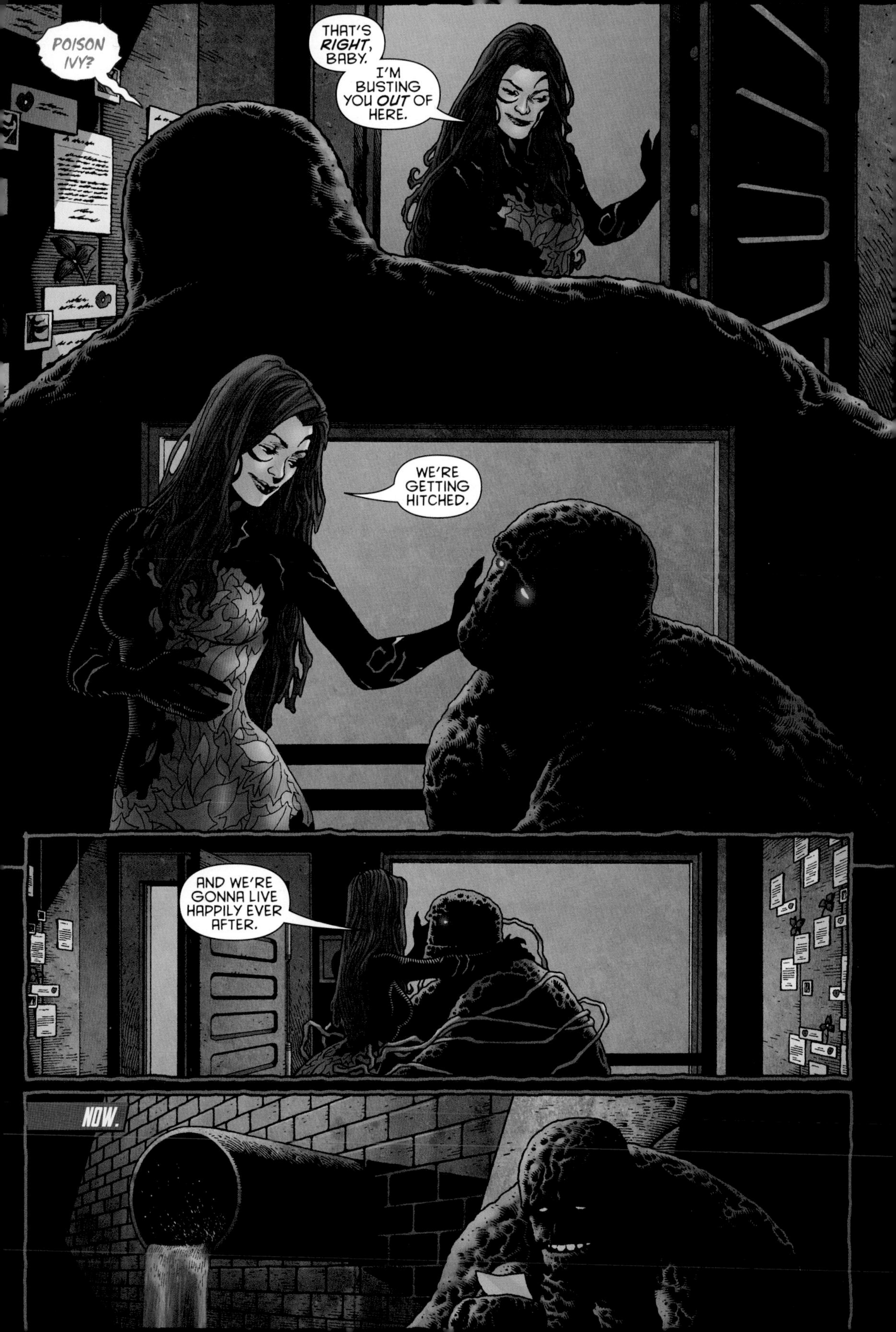
POISON IVY?
THAT'S RIGHT, BABY.
I'M BUSTING YOU OUT OF HERE.
WE'RE GETTING HITCHED.
AND WE'RE GONNA LIVE HAPPILY EVER AFTER.
NOW.

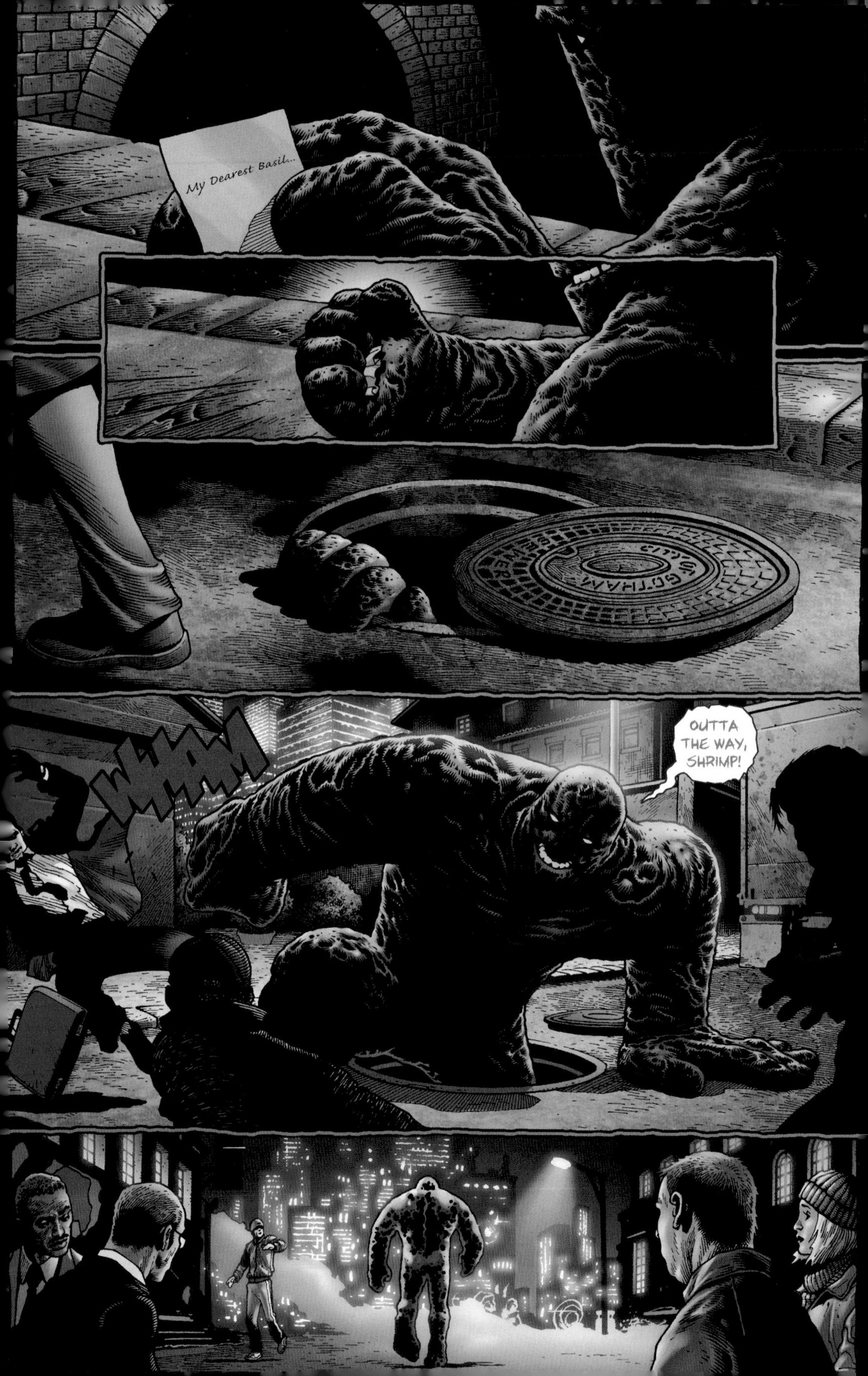
My Dearest Basil...
CITY OF GOTHAM
WHAM
OUTTA THE WAY, SHRIMP!

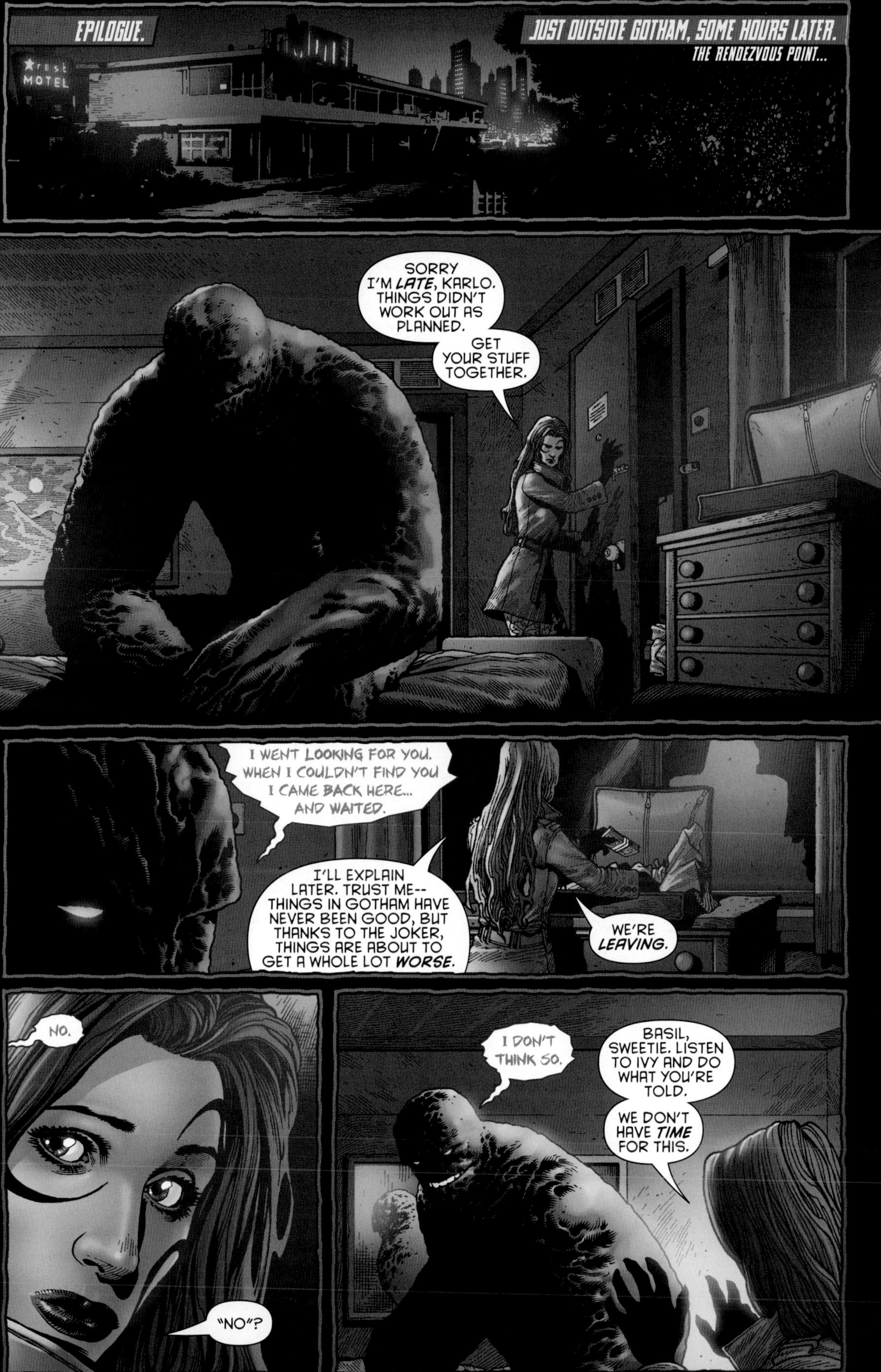
EPILOGUE.
JUST OUTSIDE GOTHAM, SOME HOURS LATER.
THE RENDEZVOUS POINT...
rest MOTEL
SORRY I'M LATE, KARLO. THINGS DIDN'T WORK OUT AS PLANNED.
GET YOUR STUFF TOGETHER.
I WENT LOOKING FOR YOU. WHEN I COULDN'T FIND YOU I CAME BACK HERE... AND WAITED.
I'LL EXPLAIN LATER. TRUST ME-- THINGS IN GOTHAM HAVE NEVER BEEN GOOD, BUT THANKS TO THE JOKER, THINGS ARE ABOUT TO GET A WHOLE LOT WORSE.
WE'RE LEAVING.
NO.
"NO"?
I DON'T THINK SO.
BASIL, SWEETIE. LISTEN TO IVY AND DO WHAT YOU'RE TOLD.
WE DON'T HAVE TIME FOR THIS.

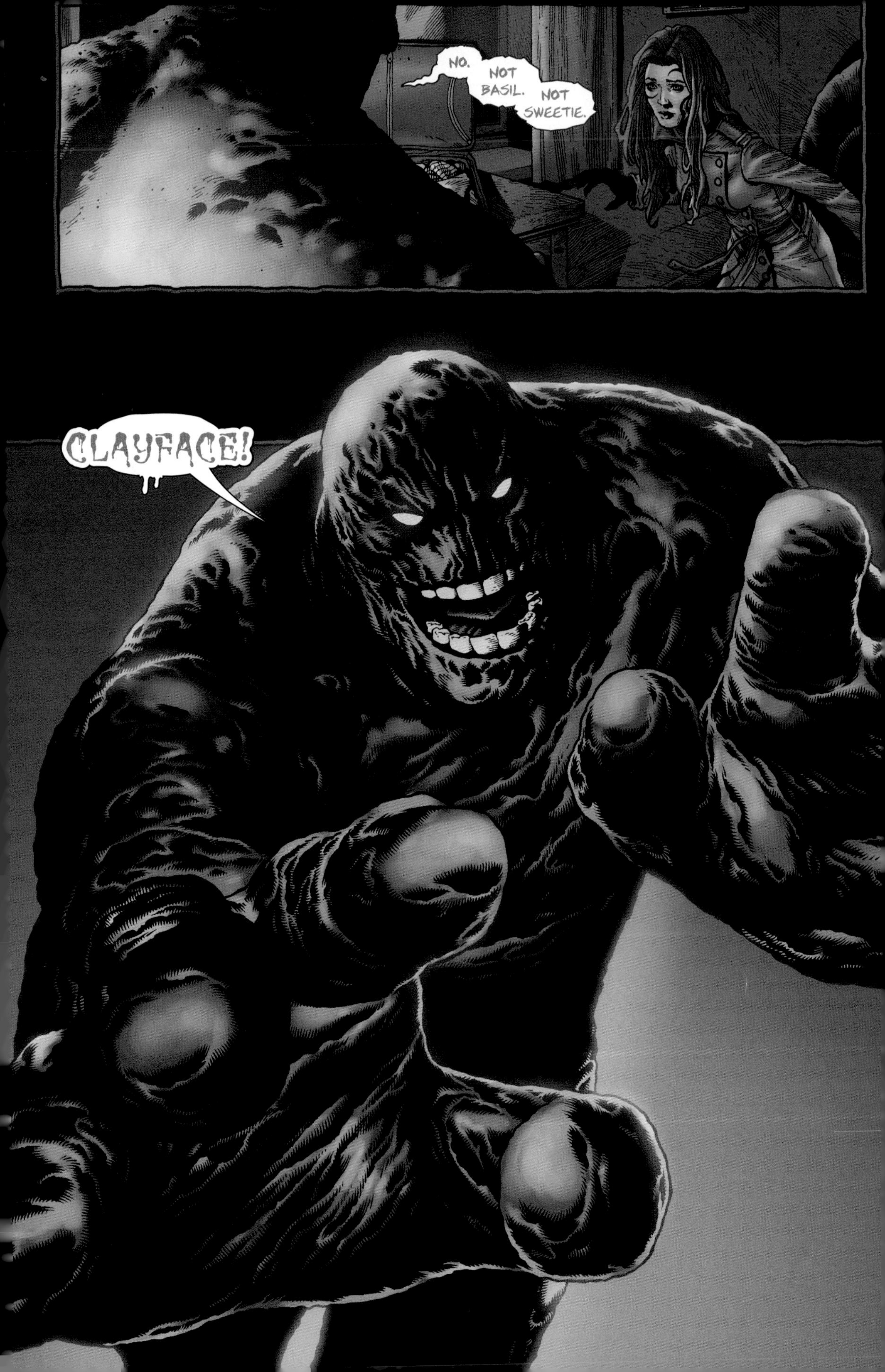
NO.
NOT BASIL.
NOT SWEETIE.
CLAYFACE!

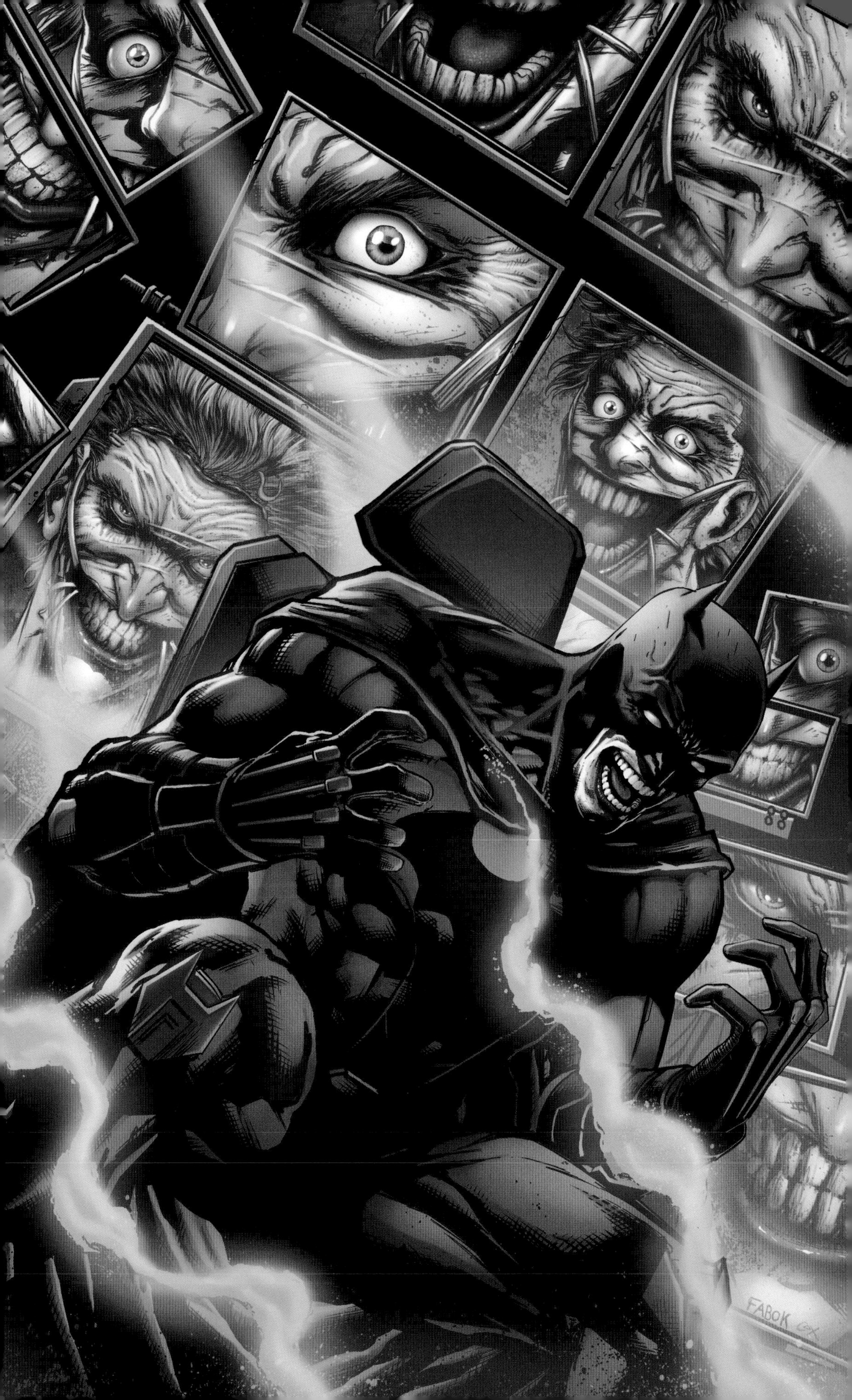
FABOK COX

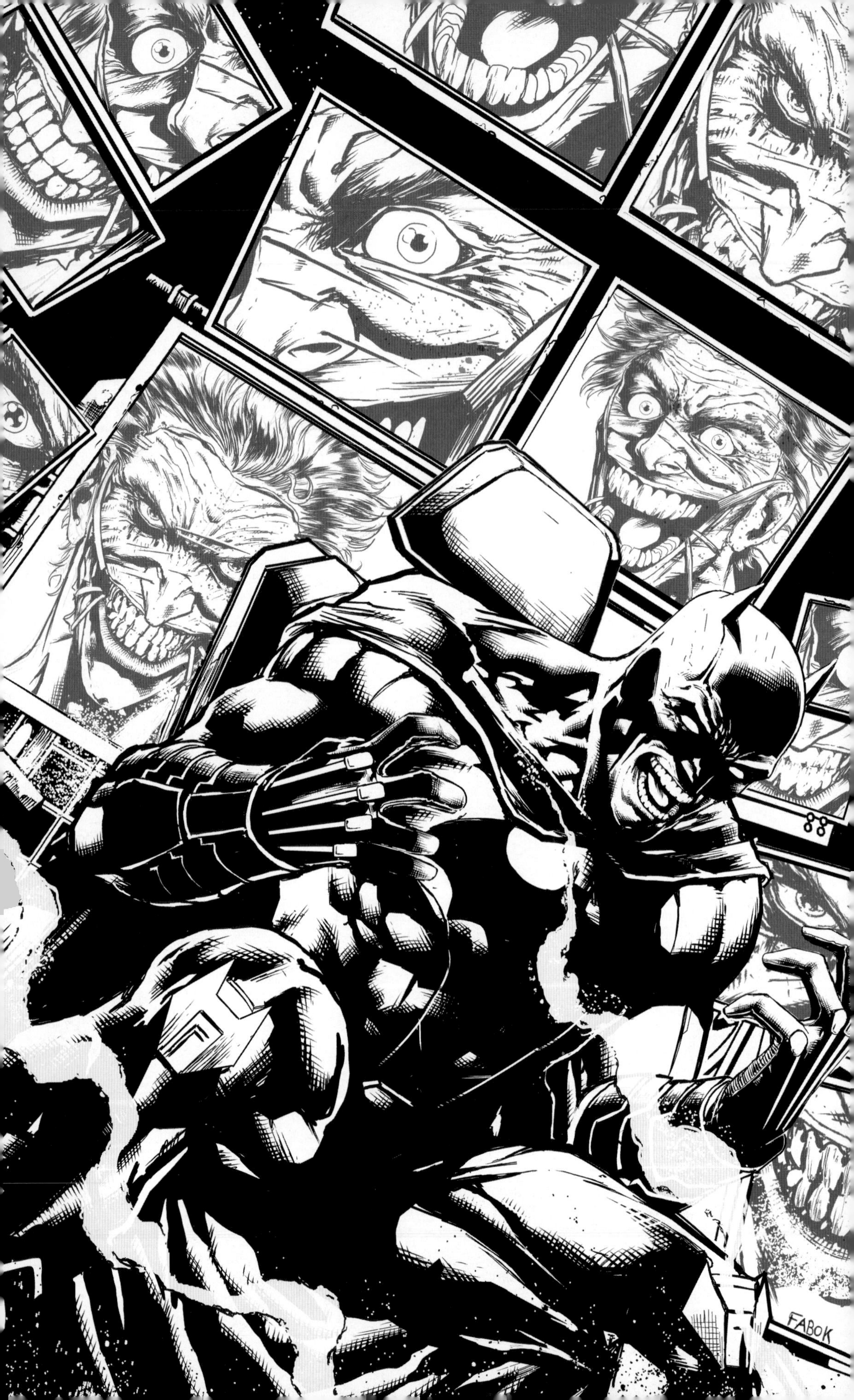
FABOK

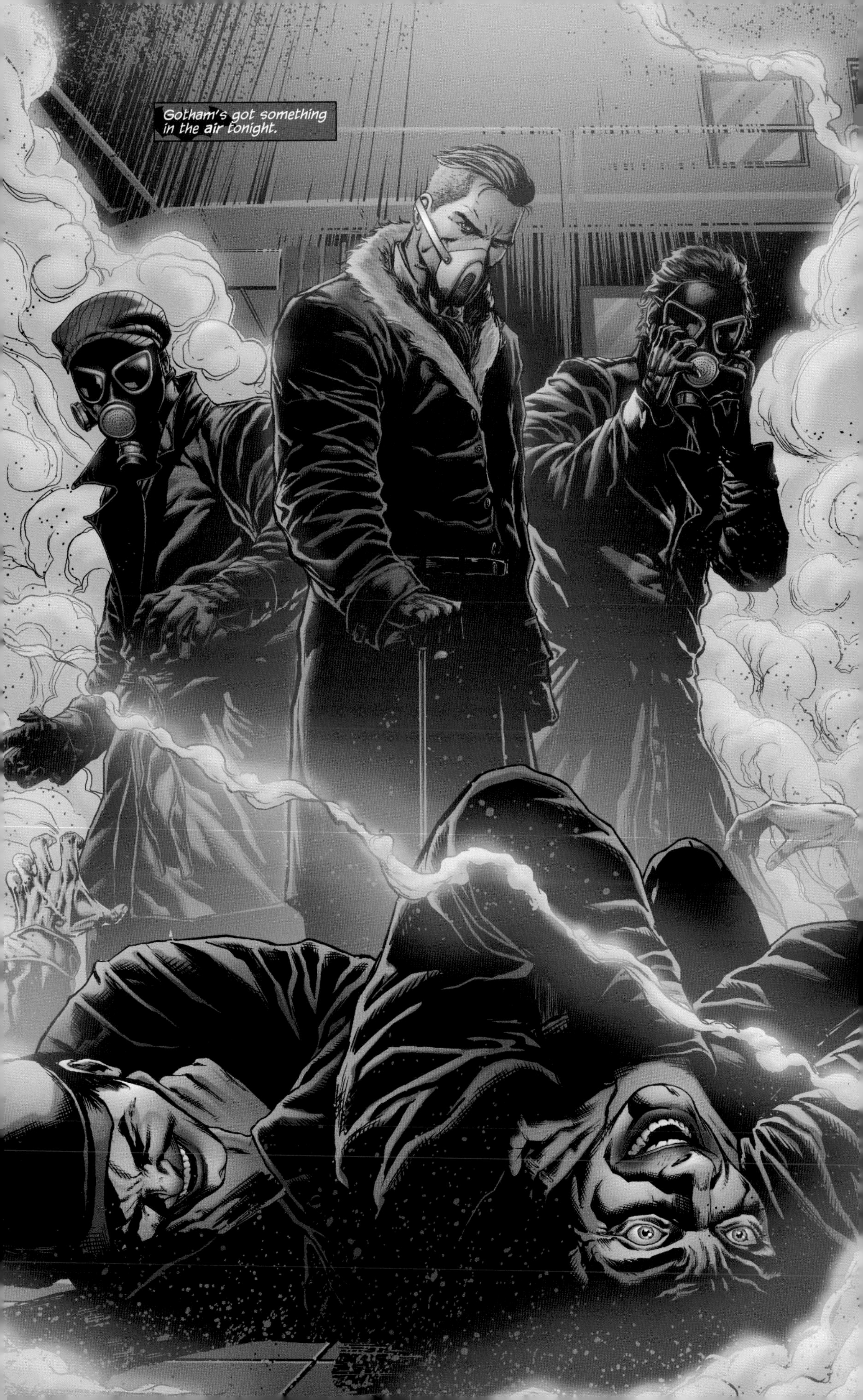
Gotham's got something in the air tonight.

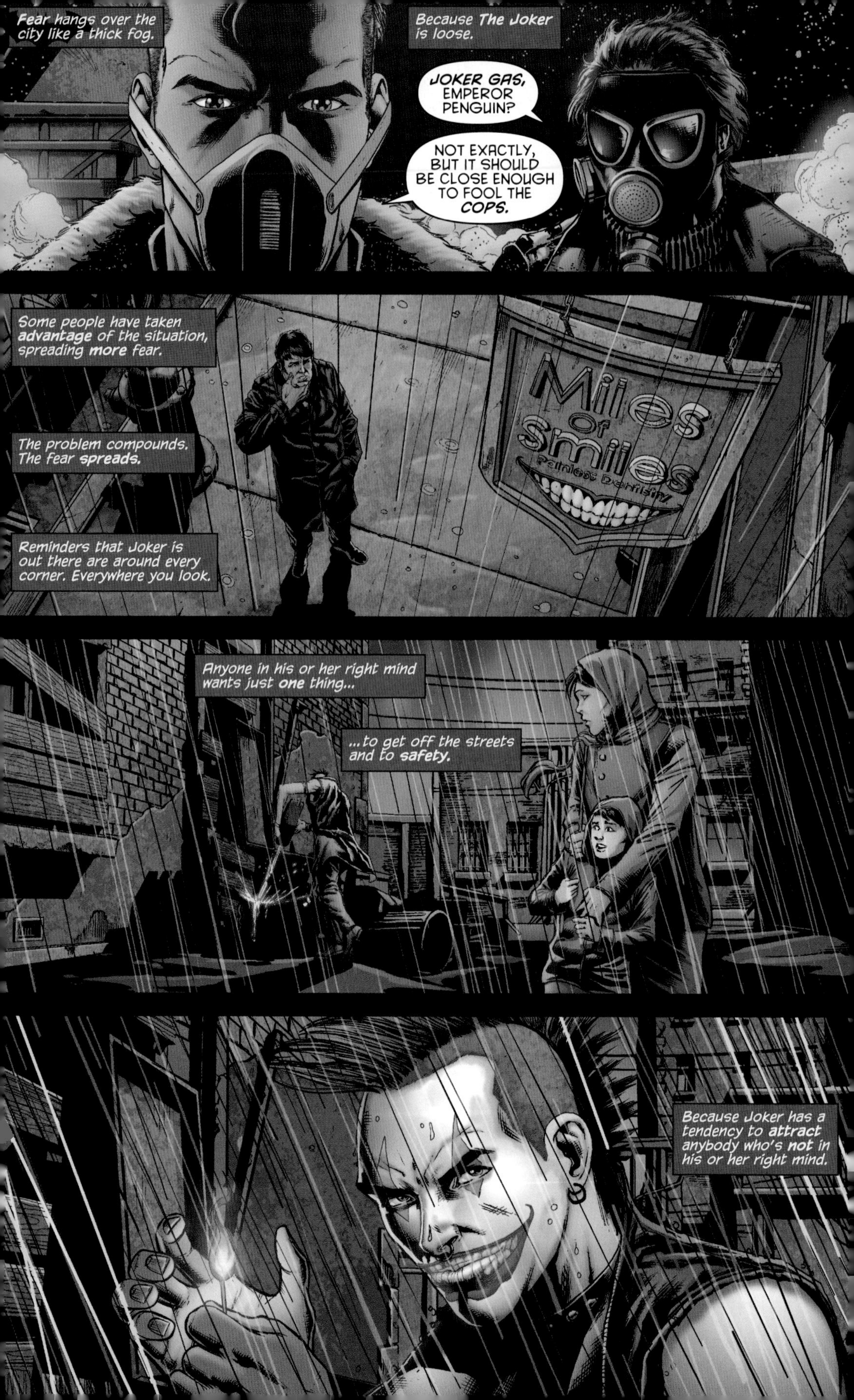
Fear hangs over the city like a thick fog.
Because The Joker is loose.
JOKER GAS, EMPEROR PENGUIN?
NOT EXACTLY, BUT IT SHOULD BE CLOSE ENOUGH TO FOOL THE COPS.
Some people have taken advantage of the situation, spreading more fear.
Miles Of Smiles Painless Dentistry
The problem compounds. The fear spreads.
Reminders that Joker is out there are around every corner. Everywhere you look.
Anyone in his or her right mind wants just one thing...
...to get off the streets and to safety.
Because Joker has a tendency to attract anybody who's not in his or her right mind.

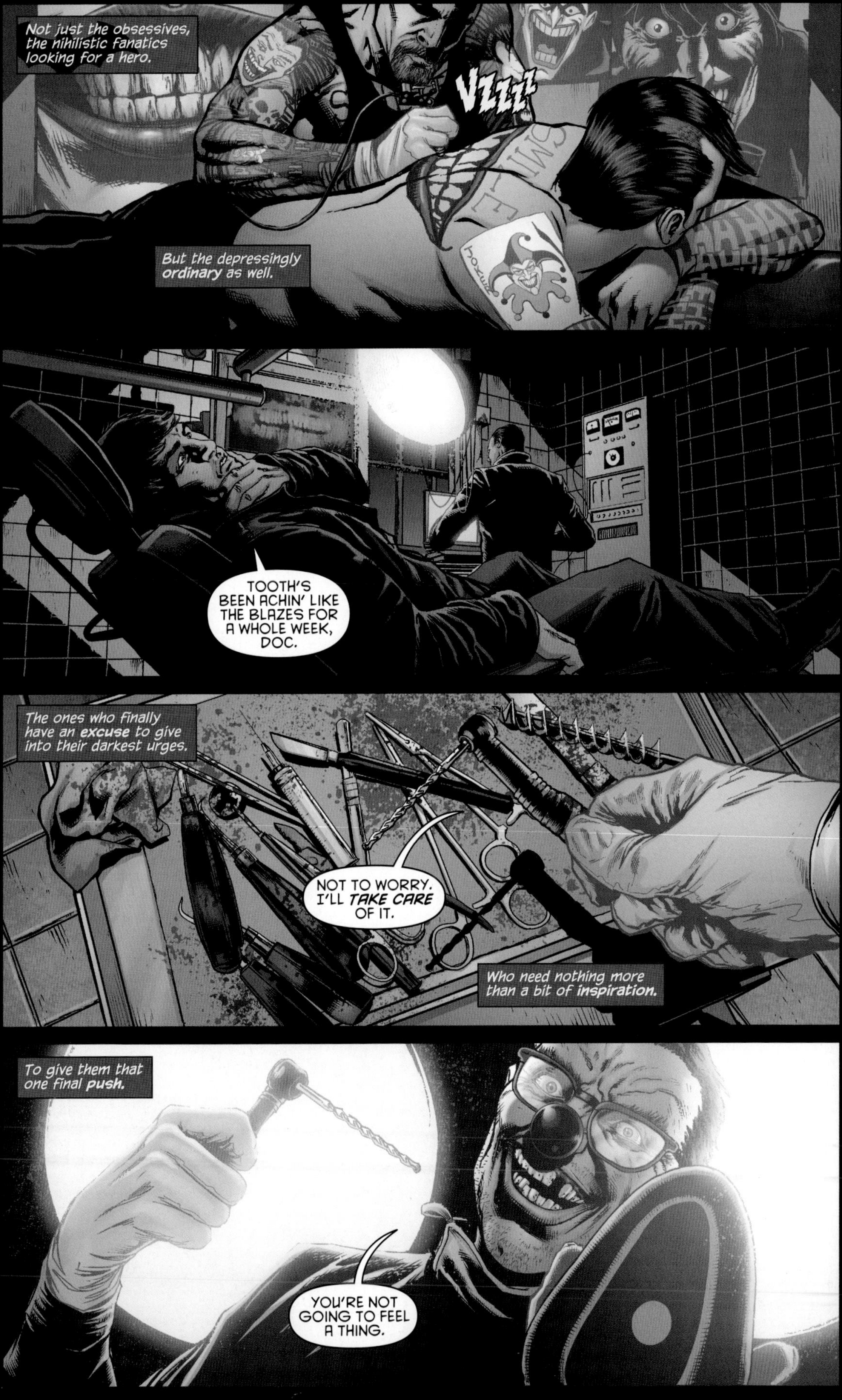
Not just the obsessives, the nihilistic fanatics looking for a hero.
VZZZZ
But the depressingly ordinary as well.
TOOTH'S BEEN ACHIN' LIKE THE BLAZES FOR A WHOLE WEEK, DOC.
The ones who finally have an excuse to give into their darkest urges.
NOT TO WORRY. I'LL TAKE CARE OF IT.
Who need nothing more than a bit of inspiration.
To give them that one final push.
YOU'RE NOT GOING TO FEEL A THING.

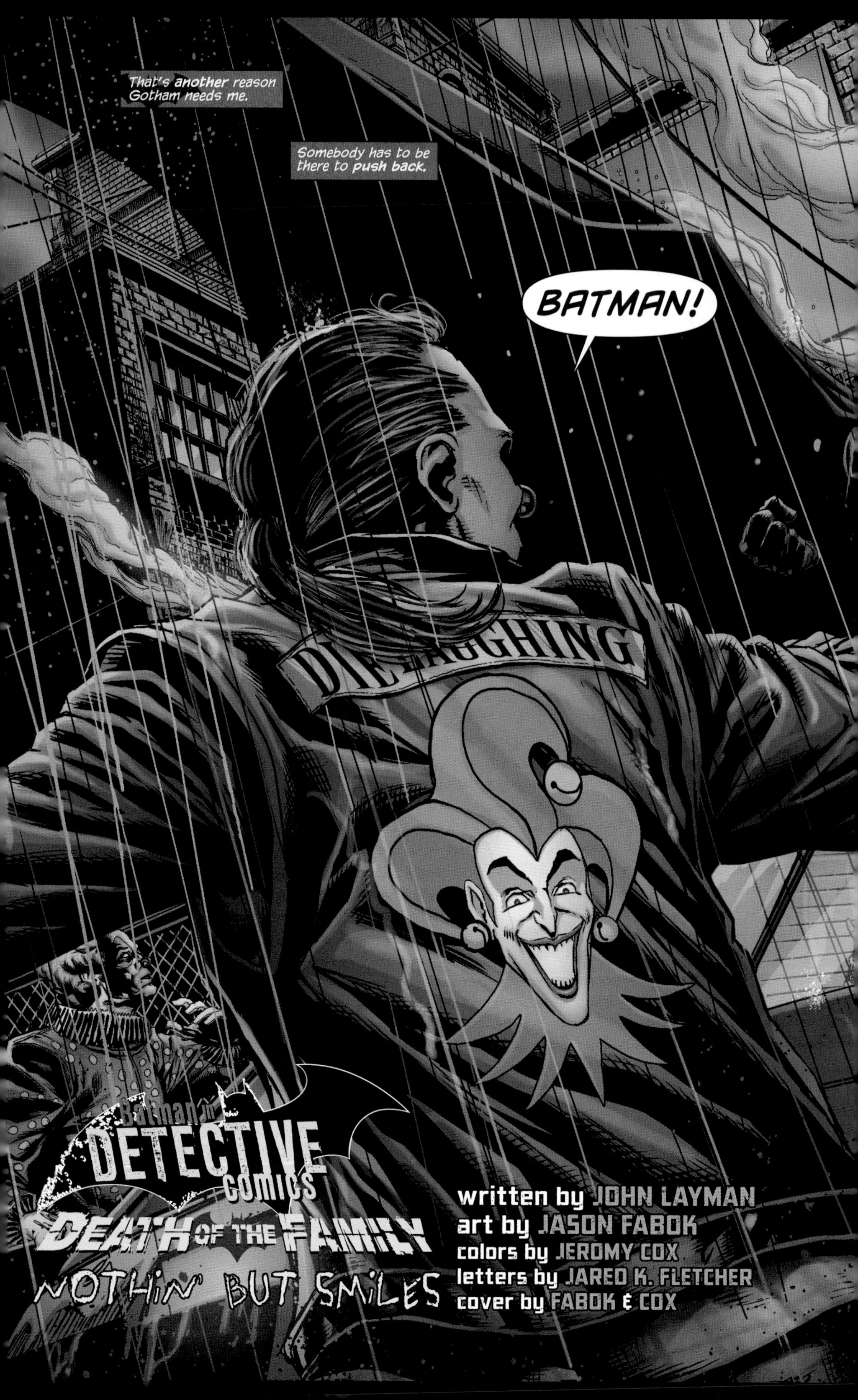

That's another reason Gotham needs me.
Somebody has to be there to push back.
BATMAN!
DIE LAUGHING
Batman in DETECTIVE COMICS
DEATH OF THE FAMILY
NOTHIN' BUT SMILES
written by JOHN LAYMAN
art by JASON FABOK
colors by JEROMY COX
letters by JARED K. FLETCHER
cover by FABOK & COX

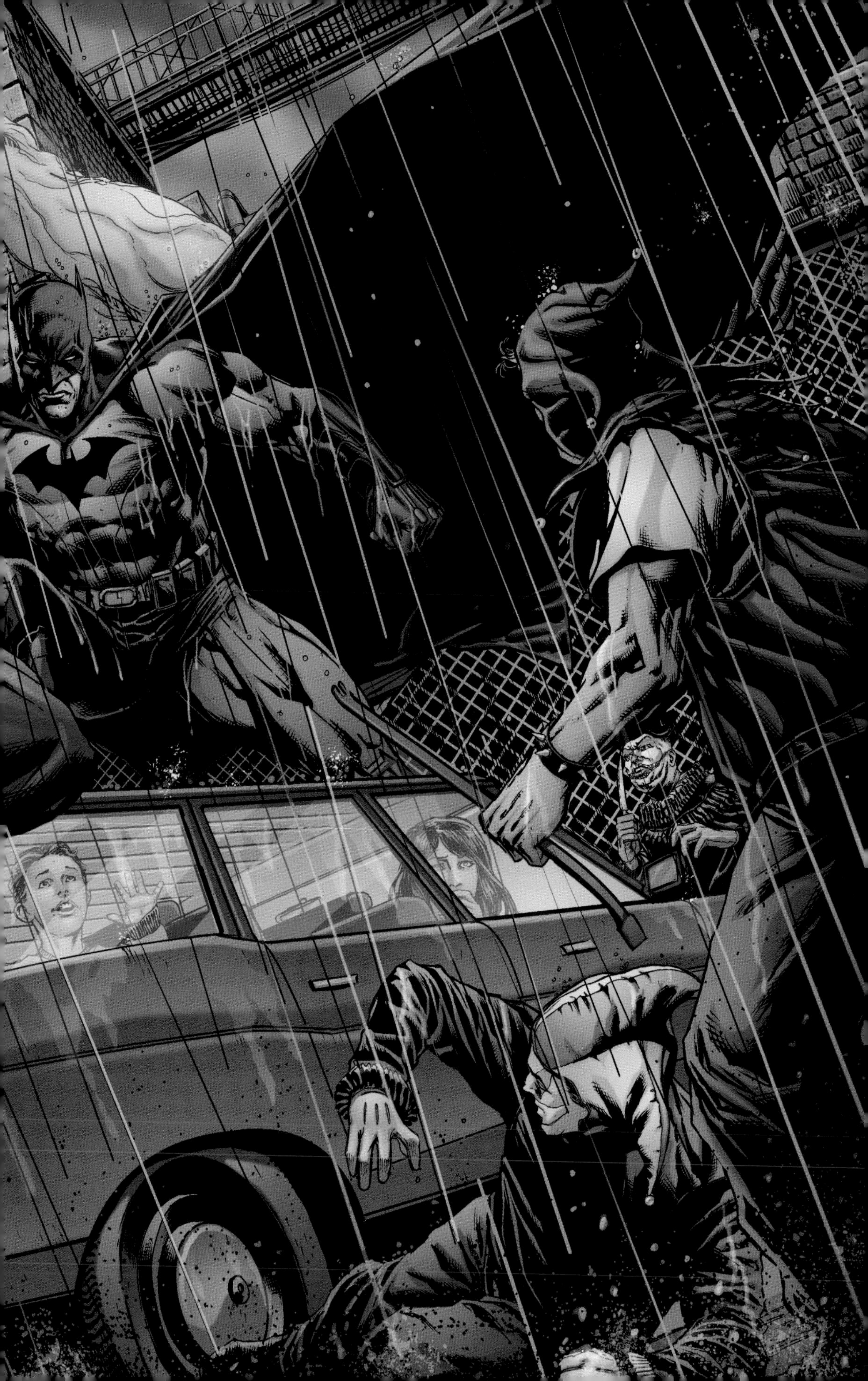

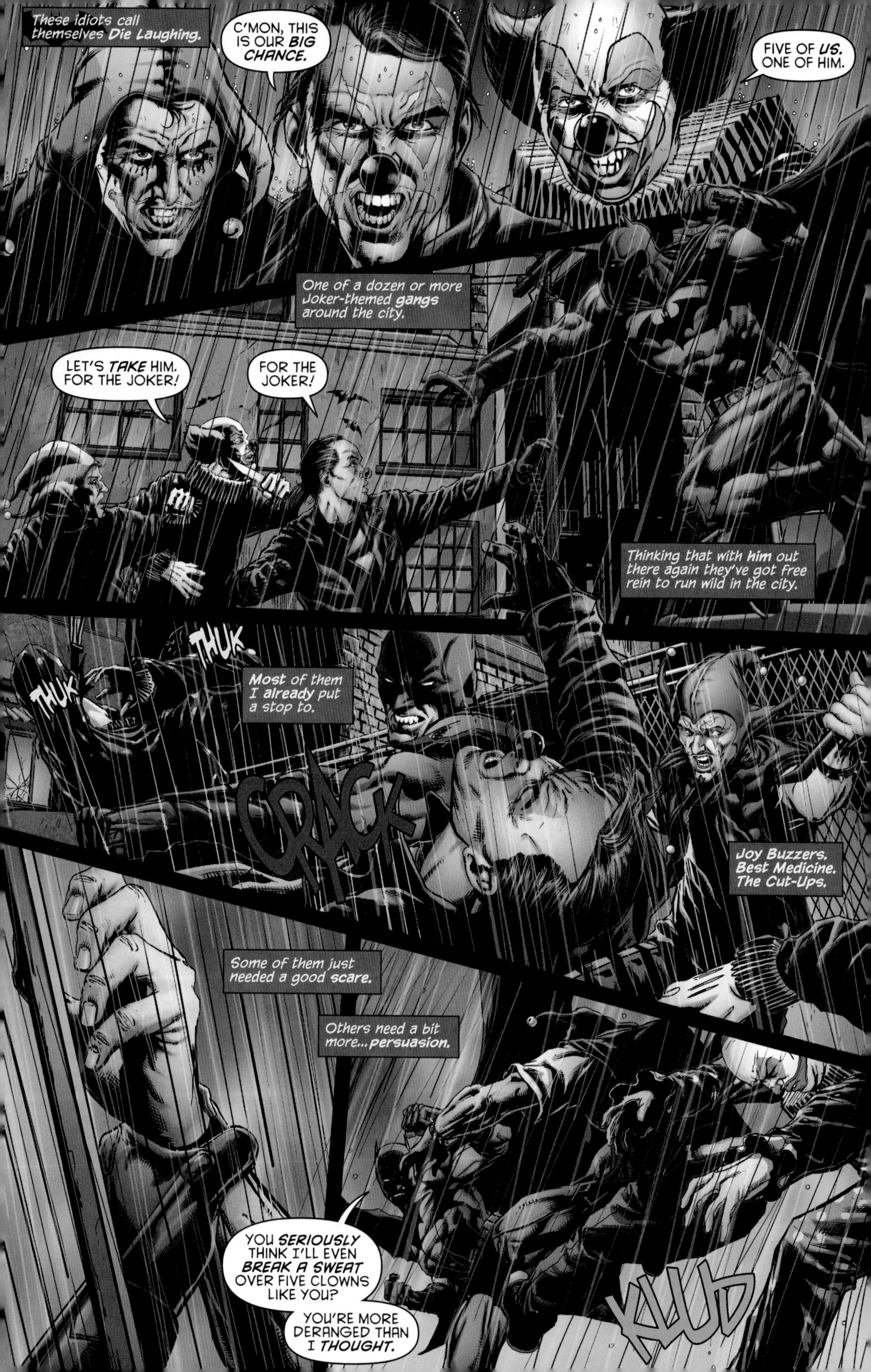

These idiots call themselves Die Laughing.
C'MON, THIS IS OUR BIG CHANCE.
FIVE OF US. ONE OF HIM.
One of a dozen or more Joker-themed gangs around the city.
LET'S TAKE HIM. FOR THE JOKER!
FOR THE JOKER!
Thinking that with him out there again they've got free rein to run wild in the city.
THUK
THUK
Most of them I already put a stop to.
CRACK
Joy Buzzers. Best Medicine. The Cut-Ups.
Some of them just needed a good scare.
Others need a bit more... persuasion.
YOU SERIOUSLY THINK I'LL EVEN BREAK A SWEAT OVER FIVE CLOWNS LIKE YOU?
YOU'RE MORE DERANGED THAN I THOUGHT.
KLUD

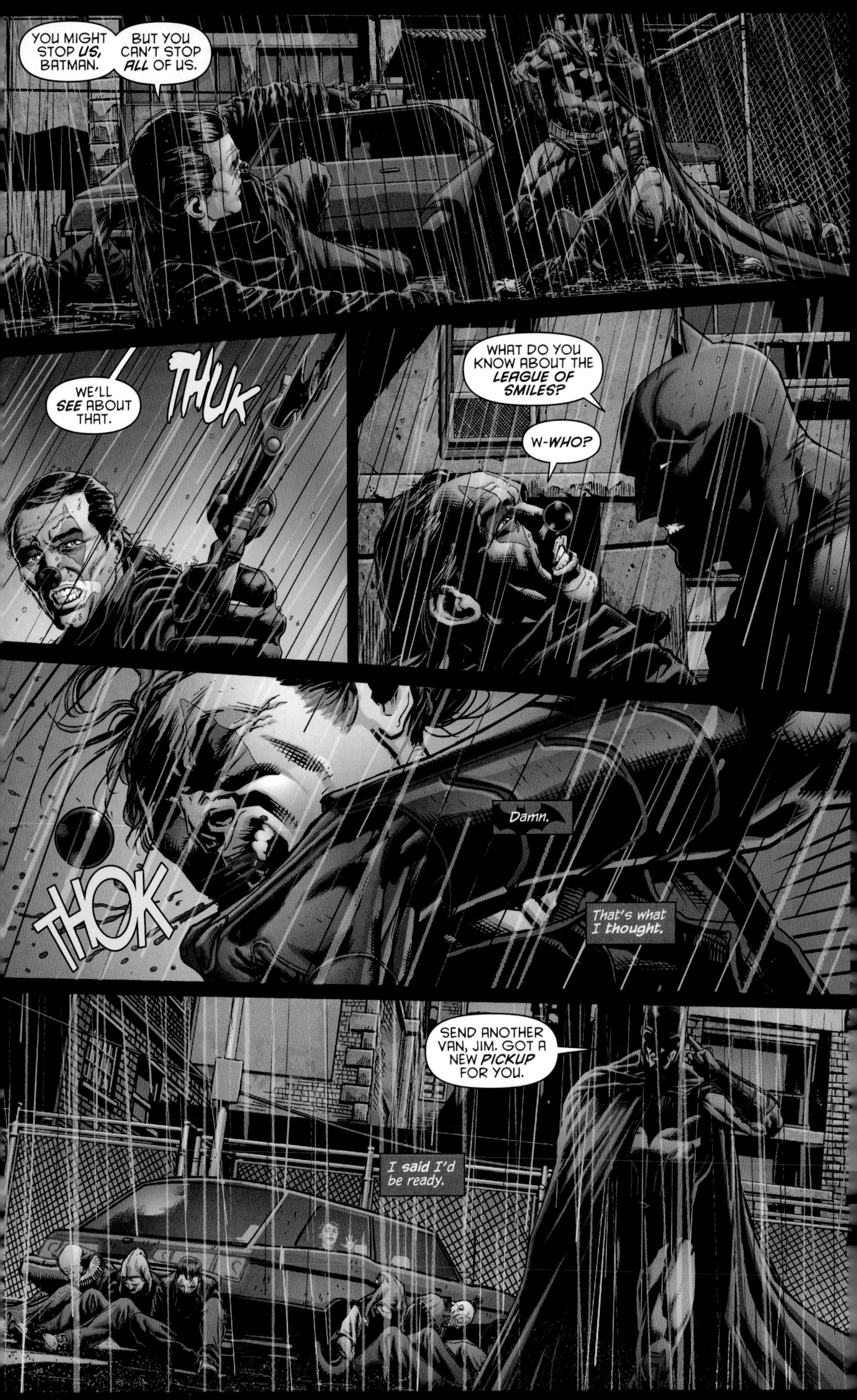

YOU MIGHT STOP *US,* BATMAN.
BUT YOU CAN'T STOP *ALL* OF US.
WE'LL *SEE* ABOUT THAT.
THUK
WHAT DO YOU KNOW ABOUT THE *LEAGUE OF SMILES?*
W-*WHO?*
Damn.
THOK
That's what *I thought.*
SEND ANOTHER VAN, JIM. GOT A NEW *PICKUP* FOR YOU.
I said I'd be ready.

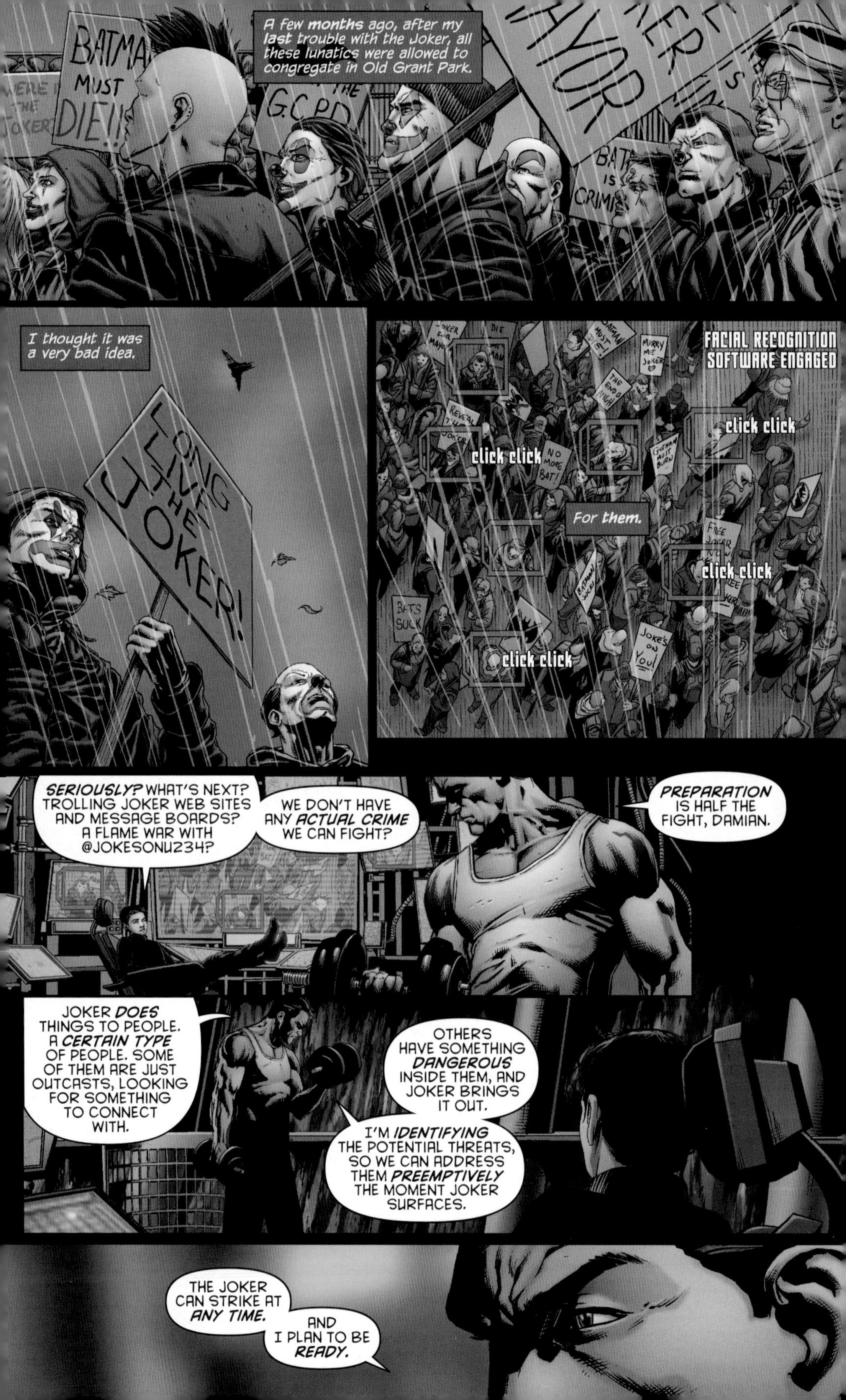

A few months ago, after my last trouble with the Joker, all these lunatics were allowed to congregate in Old Grant Park.
BATMAN MUST DIE!!
I thought it was a very bad idea.
LONG LIVE THE JOKER!
FACIAL RECOGNITION SOFTWARE ENGAGED
click click
click click
For them.
click click
click click
SERIOUSLY? WHAT'S NEXT? TROLLING JOKER WEB SITES AND MESSAGE BOARDS? A FLAME WAR WITH @JOKESONU234?
WE DON'T HAVE ANY ACTUAL CRIME WE CAN FIGHT?
PREPARATION IS HALF THE FIGHT, DAMIAN.
JOKER DOES THINGS TO PEOPLE. A CERTAIN TYPE OF PEOPLE. SOME OF THEM ARE JUST OUTCASTS, LOOKING FOR SOMETHING TO CONNECT WITH.
OTHERS HAVE SOMETHING DANGEROUS INSIDE THEM, AND JOKER BRINGS IT OUT.
I'M IDENTIFYING THE POTENTIAL THREATS, SO WE CAN ADDRESS THEM PREEMPTIVELY THE MOMENT JOKER SURFACES.
THE JOKER CAN STRIKE AT ANY TIME.
AND I PLAN TO BE READY.

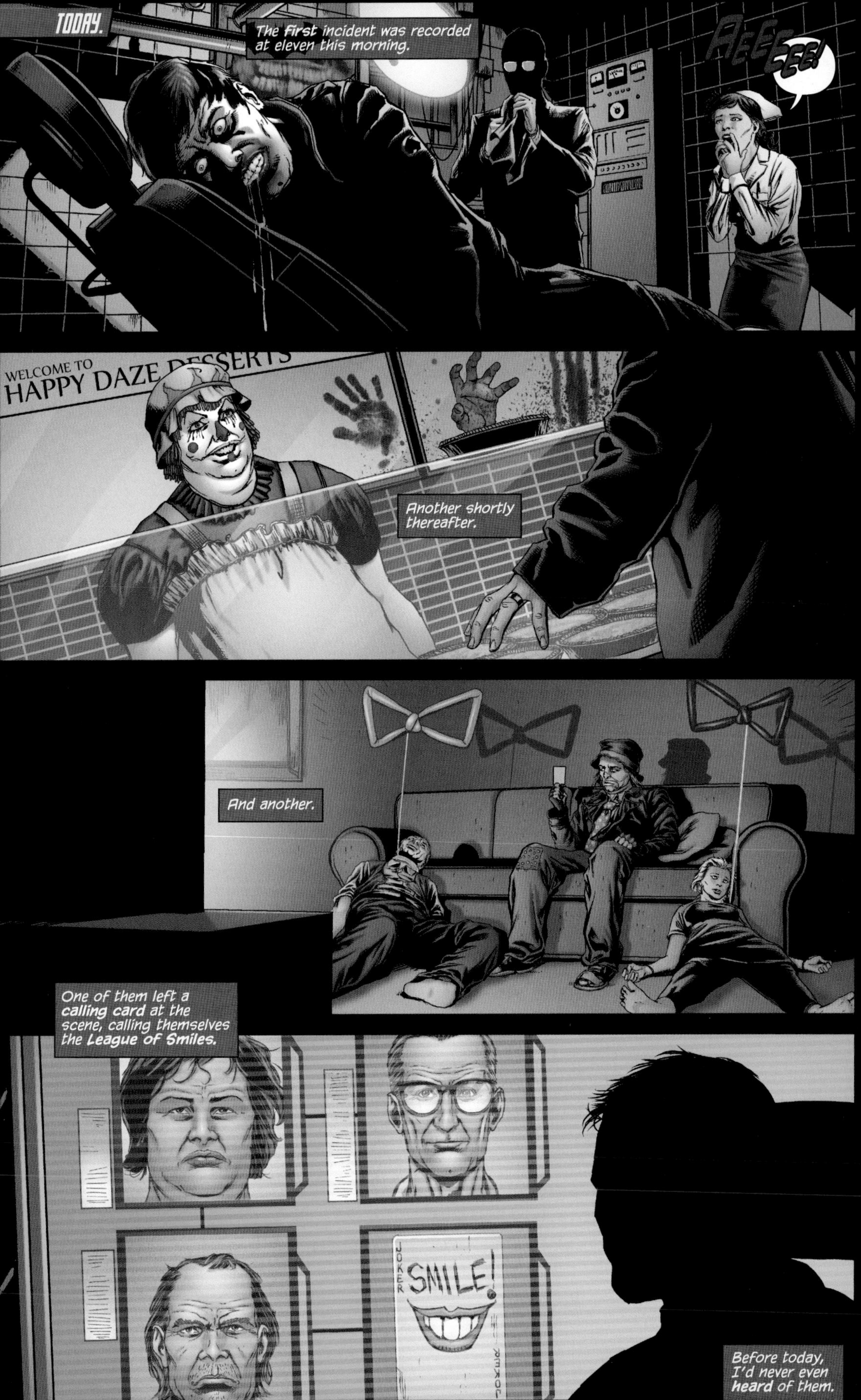
TODAY.
The first incident was recorded at eleven this morning.
AEEEEEE!
WELCOME TO HAPPY DAZE DESSERTS
Another shortly thereafter.
And another.
One of them left a calling card at the scene, calling themselves the League of Smiles.
JOKER
SMILE!
JOKER
Before today, I'd never even heard of them.

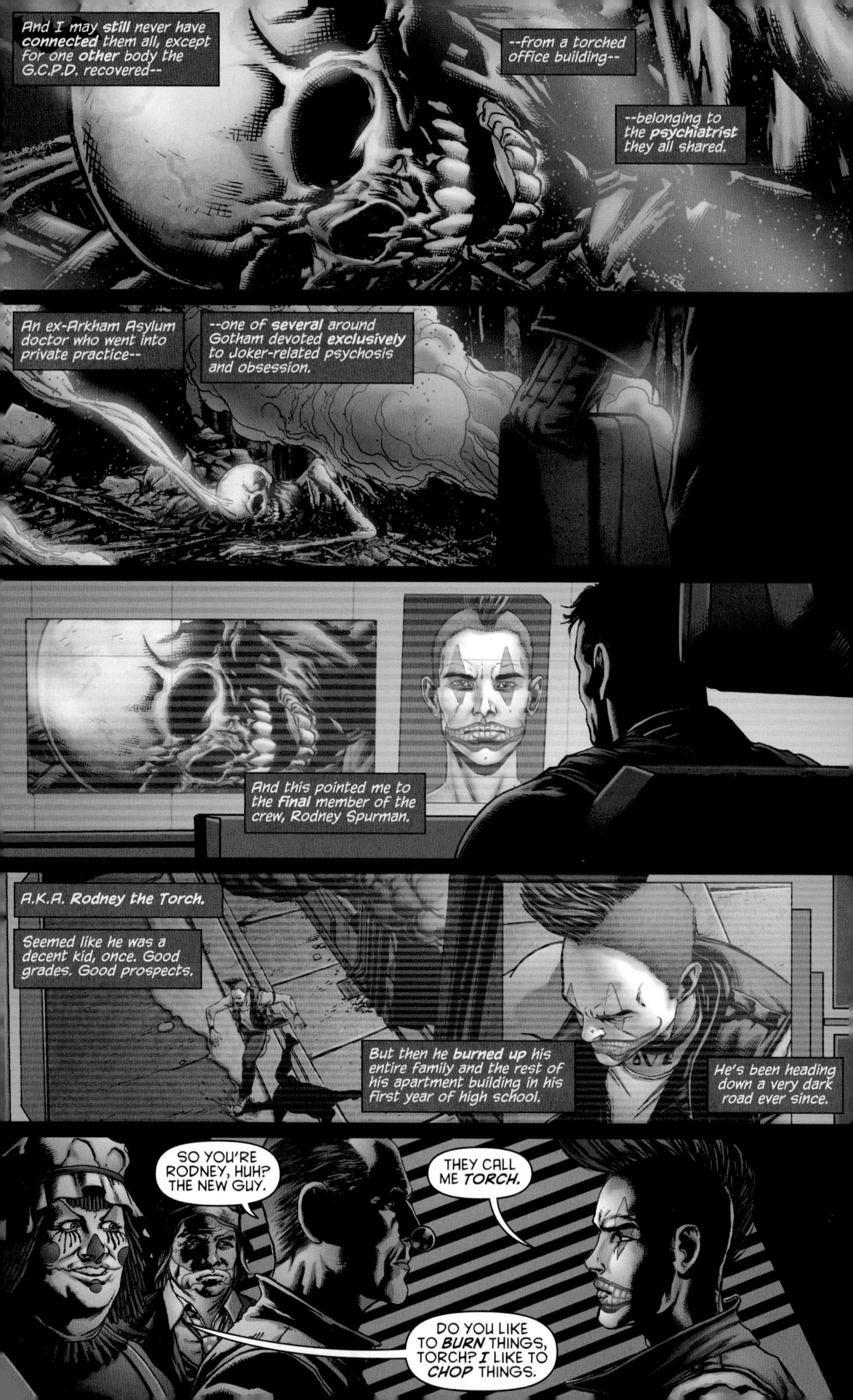
And I may still never have connected them all, except for one other body the G.C.P.D. recovered--
--from a torched office building--
--belonging to the psychiatrist they all shared.
An ex-Arkham Asylum doctor who went into private practice--
--one of several around Gotham devoted exclusively to Joker-related psychosis and obsession.
And this pointed me to the final member of the crew, Rodney Spurman.
A.K.A. Rodney the Torch.
Seemed like he was a decent kid, once. Good grades. Good prospects.
But then he burned up his entire family and the rest of his apartment building in his first year of high school.
He's been heading down a very dark road ever since.
SO YOU'RE RODNEY, HUH? THE NEW GUY.
THEY CALL ME TORCH.
DO YOU LIKE TO BURN THINGS, TORCH? I LIKE TO CHOP THINGS.

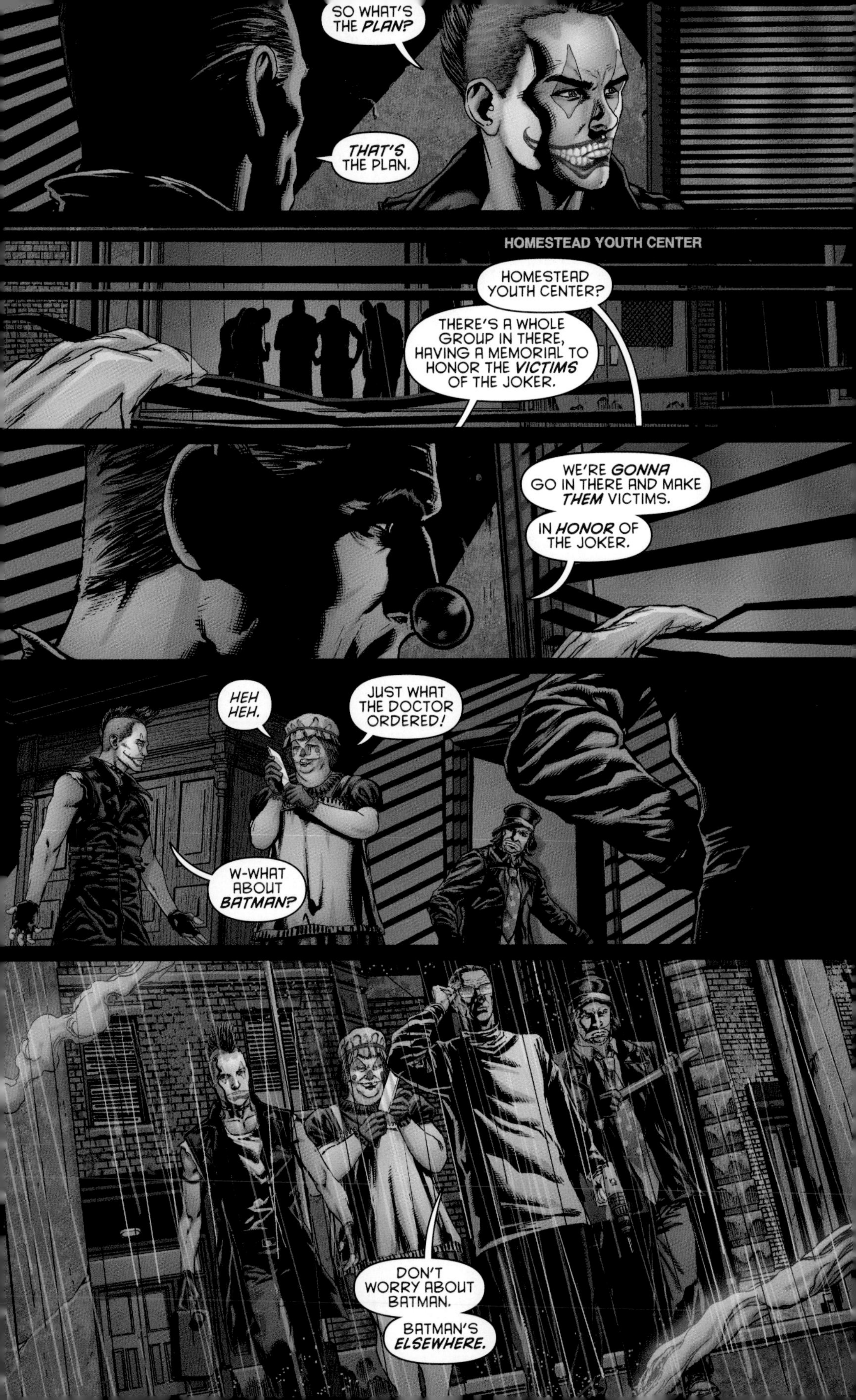
SO WHAT'S THE PLAN?
THAT'S THE PLAN.
HOMESTEAD YOUTH CENTER
HOMESTEAD YOUTH CENTER?
THERE'S A WHOLE GROUP IN THERE, HAVING A MEMORIAL TO HONOR THE VICTIMS OF THE JOKER.
WE'RE GONNA GO IN THERE AND MAKE THEM VICTIMS.
IN HONOR OF THE JOKER.
HEH HEH.
JUST WHAT THE DOCTOR ORDERED!
W-WHAT ABOUT BATMAN?
DON'T WORRY ABOUT BATMAN.
BATMAN'S ELSEWHERE.

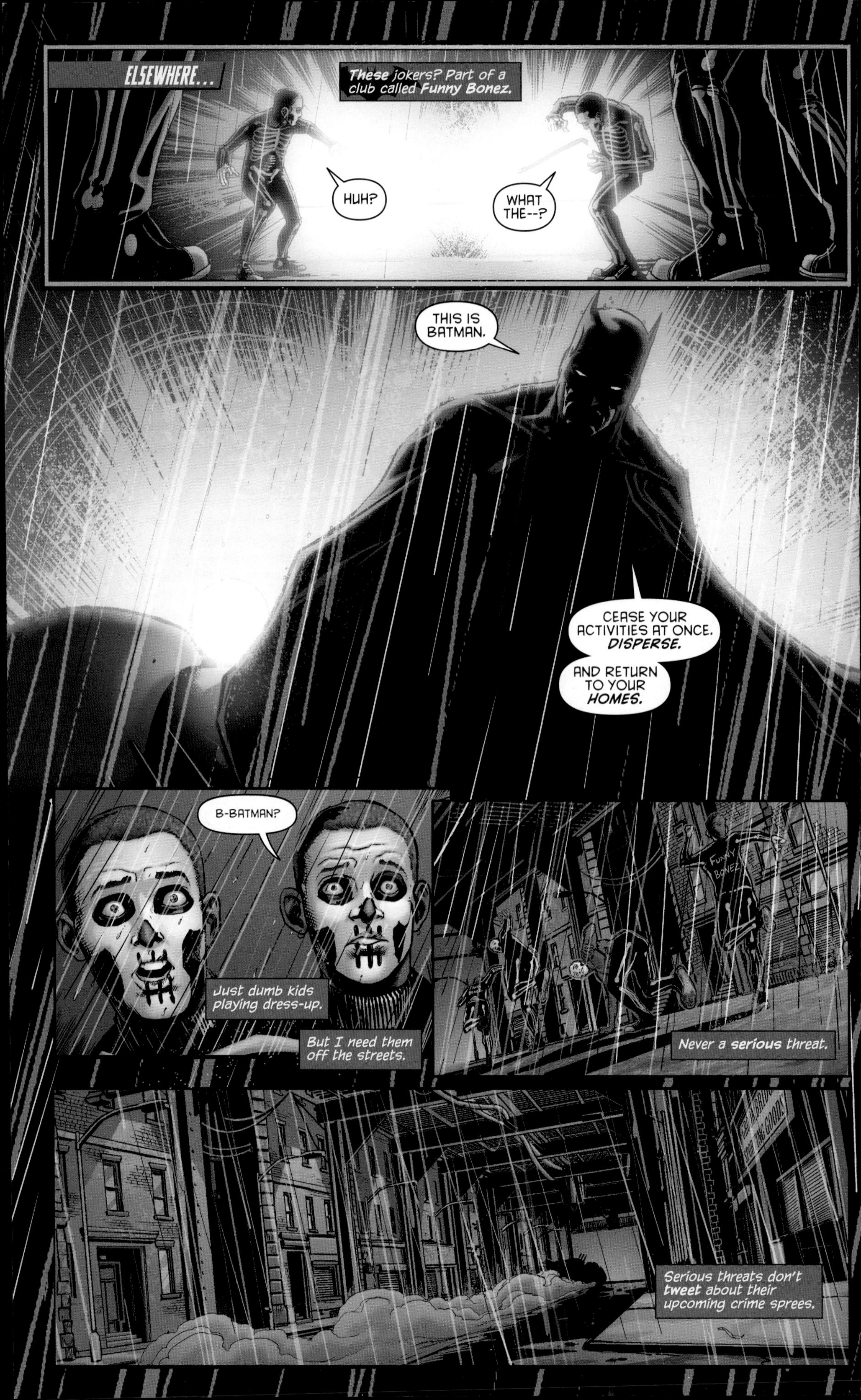
ELSEWHERE...
These jokers? Part of a club called Funny Bonez.
HUH?
WHAT THE--?
THIS IS BATMAN.
CEASE YOUR ACTIVITIES AT ONCE. DISPERSE.
AND RETURN TO YOUR HOMES.
B-BATMAN?
Just dumb kids playing dress-up.
But I need them off the streets.
FUNNY BONEZ
Never a serious threat.
Serious threats don't tweet about their upcoming crime sprees.

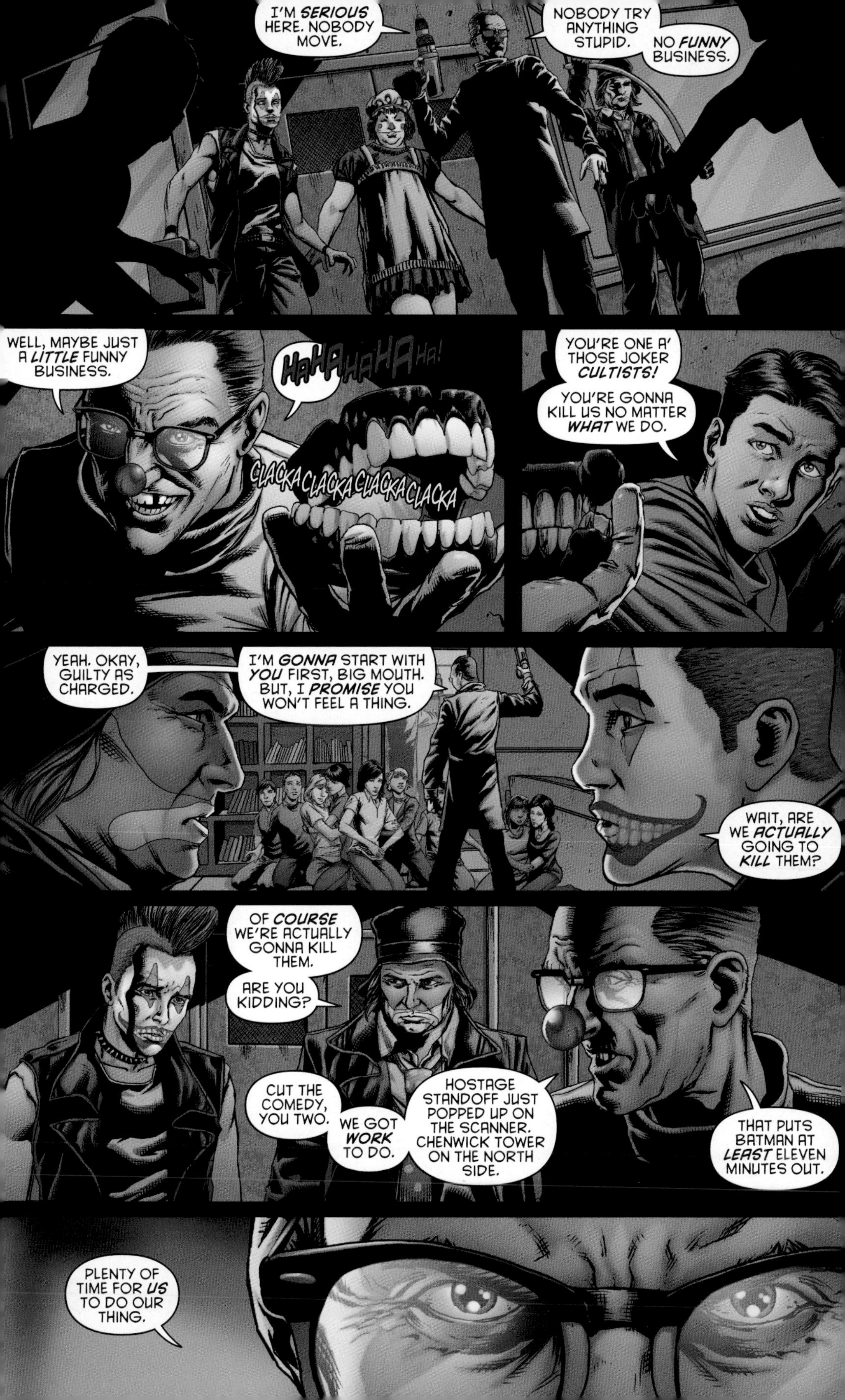
I'M SERIOUS HERE. NOBODY MOVE.
NOBODY TRY ANYTHING STUPID.
NO FUNNY BUSINESS.
WELL, MAYBE JUST A LITTLE FUNNY BUSINESS.
HAHAHAHAHA!
CLACKA CLACKA CLACKA CLACKA
YOU'RE ONE A' THOSE JOKER CULTISTS!
YOU'RE GONNA KILL US NO MATTER WHAT WE DO.
YEAH. OKAY, GUILTY AS CHARGED.
I'M GONNA START WITH YOU FIRST, BIG MOUTH. BUT, I PROMISE YOU WON'T FEEL A THING.
WAIT, ARE WE ACTUALLY GOING TO KILL THEM?
OF COURSE WE'RE ACTUALLY GONNA KILL THEM.
ARE YOU KIDDING?
CUT THE COMEDY, YOU TWO.
WE GOT WORK TO DO.
HOSTAGE STANDOFF JUST POPPED UP ON THE SCANNER. CHENWICK TOWER ON THE NORTH SIDE.
THAT PUTS BATMAN AT LEAST ELEVEN MINUTES OUT.
PLENTY OF TIME FOR US TO DO OUR THING.

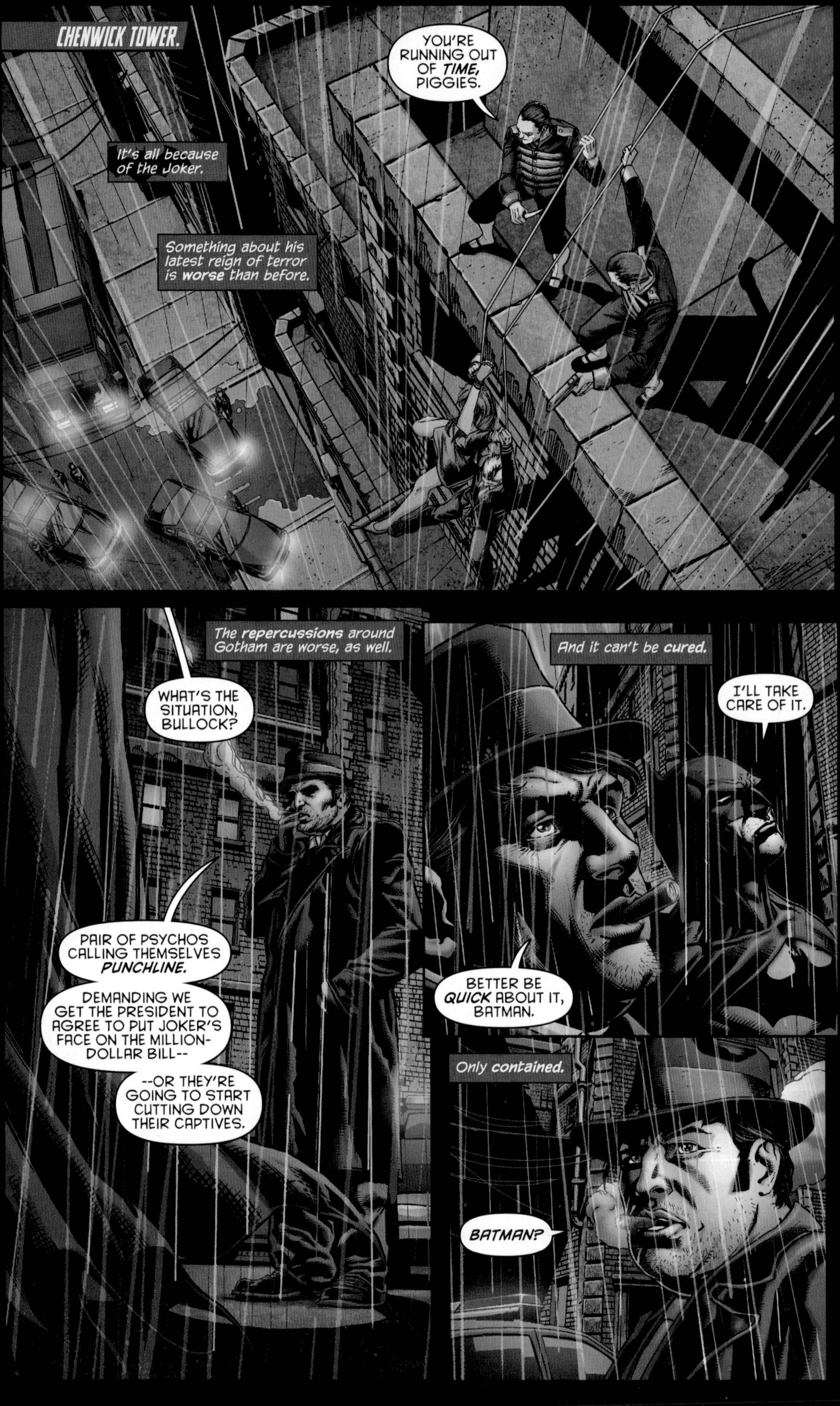
CHENWICK TOWER.
YOU'RE RUNNING OUT OF TIME, PIGGIES.
It's all because of the Joker.
Something about his latest reign of terror is worse than before.
The repercussions around Gotham are worse, as well.
WHAT'S THE SITUATION, BULLOCK?
PAIR OF PSYCHOS CALLING THEMSELVES PUNCHLINE.
DEMANDING WE GET THE PRESIDENT TO AGREE TO PUT JOKER'S FACE ON THE MILLION-DOLLAR BILL--
--OR THEY'RE GOING TO START CUTTING DOWN THEIR CAPTIVES.
And it can't be cured.
I'LL TAKE CARE OF IT.
BETTER BE QUICK ABOUT IT, BATMAN.
Only contained.
BATMAN?

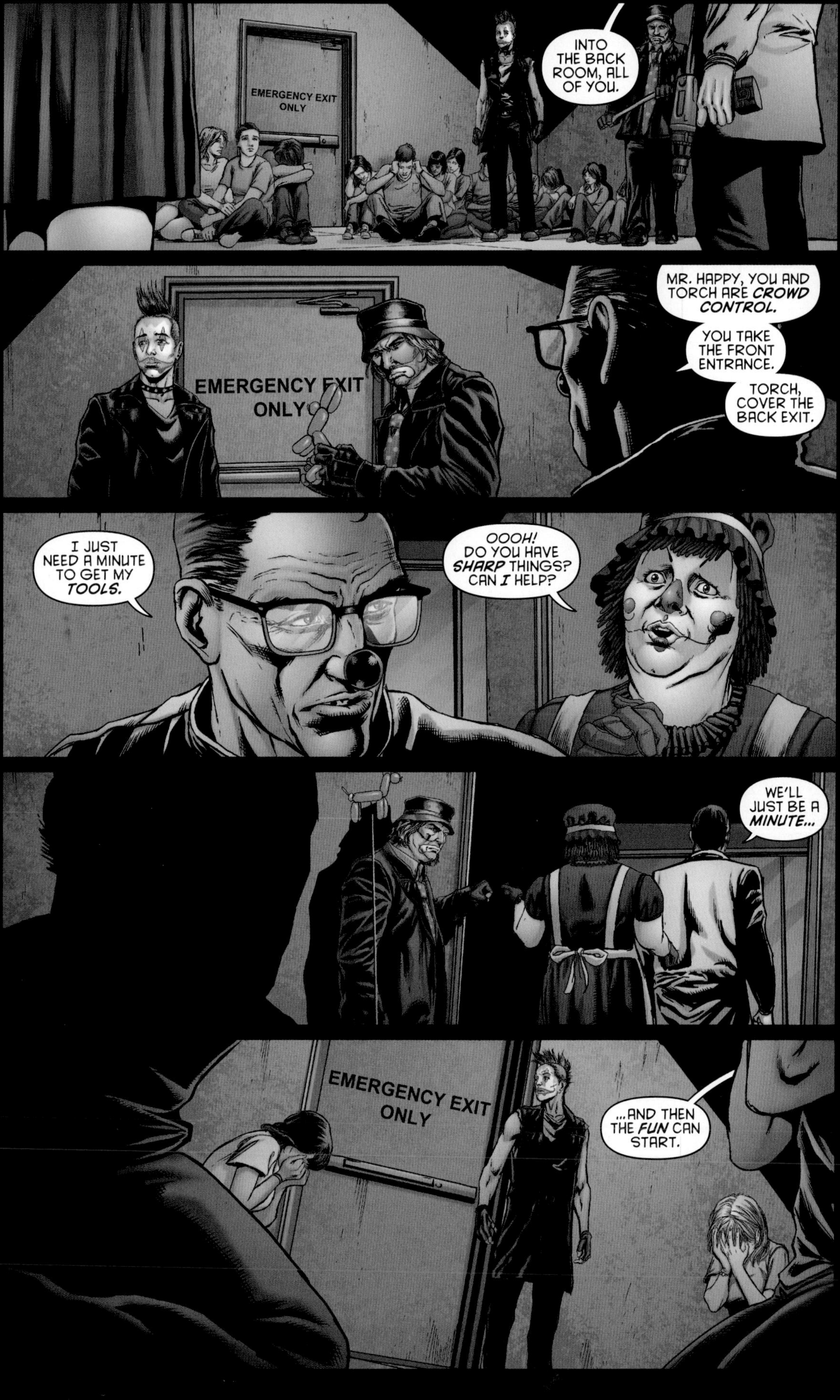
EMERGENCY EXIT ONLY
INTO THE BACK ROOM, ALL OF YOU.
MR. HAPPY, YOU AND TORCH ARE CROWD CONTROL.
YOU TAKE THE FRONT ENTRANCE.
TORCH, COVER THE BACK EXIT.
I JUST NEED A MINUTE TO GET MY TOOLS.
OOOH! DO YOU HAVE SHARP THINGS? CAN I HELP?
WE'LL JUST BE A MINUTE...
EMERGENCY EXIT ONLY
...AND THEN THE FUN CAN START.

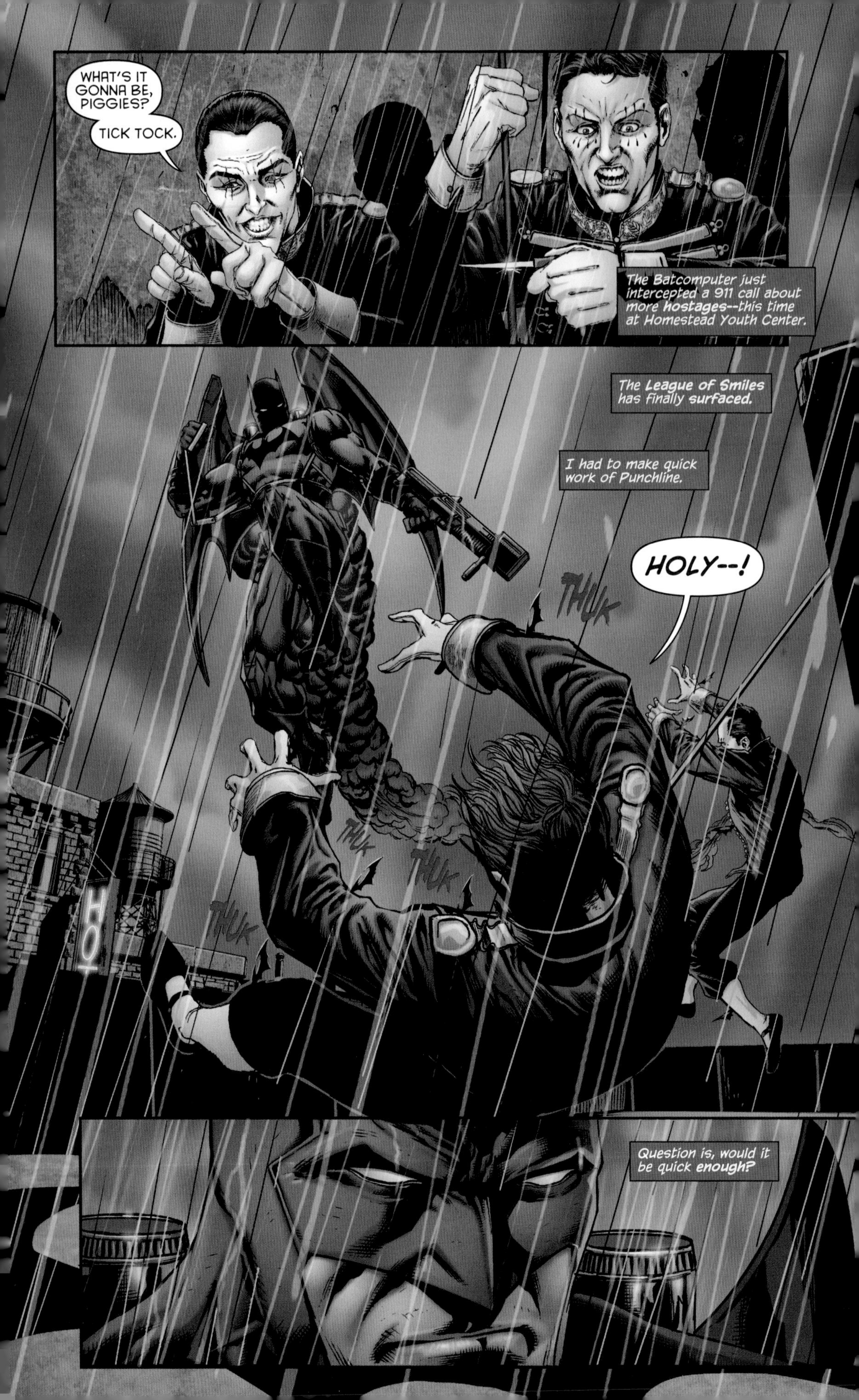
WHAT'S IT GONNA BE, PIGGIES?
TICK TOCK.
The Batcomputer just intercepted a 911 call about more hostages--this time at Homestead Youth Center.
The League of Smiles has finally surfaced.
I had to make quick work of Punchline.
HOLY--!
THUK
THUK
THUK
THUK
Question is, would it be quick enough?

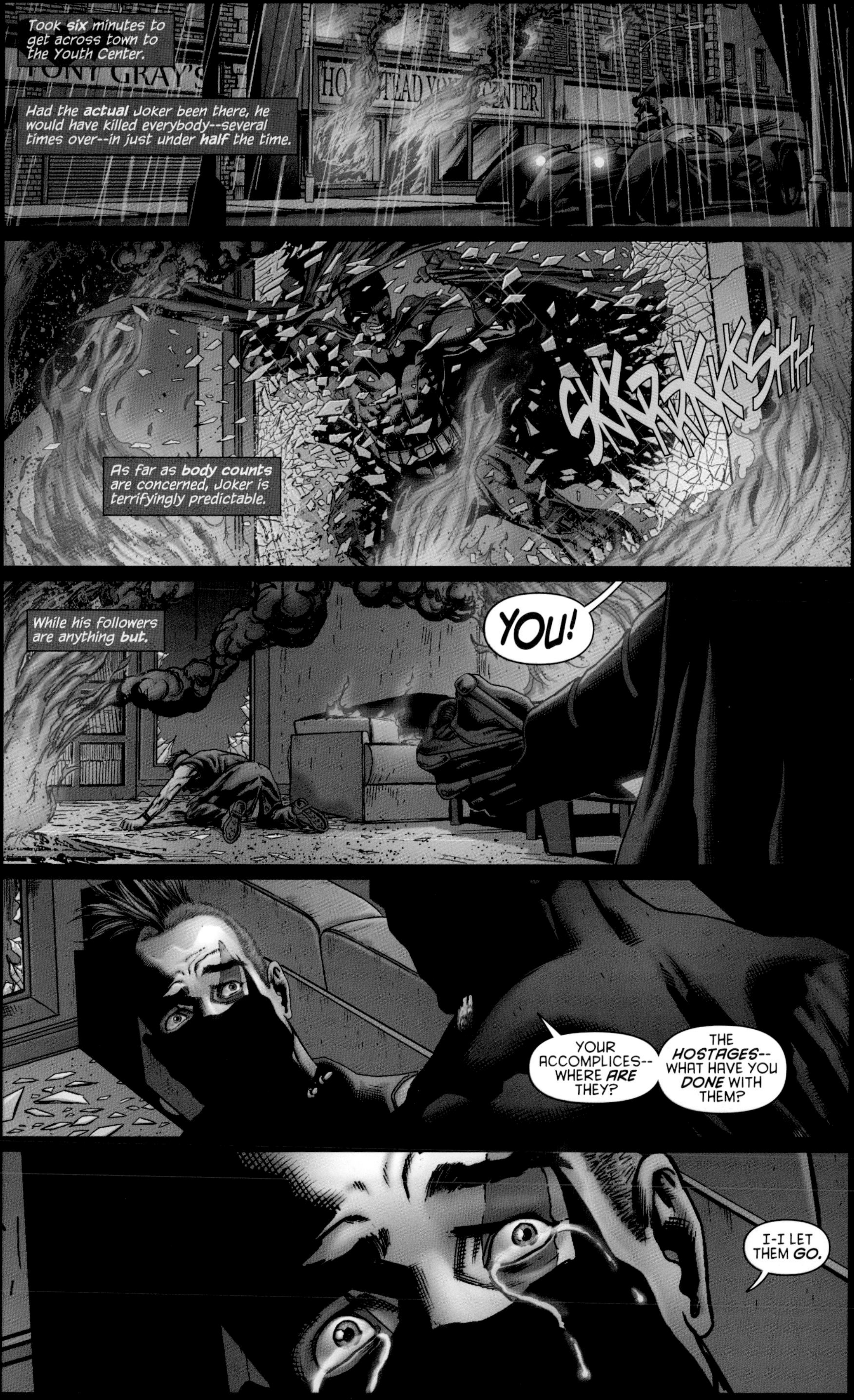
Took six minutes to get across town to the Youth Center.
TONY GRAY'S
HOMESTEAD YOUTH CENTER
Had the actual Joker been there, he would have killed everybody--several times over--in just under half the time.
SKKRRKKSHH
As far as body counts are concerned, Joker is terrifyingly predictable.
While his followers are anything but.
YOU!
YOUR ACCOMPLICES-- WHERE ARE THEY?
THE HOSTAGES-- WHAT HAVE YOU DONE WITH THEM?
I-I LET THEM GO.

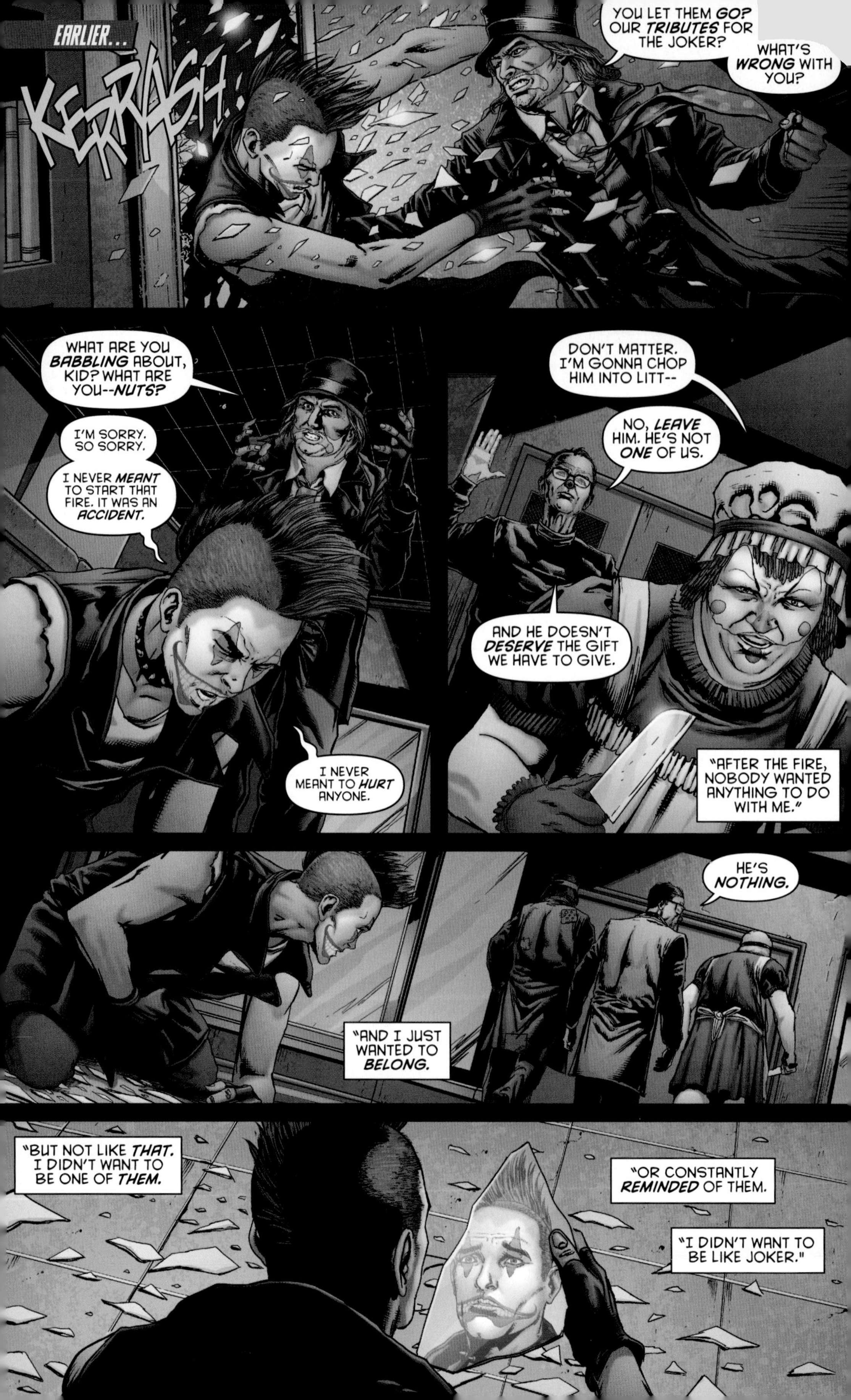
EARLIER...
KERRASH!
YOU LET THEM GO? OUR TRIBUTES FOR THE JOKER?
WHAT'S WRONG WITH YOU?
WHAT ARE YOU BABBLING ABOUT, KID? WHAT ARE YOU--NUTS?
I'M SORRY. SO SORRY.
I NEVER MEANT TO START THAT FIRE. IT WAS AN ACCIDENT.
I NEVER MEANT TO HURT ANYONE.
DON'T MATTER. I'M GONNA CHOP HIM INTO LITT--
NO, LEAVE HIM. HE'S NOT ONE OF US.
AND HE DOESN'T DESERVE THE GIFT WE HAVE TO GIVE.
"AFTER THE FIRE, NOBODY WANTED ANYTHING TO DO WITH ME."
HE'S NOTHING.
"AND I JUST WANTED TO BELONG.
"BUT NOT LIKE THAT. I DIDN'T WANT TO BE ONE OF THEM.
"OR CONSTANTLY REMINDED OF THEM.
"I DIDN'T WANT TO BE LIKE JOKER."

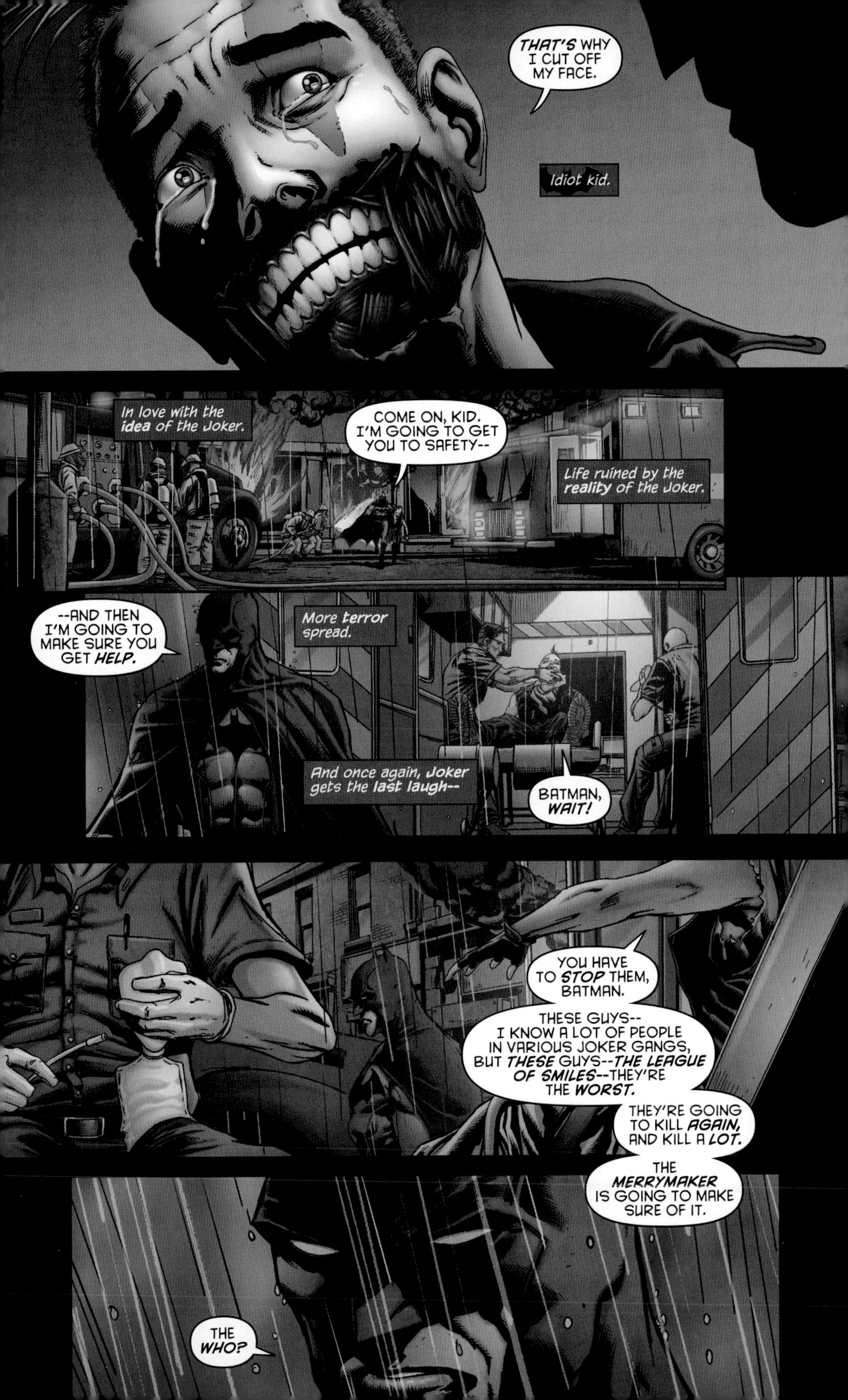
THAT'S WHY I CUT OFF MY FACE.
Idiot kid.
In love with the idea of the Joker.
COME ON, KID. I'M GOING TO GET YOU TO SAFETY--
Life ruined by the reality of the Joker.
--AND THEN I'M GOING TO MAKE SURE YOU GET HELP.
More terror spread.
And once again, Joker gets the last laugh--
BATMAN, WAIT!
YOU HAVE TO STOP THEM, BATMAN.
THESE GUYS-- I KNOW A LOT OF PEOPLE IN VARIOUS JOKER GANGS, BUT THESE GUYS--THE LEAGUE OF SMILES--THEY'RE THE WORST.
THEY'RE GOING TO KILL AGAIN, AND KILL A LOT.
THE MERRYMAKER IS GOING TO MAKE SURE OF IT.
THE WHO?

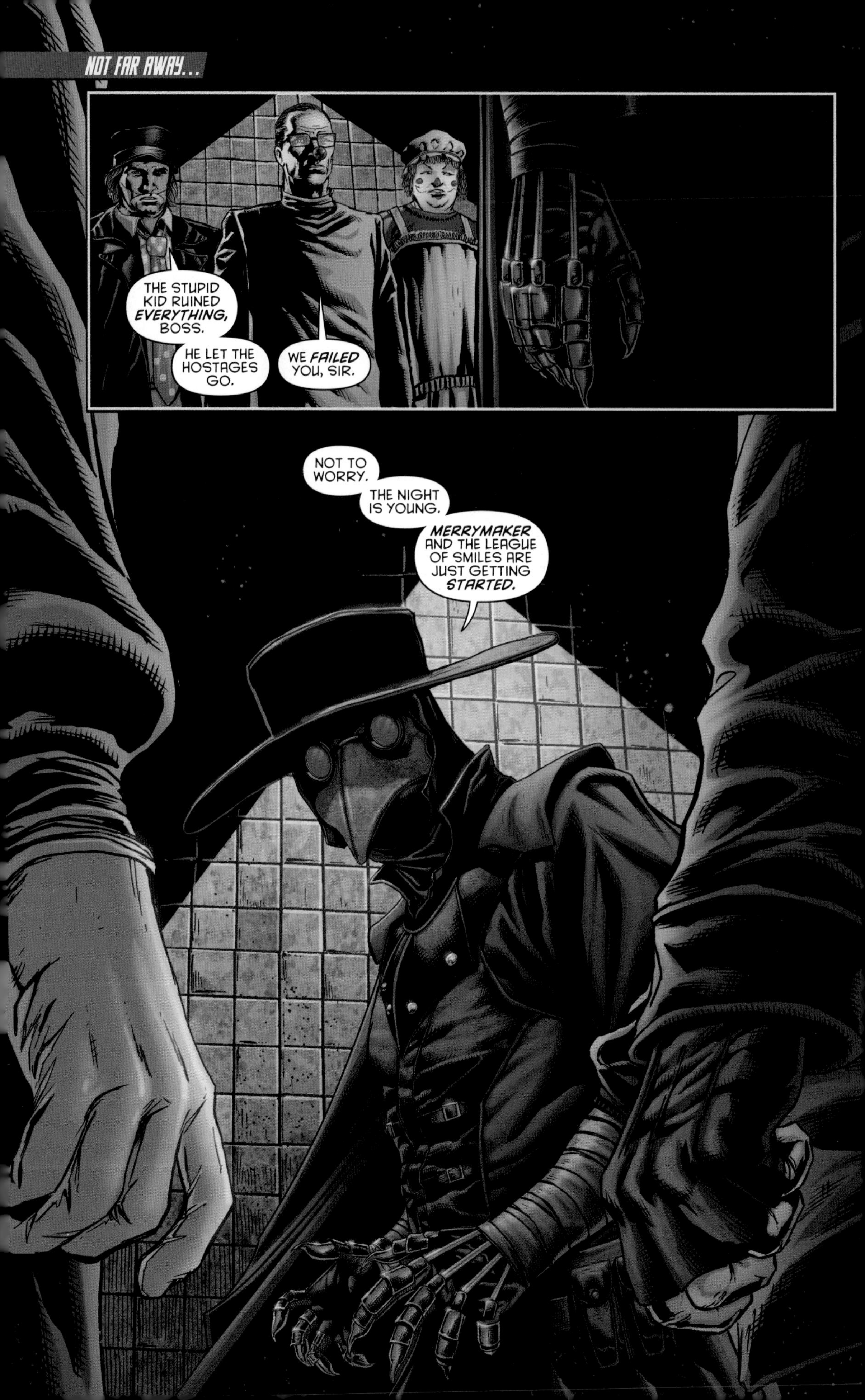
NOT FAR AWAY...
THE STUPID KID RUINED EVERYTHING, BOSS.
HE LET THE HOSTAGES GO.
WE FAILED YOU, SIR.
NOT TO WORRY.
THE NIGHT IS YOUNG.
MERRYMAKER AND THE LEAGUE OF SMILES ARE JUST GETTING STARTED.

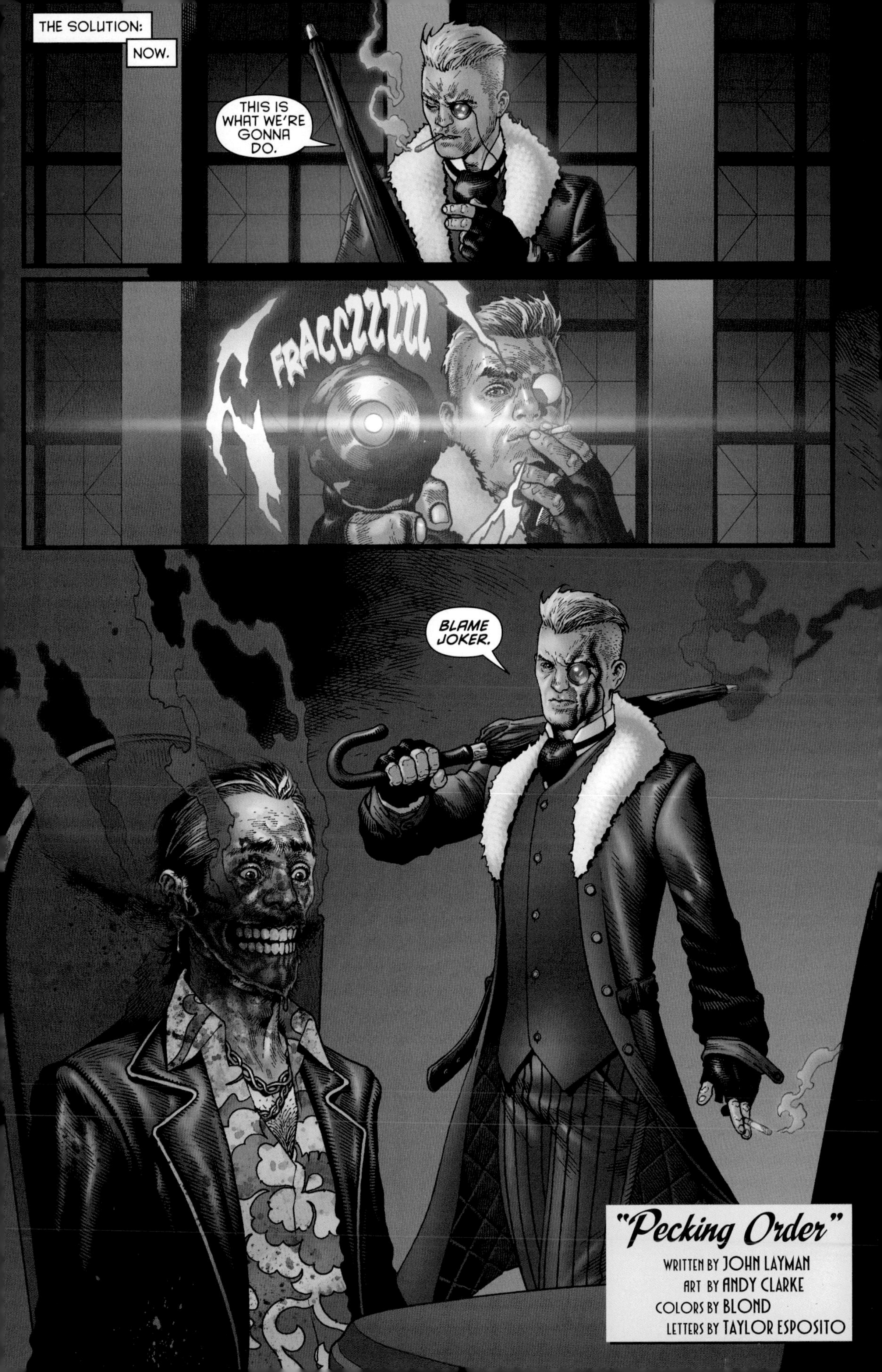
THE SOLUTION:
NOW.
THIS IS WHAT WE'RE GONNA DO.
FRACCZZZZZ
BLAME JOKER.
"Pecking Order"
WRITTEN BY JOHN LAYMAN
ART BY ANDY CLARKE
COLORS BY BLOND
LETTERS BY TAYLOR ESPOSITO

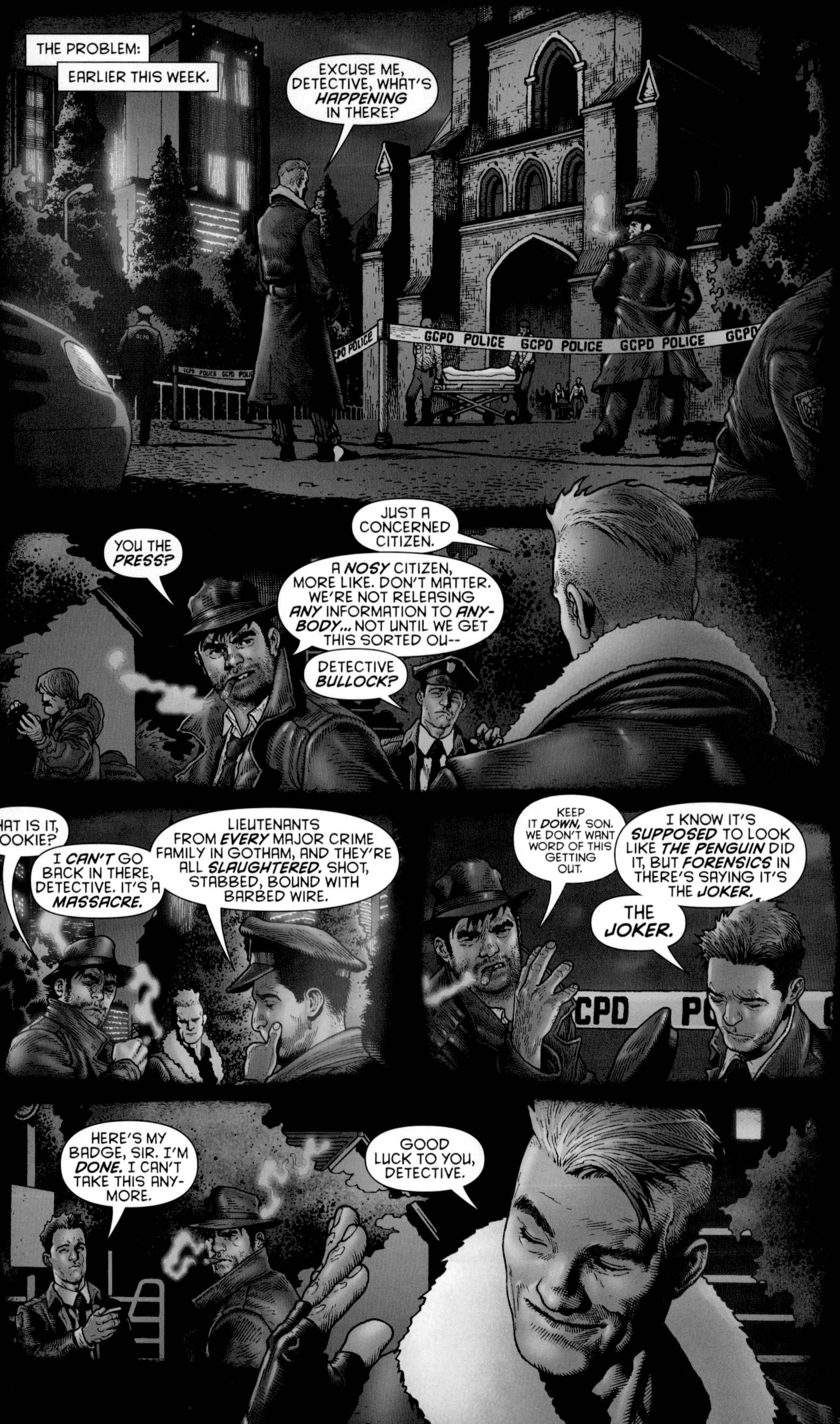

THE PROBLEM:
EARLIER THIS WEEK.
EXCUSE ME, DETECTIVE, WHAT'S HAPPENING IN THERE?
GCPD POLICE GCPD POLICE GCPD POLICE
YOU THE PRESS?
JUST A CONCERNED CITIZEN.
A NOSY CITIZEN, MORE LIKE. DON'T MATTER. WE'RE NOT RELEASING ANY INFORMATION TO ANYBODY... NOT UNTIL WE GET THIS SORTED OU--
DETECTIVE BULLOCK?
WHAT IS IT, ROOKIE?
I CAN'T GO BACK IN THERE, DETECTIVE. IT'S A MASSACRE.
LIEUTENANTS FROM EVERY MAJOR CRIME FAMILY IN GOTHAM, AND THEY'RE ALL SLAUGHTERED. SHOT, STABBED, BOUND WITH BARBED WIRE.
KEEP IT DOWN, SON. WE DON'T WANT WORD OF THIS GETTING OUT.
I KNOW IT'S SUPPOSED TO LOOK LIKE THE PENGUIN DID IT, BUT FORENSICS IN THERE'S SAYING IT'S THE JOKER.
THE JOKER.
HERE'S MY BADGE, SIR. I'M DONE. I CAN'T TAKE THIS ANYMORE.
GOOD LUCK TO YOU, DETECTIVE.

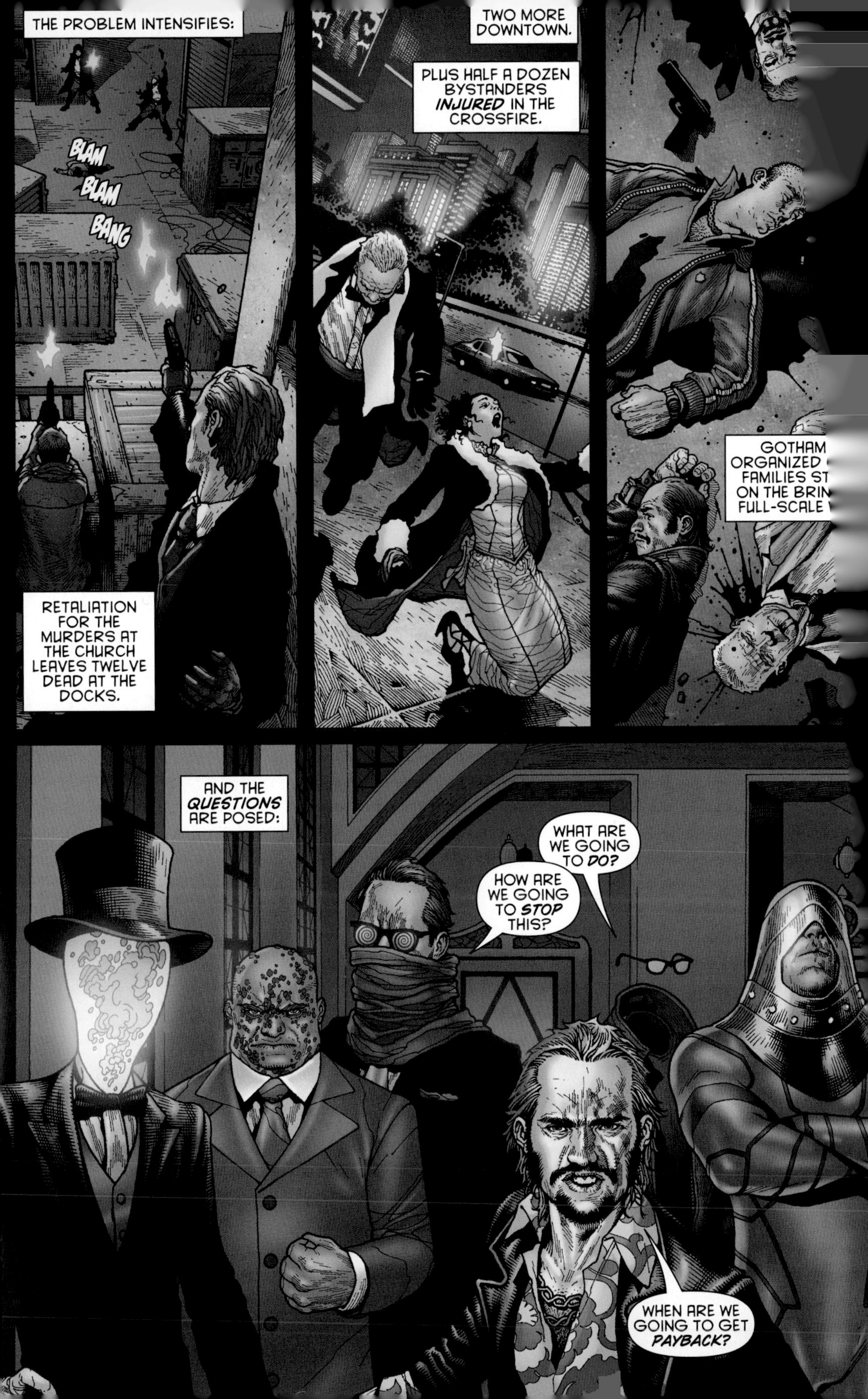
THE PROBLEM INTENSIFIES:
BLAM
BLAM
BANG
RETALIATION FOR THE MURDERS AT THE CHURCH LEAVES TWELVE DEAD AT THE DOCKS.
TWO MORE DOWNTOWN.
PLUS HALF A DOZEN BYSTANDERS *INJURED* IN THE CROSSFIRE.
GOTHAM
ORGANIZED
FAMILIES ST
ON THE BRIN
FULL-SCALE
AND THE *QUESTIONS* ARE POSED:
WHAT ARE WE GOING TO *DO?*
HOW ARE WE GOING TO *STOP* THIS?
WHEN ARE WE GOING TO GET *PAYBACK?*

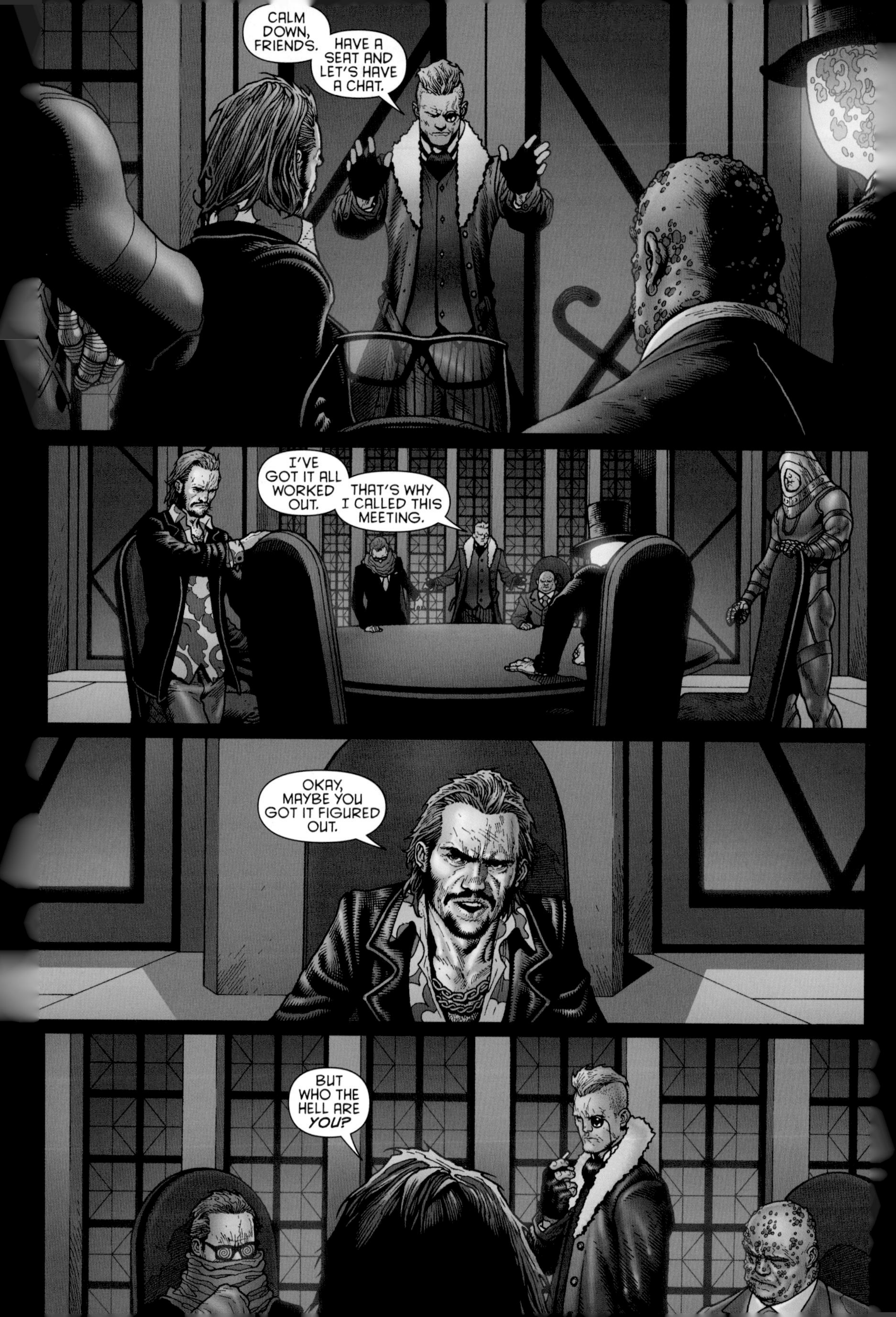
CALM DOWN, FRIENDS.
HAVE A SEAT AND LET'S HAVE A CHAT.
I'VE GOT IT ALL WORKED OUT.
THAT'S WHY I CALLED THIS MEETING.
OKAY, MAYBE YOU GOT IT FIGURED OUT.
BUT WHO THE HELL ARE *YOU?*

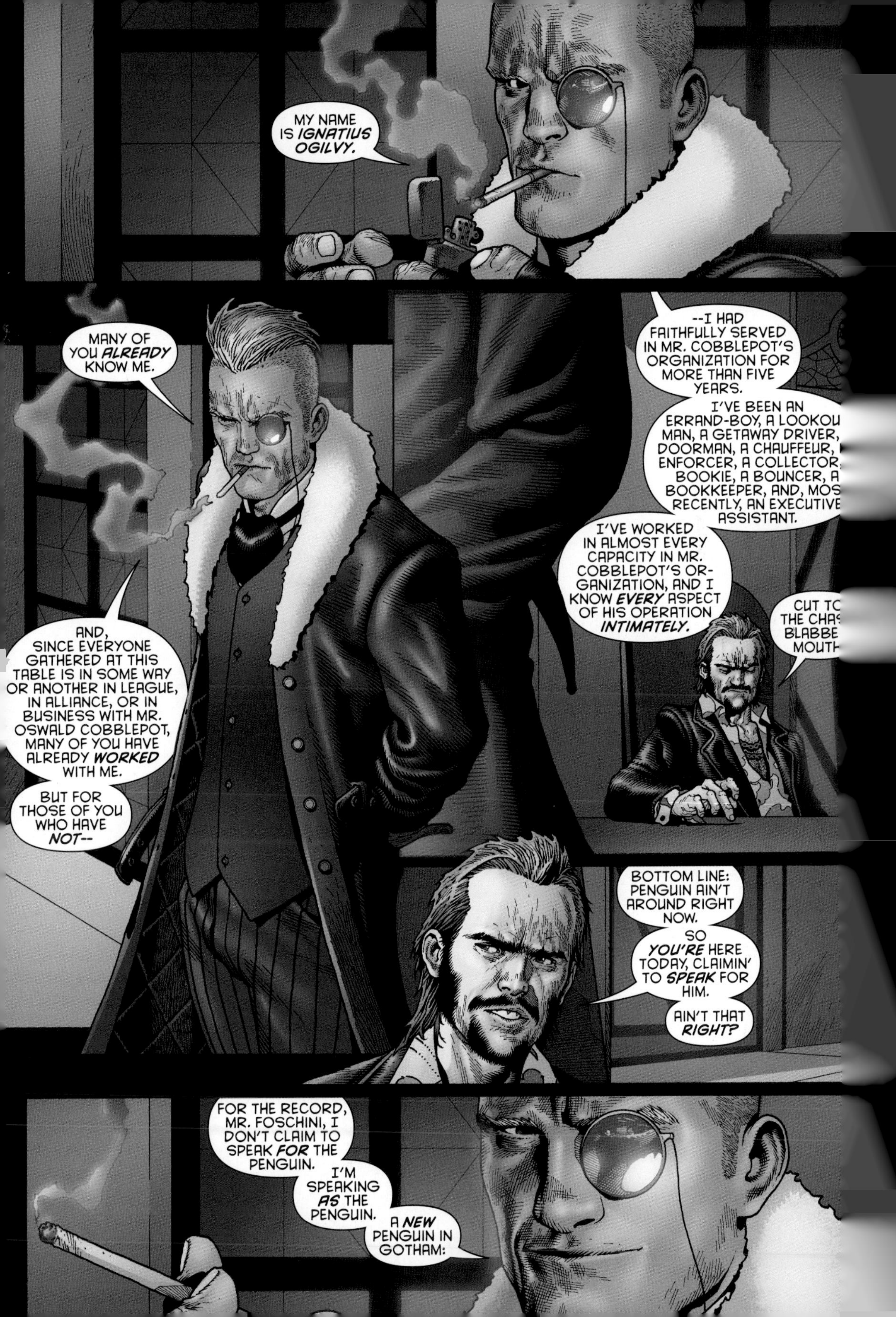

MY NAME IS IGNATIUS OGILVY.
MANY OF YOU ALREADY KNOW ME.
AND, SINCE EVERYONE GATHERED AT THIS TABLE IS IN SOME WAY OR ANOTHER IN LEAGUE, IN ALLIANCE, OR IN BUSINESS WITH MR. OSWALD COBBLEPOT, MANY OF YOU HAVE ALREADY WORKED WITH ME.
BUT FOR THOSE OF YOU WHO HAVE NOT--
--I HAD FAITHFULLY SERVED IN MR. COBBLEPOT'S ORGANIZATION FOR MORE THAN FIVE YEARS.
I'VE BEEN AN ERRAND-BOY, A LOOKOU MAN, A GETAWAY DRIVER, DOORMAN, A CHAUFFEUR, ENFORCER, A COLLECTOR, BOOKIE, A BOUNCER, A BOOKKEEPER, AND, MOS RECENTLY, AN EXECUTIVE ASSISTANT.
I'VE WORKED IN ALMOST EVERY CAPACITY IN MR. COBBLEPOT'S OR-GANIZATION, AND I KNOW EVERY ASPECT OF HIS OPERATION INTIMATELY.
CUT TO THE CHA BLABBE MOUTH
BOTTOM LINE: PENGUIN AIN'T AROUND RIGHT NOW.
SO YOU'RE HERE TODAY, CLAIMIN' TO SPEAK FOR HIM.
AIN'T THAT RIGHT?
FOR THE RECORD, MR. FOSCHINI, I DON'T CLAIM TO SPEAK FOR THE PENGUIN.
I'M SPEAKING AS THE PENGUIN.
A NEW PENGUIN IN GOTHAM:

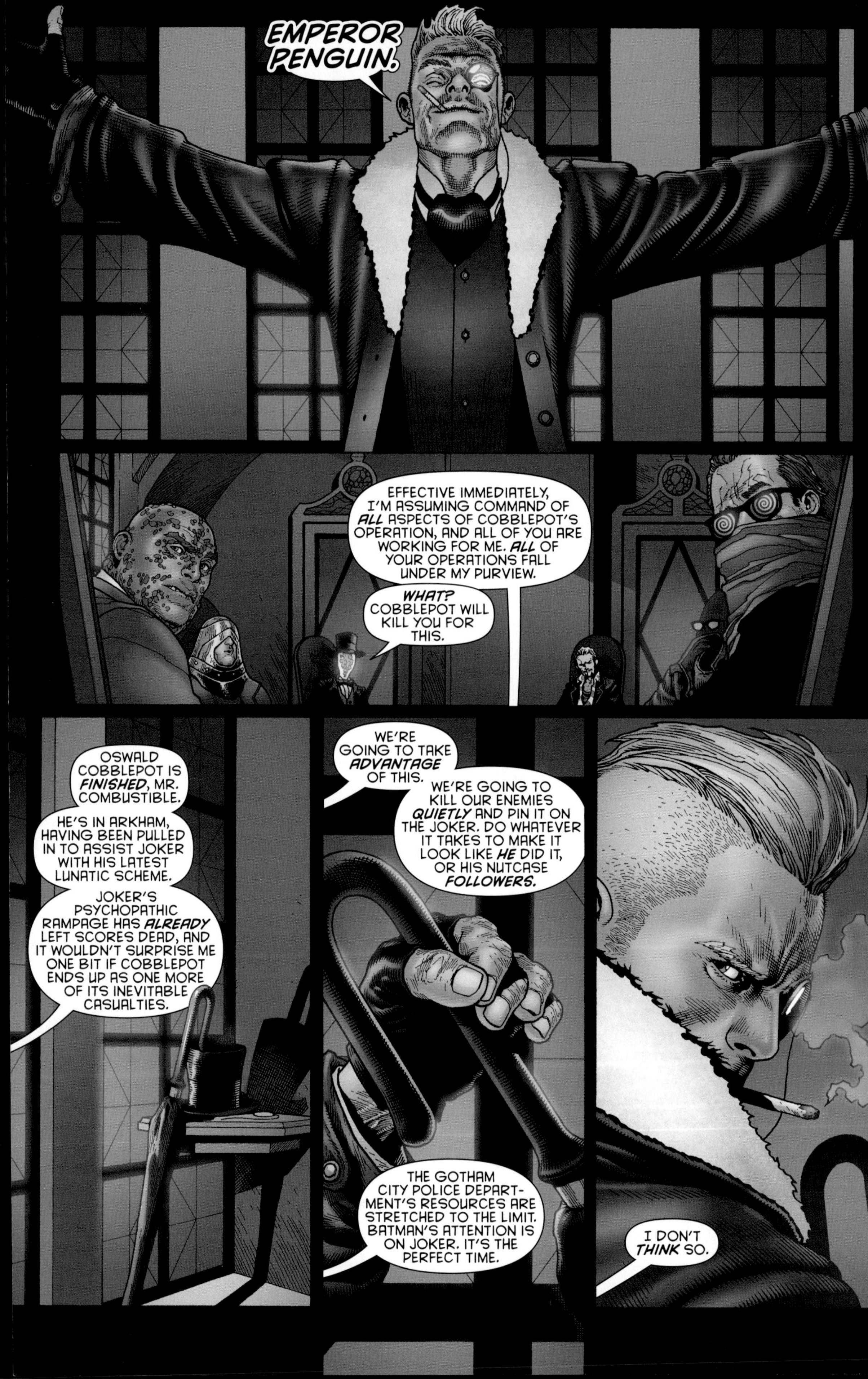
EMPEROR PENGUIN.
EFFECTIVE IMMEDIATELY, I'M ASSUMING COMMAND OF ALL ASPECTS OF COBBLEPOT'S OPERATION, AND ALL OF YOU ARE WORKING FOR ME. ALL OF YOUR OPERATIONS FALL UNDER MY PURVIEW.
WHAT? COBBLEPOT WILL KILL YOU FOR THIS.
OSWALD COBBLEPOT IS FINISHED, MR. COMBUSTIBLE.
HE'S IN ARKHAM, HAVING BEEN PULLED IN TO ASSIST JOKER WITH HIS LATEST LUNATIC SCHEME.
JOKER'S PSYCHOPATHIC RAMPAGE HAS ALREADY LEFT SCORES DEAD, AND IT WOULDN'T SURPRISE ME ONE BIT IF COBBLEPOT ENDS UP AS ONE MORE OF ITS INEVITABLE CASUALTIES.
WE'RE GOING TO TAKE ADVANTAGE OF THIS.
WE'RE GOING TO KILL OUR ENEMIES QUIETLY AND PIN IT ON THE JOKER. DO WHATEVER IT TAKES TO MAKE IT LOOK LIKE HE DID IT, OR HIS NUTCASE FOLLOWERS.
THE GOTHAM CITY POLICE DEPART-MENT'S RESOURCES ARE STRETCHED TO THE LIMIT. BATMAN'S ATTENTION IS ON JOKER. IT'S THE PERFECT TIME.
I DON'T THINK SO.

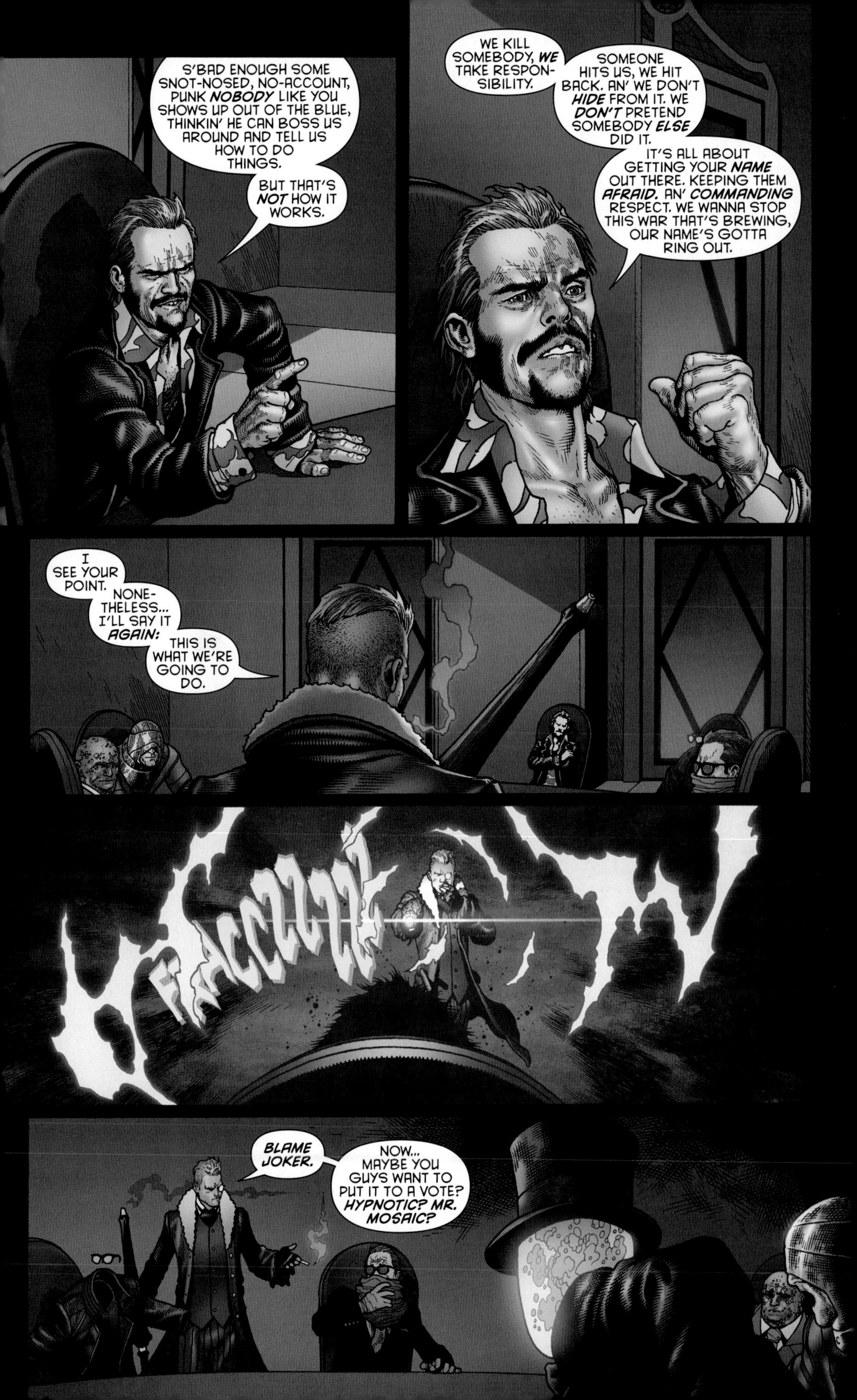
S'BAD ENOUGH SOME SNOT-NOSED, NO-ACCOUNT, PUNK NOBODY LIKE YOU SHOWS UP OUT OF THE BLUE, THINKIN' HE CAN BOSS US AROUND AND TELL US HOW TO DO THINGS.
BUT THAT'S NOT HOW IT WORKS.
WE KILL SOMEBODY, WE TAKE RESPONSIBILITY.
SOMEONE HITS US, WE HIT BACK. AN' WE DON'T HIDE FROM IT. WE DON'T PRETEND SOMEBODY ELSE DID IT.
IT'S ALL ABOUT GETTING YOUR NAME OUT THERE. KEEPING THEM AFRAID. AN' COMMANDING RESPECT. WE WANNA STOP THIS WAR THAT'S BREWING, OUR NAME'S GOTTA RING OUT.
I SEE YOUR POINT.
NONETHELESS... I'LL SAY IT AGAIN:
THIS IS WHAT WE'RE GOING TO DO.
FZACCZZZZ
BLAME JOKER.
NOW... MAYBE YOU GUYS WANT TO PUT IT TO A VOTE? HYPNOTIC? MR. MOSAIC?

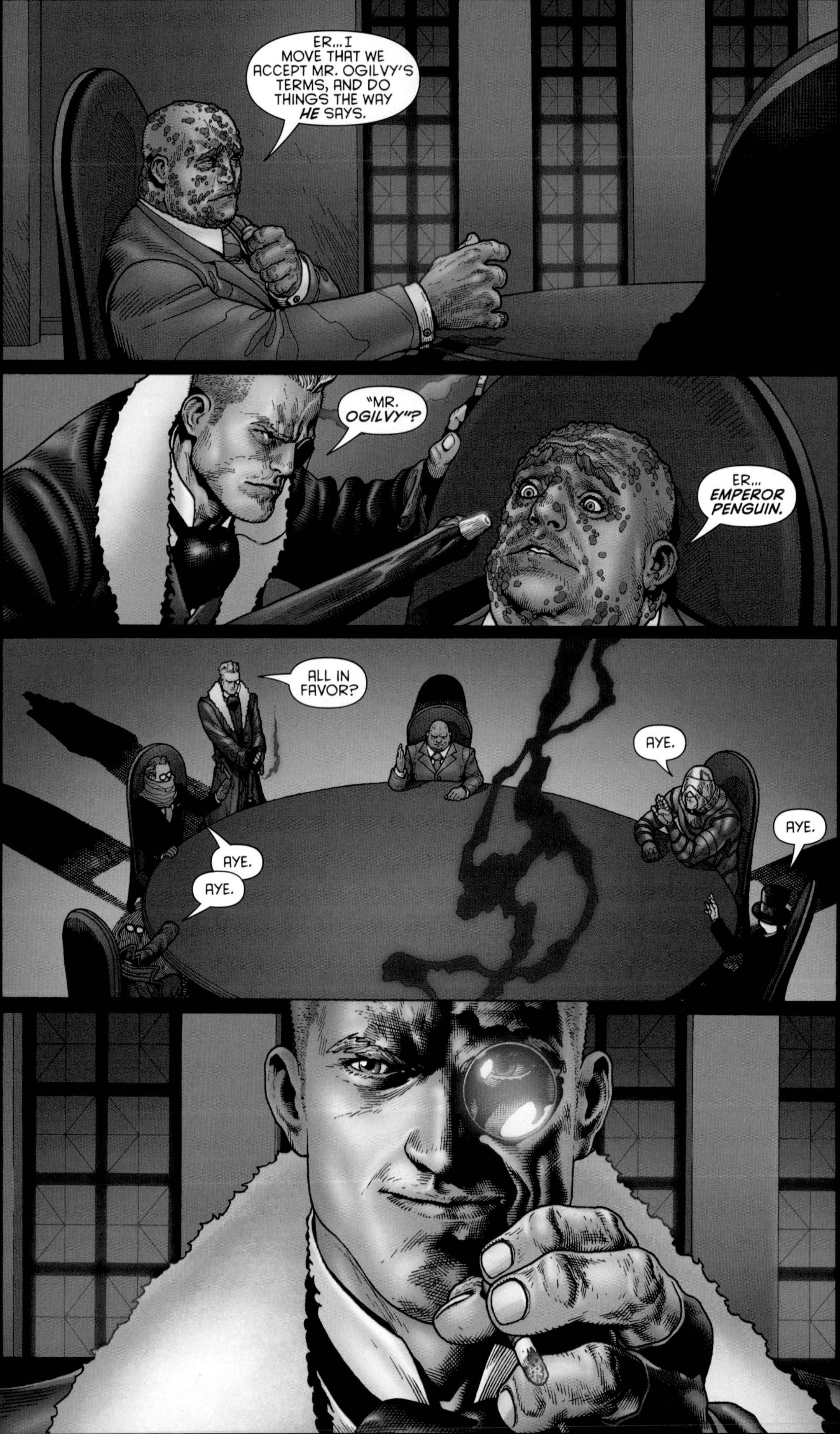
ER...I MOVE THAT WE ACCEPT MR. OGILVY'S TERMS, AND DO THINGS THE WAY HE SAYS.
"MR. OGILVY"?
ER... EMPEROR PENGUIN.
ALL IN FAVOR?
AYE.
AYE.
AYE.
AYE.

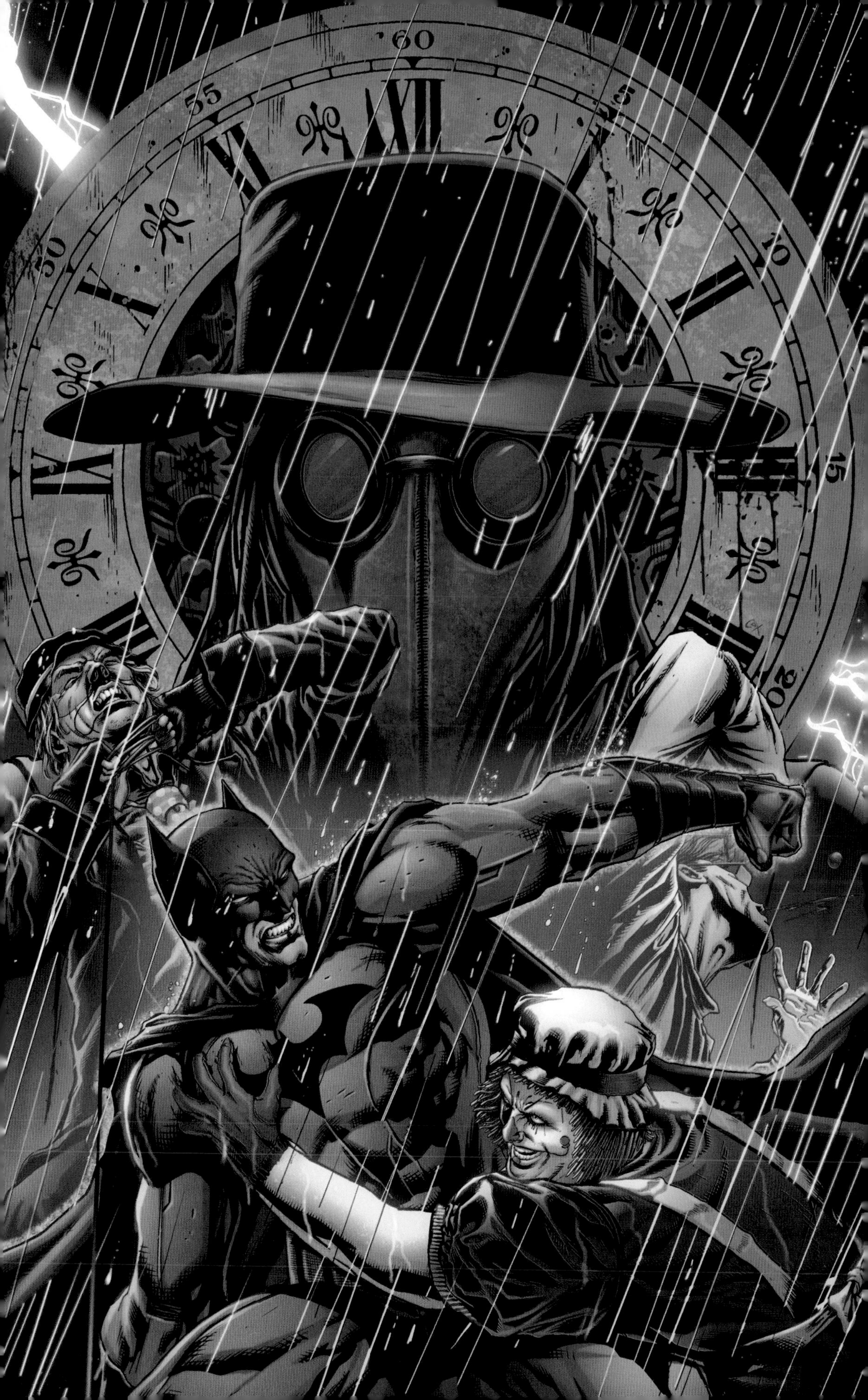

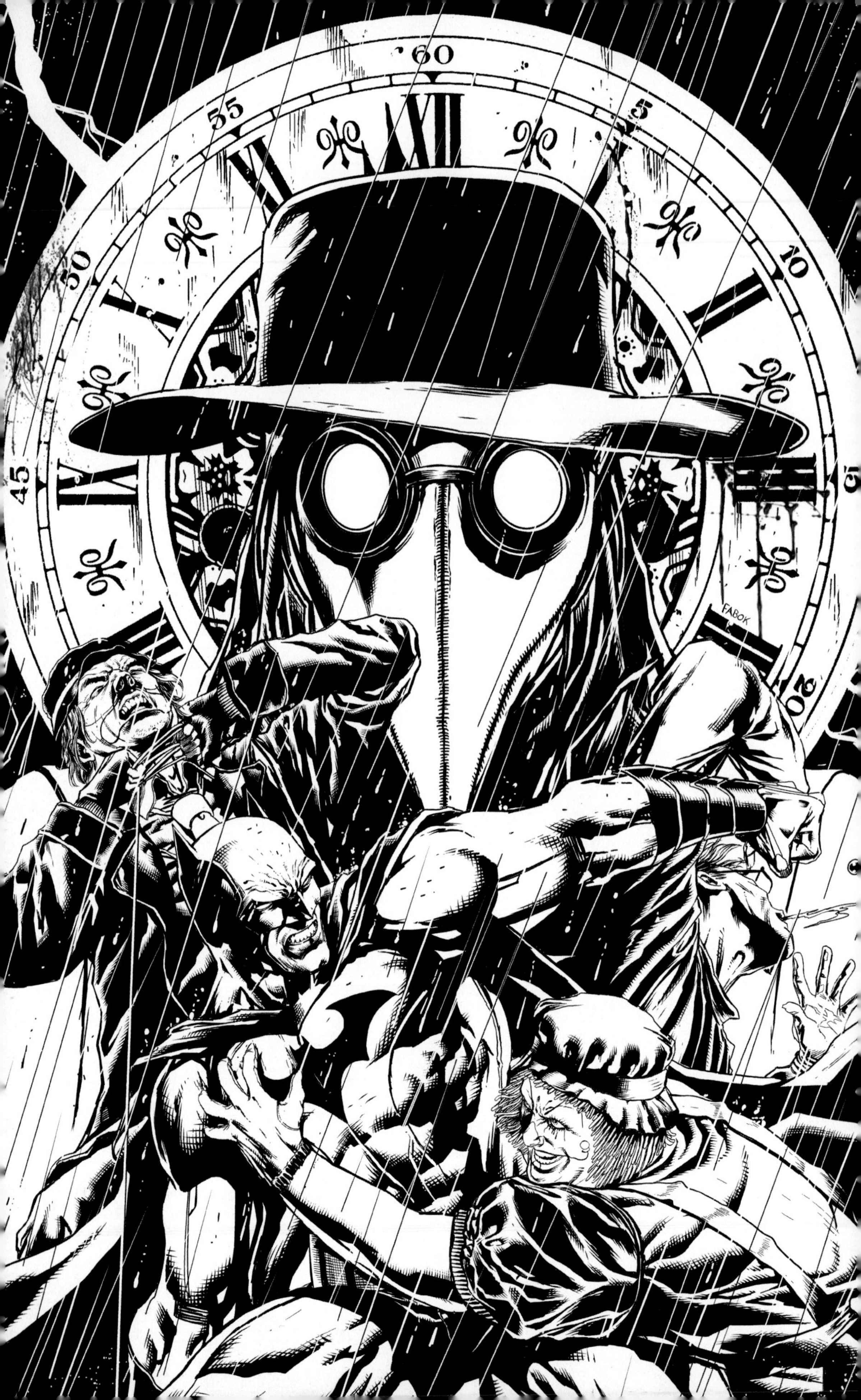
FABOK

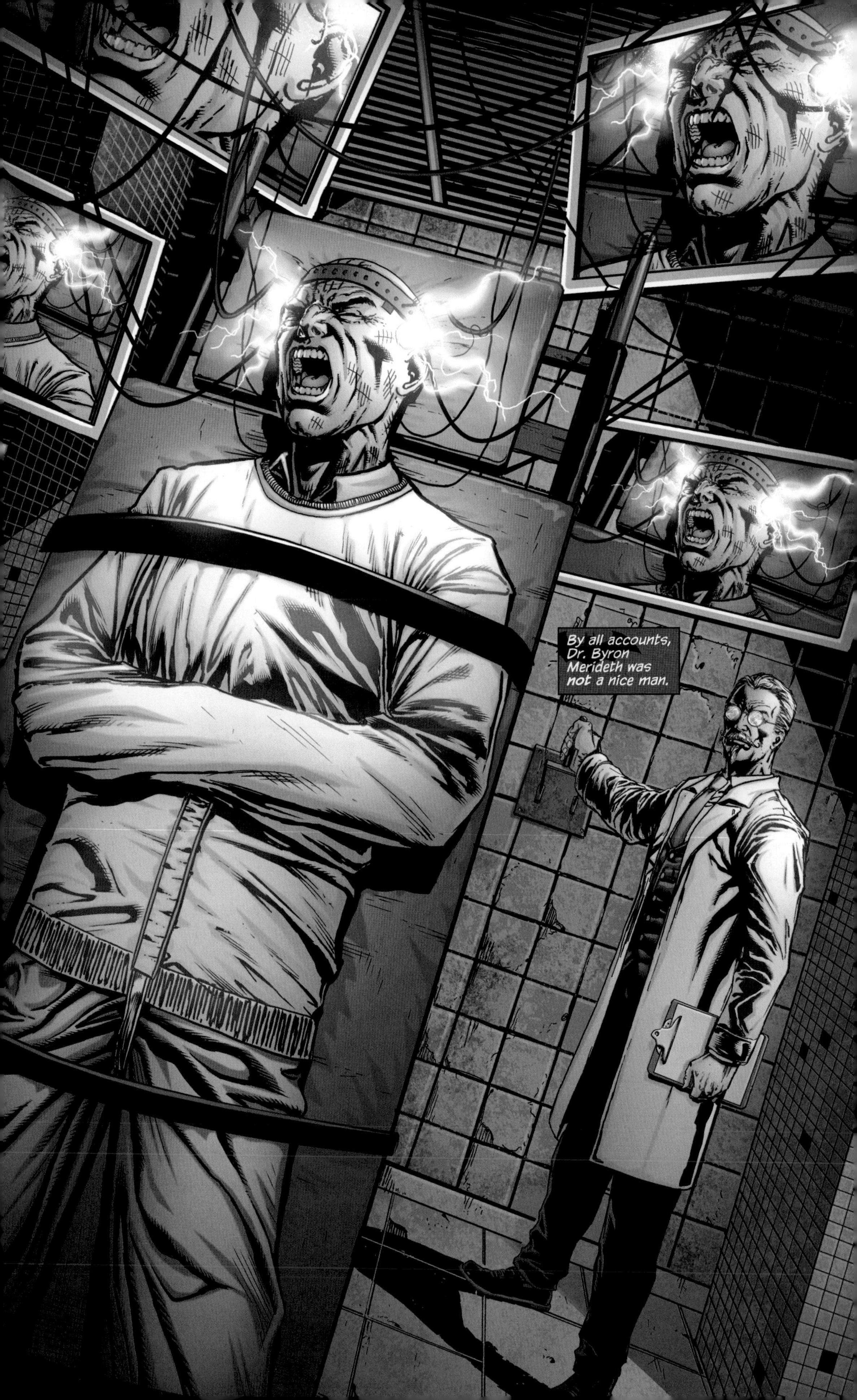
By all accounts, Dr. Byron Merideth was **not** a nice man.

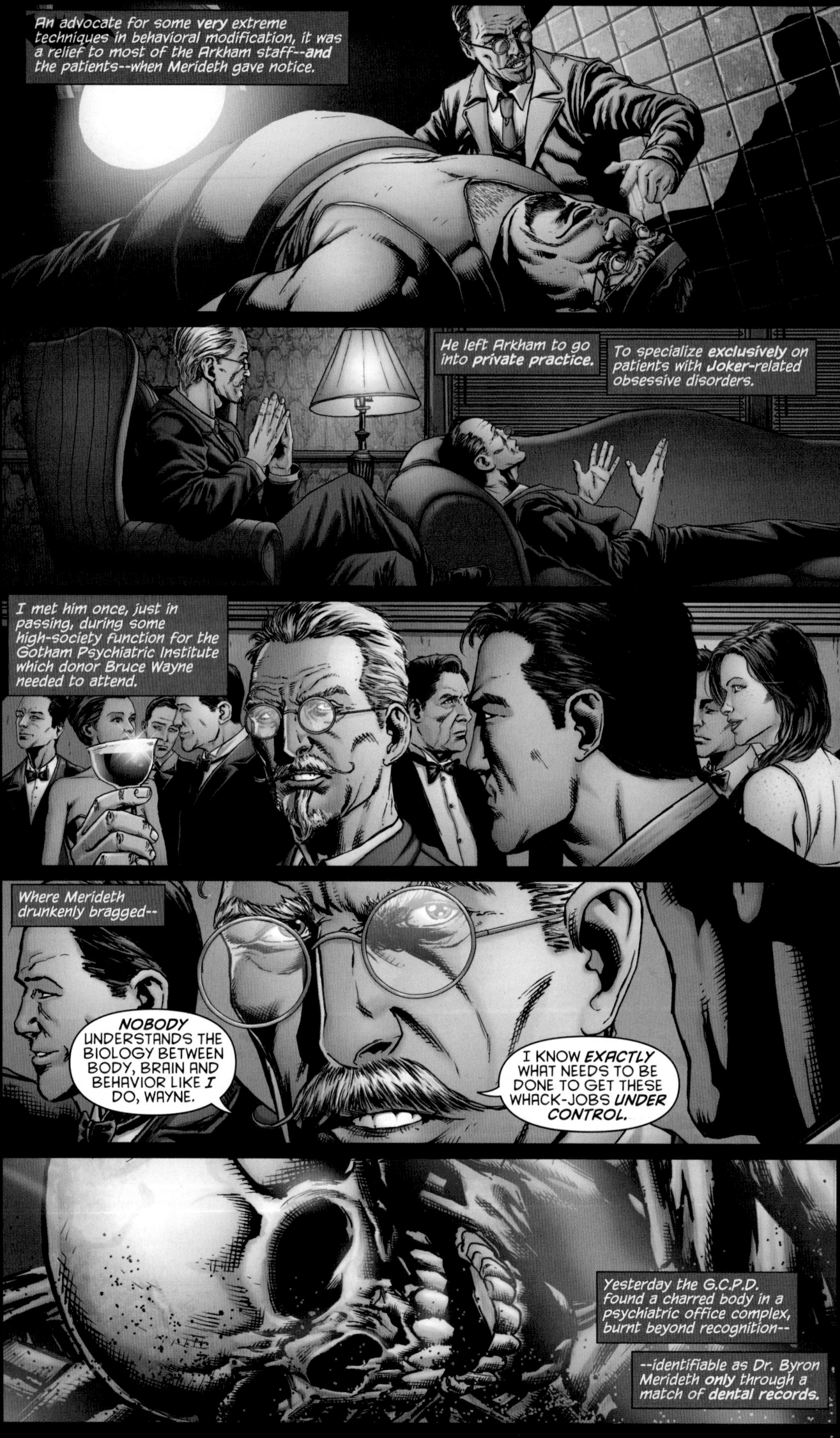
An advocate for some very extreme techniques in behavioral modification, it was a relief to most of the Arkham staff--and the patients--when Merideth gave notice.
He left Arkham to go into private practice.
To specialize exclusively on patients with Joker-related obsessive disorders.
I met him once, just in passing, during some high-society function for the Gotham Psychiatric Institute which donor Bruce Wayne needed to attend.
Where Merideth drunkenly bragged--
NOBODY UNDERSTANDS THE BIOLOGY BETWEEN BODY, BRAIN AND BEHAVIOR LIKE I DO, WAYNE.
I KNOW EXACTLY WHAT NEEDS TO BE DONE TO GET THESE WHACK-JOBS UNDER CONTROL.
Yesterday the G.C.P.D. found a charred body in a psychiatric office complex, burnt beyond recognition--
--identifiable as Dr. Byron Merideth only through a match of dental records.

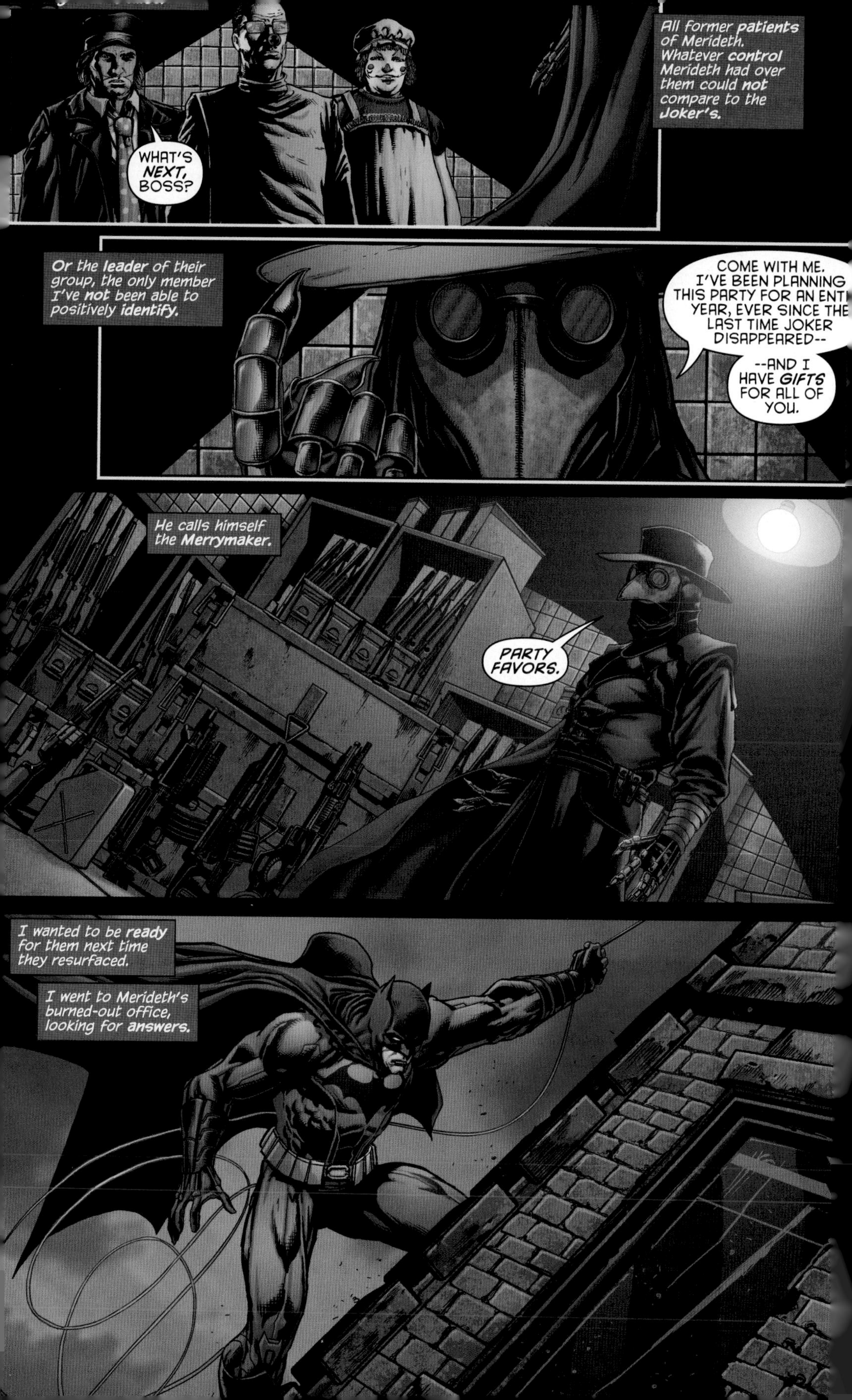
All former patients of Merideth. Whatever control Merideth had over them could not compare to the Joker's.
WHAT'S NEXT, BOSS?
Or the leader of their group, the only member I've not been able to positively identify.
COME WITH ME. I'VE BEEN PLANNING THIS PARTY FOR AN ENTI YEAR, EVER SINCE THE LAST TIME JOKER DISAPPEARED--
--AND I HAVE GIFTS FOR ALL OF YOU.
He calls himself the Merrymaker.
PARTY FAVORS.
I wanted to be ready for them next time they resurfaced.
I went to Merideth's burned-out office, looking for answers.

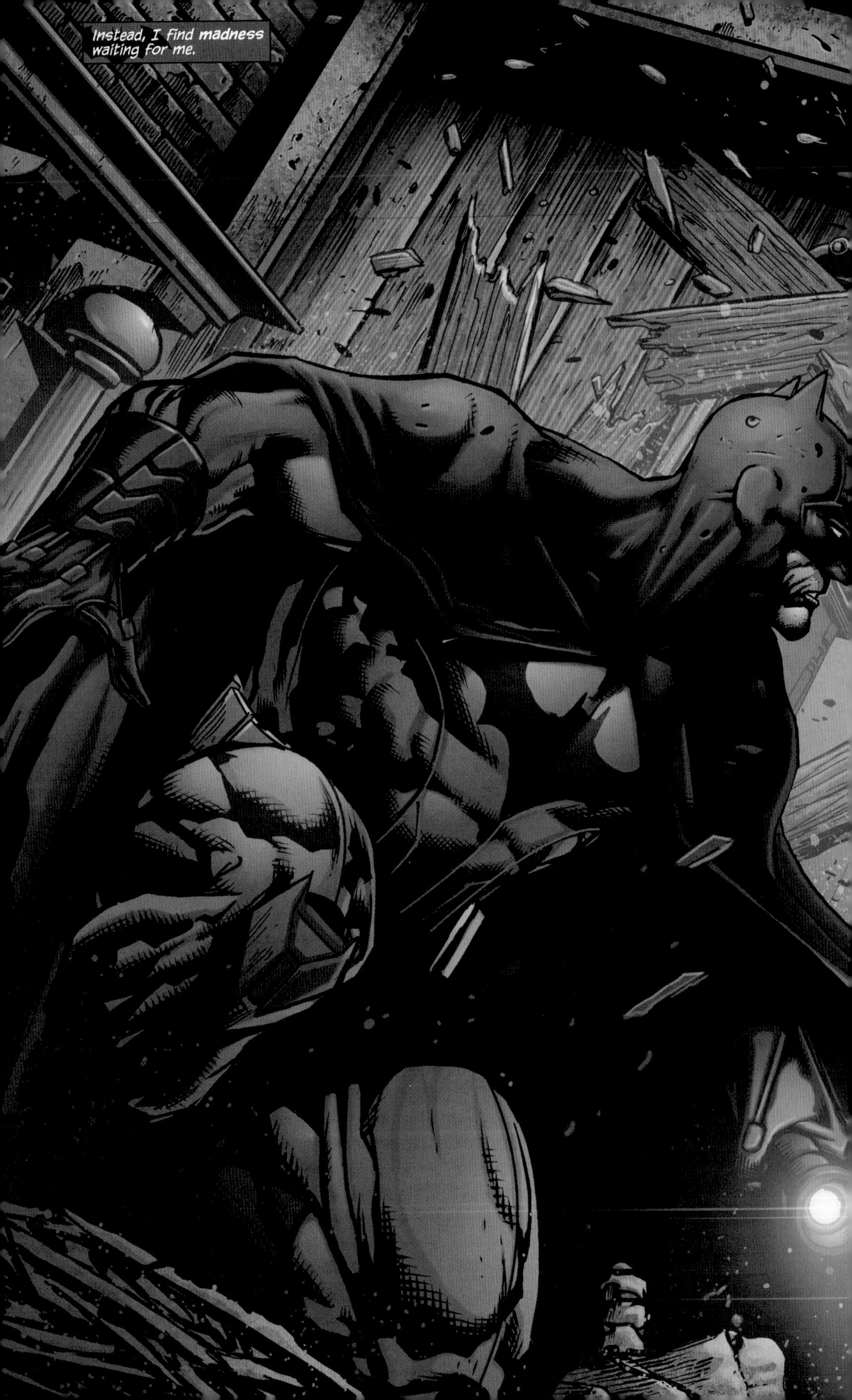
Instead, I find madness waiting for me.

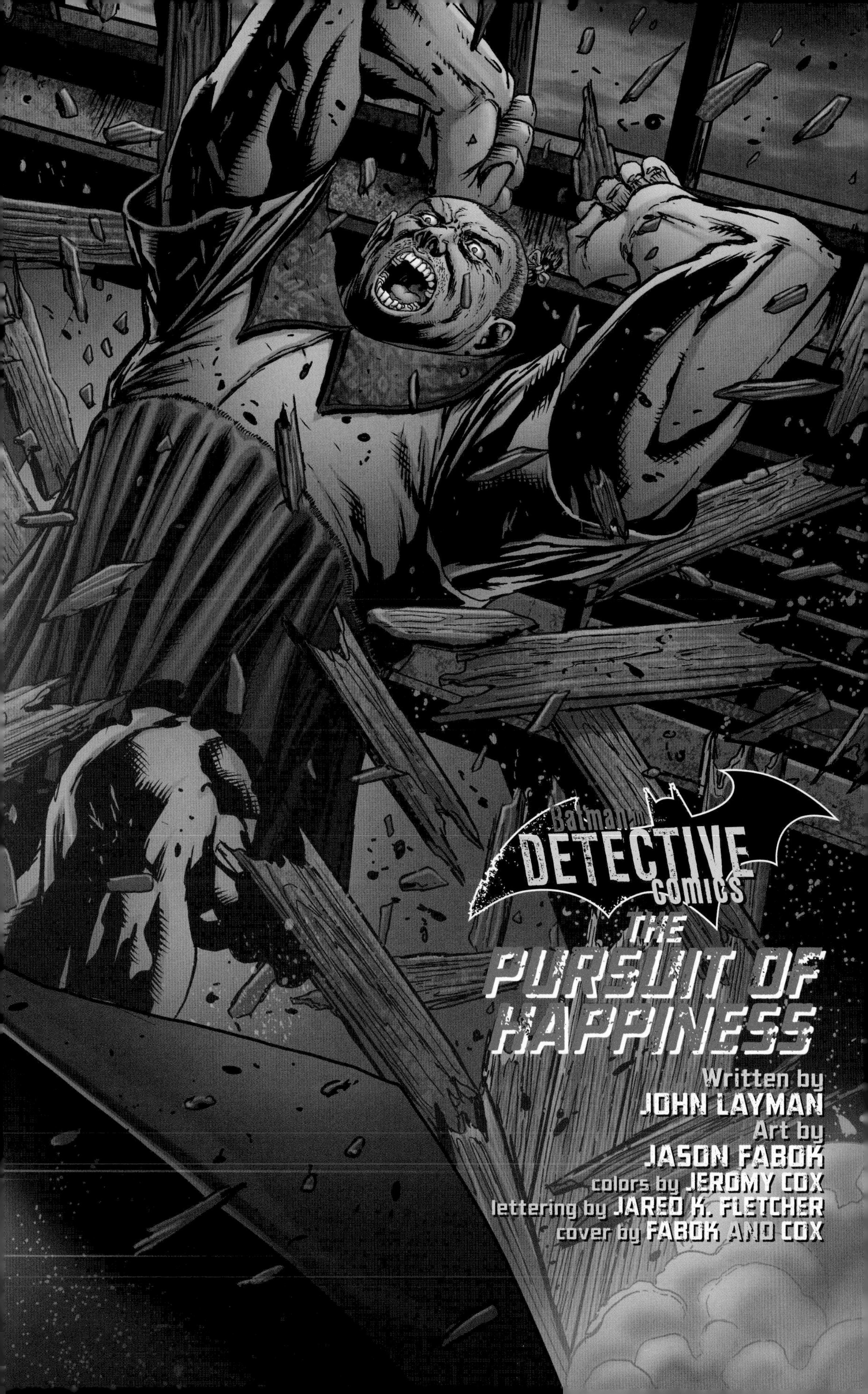

Batman
DETECTIVE COMICS
THE PURSUIT OF HAPPINESS
Written by JOHN LAYMAN
Art by JASON FABOK
colors by JEROMY COX
lettering by JARED K. FLETCHER
cover by FABOK AND COX

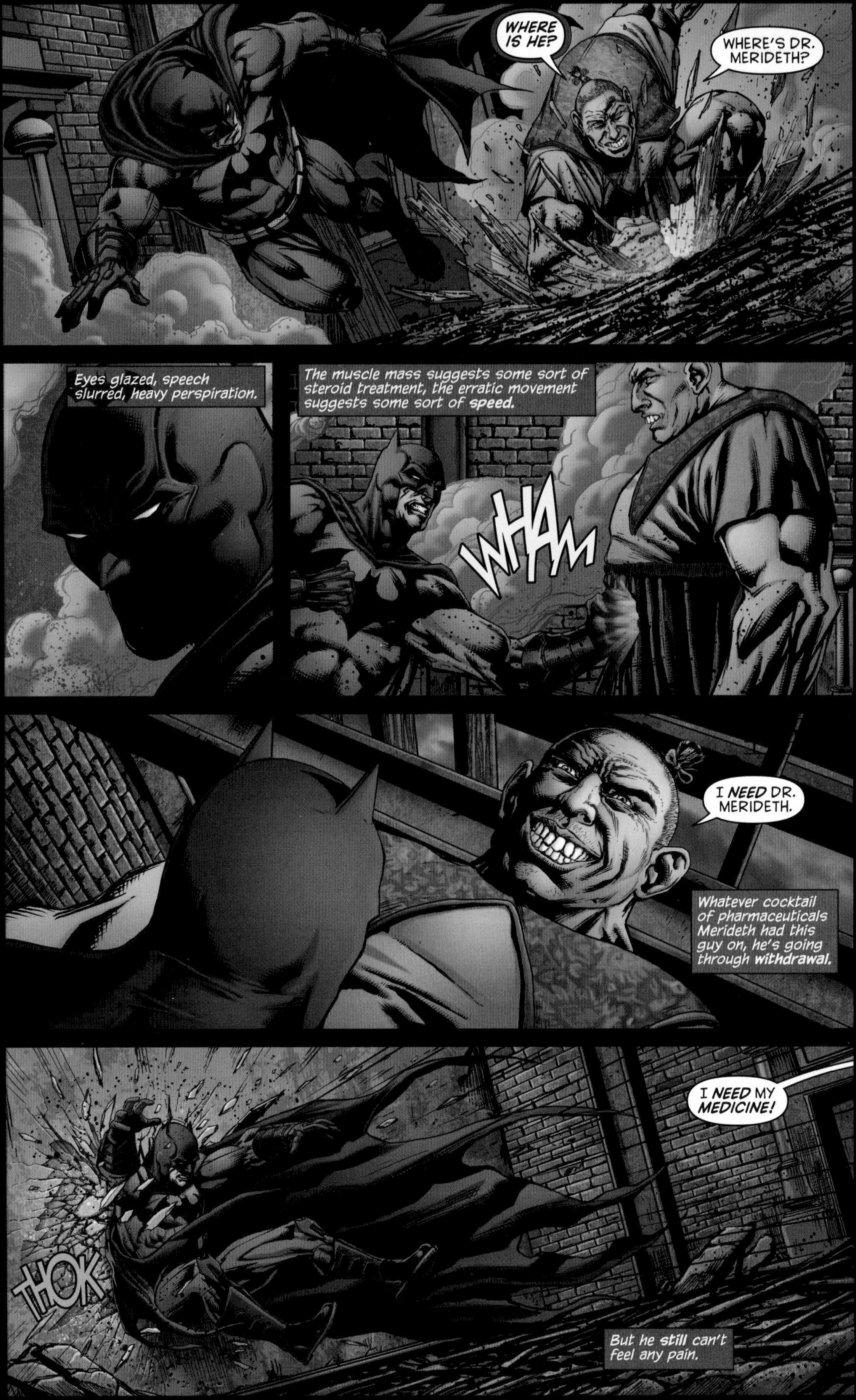
WHERE IS HE?
WHERE'S DR. MERIDETH?
Eyes glazed, speech slurred, heavy perspiration.
The muscle mass suggests some sort of steroid treatment, the erratic movement suggests some sort of **speed.**
WHAM
I **NEED** DR. MERIDETH.
Whatever cocktail of pharmaceuticals Merideth had this guy on, he's going through **withdrawal.**
I **NEED** MY **MEDICINE!**
THOK
But he **still** can't feel any pain.

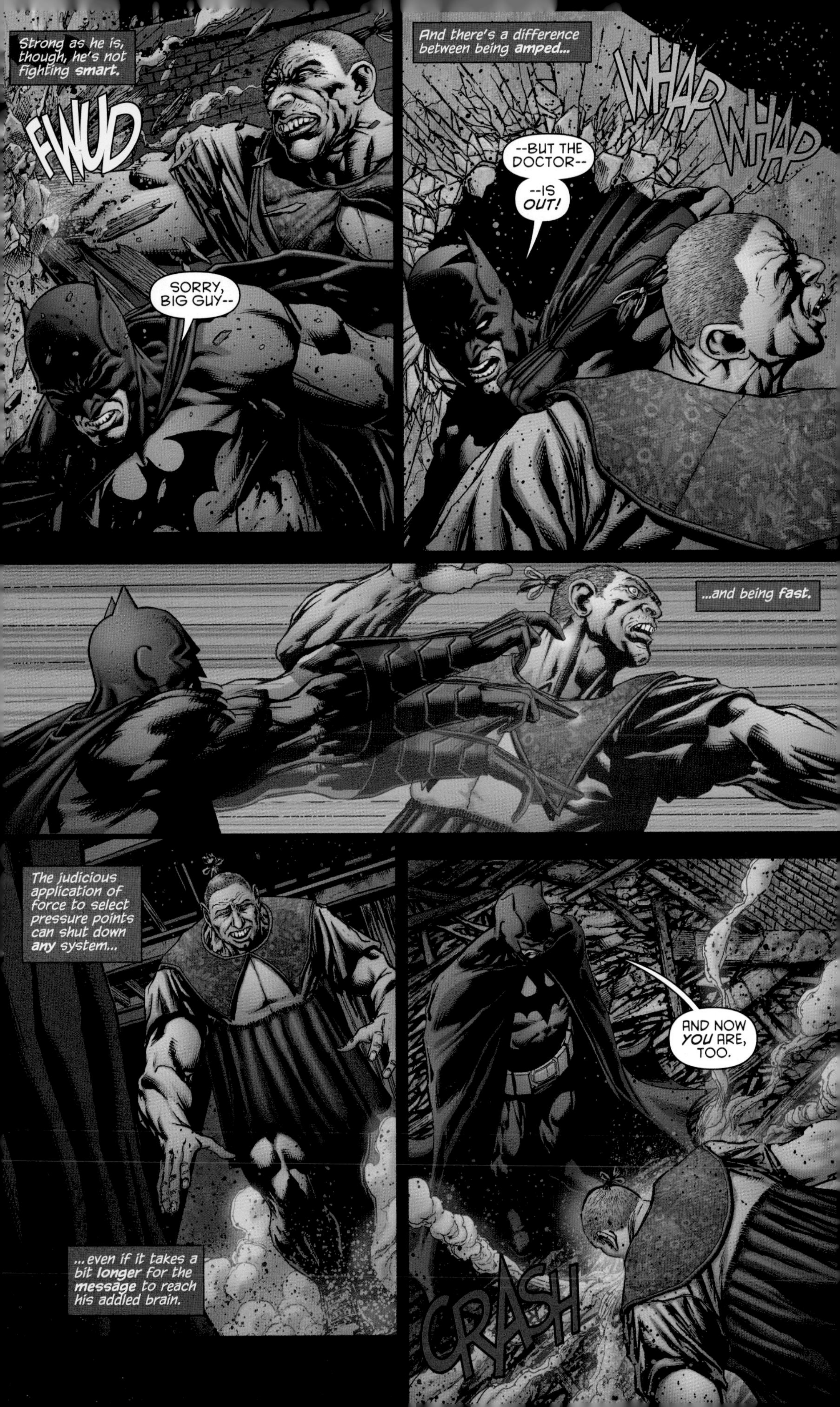
Strong as he is, though, he's not fighting smart.
FWUD
SORRY, BIG GUY--
And there's a difference between being amped...
WHAP WHAP
--BUT THE DOCTOR--
--IS OUT!
...and being fast.
The judicious application of force to select pressure points can shut down any system...
...even if it takes a bit longer for the message to reach his addled brain.
AND NOW YOU ARE, TOO.
CRASH

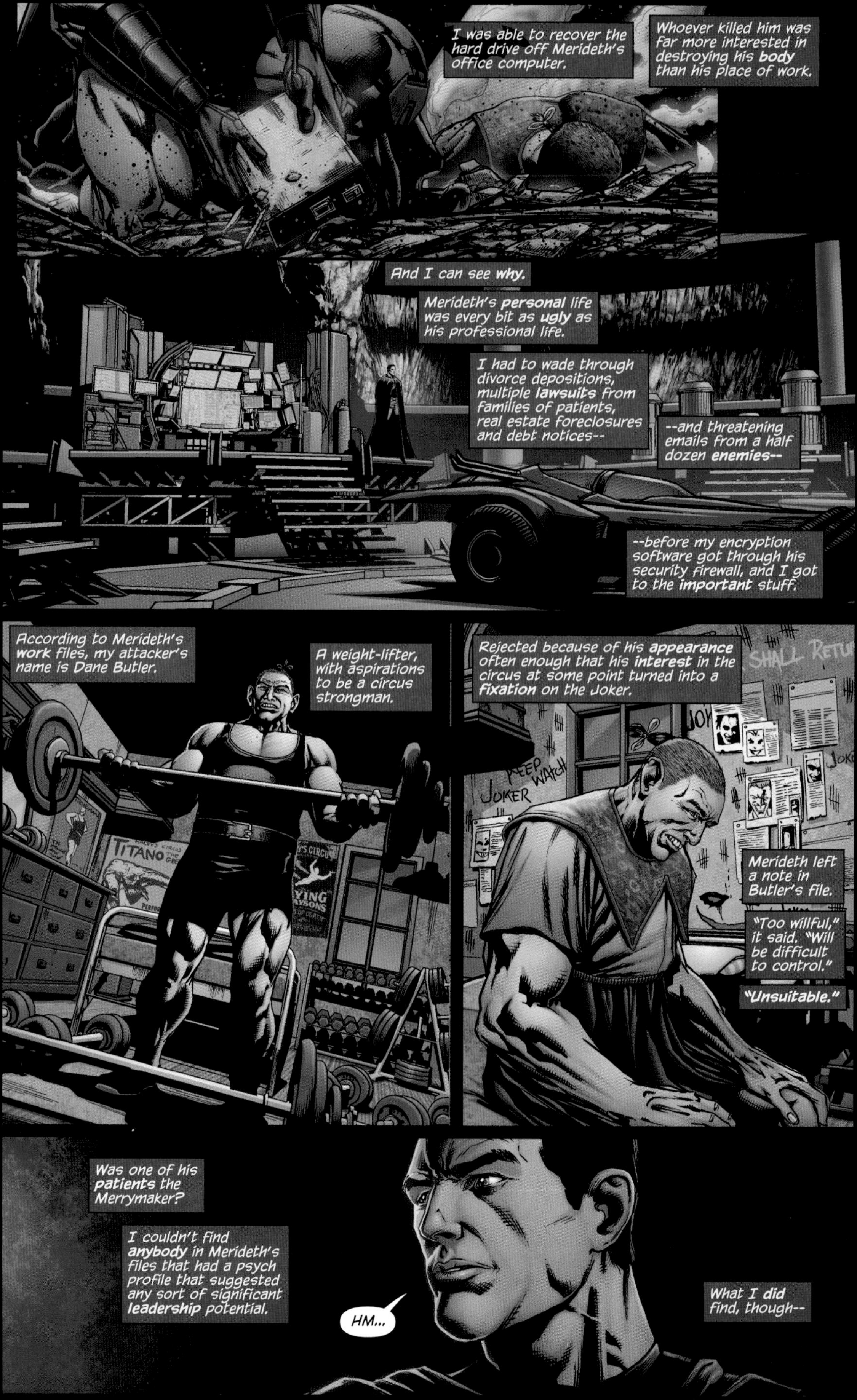
I was able to recover the hard drive off Merideth's office computer.
Whoever killed him was far more interested in destroying his body than his place of work.
And I can see why.
Merideth's personal life was every bit as ugly as his professional life.
I had to wade through divorce depositions, multiple lawsuits from families of patients, real estate foreclosures and debt notices--
--and threatening emails from a half dozen enemies--
--before my encryption software got through his security firewall, and I got to the important stuff.
According to Merideth's work files, my attacker's name is Dane Butler.
A weight-lifter, with aspirations to be a circus strongman.
TITANO
Rejected because of his appearance often enough that his interest in the circus at some point turned into a fixation on the Joker.
KEEP WATCH
JOKER
Merideth left a note in Butler's file.
"Too willful," it said. "Will be difficult to control."
"Unsuitable."
Was one of his patients the Merrymaker?
I couldn't find anybody in Merideth's files that had a psych profile that suggested any sort of significant leadership potential.
HM...
What I did find, though--

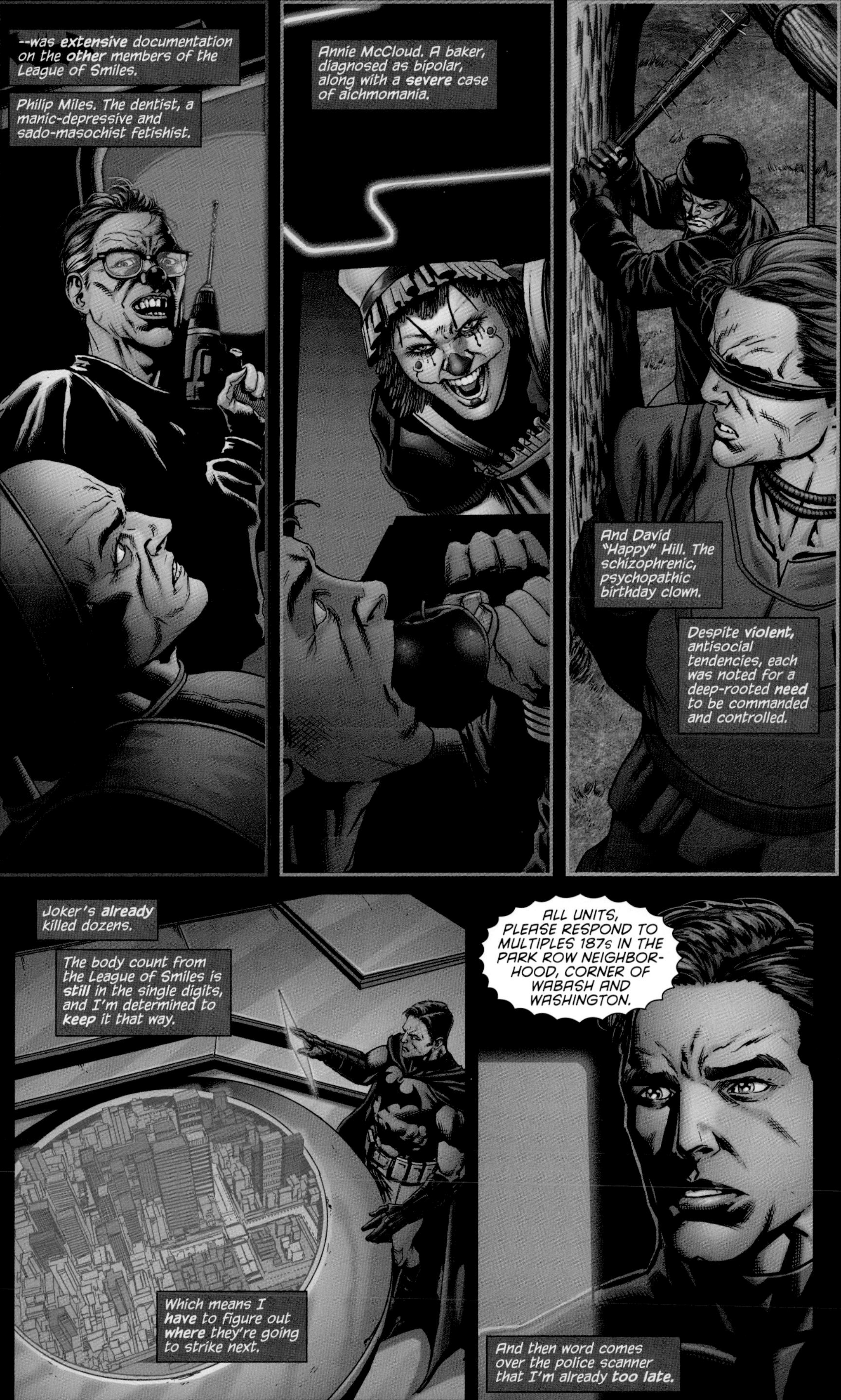
--was extensive documentation on the other members of the League of Smiles.
Philip Miles. The dentist, a manic-depressive and sado-masochist fetishist.
Annie McCloud. A baker, diagnosed as bipolar, along with a severe case of aichmomania.
And David "Happy" Hill. The schizophrenic, psychopathic birthday clown.
Despite violent, antisocial tendencies, each was noted for a deep-rooted need to be commanded and controlled.
Joker's already killed dozens.
The body count from the League of Smiles is still in the single digits, and I'm determined to keep it that way.
Which means I have to figure out where they're going to strike next.
ALL UNITS, PLEASE RESPOND TO MULTIPLES 187s IN THE PARK ROW NEIGHBOR-HOOD, CORNER OF WABASH AND WASHINGTON.
And then word comes over the police scanner that I'm already too late.

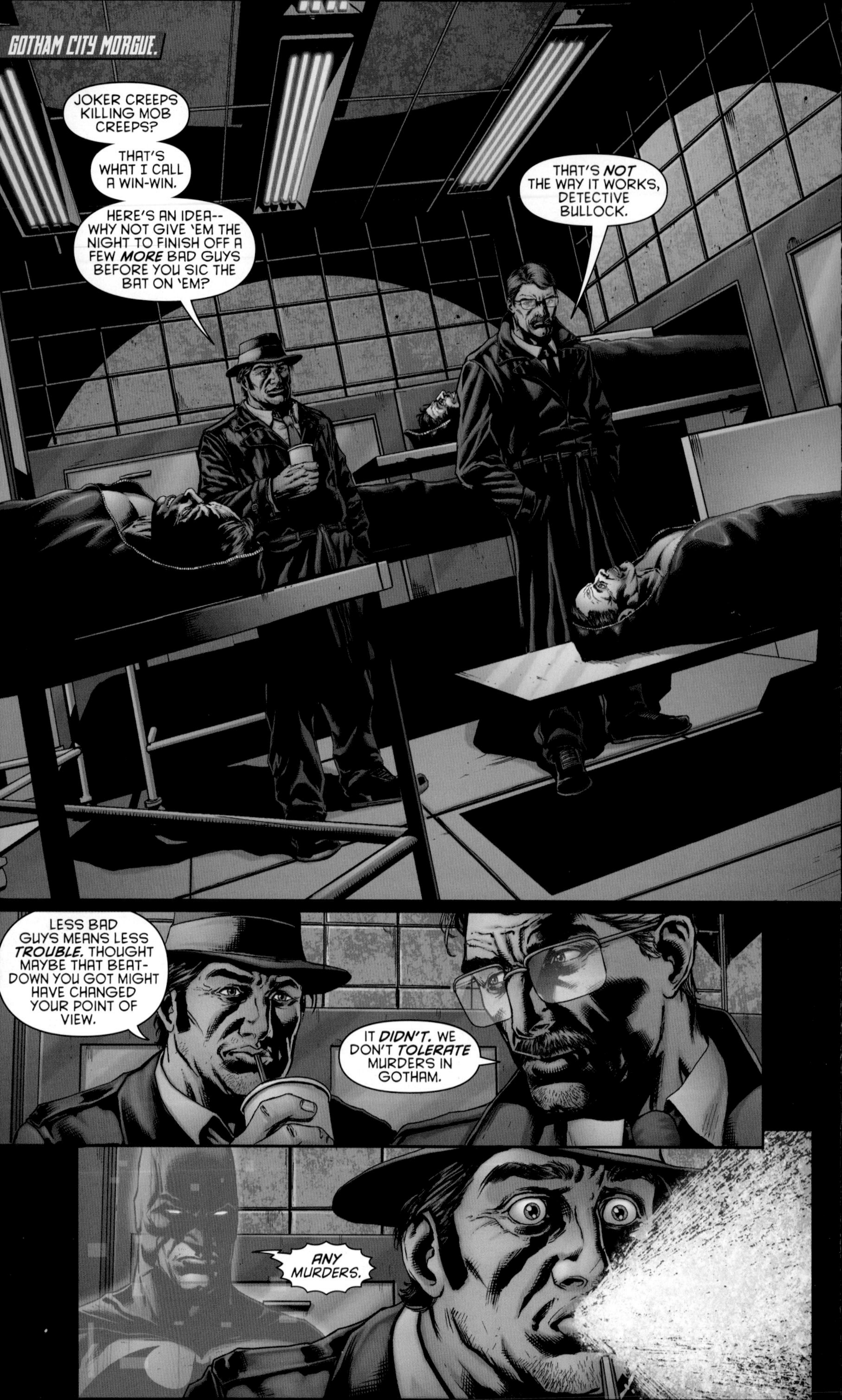
GOTHAM CITY MORGUE.
JOKER CREEPS KILLING MOB CREEPS?
THAT'S WHAT I CALL A WIN-WIN.
HERE'S AN IDEA-- WHY NOT GIVE 'EM THE NIGHT TO FINISH OFF A FEW MORE BAD GUYS BEFORE YOU SIC THE BAT ON 'EM?
THAT'S NOT THE WAY IT WORKS, DETECTIVE BULLOCK.
LESS BAD GUYS MEANS LESS TROUBLE. THOUGHT MAYBE THAT BEAT-DOWN YOU GOT MIGHT HAVE CHANGED YOUR POINT OF VIEW.
IT DIDN'T. WE DON'T TOLERATE MURDERS IN GOTHAM.
ANY MURDERS.

WHAT IS THIS, GORDON? I RECOGNIZE SOME OF THESE BODIES. ENFORCERS AND CAPOS FROM THE FOSCHINI FAMILY.

CORRECT. FOUND THEIR BODIES IN AN ABANDONED WAREHOUSE.

IT'S EITHER THE WORK OF THE JOKER OR ONE OF HIS SURROGATE FOLLOWER GROUPS. THE LEAGUE OF SMILES, ISN'T THAT WHAT THEY'RE CALLING THEMSELVES?

W-WHAT IS THIS?

NO, THIS IS AN ORGANIZED CRIME HIT, DESIGNED TO LOOK LIKE IT WAS PERPETRATED BY JOKER OR THE LEAGUE OF SMILES.

JOKER'S MURDERS ARE MEANT TO SEND A MESSAGE...HIS FOLLOWERS SIMPLY WANT TO SOW TERROR.

THESE MURDERS ARE DESIGNED TO SEND A DIFFERENT MESSAGE, AND NOT FOR US.

AND THE ANALYSIS I'M RUNNING ON THE BODIES SHOWS A SIGNIFICANTLY DIFFERENT CHEMICAL COMPOSITION THAN THAT OF STANDARD JOKER GAS.

NOT A JOKER KILLING?! LOOK AT THE BODIES! LOOK AT THEIR SMILES!

NOT RELATED, BULLOCK.

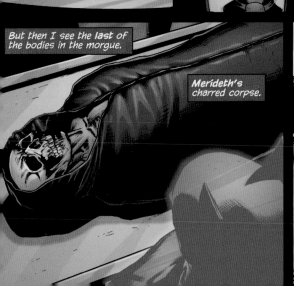

But then I see the last of the bodies in the morgue.

Merideth's charred corpse.

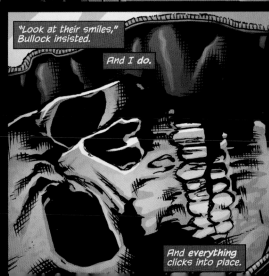

"Look at their smiles," Bullock insisted.

And I do.

And everything clicks into place.

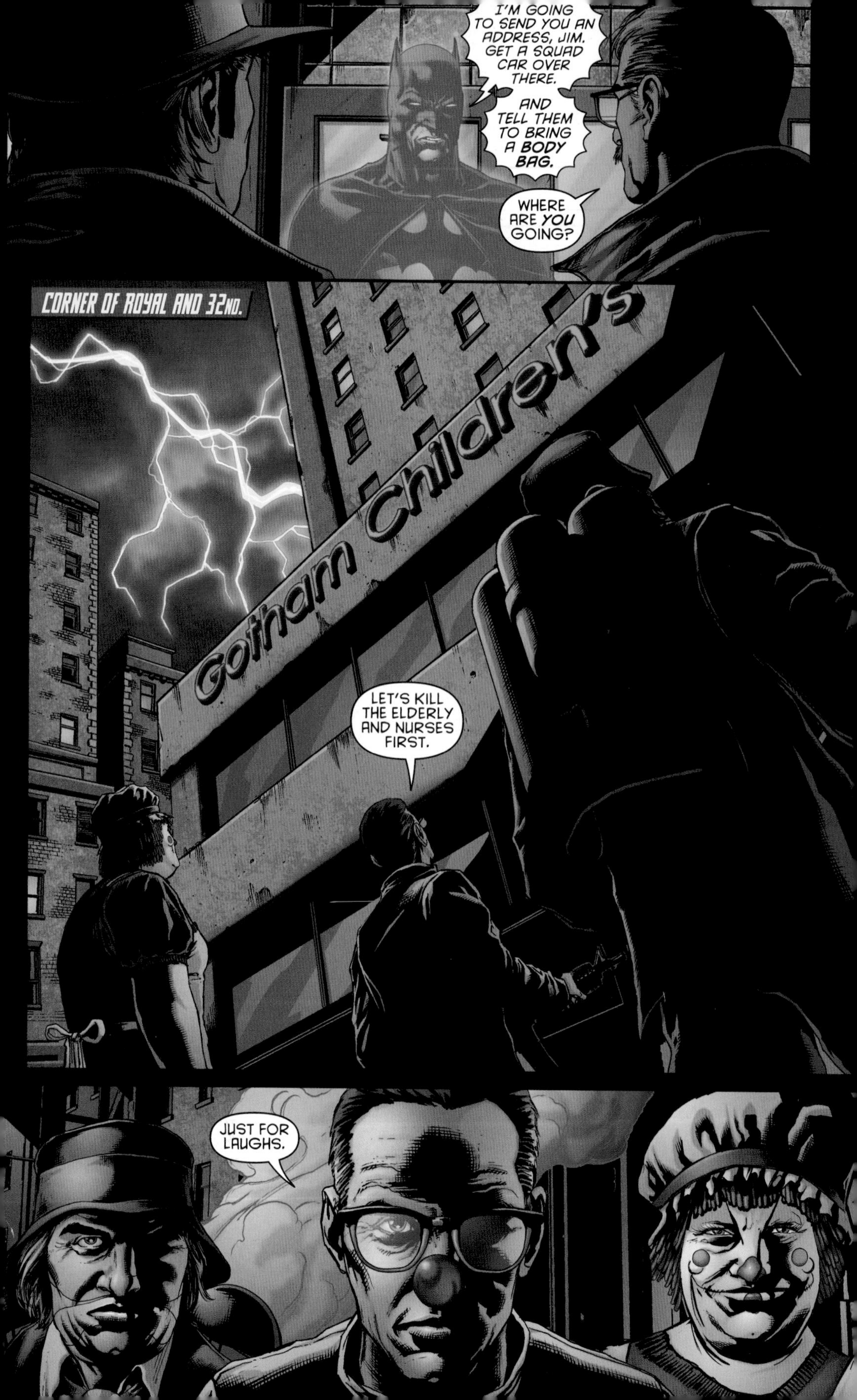
I'M GOING TO SEND YOU AN ADDRESS, JIM. GET A SQUAD CAR OVER THERE.
AND TELL THEM TO BRING A BODY BAG.
WHERE ARE YOU GOING?
CORNER OF ROYAL AND 32ND.
Gotham Children's
LET'S KILL THE ELDERLY AND NURSES FIRST.
JUST FOR LAUGHS.

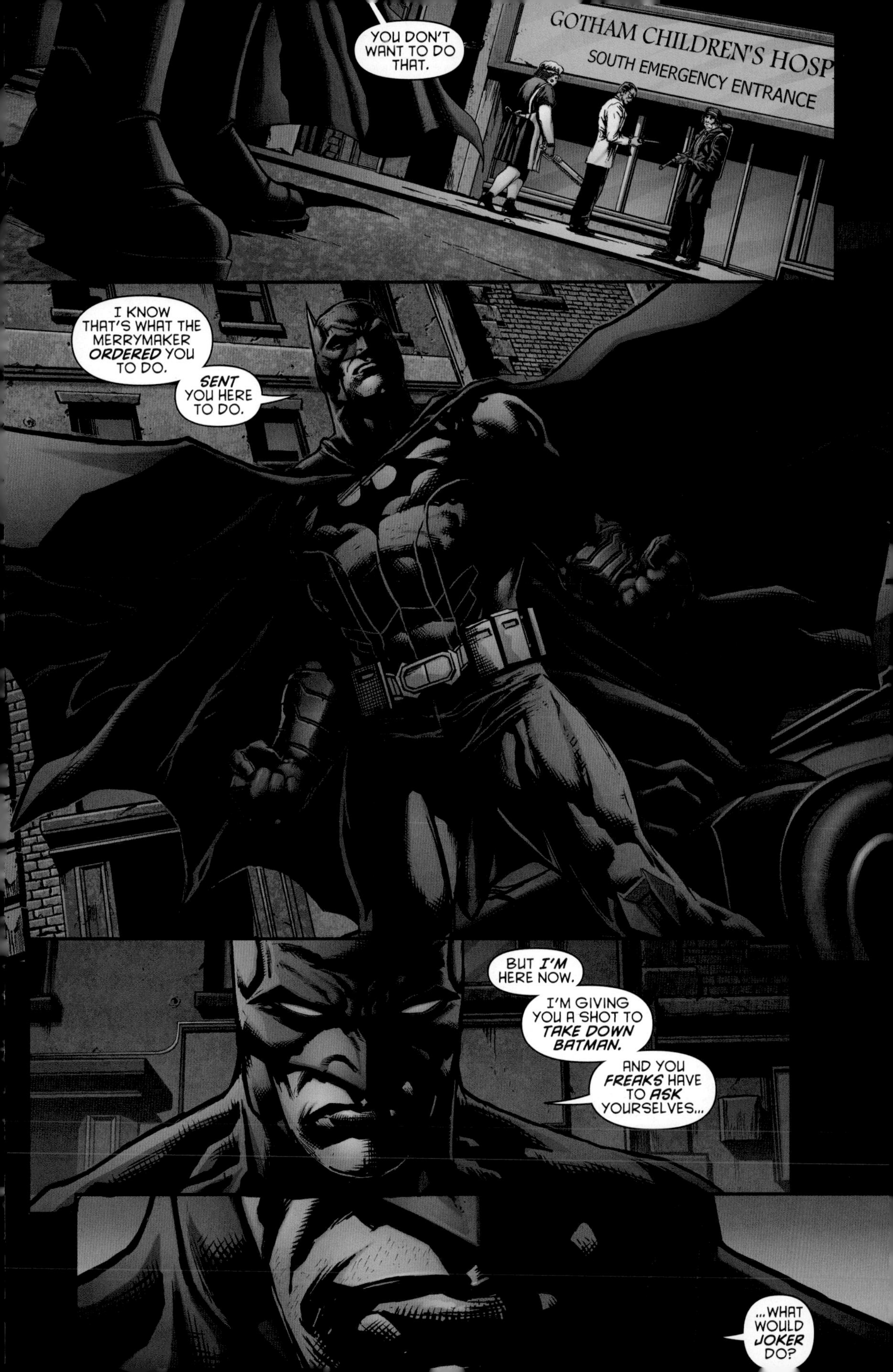
YOU DON'T WANT TO DO THAT.
GOTHAM CHILDREN'S HOSP
SOUTH EMERGENCY ENTRANCE
I KNOW THAT'S WHAT THE MERRYMAKER ORDERED YOU TO DO.
SENT YOU HERE TO DO.
BUT I'M HERE NOW.
I'M GIVING YOU A SHOT TO TAKE DOWN BATMAN.
AND YOU FREAKS HAVE TO ASK YOURSELVES...
...WHAT WOULD JOKER DO?

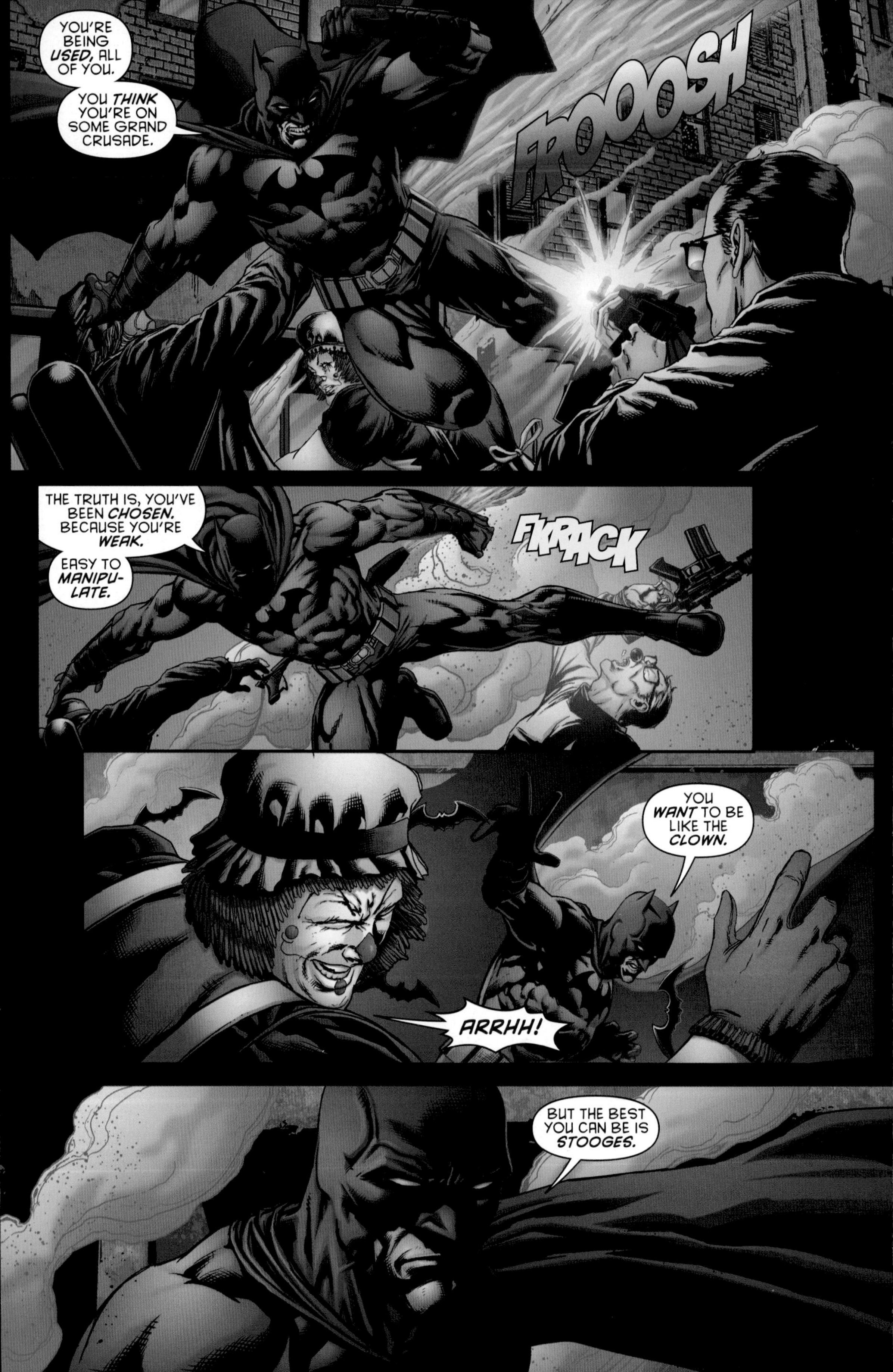
YOU'RE BEING USED, ALL OF YOU.
YOU THINK YOU'RE ON SOME GRAND CRUSADE.
FROOOSH
THE TRUTH IS, YOU'VE BEEN CHOSEN. BECAUSE YOU'RE WEAK.
EASY TO MANIPU-LATE.
FKRACK
YOU WANT TO BE LIKE THE CLOWN.
ARRHH!
BUT THE BEST YOU CAN BE IS STOOGES.

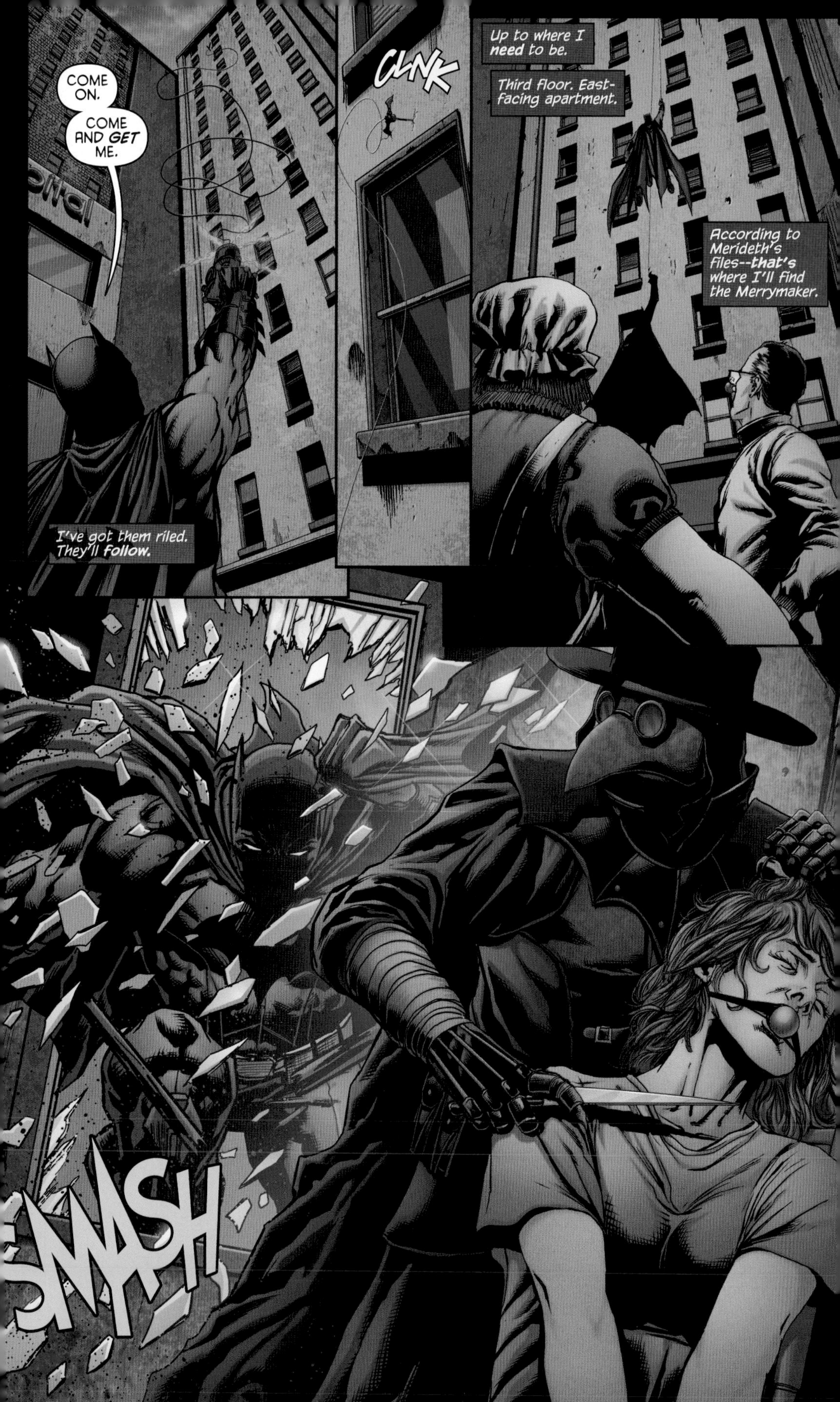
COME ON.
COME AND GET ME.
I've got them riled. They'll follow.
CLNK
Up to where I need to be.
Third floor. East-facing apartment.
According to Merideth's files--that's where I'll find the Merrymaker.
SMASH

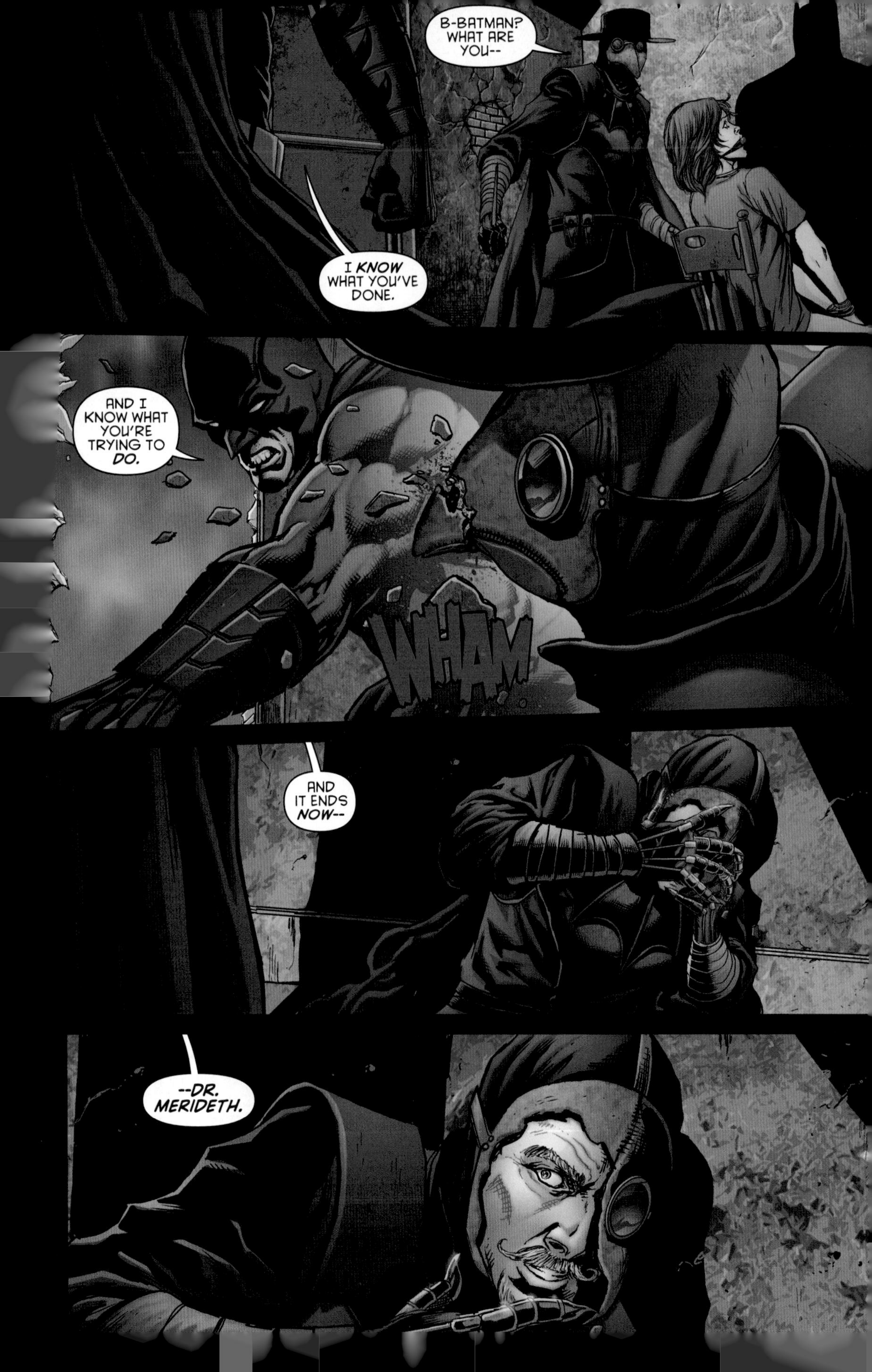
B-BATMAN? WHAT ARE YOU--
I KNOW WHAT YOU'VE DONE.
AND I KNOW WHAT YOU'RE TRYING TO DO.
WHAM
AND IT ENDS NOW--
--DR. MERIDETH.

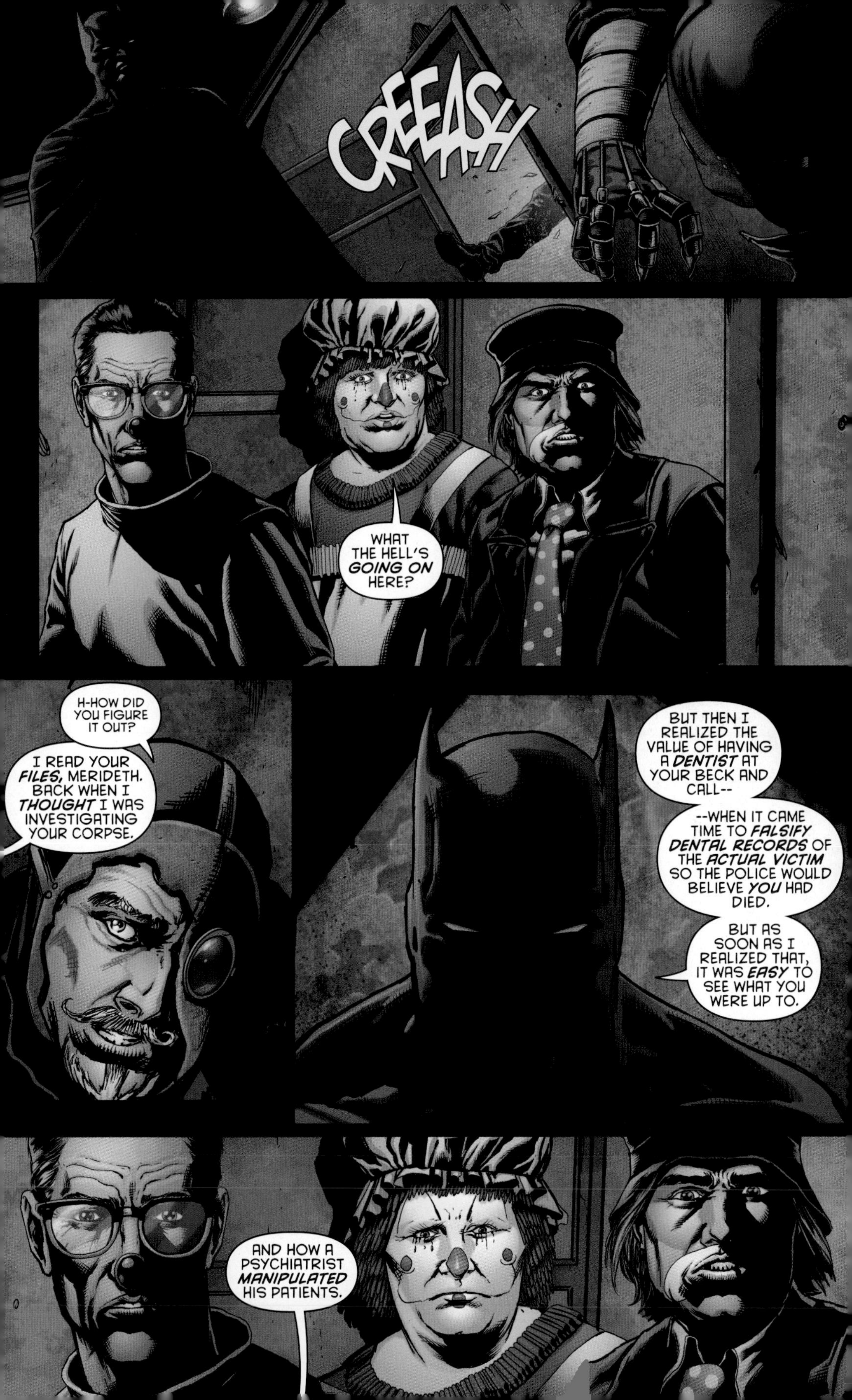
CREEASH
WHAT THE HELL'S GOING ON HERE?
H-HOW DID YOU FIGURE IT OUT?
I READ YOUR FILES, MERIDETH. BACK WHEN I THOUGHT I WAS INVESTIGATING YOUR CORPSE.
BUT THEN I REALIZED THE VALUE OF HAVING A DENTIST AT YOUR BECK AND CALL--
--WHEN IT CAME TIME TO FALSIFY DENTAL RECORDS OF THE ACTUAL VICTIM SO THE POLICE WOULD BELIEVE YOU HAD DIED.
BUT AS SOON AS I REALIZED THAT, IT WAS EASY TO SEE WHAT YOU WERE UP TO.
AND HOW A PSYCHIATRIST MANIPULATED HIS PATIENTS.

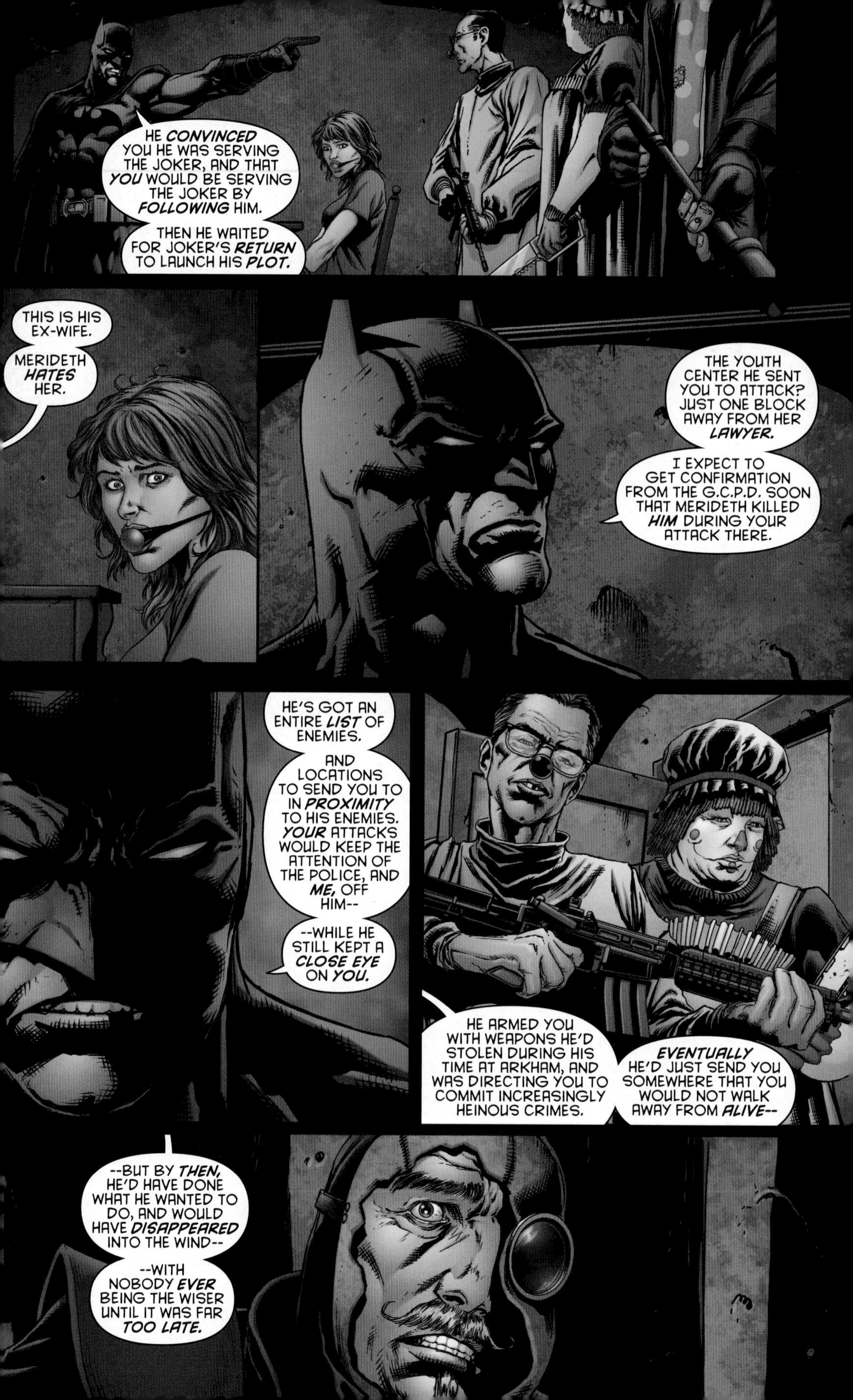

HE CONVINCED YOU HE WAS SERVING THE JOKER, AND THAT YOU WOULD BE SERVING THE JOKER BY FOLLOWING HIM.
THEN HE WAITED FOR JOKER'S RETURN TO LAUNCH HIS PLOT.
THIS IS HIS EX-WIFE.
MERIDETH HATES HER.
THE YOUTH CENTER HE SENT YOU TO ATTACK? JUST ONE BLOCK AWAY FROM HER LAWYER.
I EXPECT TO GET CONFIRMATION FROM THE G.C.P.D. SOON THAT MERIDETH KILLED HIM DURING YOUR ATTACK THERE.
HE'S GOT AN ENTIRE LIST OF ENEMIES.
AND LOCATIONS TO SEND YOU TO IN PROXIMITY TO HIS ENEMIES. YOUR ATTACKS WOULD KEEP THE ATTENTION OF THE POLICE, AND ME, OFF HIM--
--WHILE HE STILL KEPT A CLOSE EYE ON YOU.
HE ARMED YOU WITH WEAPONS HE'D STOLEN DURING HIS TIME AT ARKHAM, AND WAS DIRECTING YOU TO COMMIT INCREASINGLY HEINOUS CRIMES.
EVENTUALLY HE'D JUST SEND YOU SOMEWHERE THAT YOU WOULD NOT WALK AWAY FROM ALIVE--
--BUT BY THEN, HE'D HAVE DONE WHAT HE WANTED TO DO, AND WOULD HAVE DISAPPEARED INTO THE WIND--
--WITH NOBODY EVER BEING THE WISER UNTIL IT WAS FAR TOO LATE.

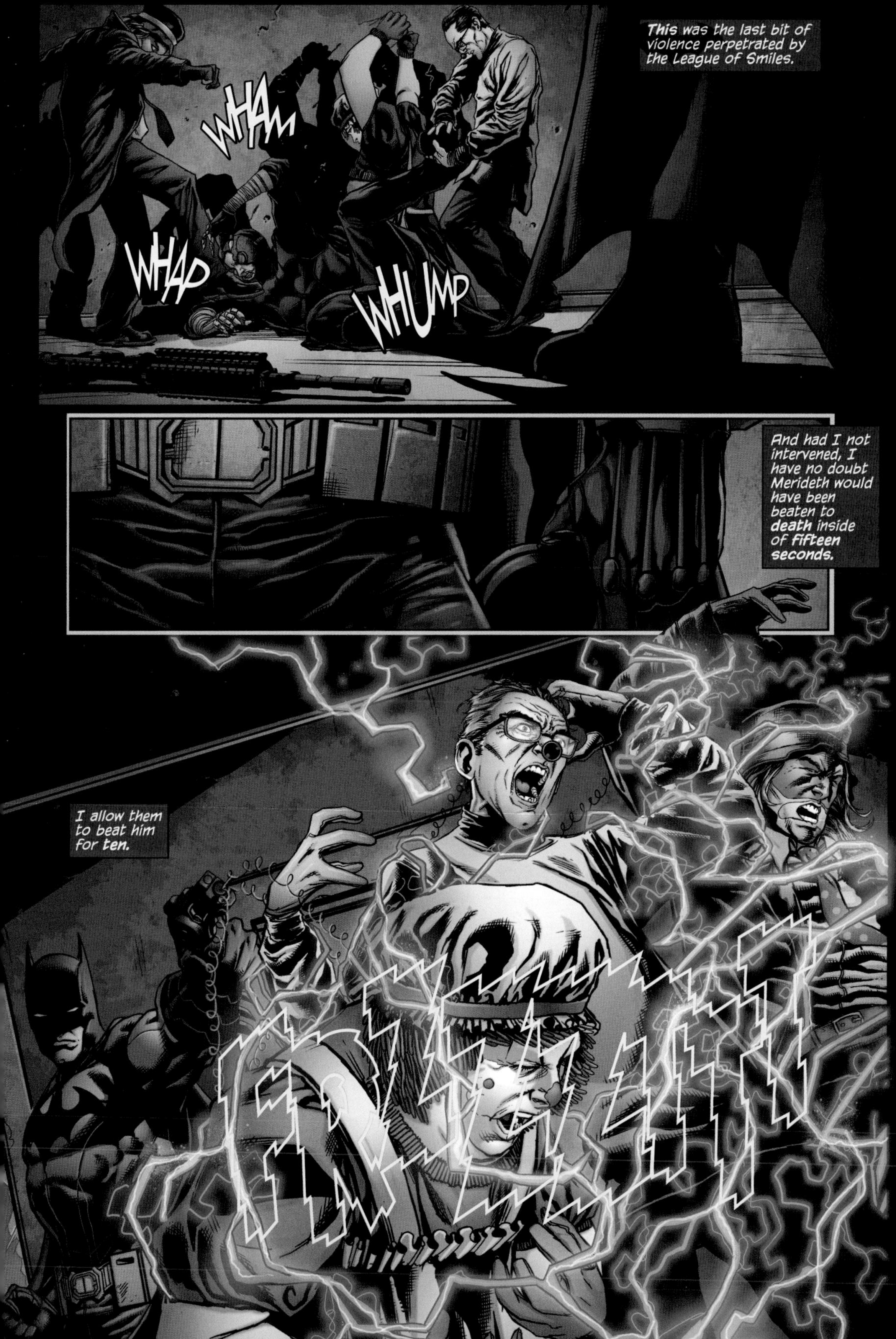
This was the last bit of violence perpetrated by the League of Smiles.
WHAM
WHAP
WHUMP
And had I not intervened, I have no doubt Merideth would have been beaten to death inside of fifteen seconds.
I allow them to beat him for ten.

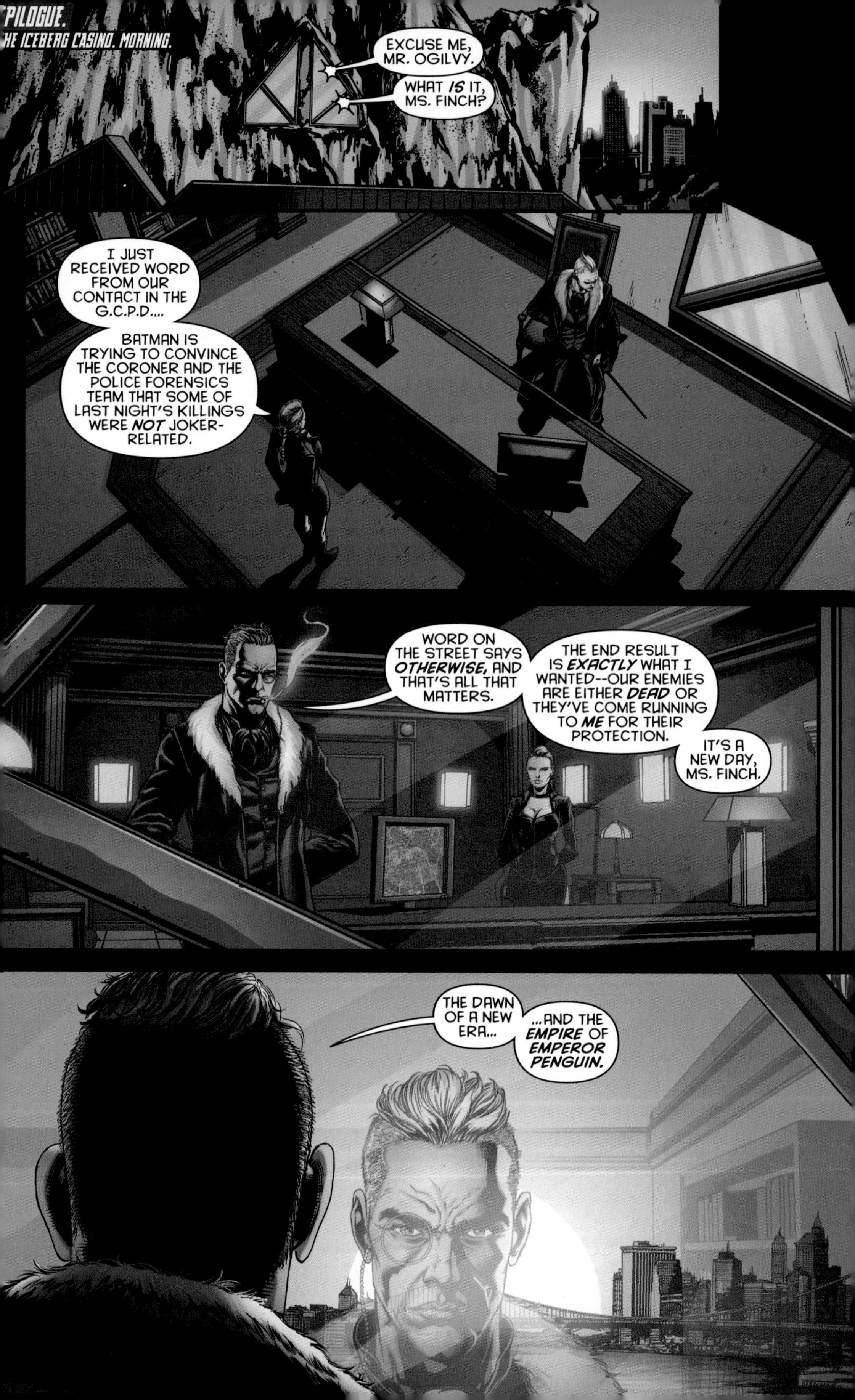
PILOGUE.
HE ICEBERG CASINO. MORNING.
EXCUSE ME, MR. OGILVY.
WHAT IS IT, MS. FINCH?
I JUST RECEIVED WORD FROM OUR CONTACT IN THE G.C.P.D....
BATMAN IS TRYING TO CONVINCE THE CORONER AND THE POLICE FORENSICS TEAM THAT SOME OF LAST NIGHT'S KILLINGS WERE NOT JOKER-RELATED.
WORD ON THE STREET SAYS OTHERWISE, AND THAT'S ALL THAT MATTERS.
THE END RESULT IS EXACTLY WHAT I WANTED--OUR ENEMIES ARE EITHER DEAD OR THEY'VE COME RUNNING TO ME FOR THEIR PROTECTION.
IT'S A NEW DAY, MS. FINCH.
THE DAWN OF A NEW ERA...
...AND THE EMPIRE OF EMPEROR PENGUIN.

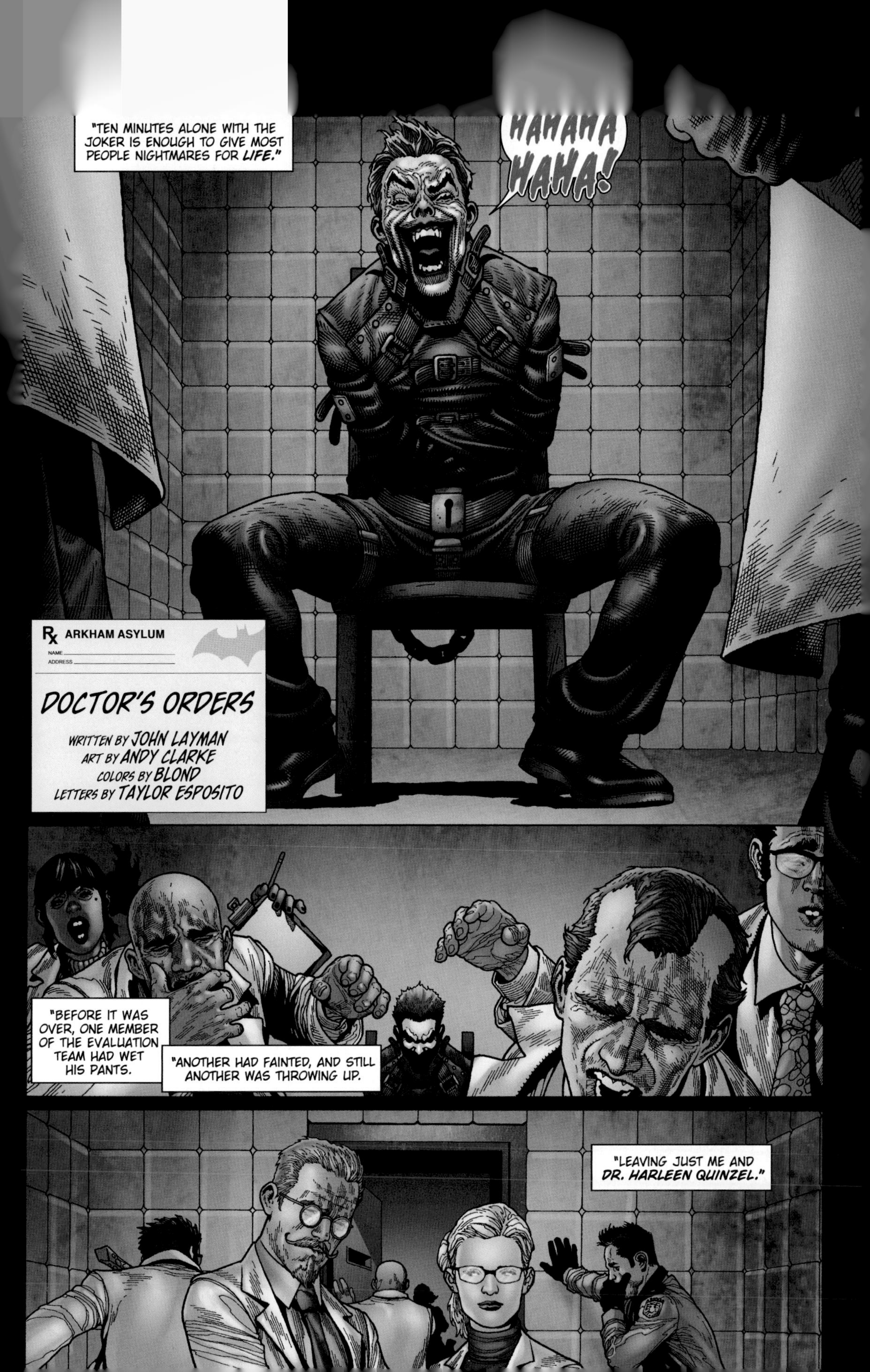
"TEN MINUTES ALONE WITH THE JOKER IS ENOUGH TO GIVE MOST PEOPLE NIGHTMARES FOR LIFE."
HAHAHA HAHA!
ARKHAM ASYLUM
NAME
ADDRESS
DOCTOR'S ORDERS
WRITTEN BY JOHN LAYMAN
ART BY ANDY CLARKE
COLORS BY BLOND
LETTERS BY TAYLOR ESPOSITO
"BEFORE IT WAS OVER, ONE MEMBER OF THE EVALUATION TEAM HAD WET HIS PANTS.
"ANOTHER HAD FAINTED, AND STILL ANOTHER WAS THROWING UP.
"LEAVING JUST ME AND DR. HARLEEN QUINZEL."

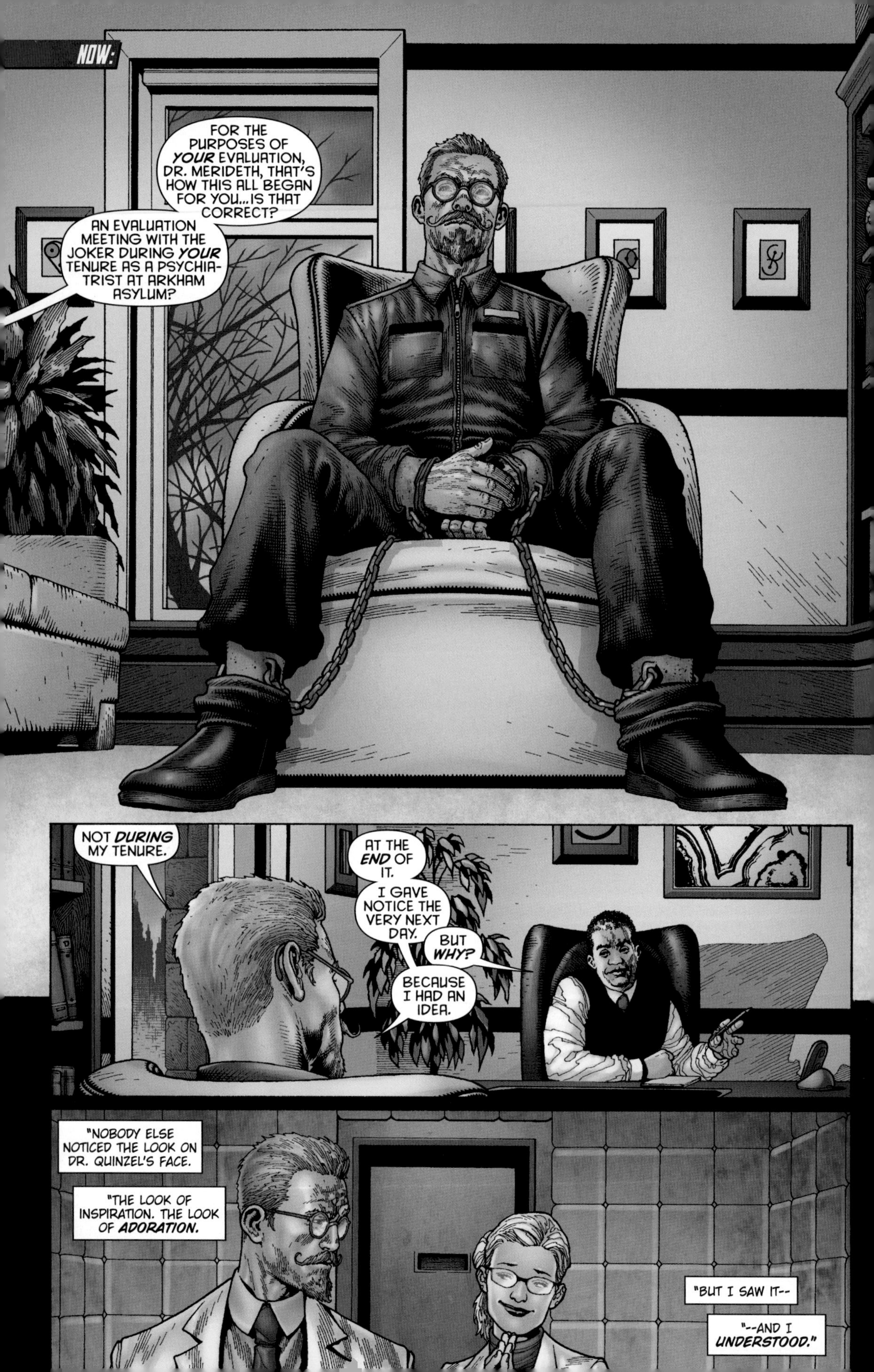
NOW:
FOR THE PURPOSES OF *YOUR* EVALUATION, DR. MERIDETH, THAT'S HOW THIS ALL BEGAN FOR YOU...IS THAT CORRECT?
AN EVALUATION MEETING WITH THE JOKER DURING *YOUR* TENURE AS A PSYCHIATRIST AT ARKHAM ASYLUM?
NOT *DURING* MY TENURE.
AT THE *END* OF IT.
I GAVE NOTICE THE VERY NEXT DAY.
BUT *WHY?*
BECAUSE I HAD AN IDEA.
"NOBODY ELSE NOTICED THE LOOK ON DR. QUINZEL'S FACE.
"THE LOOK OF INSPIRATION. THE LOOK OF *ADORATION.*
"BUT I SAW IT--
"--AND I *UNDERSTOOD.*"

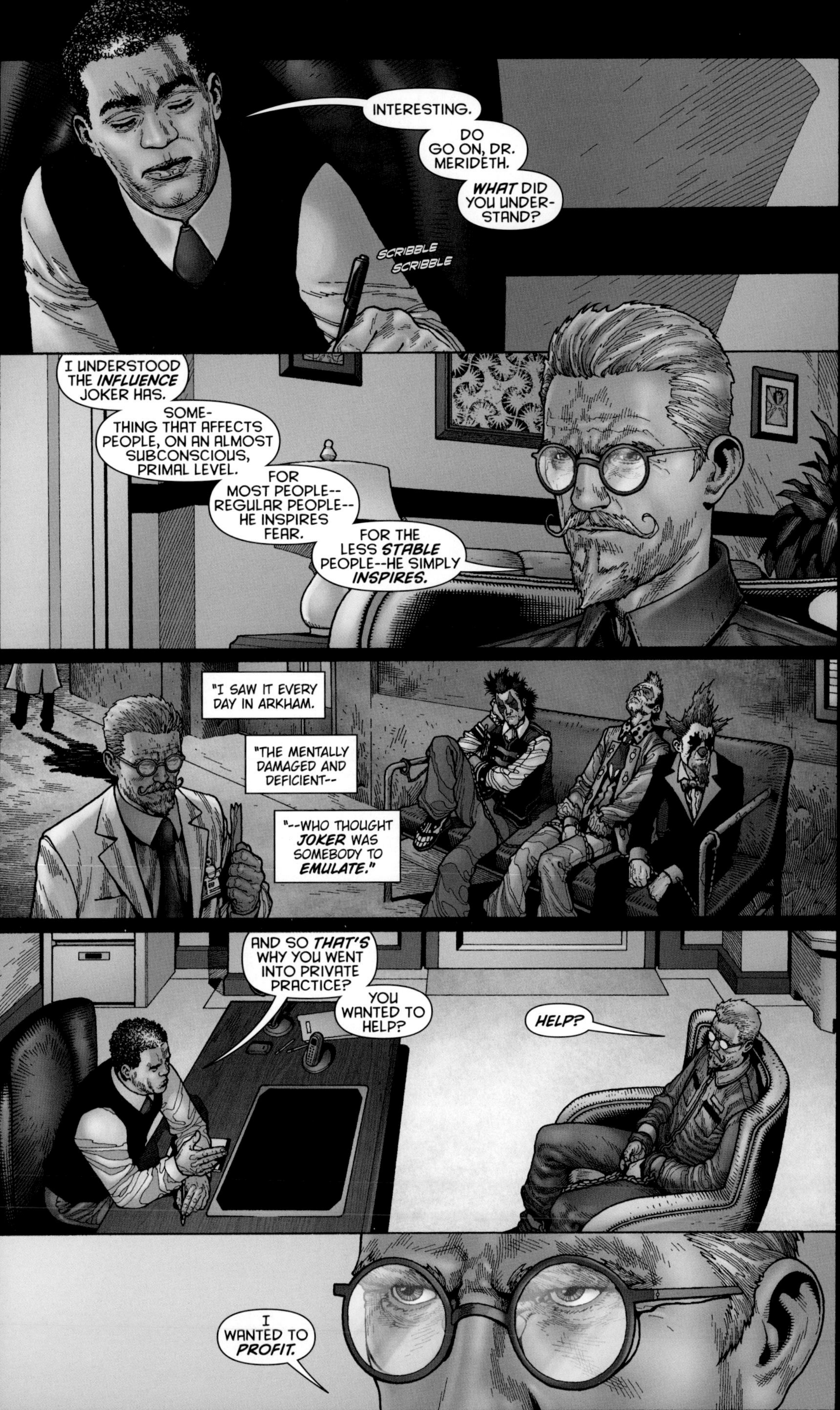
INTERESTING.
DO GO ON, DR. MERIDETH.
WHAT DID YOU UNDER-STAND?
SCRIBBLE SCRIBBLE
I UNDERSTOOD THE *INFLUENCE* JOKER HAS.
SOME-THING THAT AFFECTS PEOPLE, ON AN ALMOST SUBCONSCIOUS, PRIMAL LEVEL.
FOR MOST PEOPLE-- REGULAR PEOPLE-- HE INSPIRES FEAR.
FOR THE LESS *STABLE* PEOPLE--HE SIMPLY *INSPIRES.*
"I SAW IT EVERY DAY IN ARKHAM.
"THE MENTALLY DAMAGED AND DEFICIENT--
"--WHO THOUGHT *JOKER* WAS SOMEBODY TO *EMULATE.*"
AND SO *THAT'S* WHY YOU WENT INTO PRIVATE PRACTICE?
YOU WANTED TO HELP?
HELP?
I WANTED TO *PROFIT.*

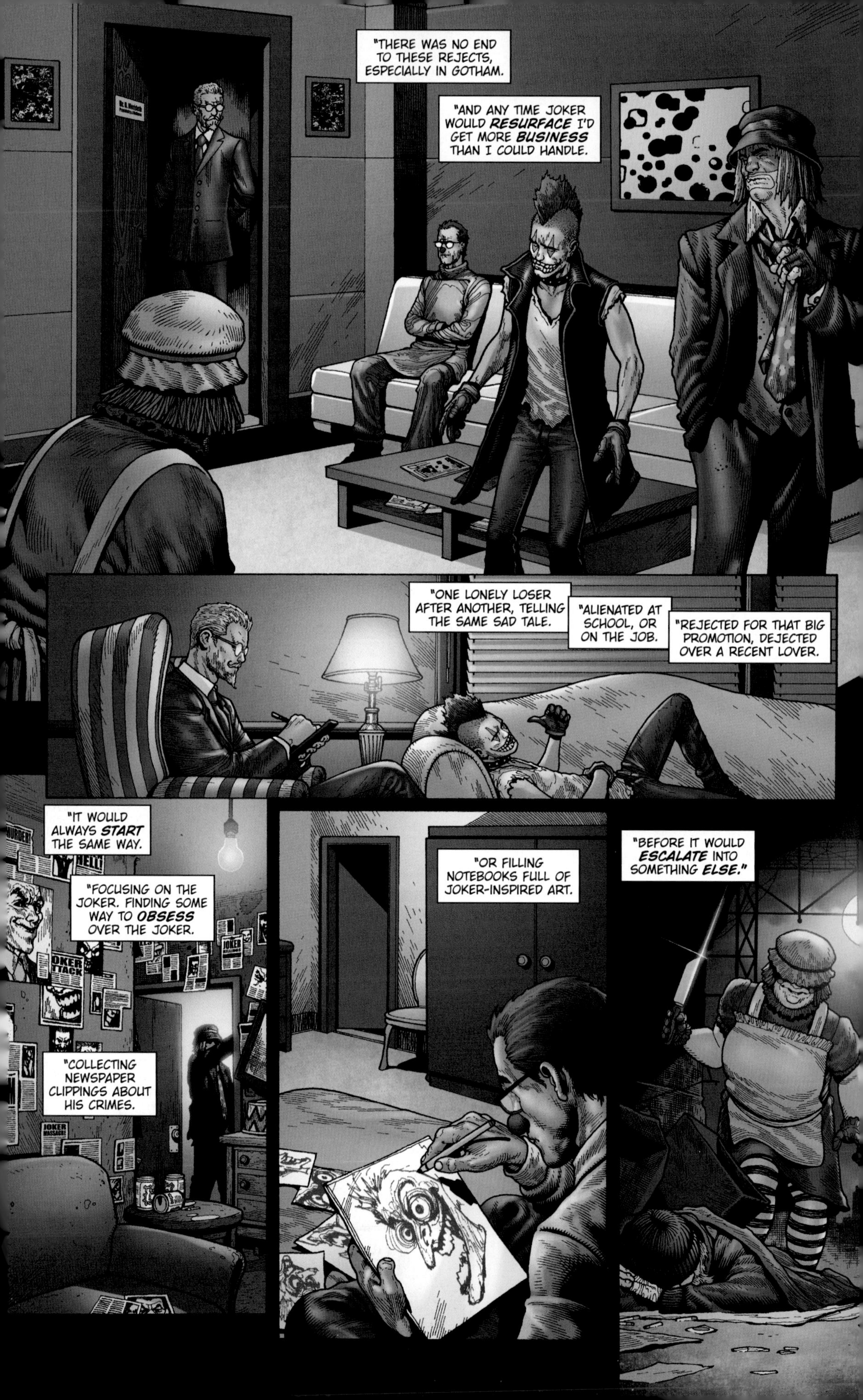

"THERE WAS NO END TO THESE REJECTS, ESPECIALLY IN GOTHAM.
"AND ANY TIME JOKER WOULD RESURFACE I'D GET MORE BUSINESS THAN I COULD HANDLE.
"ONE LONELY LOSER AFTER ANOTHER, TELLING THE SAME SAD TALE.
"ALIENATED AT SCHOOL, OR ON THE JOB.
"REJECTED FOR THAT BIG PROMOTION, DEJECTED OVER A RECENT LOVER.
"IT WOULD ALWAYS START THE SAME WAY.
"FOCUSING ON THE JOKER. FINDING SOME WAY TO OBSESS OVER THE JOKER.
"COLLECTING NEWSPAPER CLIPPINGS ABOUT HIS CRIMES.
"OR FILLING NOTEBOOKS FULL OF JOKER-INSPIRED ART.
"BEFORE IT WOULD ESCALATE INTO SOMETHING ELSE."

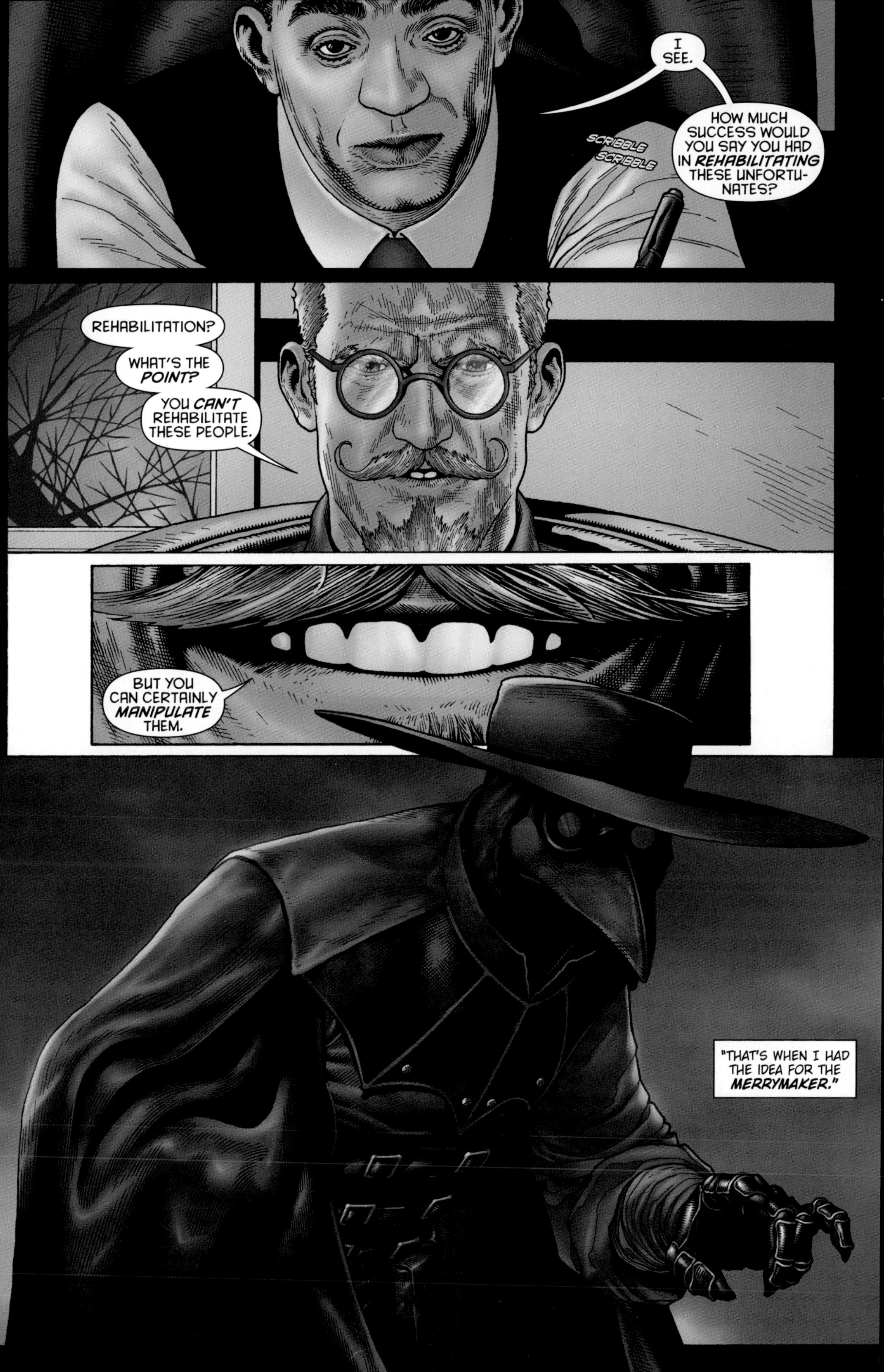
I SEE.
HOW MUCH SUCCESS WOULD YOU SAY YOU HAD IN ***REHABILITATING*** THESE UNFORTU-NATES?
SCRIBBLE SCRIBBLE
REHABILITATION?
WHAT'S THE ***POINT?***
YOU ***CAN'T*** REHABILITATE THESE PEOPLE.
BUT YOU CAN CERTAINLY ***MANIPULATE*** THEM.
"THAT'S WHEN I HAD THE IDEA FOR THE ***MERRYMAKER.***"

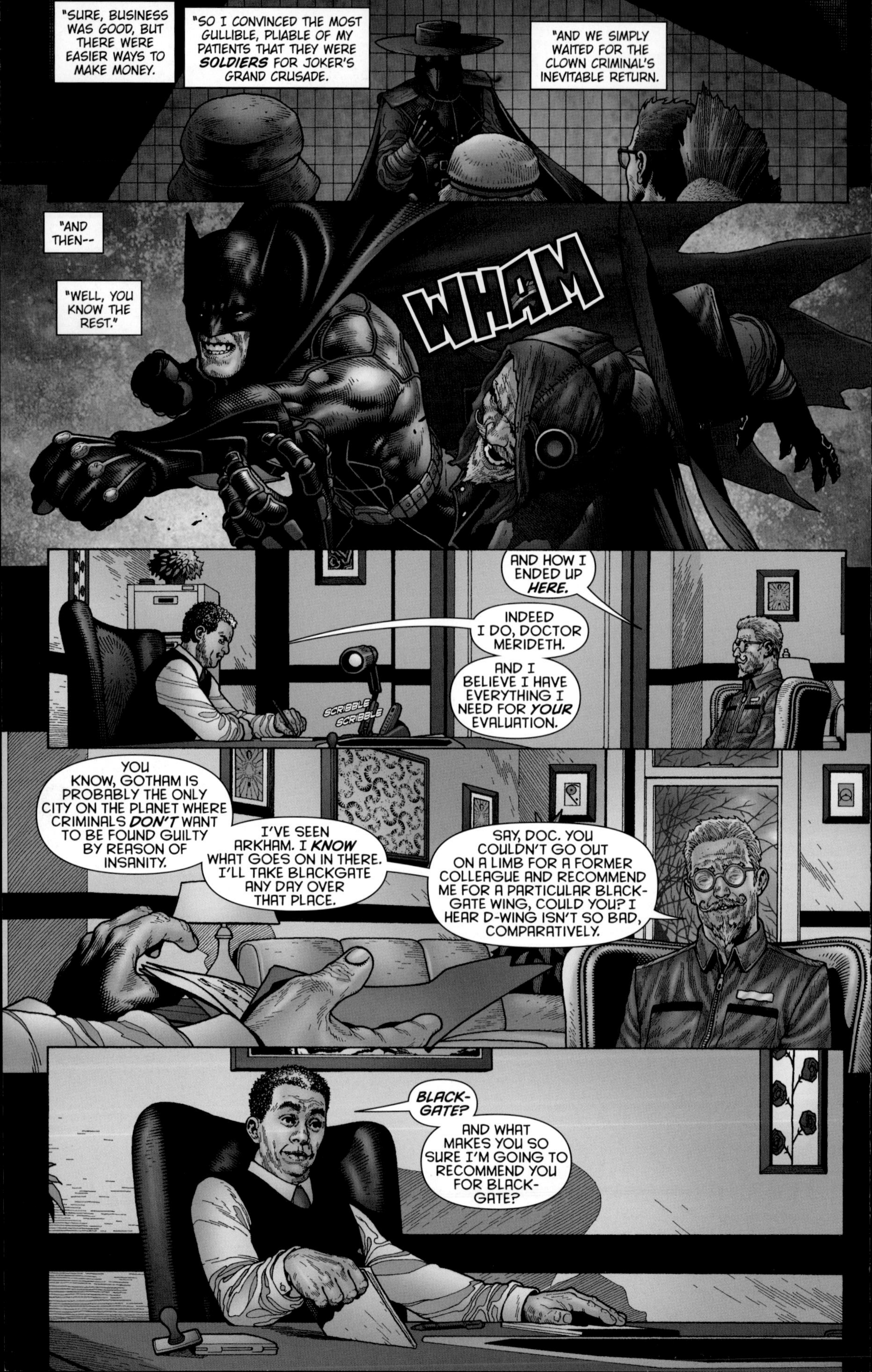
"SURE, BUSINESS WAS GOOD, BUT THERE WERE EASIER WAYS TO MAKE MONEY.
"SO I CONVINCED THE MOST GULLIBLE, PLIABLE OF MY PATIENTS THAT THEY WERE SOLDIERS FOR JOKER'S GRAND CRUSADE.
"AND WE SIMPLY WAITED FOR THE CLOWN CRIMINAL'S INEVITABLE RETURN.
"AND THEN--
"WELL, YOU KNOW THE REST."
WHAM
AND HOW I ENDED UP HERE.
INDEED I DO, DOCTOR MERIDETH.
AND I BELIEVE I HAVE EVERYTHING I NEED FOR YOUR EVALUATION.
SCRIBBLE SCRIBBLE
YOU KNOW, GOTHAM IS PROBABLY THE ONLY CITY ON THE PLANET WHERE CRIMINALS DON'T WANT TO BE FOUND GUILTY BY REASON OF INSANITY.
I'VE SEEN ARKHAM. I KNOW WHAT GOES ON IN THERE. I'LL TAKE BLACKGATE ANY DAY OVER THAT PLACE.
SAY, DOC. YOU COULDN'T GO OUT ON A LIMB FOR A FORMER COLLEAGUE AND RECOMMEND ME FOR A PARTICULAR BLACK-GATE WING, COULD YOU? I HEAR D-WING ISN'T SO BAD, COMPARATIVELY.
BLACK-GATE?
AND WHAT MAKES YOU SO SURE I'M GOING TO RECOMMEND YOU FOR BLACK-GATE?

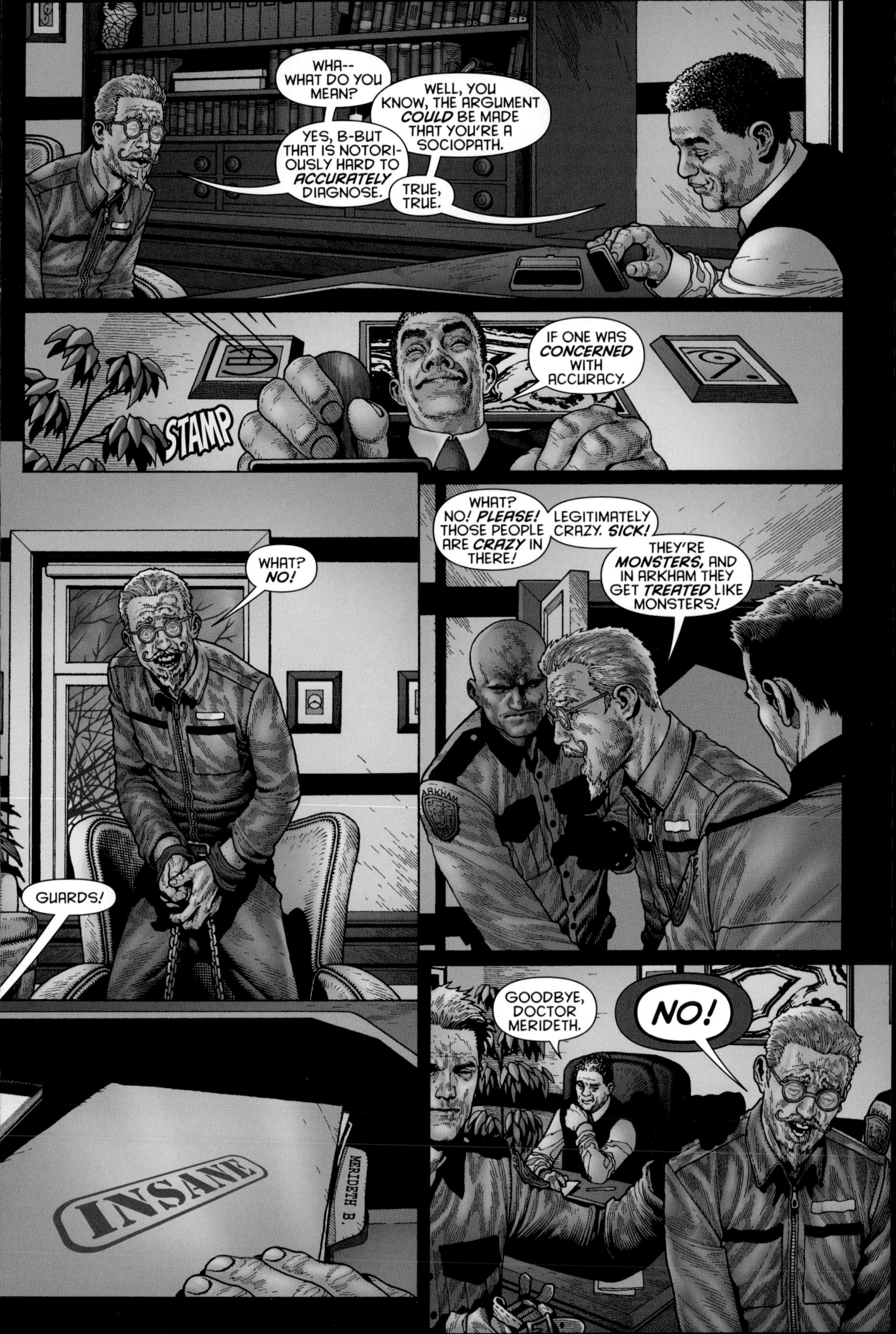
WHA-- WHAT DO YOU MEAN?
WELL, YOU KNOW, THE ARGUMENT COULD BE MADE THAT YOU'RE A SOCIOPATH.
YES, B-BUT THAT IS NOTORIOUSLY HARD TO ACCURATELY DIAGNOSE.
TRUE, TRUE.
STAMP
IF ONE WAS CONCERNED WITH ACCURACY.
WHAT? NO!
GUARDS!
WHAT? NO! PLEASE! THOSE PEOPLE ARE CRAZY IN THERE!
LEGITIMATELY CRAZY. SICK!
THEY'RE MONSTERS, AND IN ARKHAM THEY GET TREATED LIKE MONSTERS!
ARKHAM
INSANE
MERIDETH B.
GOODBYE, DOCTOR MERIDETH.
NO!

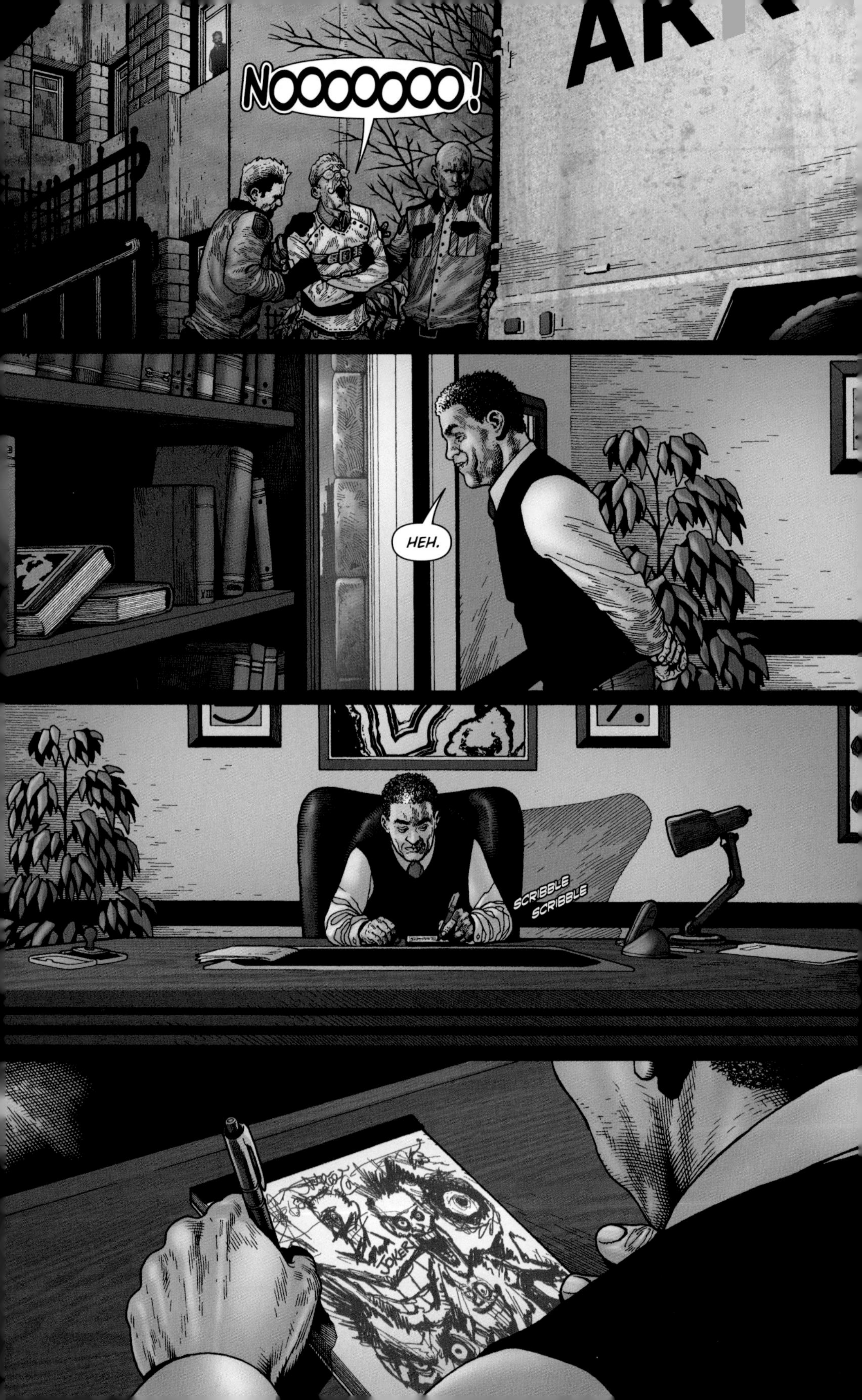
NOOOOOOO!
HEH.
SCRIBBLE
SCRIBBLE
JOKER

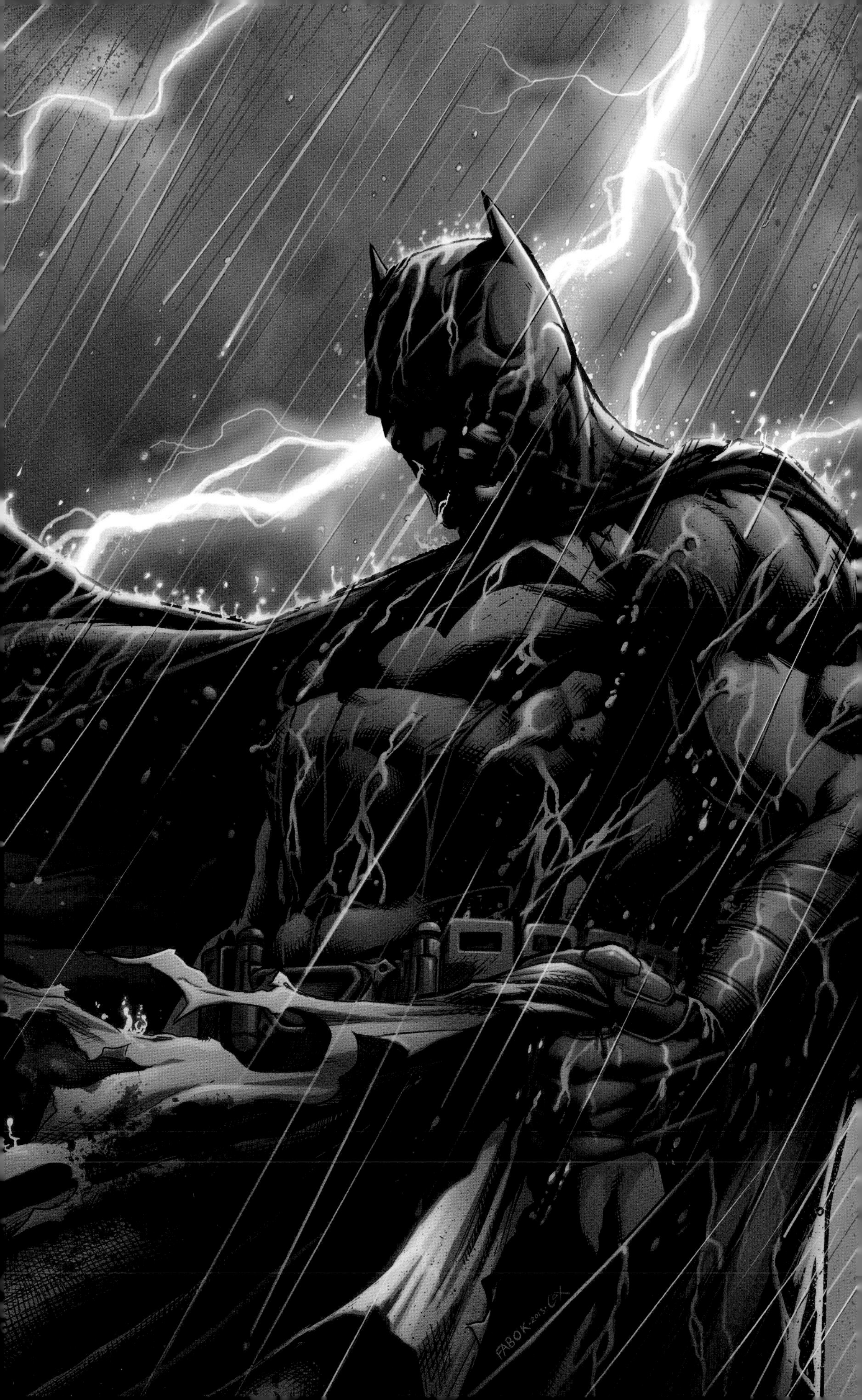
FABOK · 2013 · COX

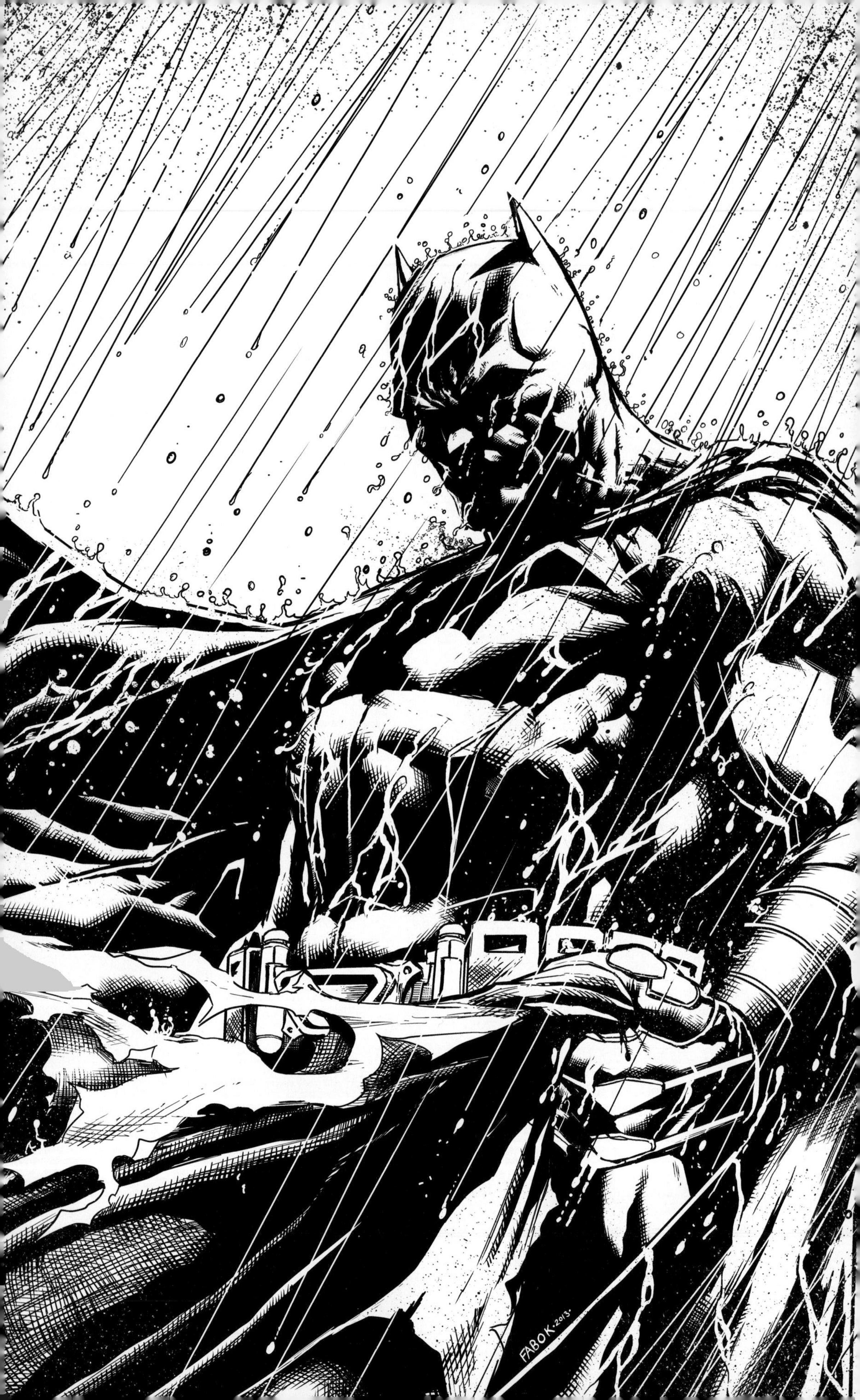
FABOK 2013.

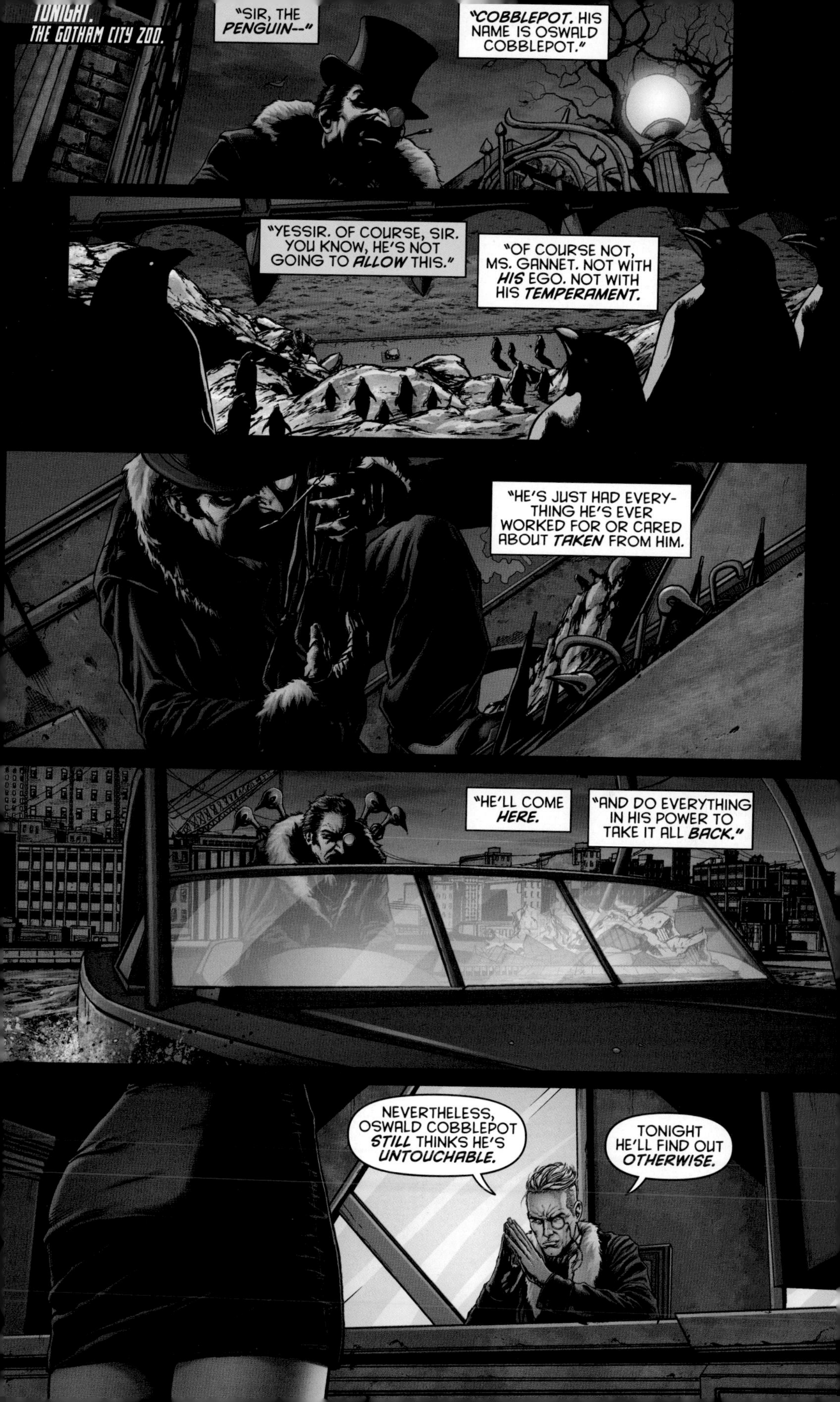
TONIGHT.
THE GOTHAM CITY ZOO.
"SIR, THE PENGUIN--"
"COBBLEPOT. HIS NAME IS OSWALD COBBLEPOT."
"YESSIR. OF COURSE, SIR. YOU KNOW, HE'S NOT GOING TO ALLOW THIS."
"OF COURSE NOT, MS. GANNET. NOT WITH HIS EGO. NOT WITH HIS TEMPERAMENT.
"HE'S JUST HAD EVERY-THING HE'S EVER WORKED FOR OR CARED ABOUT TAKEN FROM HIM.
"HE'LL COME HERE.
"AND DO EVERYTHING IN HIS POWER TO TAKE IT ALL BACK."
NEVERTHELESS, OSWALD COBBLEPOT STILL THINKS HE'S UNTOUCHABLE.
TONIGHT HE'LL FIND OUT OTHERWISE.

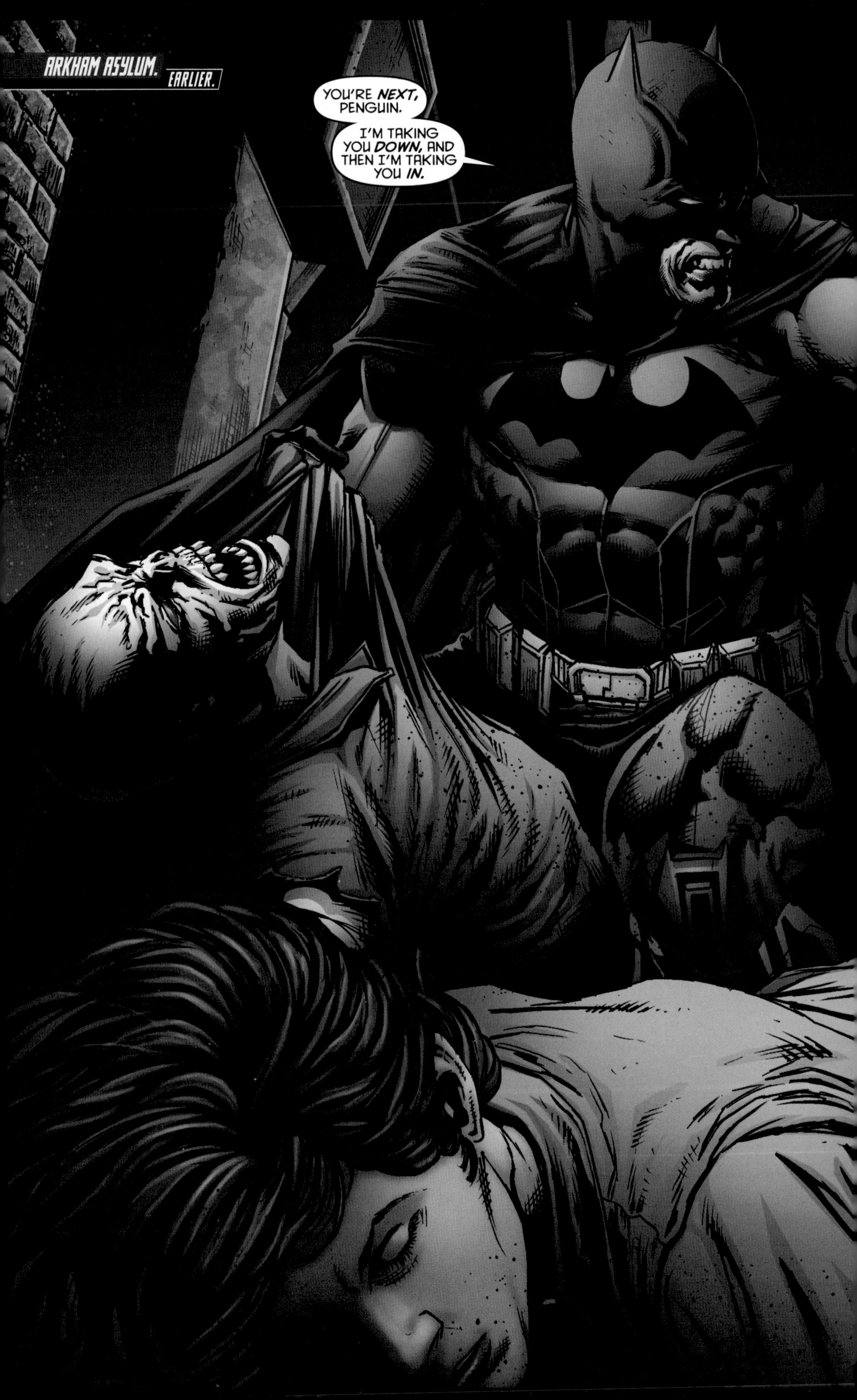
ARKHAM ASYLUM.
EARLIER.
YOU'RE NEXT, PENGUIN.
I'M TAKING YOU DOWN, AND THEN I'M TAKING YOU IN.

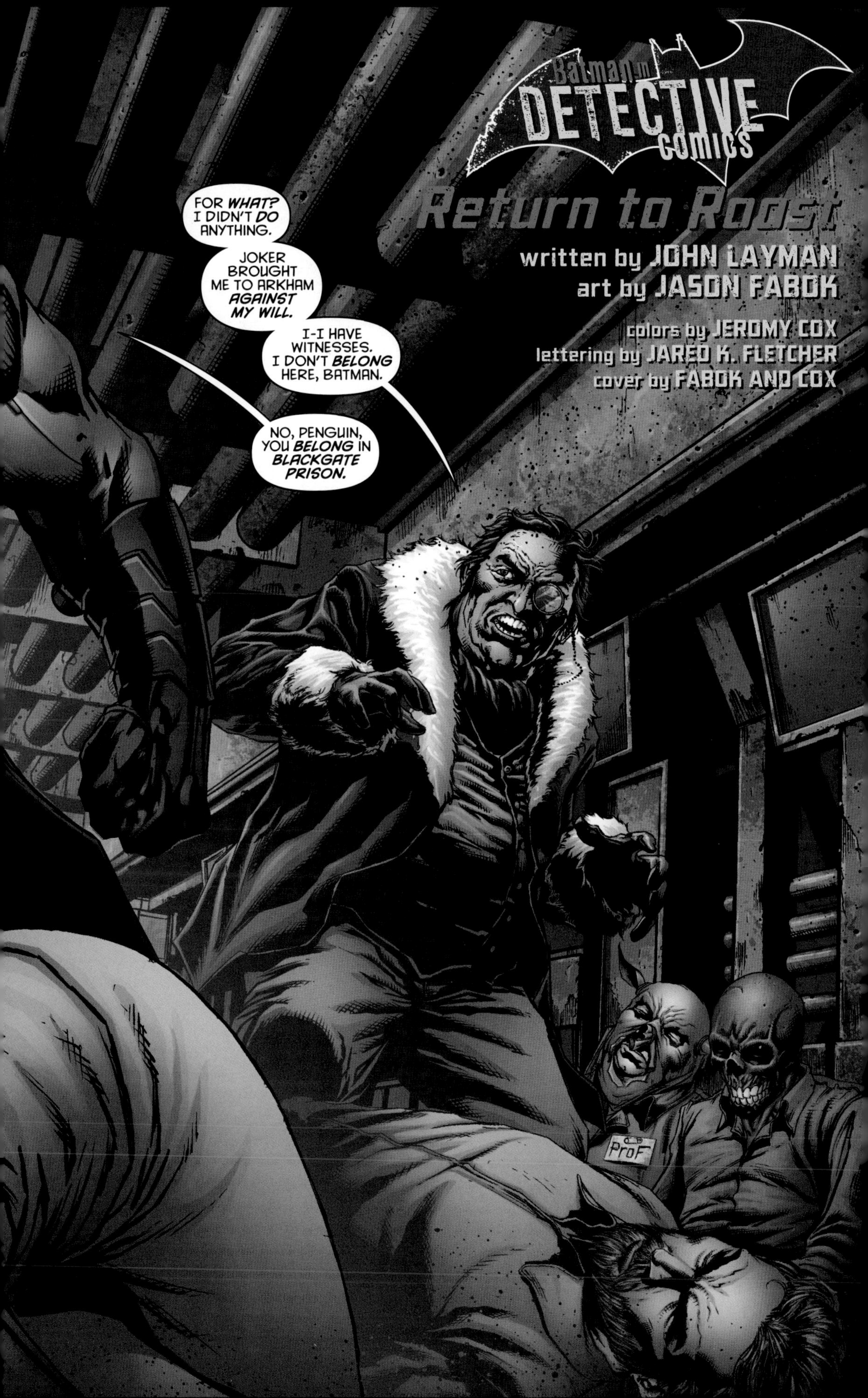
Batman in DETECTIVE COMICS
Return to Roost
written by JOHN LAYMAN
art by JASON FABOK
colors by JEROMY COX
lettering by JARED K. FLETCHER
cover by FABOK AND COX
FOR WHAT? I DIDN'T DO ANYTHING.
JOKER BROUGHT ME TO ARKHAM AGAINST MY WILL.
I-I HAVE WITNESSES. I DON'T BELONG HERE, BATMAN.
NO, PENGUIN, YOU BELONG IN BLACKGATE PRISON.
ProF

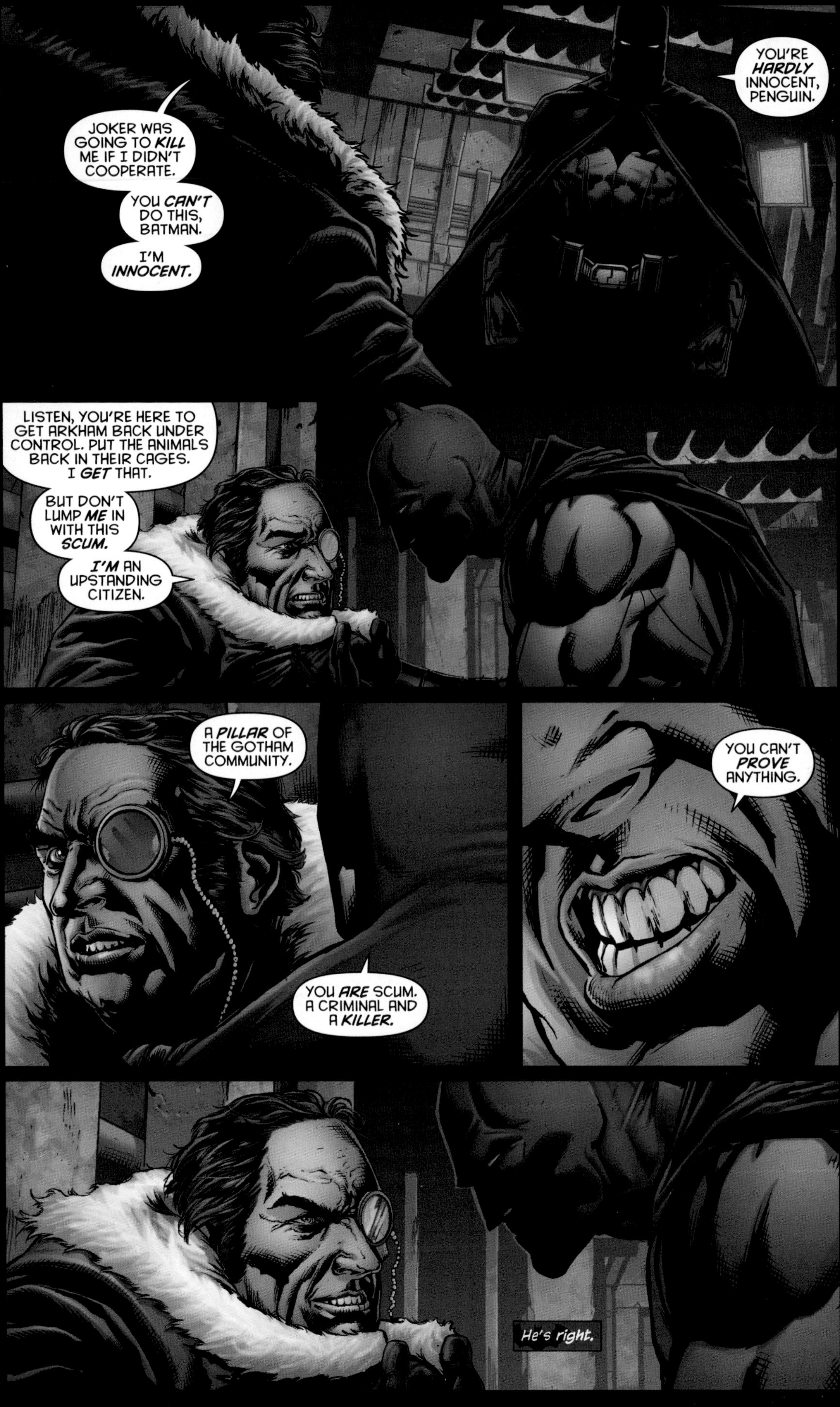
JOKER WAS GOING TO KILL ME IF I DIDN'T COOPERATE.
YOU CAN'T DO THIS, BATMAN.
I'M INNOCENT.
YOU'RE HARDLY INNOCENT, PENGUIN.
LISTEN, YOU'RE HERE TO GET ARKHAM BACK UNDER CONTROL. PUT THE ANIMALS BACK IN THEIR CAGES. I GET THAT.
BUT DON'T LUMP ME IN WITH THIS SCUM.
I'M AN UPSTANDING CITIZEN.
A PILLAR OF THE GOTHAM COMMUNITY.
YOU ARE SCUM. A CRIMINAL AND A KILLER.
YOU CAN'T PROVE ANYTHING.
He's right.

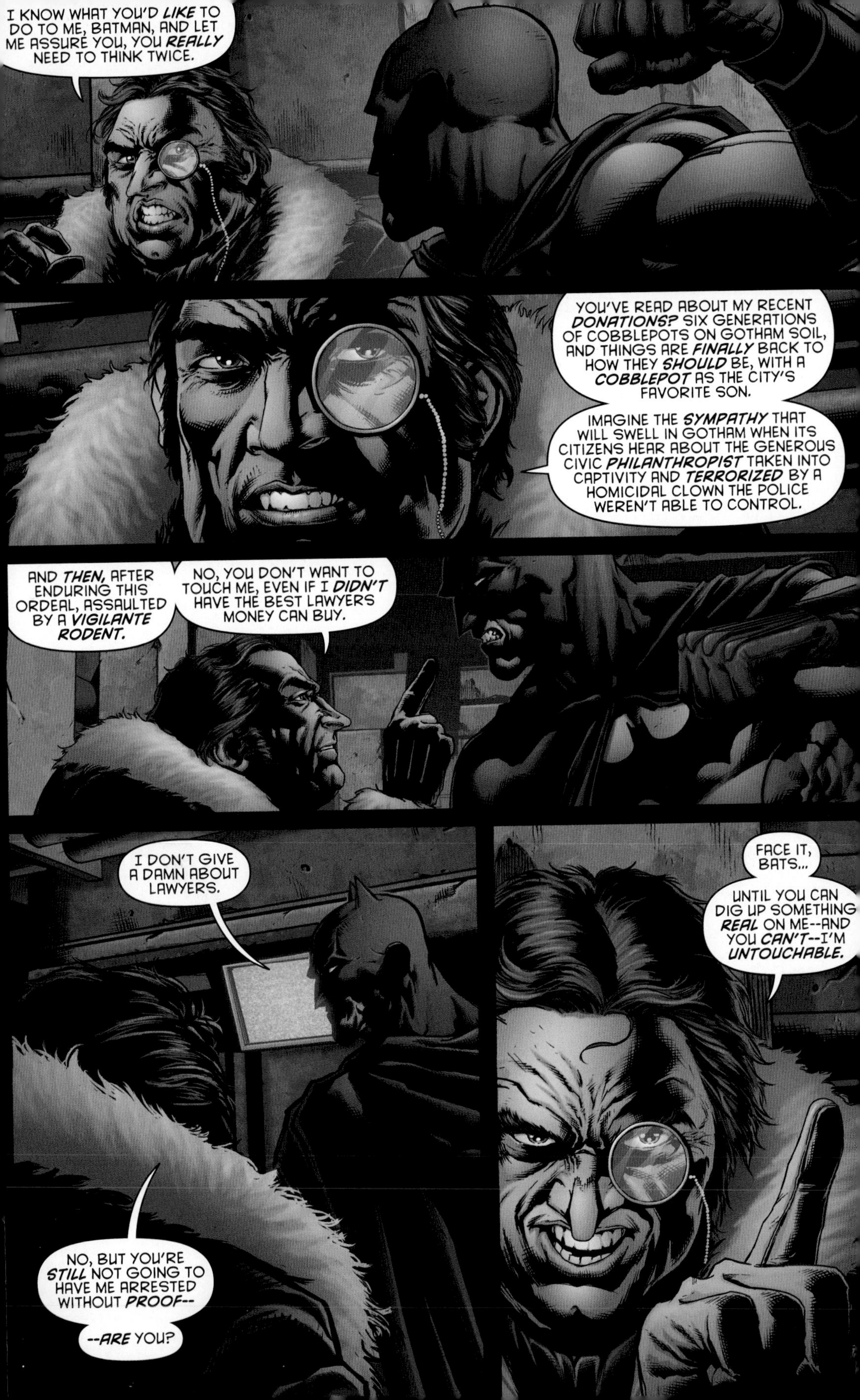
I KNOW WHAT YOU'D LIKE TO DO TO ME, BATMAN, AND LET ME ASSURE YOU, YOU REALLY NEED TO THINK TWICE.
YOU'VE READ ABOUT MY RECENT DONATIONS? SIX GENERATIONS OF COBBLEPOTS ON GOTHAM SOIL, AND THINGS ARE FINALLY BACK TO HOW THEY SHOULD BE, WITH A COBBLEPOT AS THE CITY'S FAVORITE SON.
IMAGINE THE SYMPATHY THAT WILL SWELL IN GOTHAM WHEN ITS CITIZENS HEAR ABOUT THE GENEROUS CIVIC PHILANTHROPIST TAKEN INTO CAPTIVITY AND TERRORIZED BY A HOMICIDAL CLOWN THE POLICE WEREN'T ABLE TO CONTROL.
AND THEN, AFTER ENDURING THIS ORDEAL, ASSAULTED BY A VIGILANTE RODENT.
NO, YOU DON'T WANT TO TOUCH ME, EVEN IF I DIDN'T HAVE THE BEST LAWYERS MONEY CAN BUY.
I DON'T GIVE A DAMN ABOUT LAWYERS.
NO, BUT YOU'RE STILL NOT GOING TO HAVE ME ARRESTED WITHOUT PROOF--
--ARE YOU?
FACE IT, BATS...
UNTIL YOU CAN DIG UP SOMETHING REAL ON ME--AND YOU CAN'T--I'M UNTOUCHABLE.

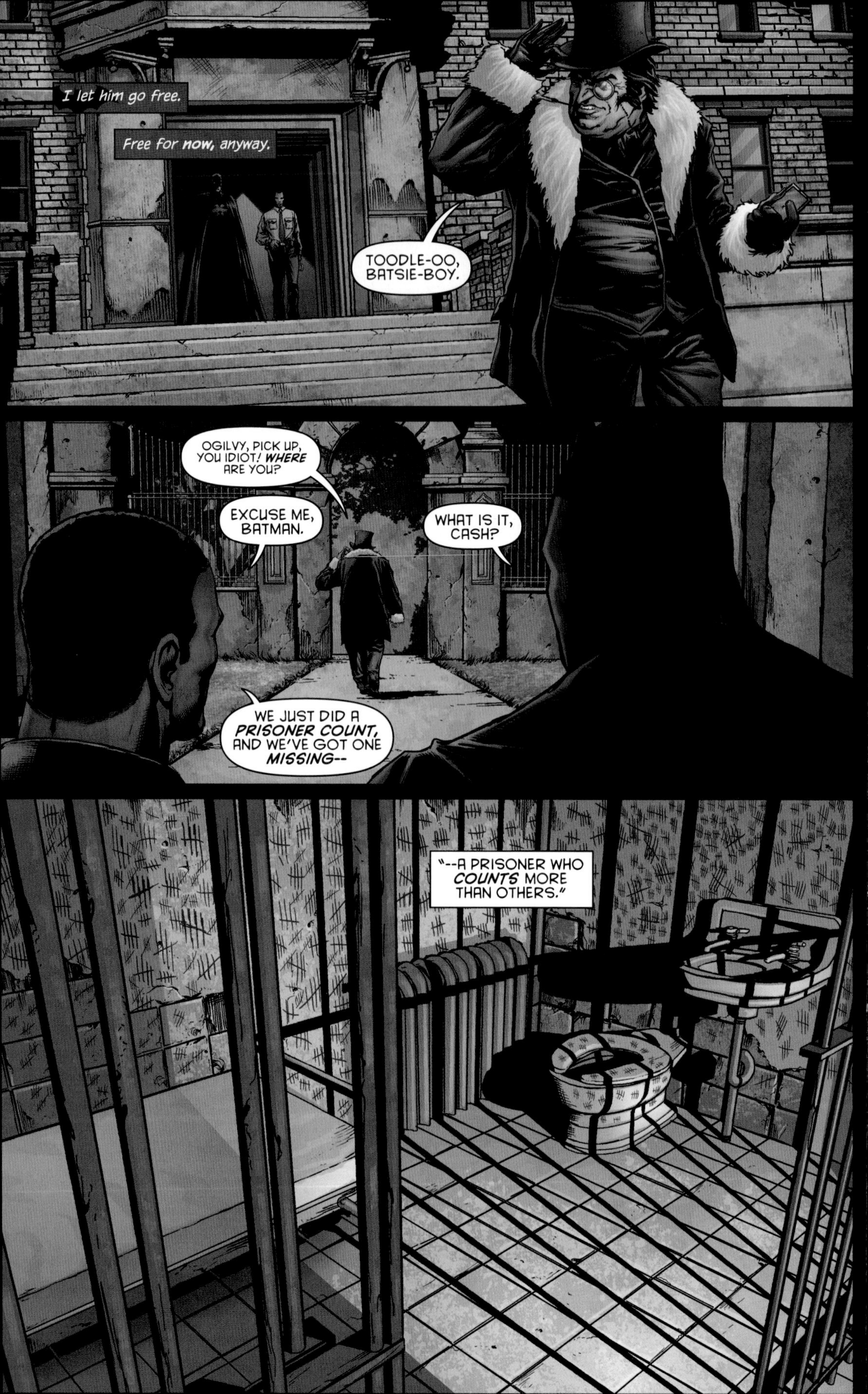
I let him go free.
Free for **now,** anyway.
TOODLE-OO, BATSIE-BOY.
OGILVY, PICK UP, YOU IDIOT! *WHERE* ARE YOU?
EXCUSE ME, BATMAN.
WHAT IS IT, CASH?
WE JUST DID A *PRISONER COUNT,* AND WE'VE GOT ONE *MISSING--*
"--A PRISONER WHO *COUNTS* MORE THAN OTHERS."

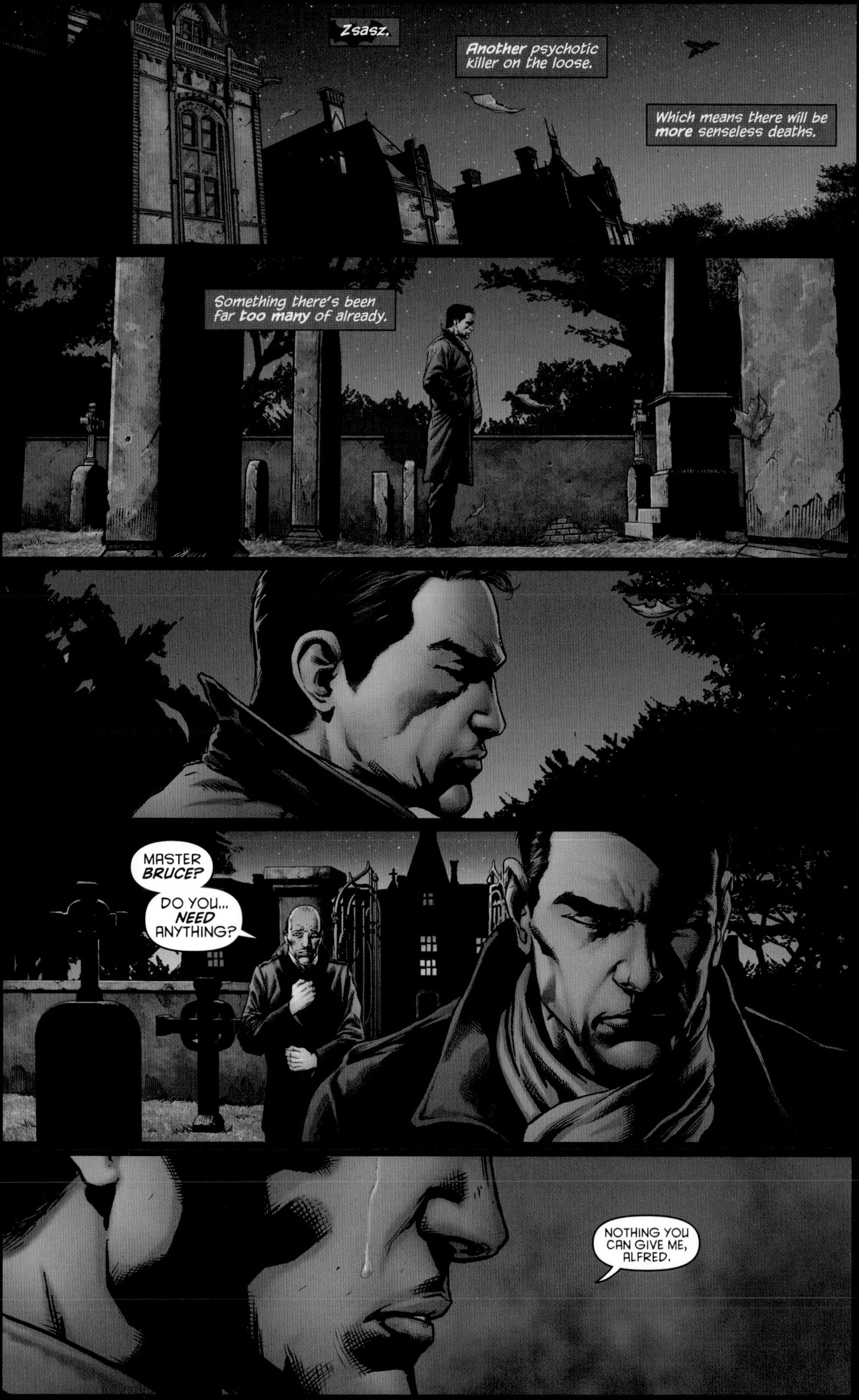
Zsasz.
Another psychotic killer on the loose.
Which means there will be more senseless deaths.
Something there's been far too many of already.
MASTER BRUCE?
DO YOU... NEED ANYTHING?
NOTHING YOU CAN GIVE ME, ALFRED.

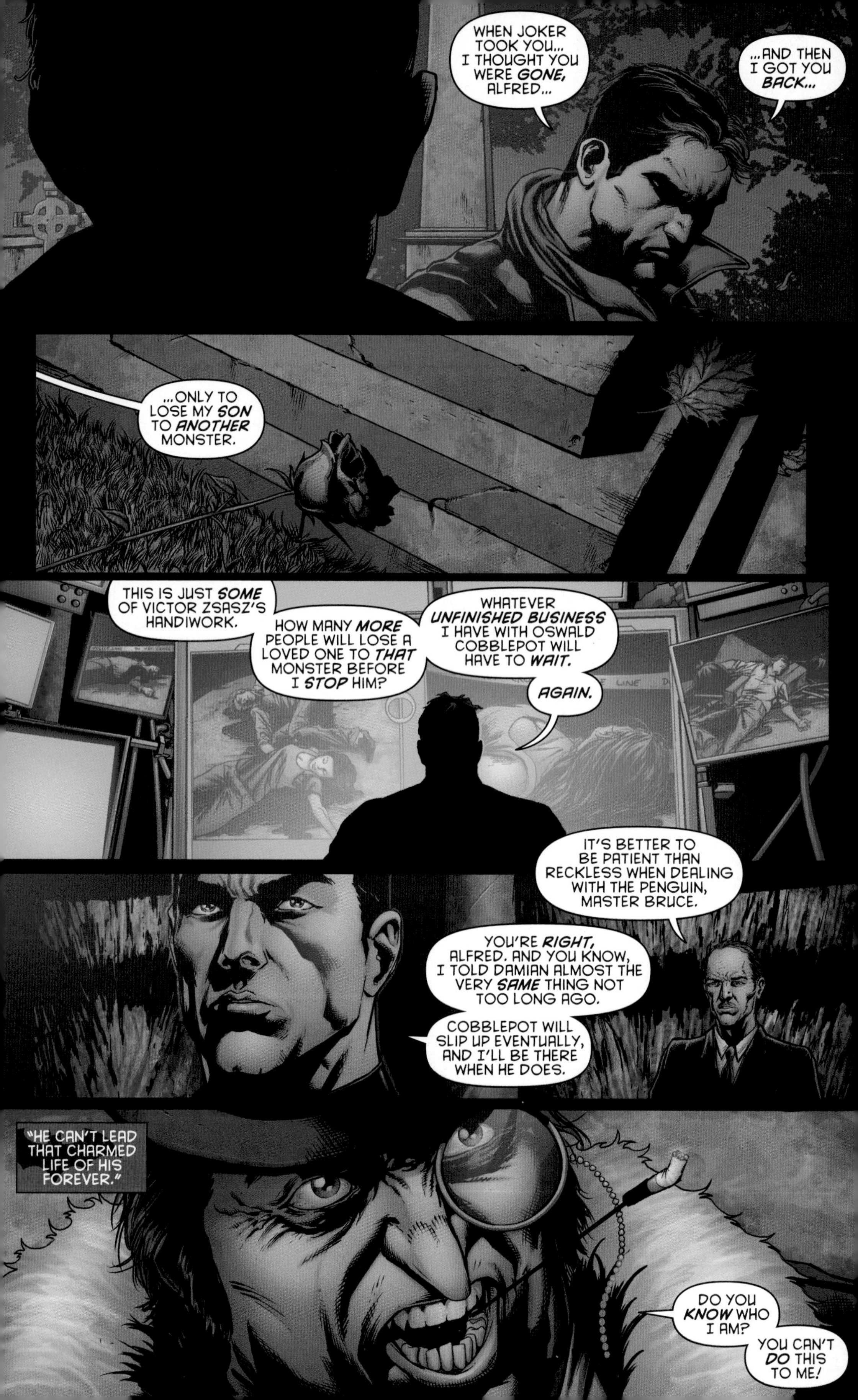
WHEN JOKER TOOK YOU... I THOUGHT YOU WERE GONE, ALFRED...
...AND THEN I GOT YOU BACK...
...ONLY TO LOSE MY SON TO ANOTHER MONSTER.
THIS IS JUST SOME OF VICTOR ZSASZ'S HANDIWORK.
HOW MANY MORE PEOPLE WILL LOSE A LOVED ONE TO THAT MONSTER BEFORE I STOP HIM?
WHATEVER UNFINISHED BUSINESS I HAVE WITH OSWALD COBBLEPOT WILL HAVE TO WAIT.
AGAIN.
IT'S BETTER TO BE PATIENT THAN RECKLESS WHEN DEALING WITH THE PENGUIN, MASTER BRUCE.
YOU'RE RIGHT, ALFRED. AND YOU KNOW, I TOLD DAMIAN ALMOST THE VERY SAME THING NOT TOO LONG AGO.
COBBLEPOT WILL SLIP UP EVENTUALLY, AND I'LL BE THERE WHEN HE DOES.
"HE CAN'T LEAD THAT CHARMED LIFE OF HIS FOREVER."
DO YOU KNOW WHO I AM?
YOU CAN'T DO THIS TO ME!

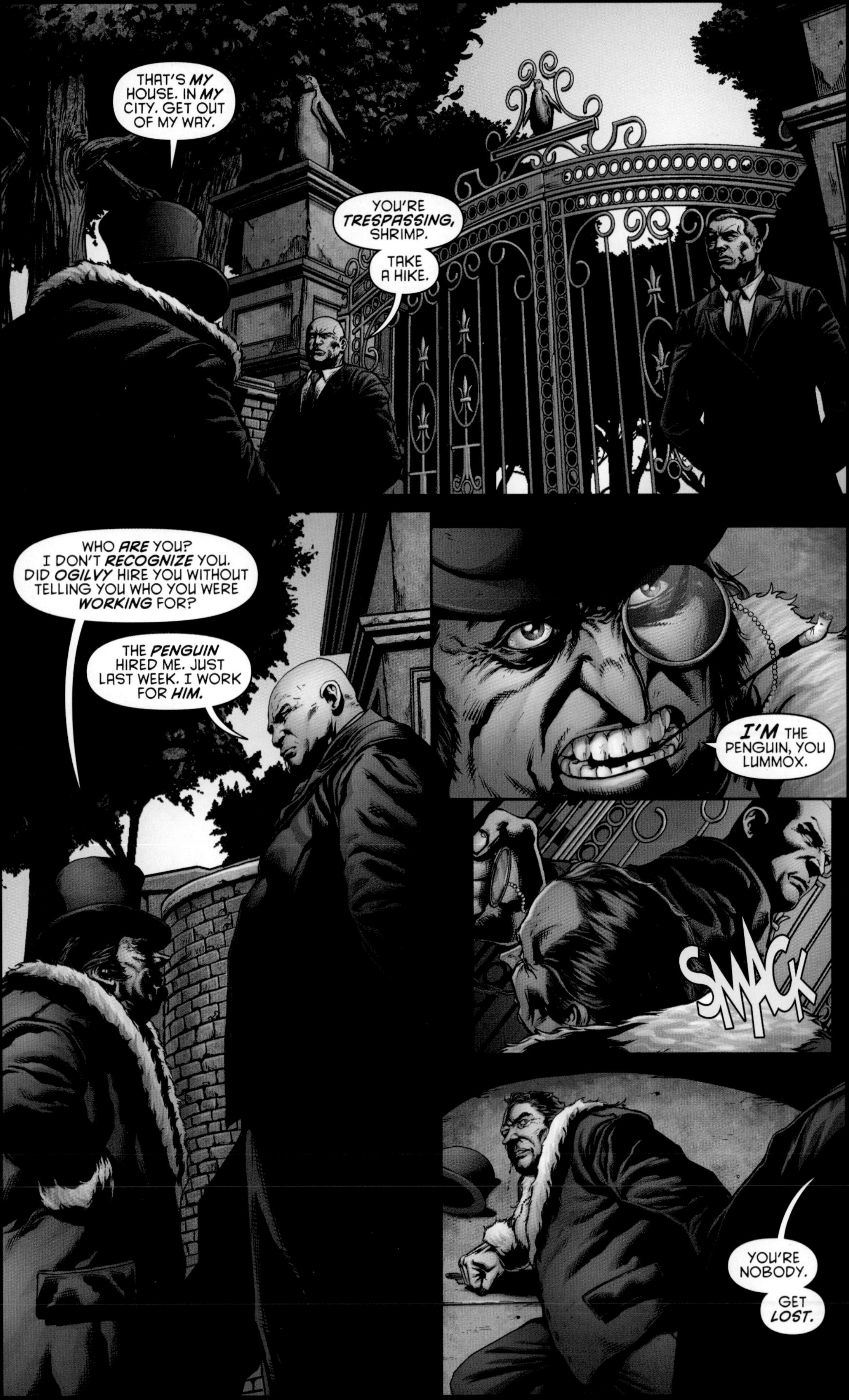
THAT'S *MY* HOUSE. IN *MY* CITY. GET OUT OF MY WAY.
YOU'RE *TRESPASSING,* SHRIMP.
TAKE A HIKE.
WHO *ARE* YOU? I DON'T *RECOGNIZE* YOU. DID *OGILVY* HIRE YOU WITHOUT TELLING YOU WHO YOU WERE *WORKING* FOR?
THE *PENGUIN* HIRED ME. JUST LAST WEEK. I WORK FOR *HIM.*
I'M THE PENGUIN, YOU LUMMOX.
SMACK
YOU'RE NOBODY.
GET *LOST.*

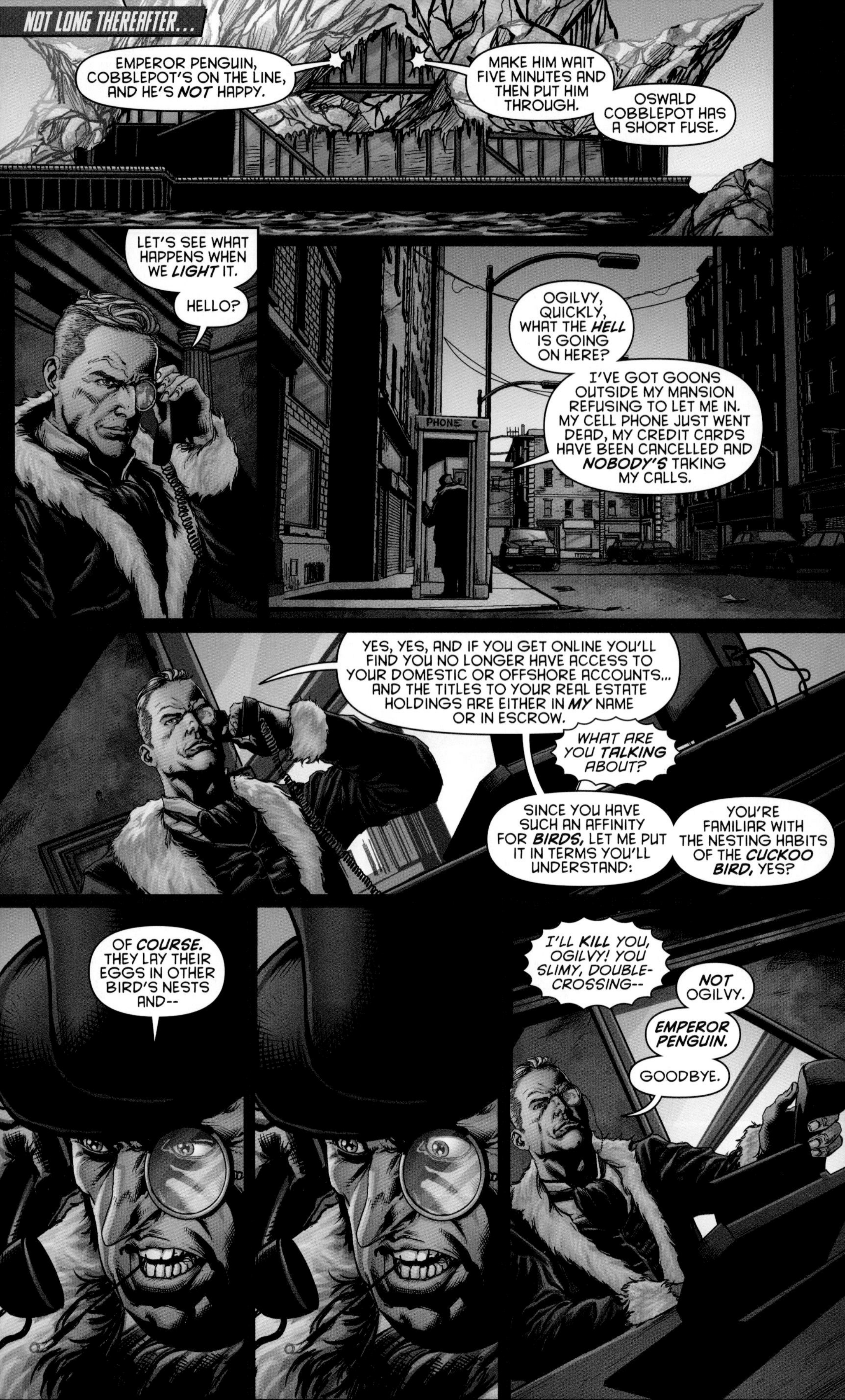
NOT LONG THEREAFTER...
EMPEROR PENGUIN, COBBLEPOT'S ON THE LINE, AND HE'S NOT HAPPY.
MAKE HIM WAIT FIVE MINUTES AND THEN PUT HIM THROUGH.
OSWALD COBBLEPOT HAS A SHORT FUSE.
LET'S SEE WHAT HAPPENS WHEN WE LIGHT IT.
HELLO?
OGILVY, QUICKLY, WHAT THE HELL IS GOING ON HERE?
I'VE GOT GOONS OUTSIDE MY MANSION REFUSING TO LET ME IN. MY CELL PHONE JUST WENT DEAD, MY CREDIT CARDS HAVE BEEN CANCELLED AND NOBODY'S TAKING MY CALLS.
PHONE
YES, YES, AND IF YOU GET ONLINE YOU'LL FIND YOU NO LONGER HAVE ACCESS TO YOUR DOMESTIC OR OFFSHORE ACCOUNTS... AND THE TITLES TO YOUR REAL ESTATE HOLDINGS ARE EITHER IN MY NAME OR IN ESCROW.
WHAT ARE YOU TALKING ABOUT?
SINCE YOU HAVE SUCH AN AFFINITY FOR BIRDS, LET ME PUT IT IN TERMS YOU'LL UNDERSTAND:
YOU'RE FAMILIAR WITH THE NESTING HABITS OF THE CUCKOO BIRD, YES?
OF COURSE. THEY LAY THEIR EGGS IN OTHER BIRD'S NESTS AND--
I'LL KILL YOU, OGILVY! YOU SLIMY, DOUBLE-CROSSING--
NOT OGILVY.
EMPEROR PENGUIN.
GOODBYE.

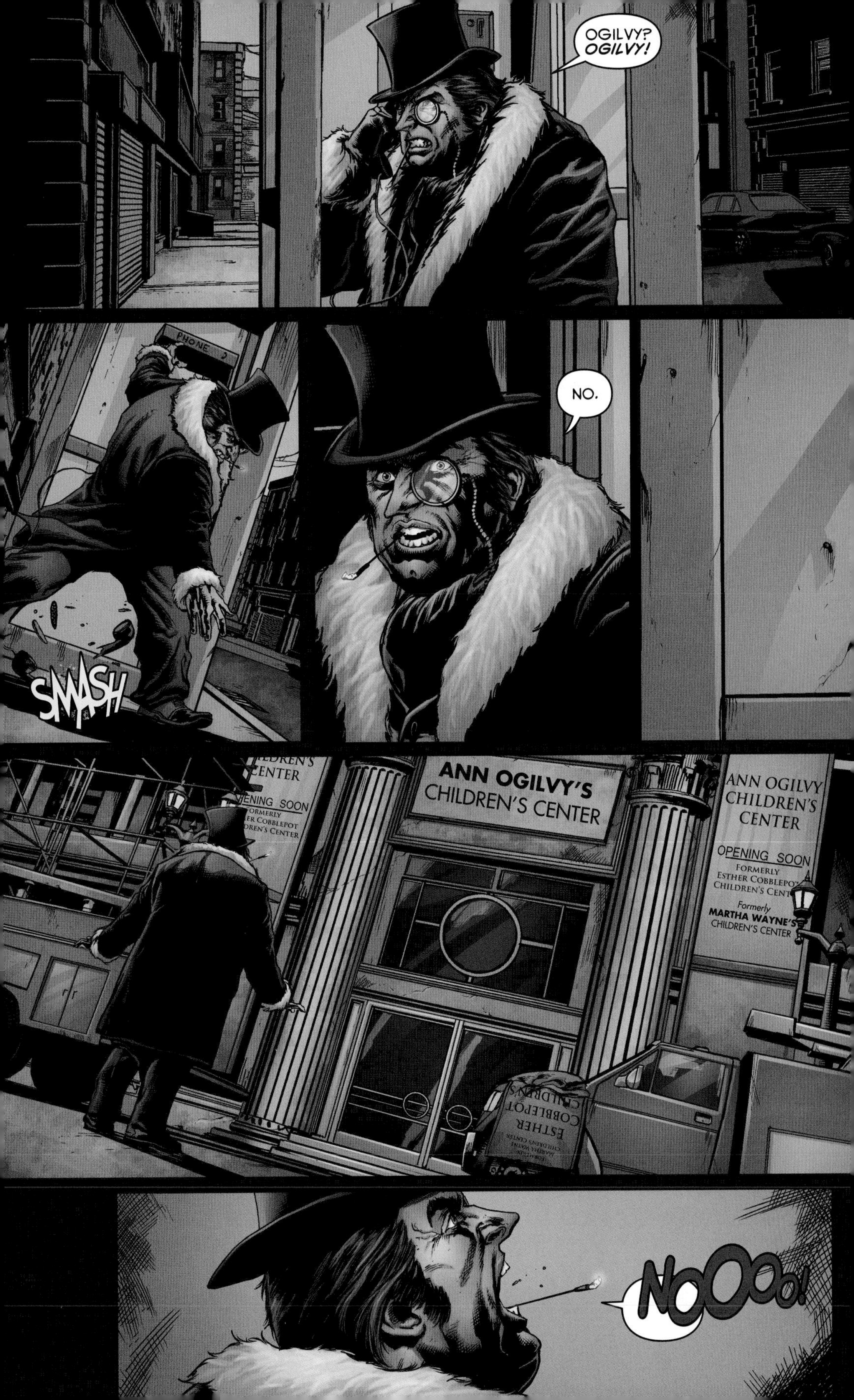
OGILVY? OGILVY!
PHONE
SMASH
NO.
ANN OGILVY'S CHILDREN'S CENTER
ANN OGILVY CHILDREN'S CENTER
OPENING SOON
Formerly
ESTHER COBBLEPOT
Formerly
MARTHA WAYNE'S
CHILDREN'S CENTER
NOOOO!

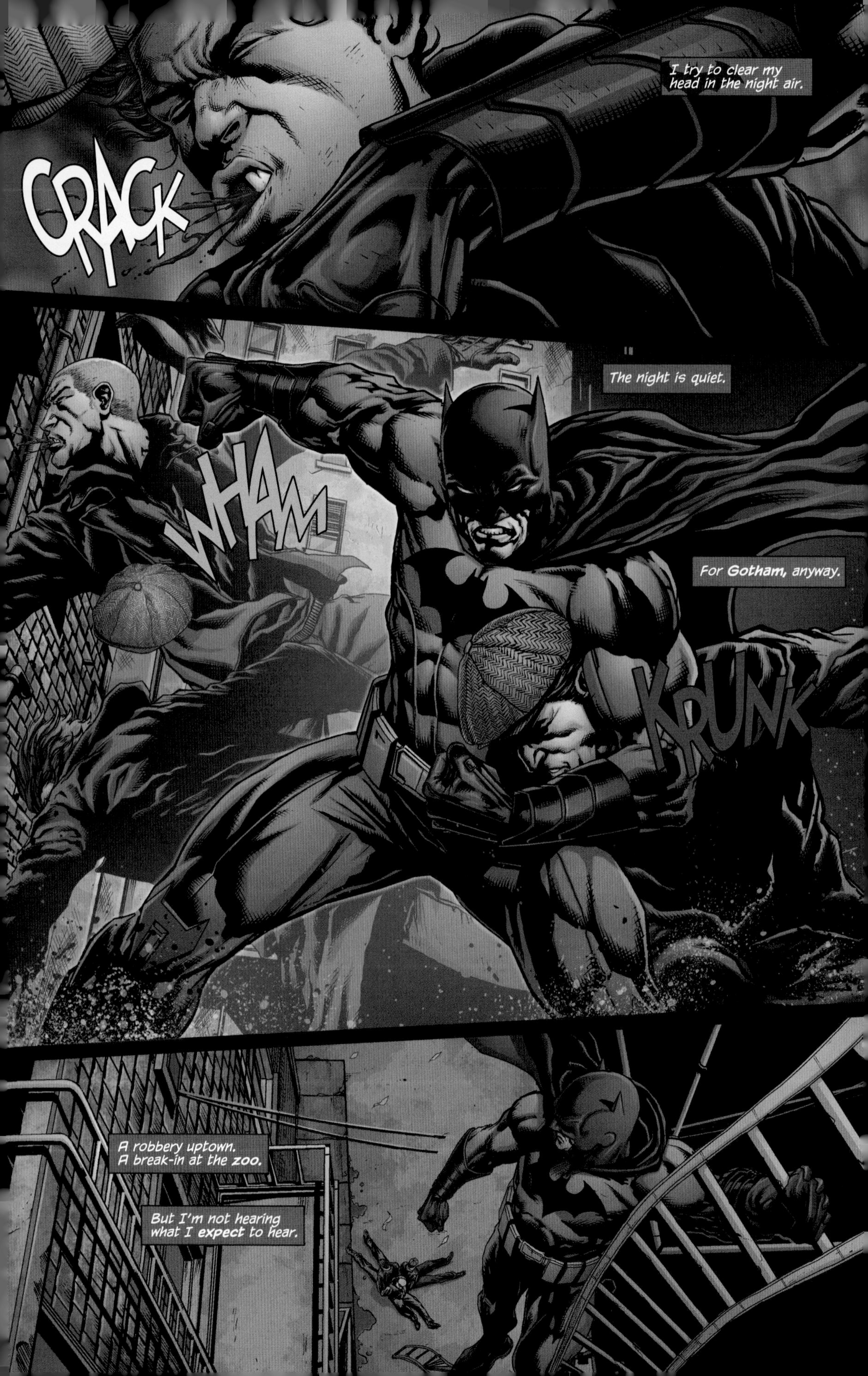

I try to clear my head in the night air.
CRACK
The night is quiet.
WHAM
For Gotham, anyway.
KRUNK
A robbery uptown. A break-in at the zoo.
But I'm not hearing what I expect to hear.

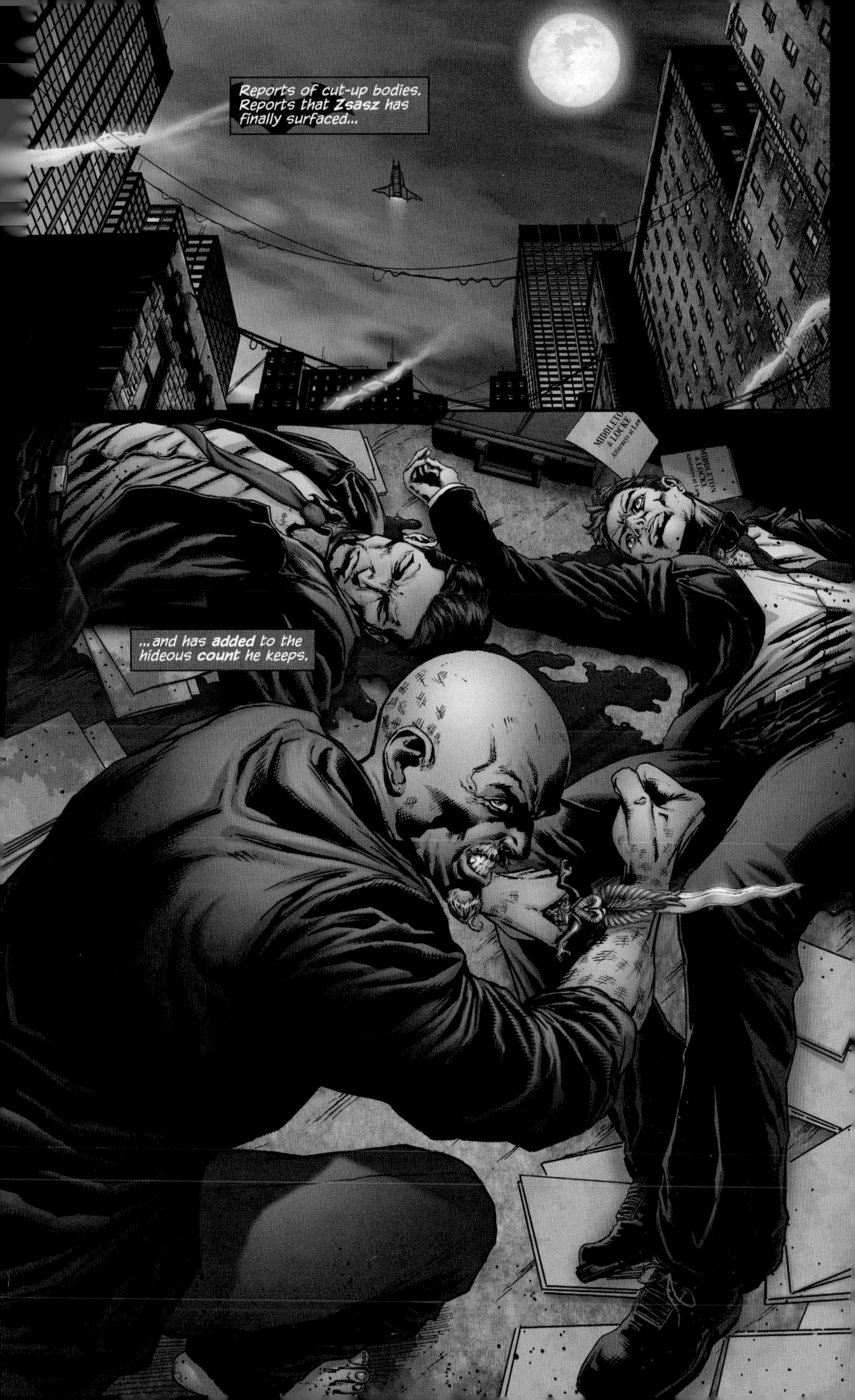
Reports of cut-up bodies. Reports that **Zsasz** has finally surfaced...
MIDDLETON & LOCKE Attorneys at Law
...and has **added** to the hideous **count** he keeps.

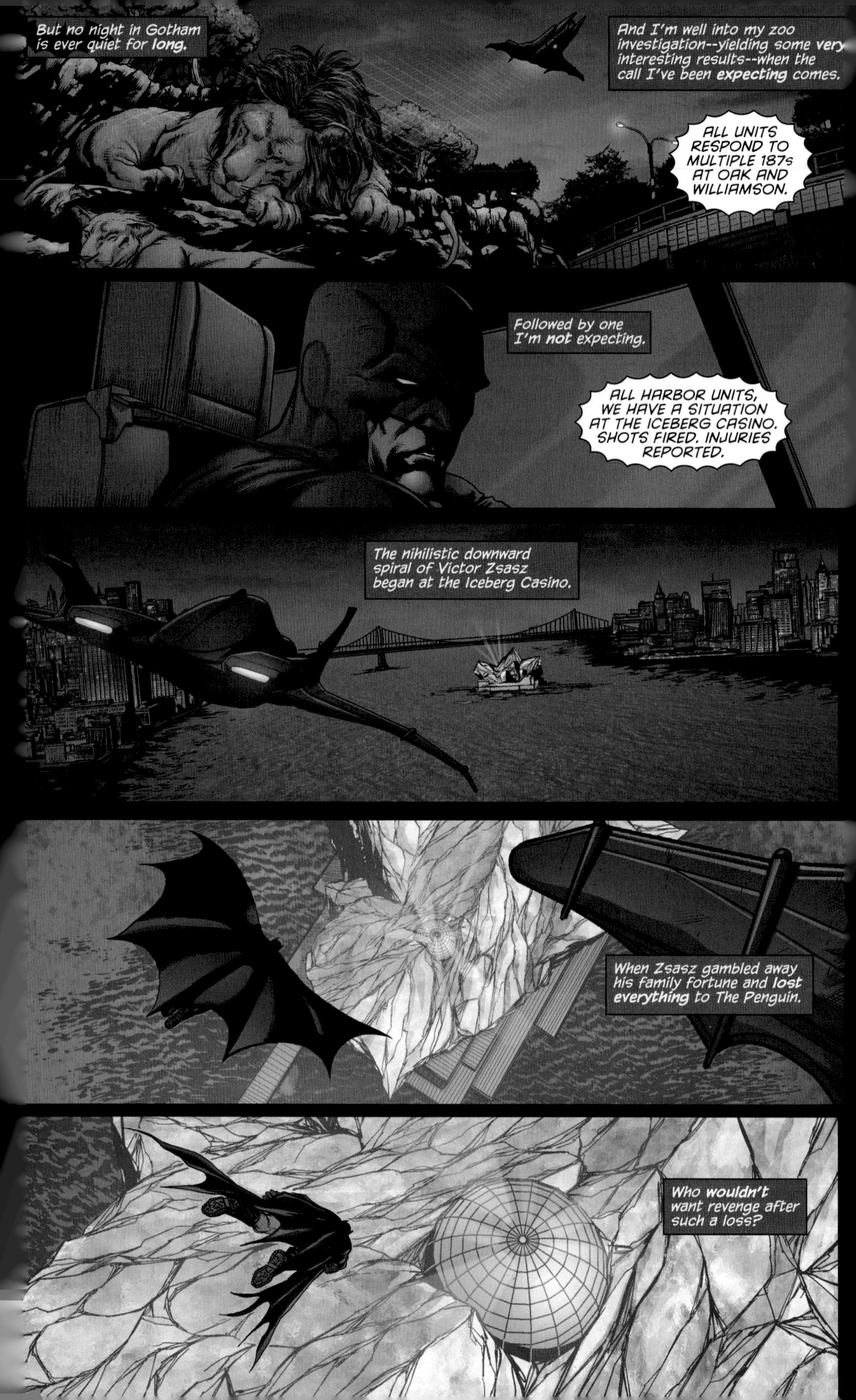
But no night in Gotham is ever quiet for long.
And I'm well into my zoo investigation--yielding some very interesting results--when the call I've been expecting comes.
ALL UNITS RESPOND TO MULTIPLE 187s AT OAK AND WILLIAMSON.
Followed by one I'm not expecting.
ALL HARBOR UNITS, WE HAVE A SITUATION AT THE ICEBERG CASINO. SHOTS FIRED. INJURIES REPORTED.
The nihilistic downward spiral of Victor Zsasz began at the Iceberg Casino.
When Zsasz gambled away his family fortune and lost everything to The Penguin.
Who wouldn't want revenge after such a loss?

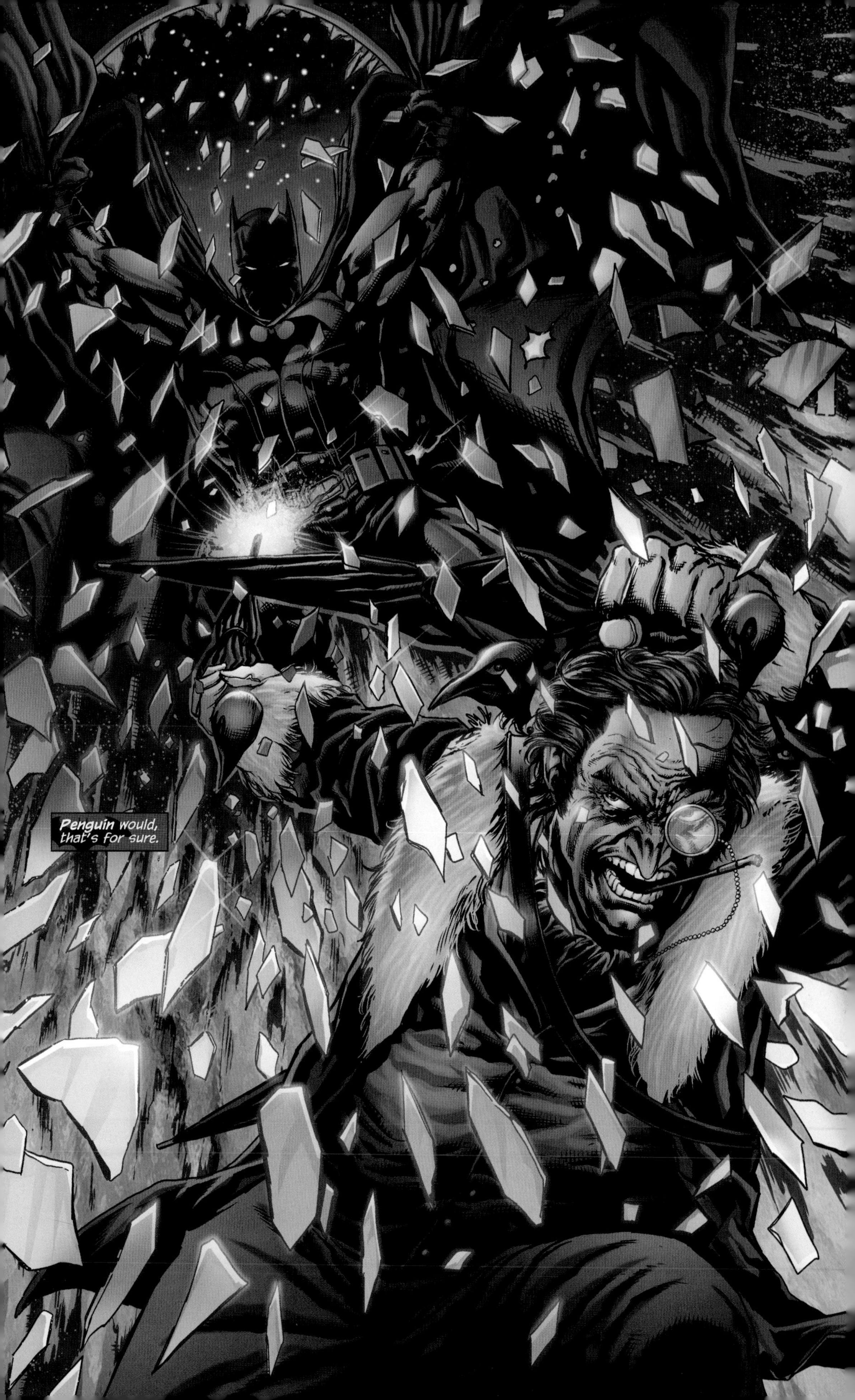
Penguin would, that's for sure.

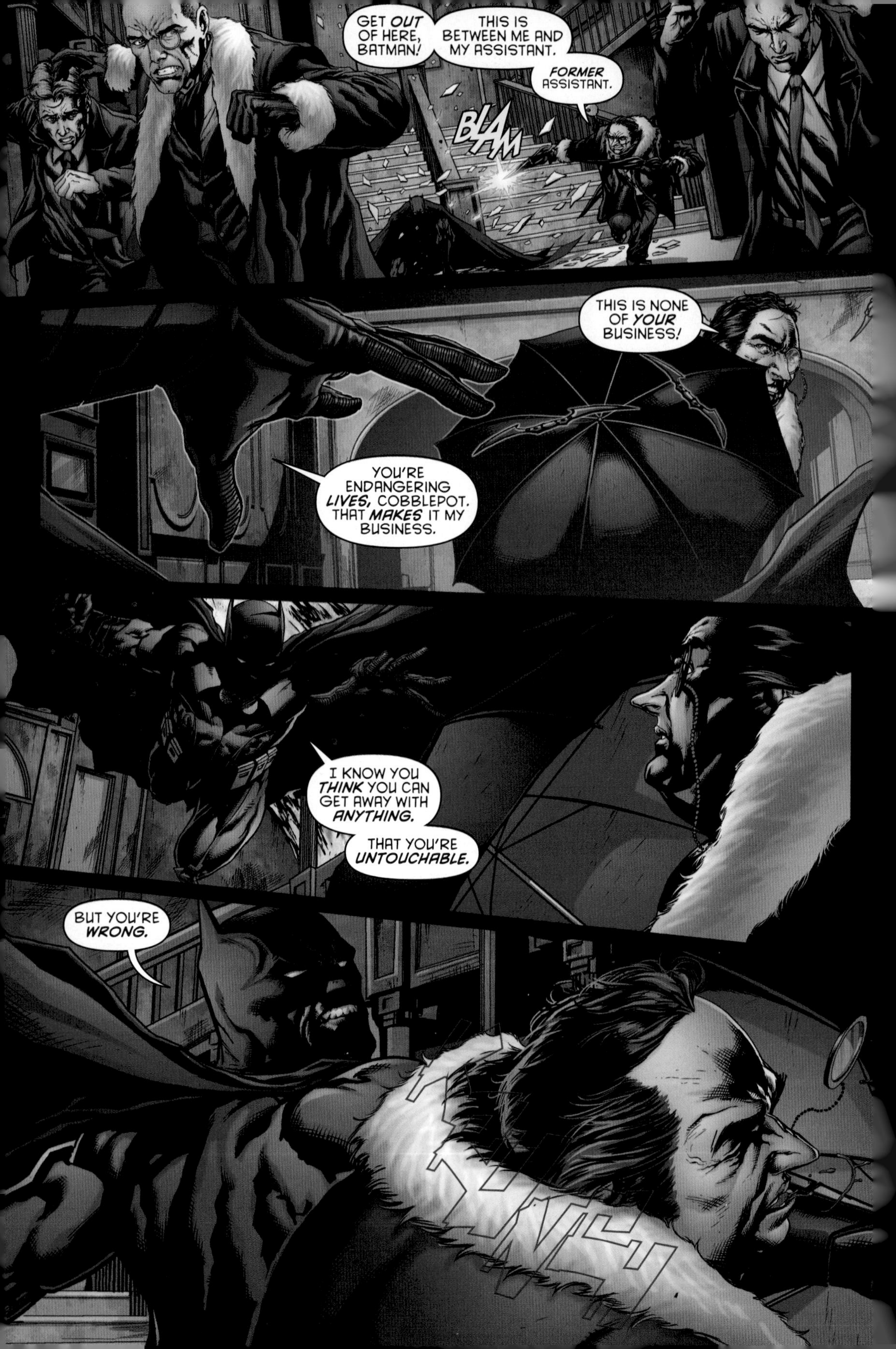
GET *OUT* OF HERE, BATMAN!
THIS IS BETWEEN ME AND MY ASSISTANT.
FORMER ASSISTANT.
BLAM
THIS IS NONE OF *YOUR* BUSINESS!
YOU'RE ENDANGERING *LIVES,* COBBLEPOT. THAT *MAKES* IT MY BUSINESS.
I KNOW YOU *THINK* YOU CAN GET AWAY WITH *ANYTHING.*
THAT YOU'RE *UNTOUCHABLE.*
BUT YOU'RE *WRONG.*

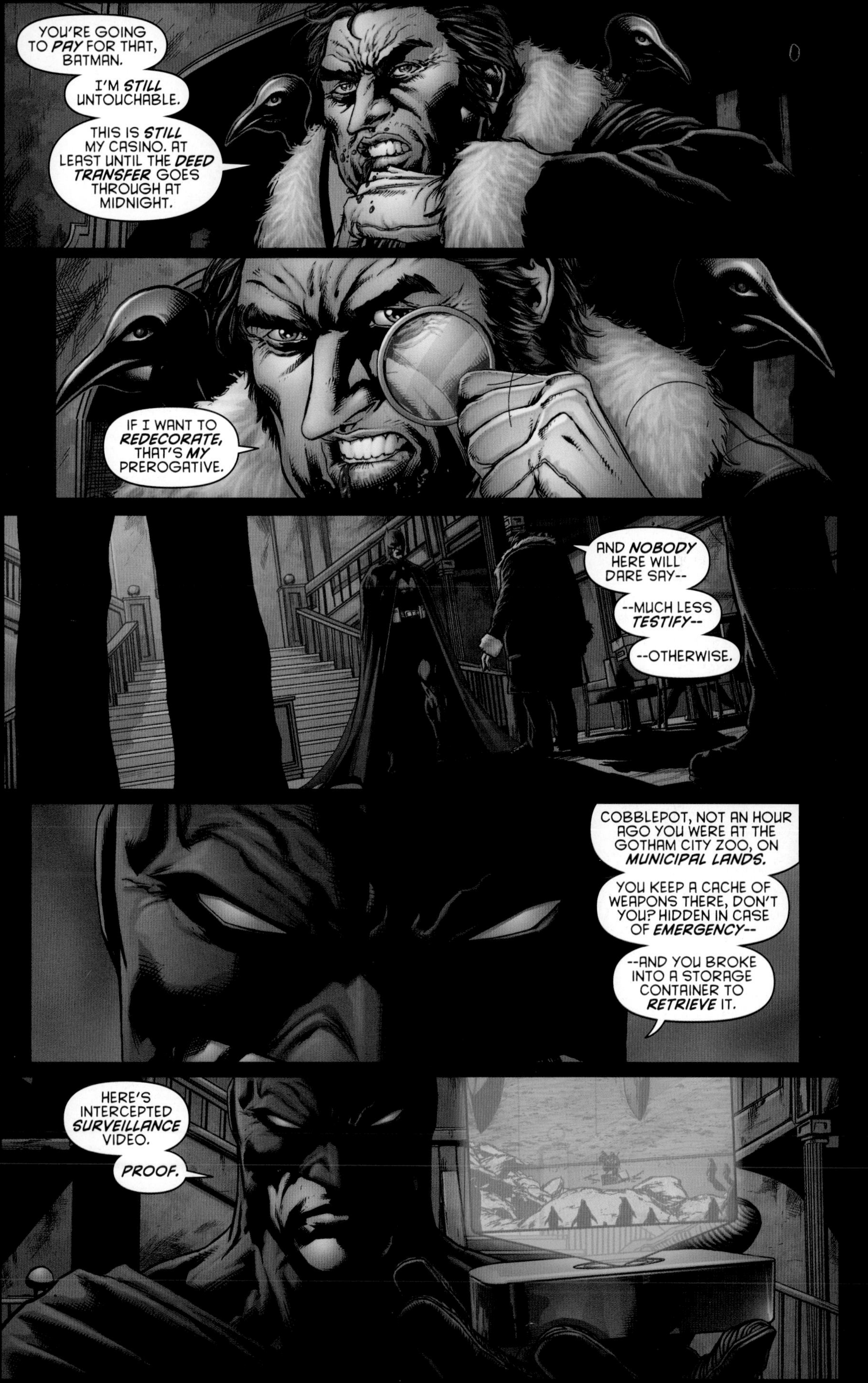
YOU'RE GOING TO *PAY* FOR THAT, BATMAN.
I'M *STILL* UNTOUCHABLE.
THIS IS *STILL* MY CASINO. AT LEAST UNTIL THE *DEED TRANSFER* GOES THROUGH AT MIDNIGHT.
IF I WANT TO *REDECORATE,* THAT'S *MY* PREROGATIVE.
AND *NOBODY* HERE WILL DARE SAY--
--MUCH LESS *TESTIFY*--
--OTHERWISE.
COBBLEPOT, NOT AN HOUR AGO YOU WERE AT THE GOTHAM CITY ZOO, ON *MUNICIPAL LANDS.*
YOU KEEP A CACHE OF WEAPONS THERE, DON'T YOU? HIDDEN IN CASE OF *EMERGENCY*--
--AND YOU BROKE INTO A STORAGE CONTAINER TO *RETRIEVE* IT.
HERE'S INTERCEPTED *SURVEILLANCE* VIDEO.
PROOF.

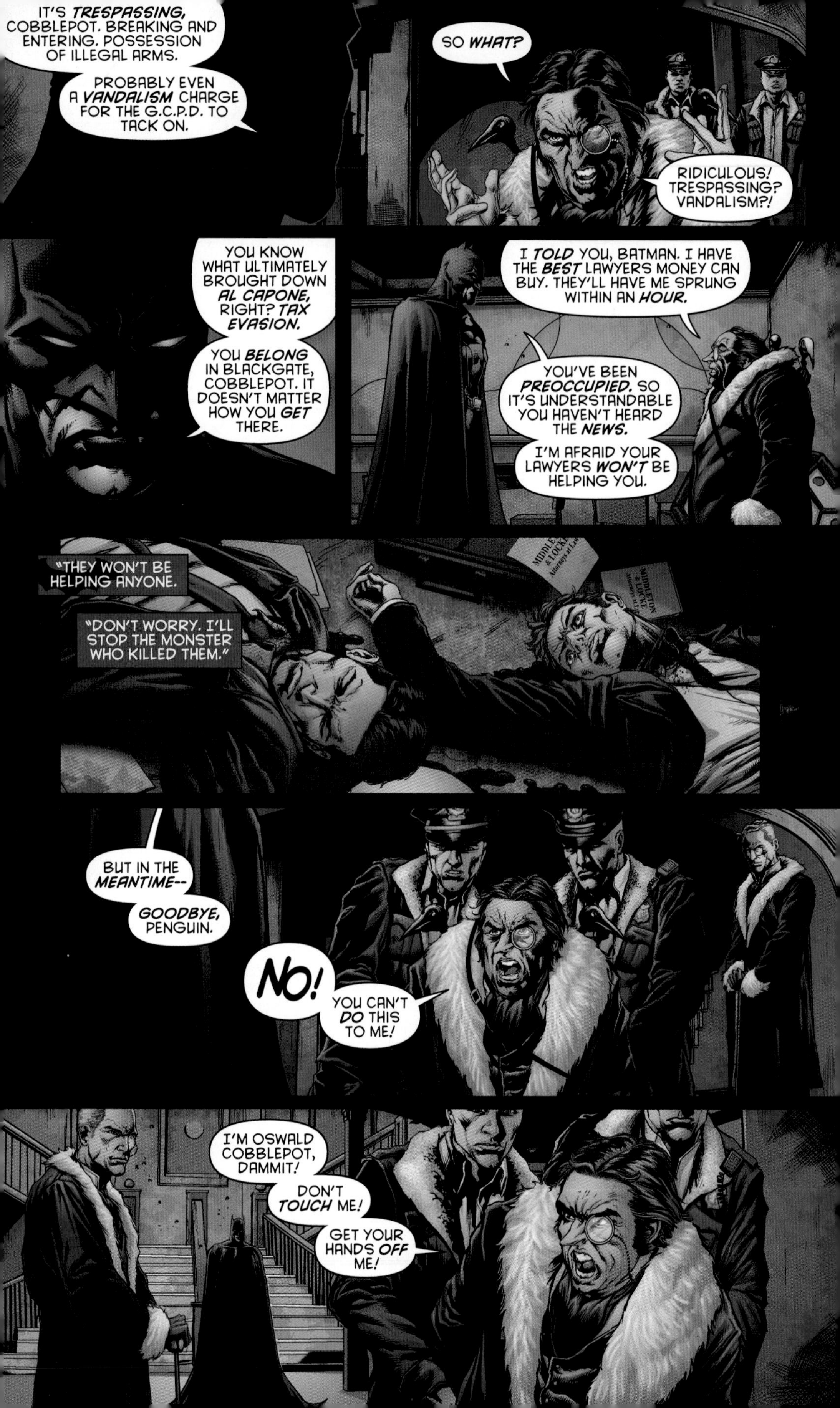
IT'S TRESPASSING, COBBLEPOT. BREAKING AND ENTERING. POSSESSION OF ILLEGAL ARMS.
PROBABLY EVEN A VANDALISM CHARGE FOR THE G.C.P.D. TO TACK ON.
SO WHAT?
RIDICULOUS! TRESPASSING? VANDALISM?!
YOU KNOW WHAT ULTIMATELY BROUGHT DOWN AL CAPONE, RIGHT? TAX EVASION.
YOU BELONG IN BLACKGATE, COBBLEPOT. IT DOESN'T MATTER HOW YOU GET THERE.
I TOLD YOU, BATMAN. I HAVE THE BEST LAWYERS MONEY CAN BUY. THEY'LL HAVE ME SPRUNG WITHIN AN HOUR.
YOU'VE BEEN PREOCCUPIED. SO IT'S UNDERSTANDABLE YOU HAVEN'T HEARD THE NEWS.
I'M AFRAID YOUR LAWYERS WON'T BE HELPING YOU.
"THEY WON'T BE HELPING ANYONE.
"DON'T WORRY. I'LL STOP THE MONSTER WHO KILLED THEM."
BUT IN THE MEANTIME--
GOODBYE, PENGUIN.
NO!
YOU CAN'T DO THIS TO ME!
I'M OSWALD COBBLEPOT, DAMMIT!
DON'T TOUCH ME!
GET YOUR HANDS OFF ME!

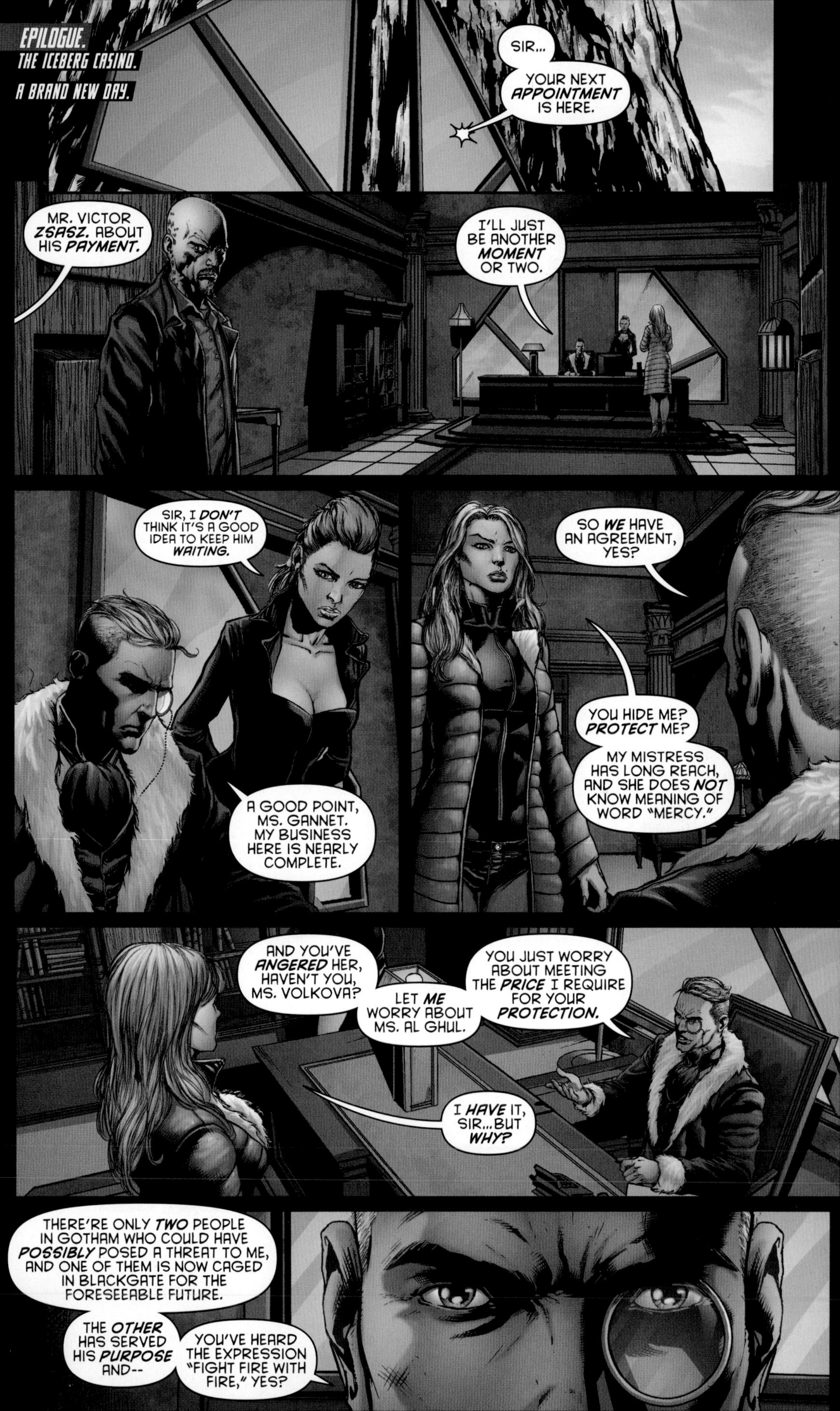
EPILOGUE.
THE ICEBERG CASINO.
A BRAND NEW DAY.
SIR...
YOUR NEXT APPOINTMENT IS HERE.
MR. VICTOR ZSASZ. ABOUT HIS PAYMENT.
I'LL JUST BE ANOTHER MOMENT OR TWO.
SIR, I DON'T THINK IT'S A GOOD IDEA TO KEEP HIM WAITING.
A GOOD POINT, MS. GANNET. MY BUSINESS HERE IS NEARLY COMPLETE.
SO WE HAVE AN AGREEMENT, YES?
YOU HIDE ME? PROTECT ME?
MY MISTRESS HAS LONG REACH, AND SHE DOES NOT KNOW MEANING OF WORD "MERCY."
AND YOU'VE ANGERED HER, HAVEN'T YOU, MS. VOLKOVA?
LET ME WORRY ABOUT MS. AL GHUL.
YOU JUST WORRY ABOUT MEETING THE PRICE I REQUIRE FOR YOUR PROTECTION.
I HAVE IT, SIR...BUT WHY?
THERE'RE ONLY TWO PEOPLE IN GOTHAM WHO COULD HAVE POSSIBLY POSED A THREAT TO ME, AND ONE OF THEM IS NOW CAGED IN BLACKGATE FOR THE FORESEEABLE FUTURE.
THE OTHER HAS SERVED HIS PURPOSE AND--
YOU'VE HEARD THE EXPRESSION "FIGHT FIRE WITH FIRE," YES?

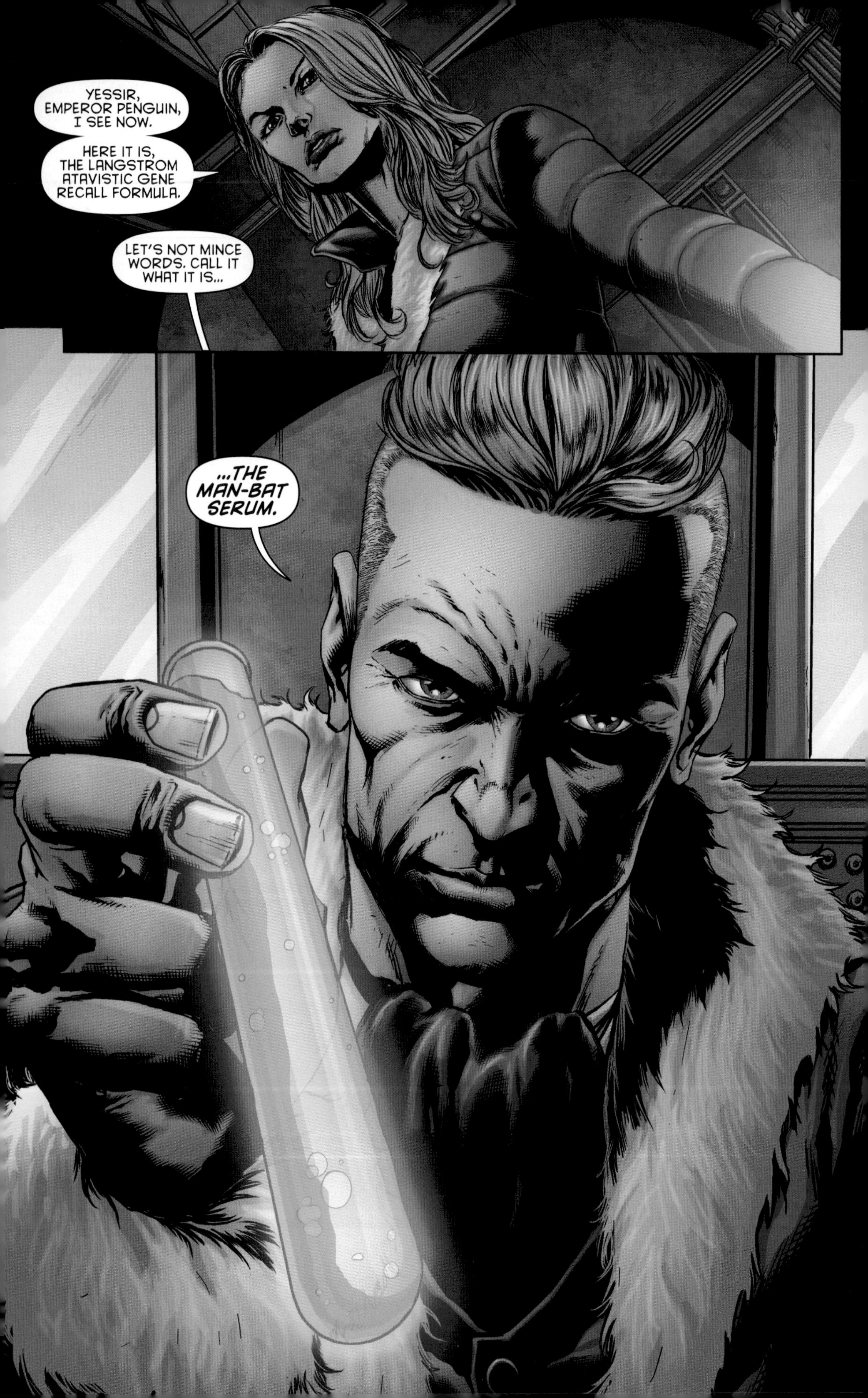
YESSIR, EMPEROR PENGUIN, I SEE NOW.
HERE IT IS, THE LANGSTROM ATAVISTIC GENE RECALL FORMULA.
LET'S NOT MINCE WORDS. CALL IT WHAT IT IS...
...THE MAN-BAT SERUM.

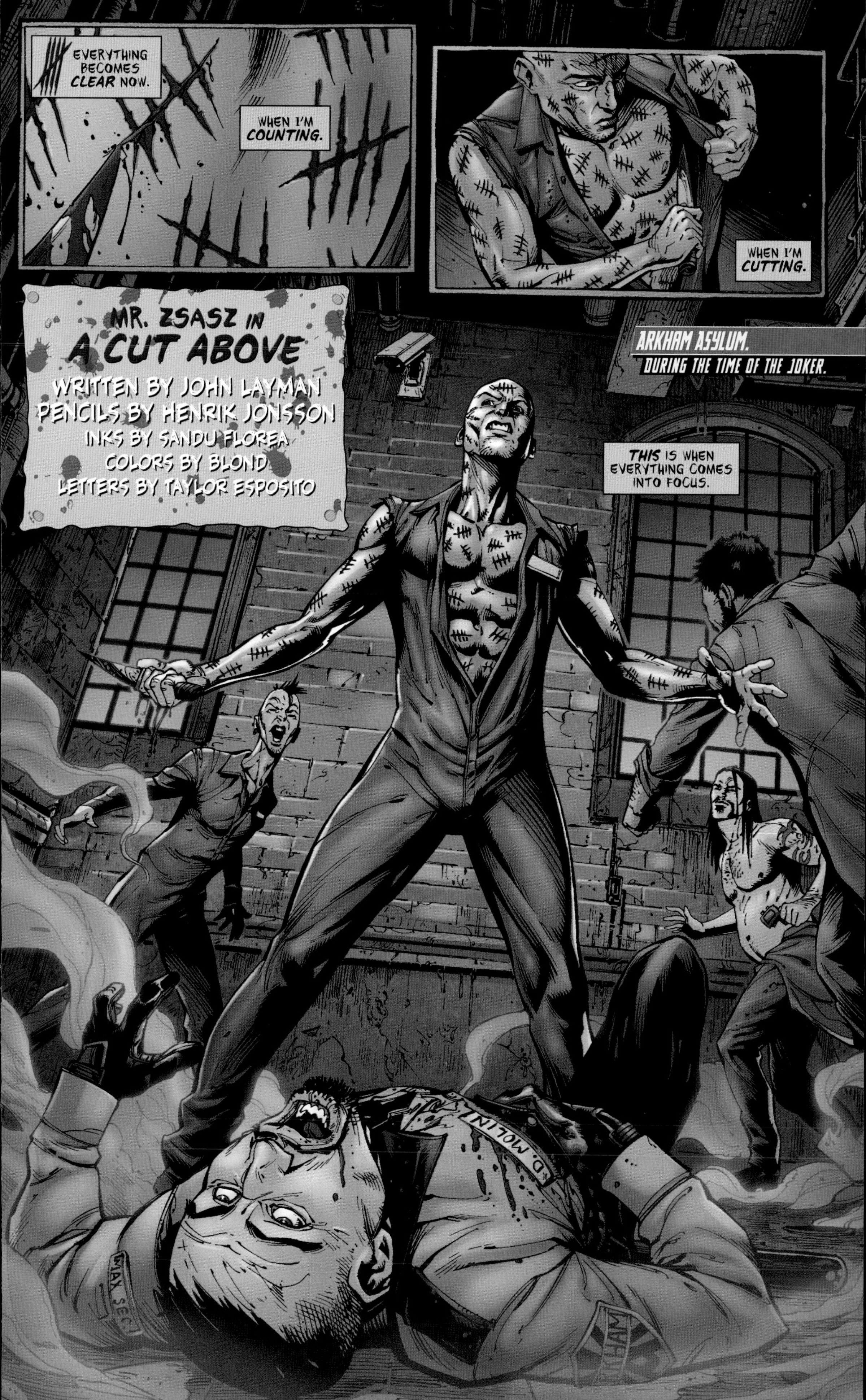
EVERYTHING BECOMES CLEAR NOW.
WHEN I'M COUNTING.
WHEN I'M CUTTING.
MR. ZSASZ IN
A CUT ABOVE
WRITTEN BY JOHN LAYMAN
PENCILS BY HENRIK JONSSON
INKS BY SANDU FLOREA
COLORS BY BLOND
LETTERS BY TAYLOR ESPOSITO
ARKHAM ASYLUM.
DURING THE TIME OF THE JOKER.
THIS IS WHEN EVERYTHING COMES INTO FOCUS.

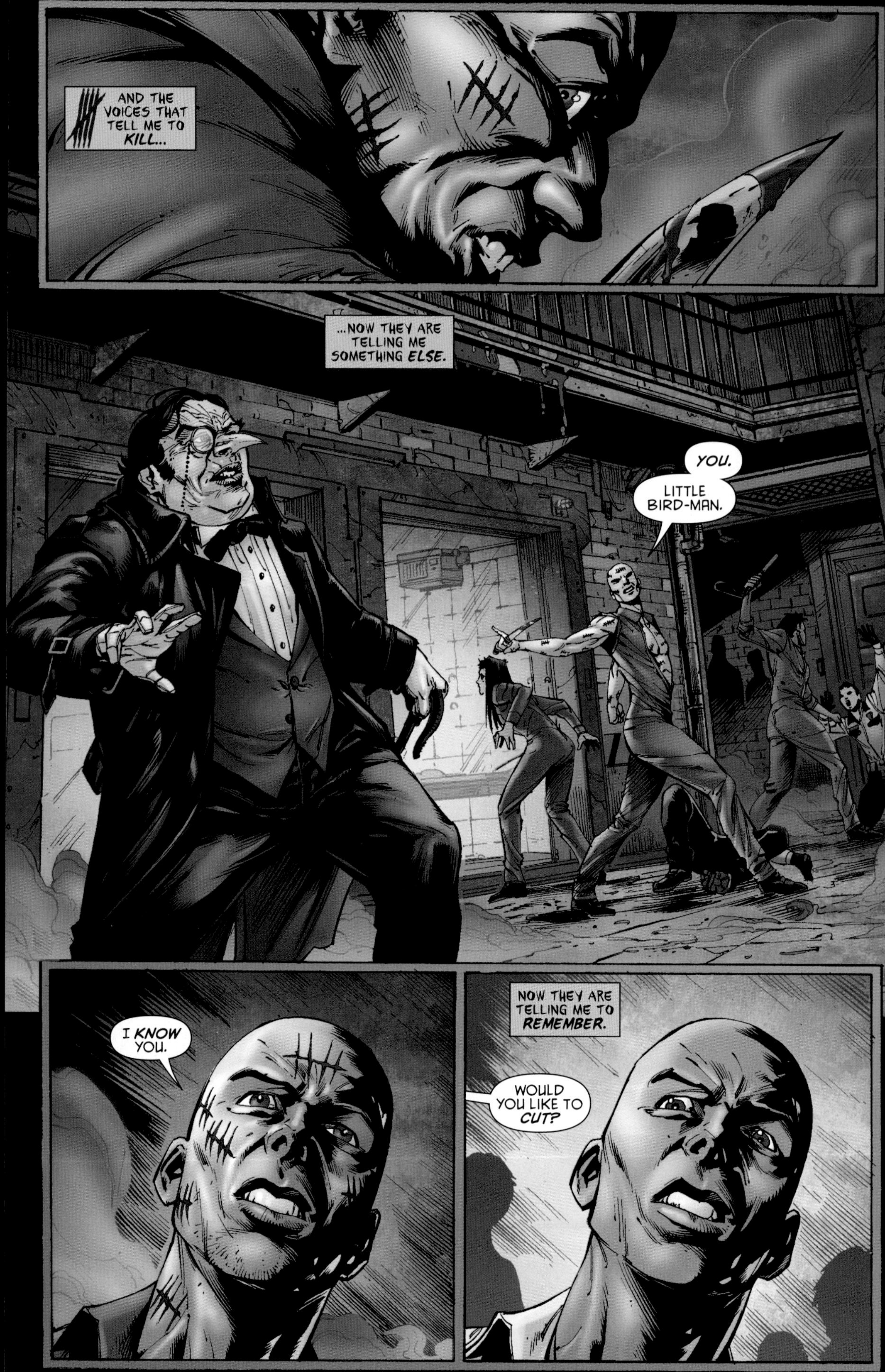
AND THE VOICES THAT TELL ME TO KILL...
...NOW THEY ARE TELLING ME SOMETHING ELSE.
YOU.
LITTLE BIRD-MAN.
I KNOW YOU.
NOW THEY ARE TELLING ME TO REMEMBER.
WOULD YOU LIKE TO CUT?

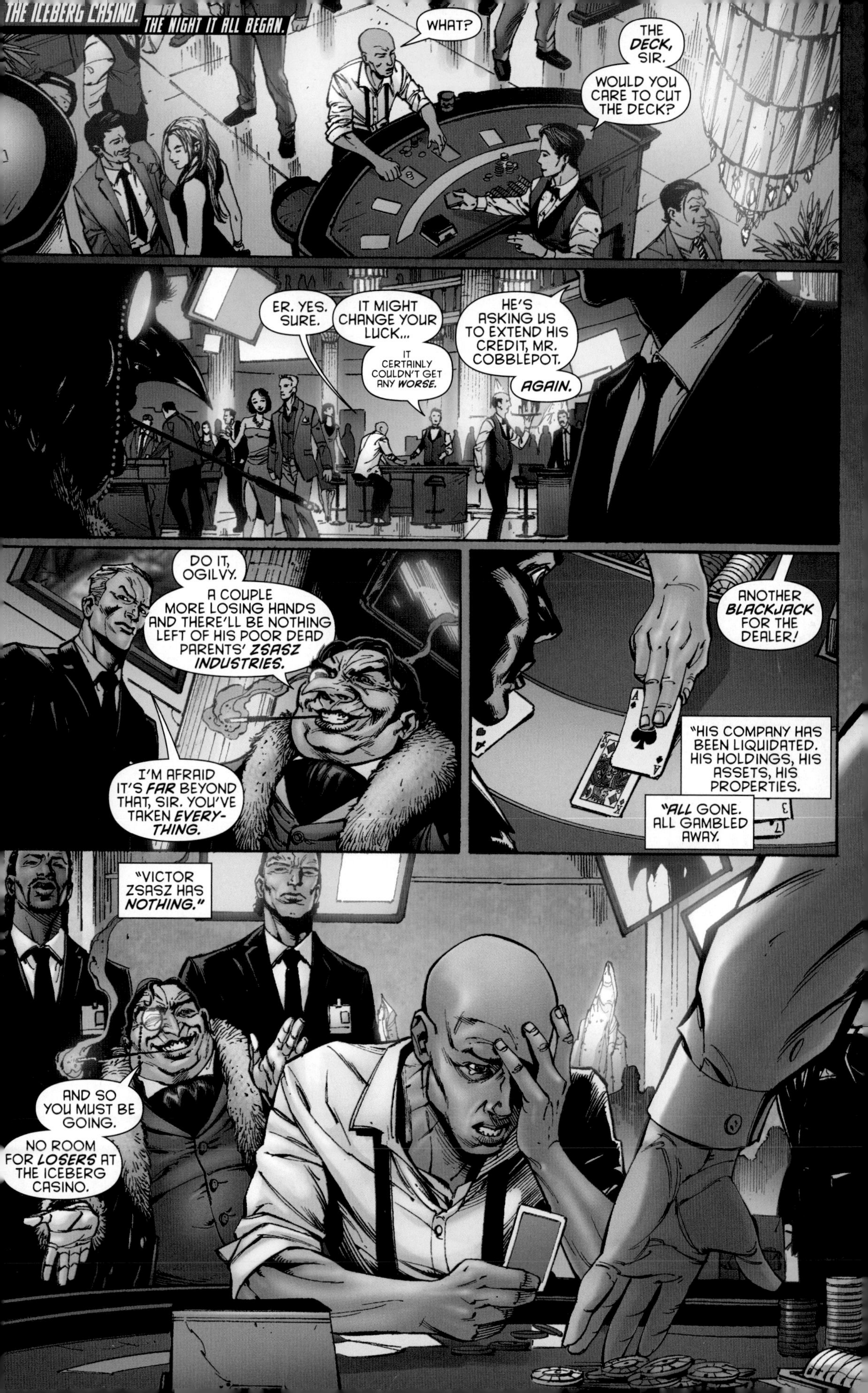
THE ICEBERG CASINO.
THE NIGHT IT ALL BEGAN.
WHAT?
THE DECK, SIR.
WOULD YOU CARE TO CUT THE DECK?
ER. YES. SURE.
IT MIGHT CHANGE YOUR LUCK...
IT CERTAINLY COULDN'T GET ANY WORSE.
HE'S ASKING US TO EXTEND HIS CREDIT, MR. COBBLEPOT.
AGAIN.
DO IT, OGILVY.
A COUPLE MORE LOSING HANDS AND THERE'LL BE NOTHING LEFT OF HIS POOR DEAD PARENTS' ZSASZ INDUSTRIES.
I'M AFRAID IT'S FAR BEYOND THAT, SIR. YOU'VE TAKEN EVERYTHING.
ANOTHER BLACKJACK FOR THE DEALER!
"HIS COMPANY HAS BEEN LIQUIDATED. HIS HOLDINGS, HIS ASSETS, HIS PROPERTIES.
"ALL GONE. ALL GAMBLED AWAY.
"VICTOR ZSASZ HAS NOTHING."
AND SO YOU MUST BE GOING.
NO ROOM FOR LOSERS AT THE ICEBERG CASINO.

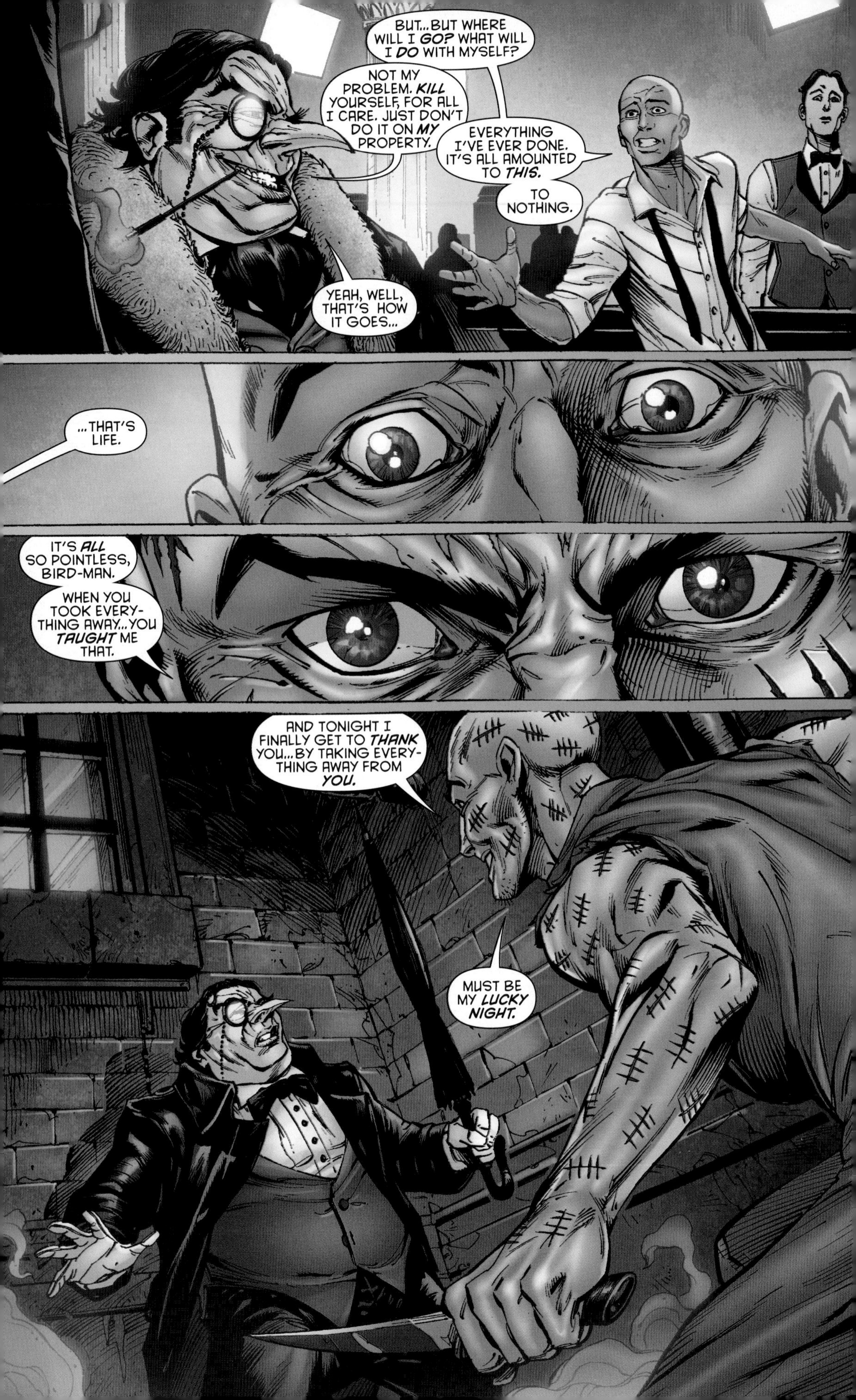
BUT...BUT WHERE WILL I GO? WHAT WILL I DO WITH MYSELF?
NOT MY PROBLEM. KILL YOURSELF, FOR ALL I CARE. JUST DON'T DO IT ON MY PROPERTY.
EVERYTHING I'VE EVER DONE. IT'S ALL AMOUNTED TO THIS.
TO NOTHING.
YEAH, WELL, THAT'S HOW IT GOES...
...THAT'S LIFE.
IT'S ALL SO POINTLESS, BIRD-MAN.
WHEN YOU TOOK EVERYTHING AWAY...YOU TAUGHT ME THAT.
AND TONIGHT I FINALLY GET TO THANK YOU...BY TAKING EVERYTHING AWAY FROM YOU.
MUST BE MY LUCKY NIGHT.

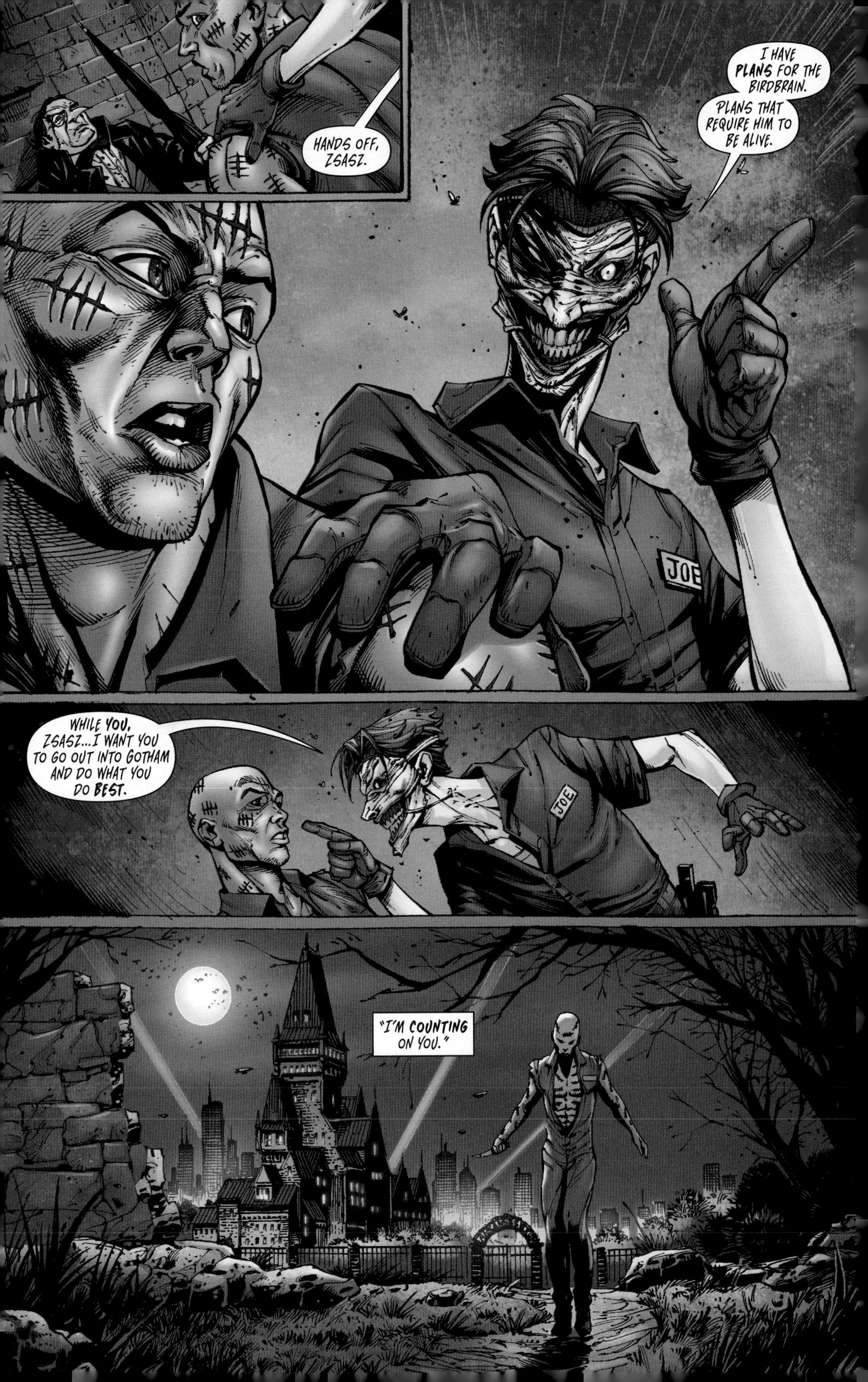
HANDS OFF, ZSASZ.
I HAVE PLANS FOR THE BIRDBRAIN.
PLANS THAT REQUIRE HIM TO BE ALIVE.
JOE
WHILE YOU, ZSASZ...I WANT YOU TO GO OUT INTO GOTHAM AND DO WHAT YOU DO BEST.
JOE
"I'M COUNTING ON YOU."

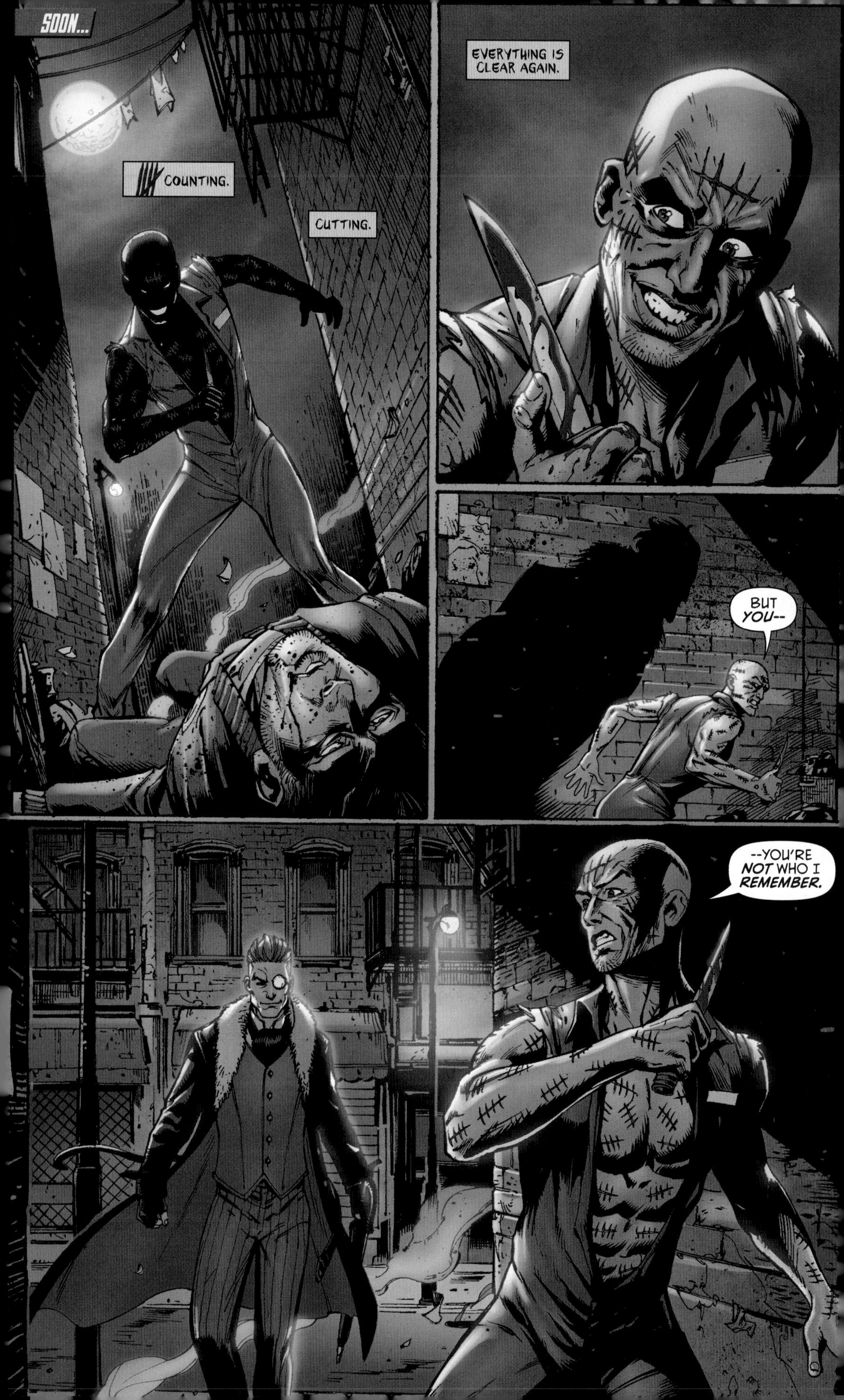
SOON...
COUNTING.
CUTTING.
EVERYTHING IS CLEAR AGAIN.
BUT YOU--
--YOU'RE NOT WHO I REMEMBER.

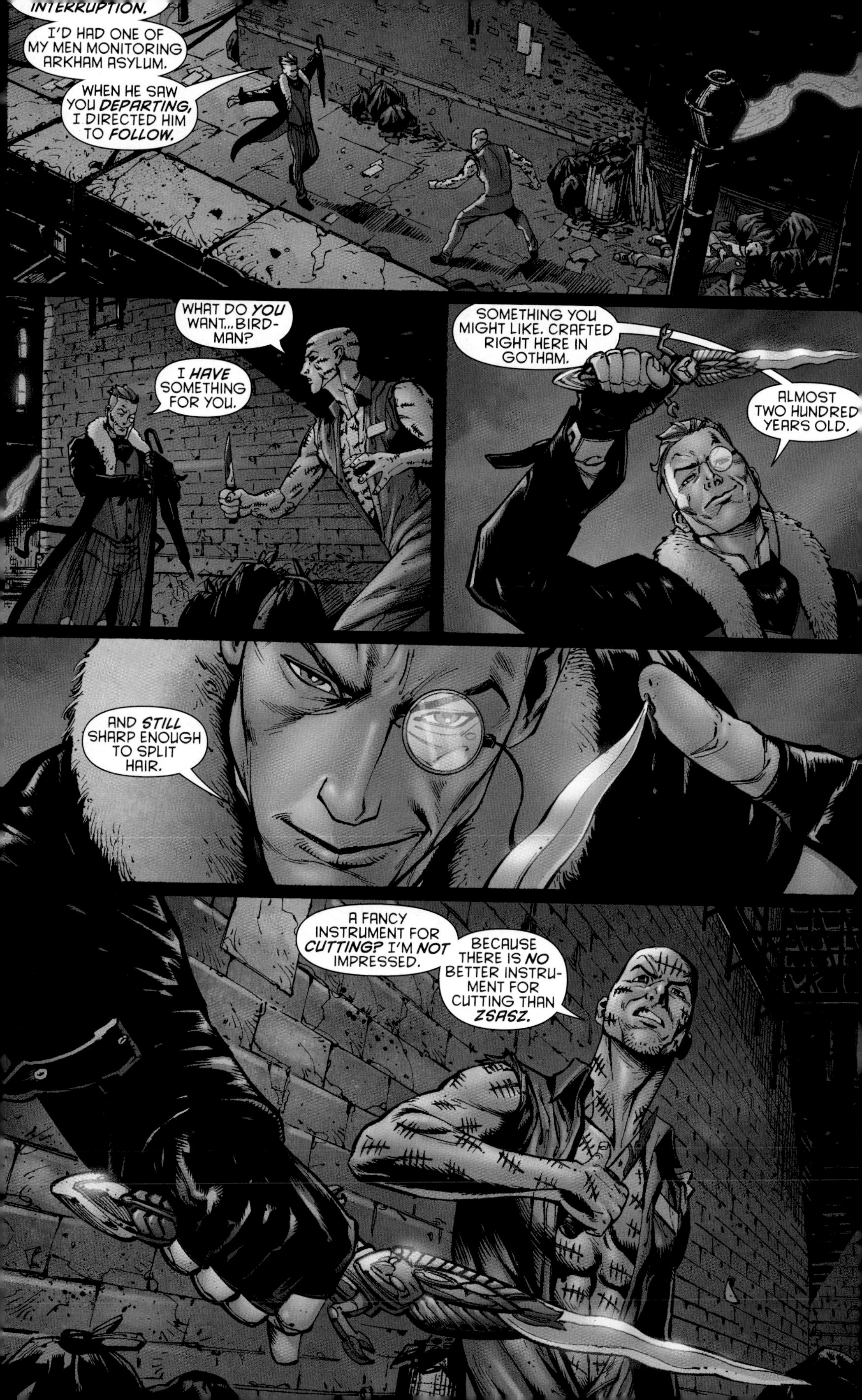
INTERRUPTION.
I'D HAD ONE OF MY MEN MONITORING ARKHAM ASYLUM.
WHEN HE SAW YOU DEPARTING, I DIRECTED HIM TO FOLLOW.
WHAT DO YOU WANT...BIRD-MAN?
I HAVE SOMETHING FOR YOU.
SOMETHING YOU MIGHT LIKE. CRAFTED RIGHT HERE IN GOTHAM.
ALMOST TWO HUNDRED YEARS OLD.
AND STILL SHARP ENOUGH TO SPLIT HAIR.
A FANCY INSTRUMENT FOR CUTTING? I'M NOT IMPRESSED.
BECAUSE THERE IS NO BETTER INSTRU-MENT FOR CUTTING THAN ZSASZ.

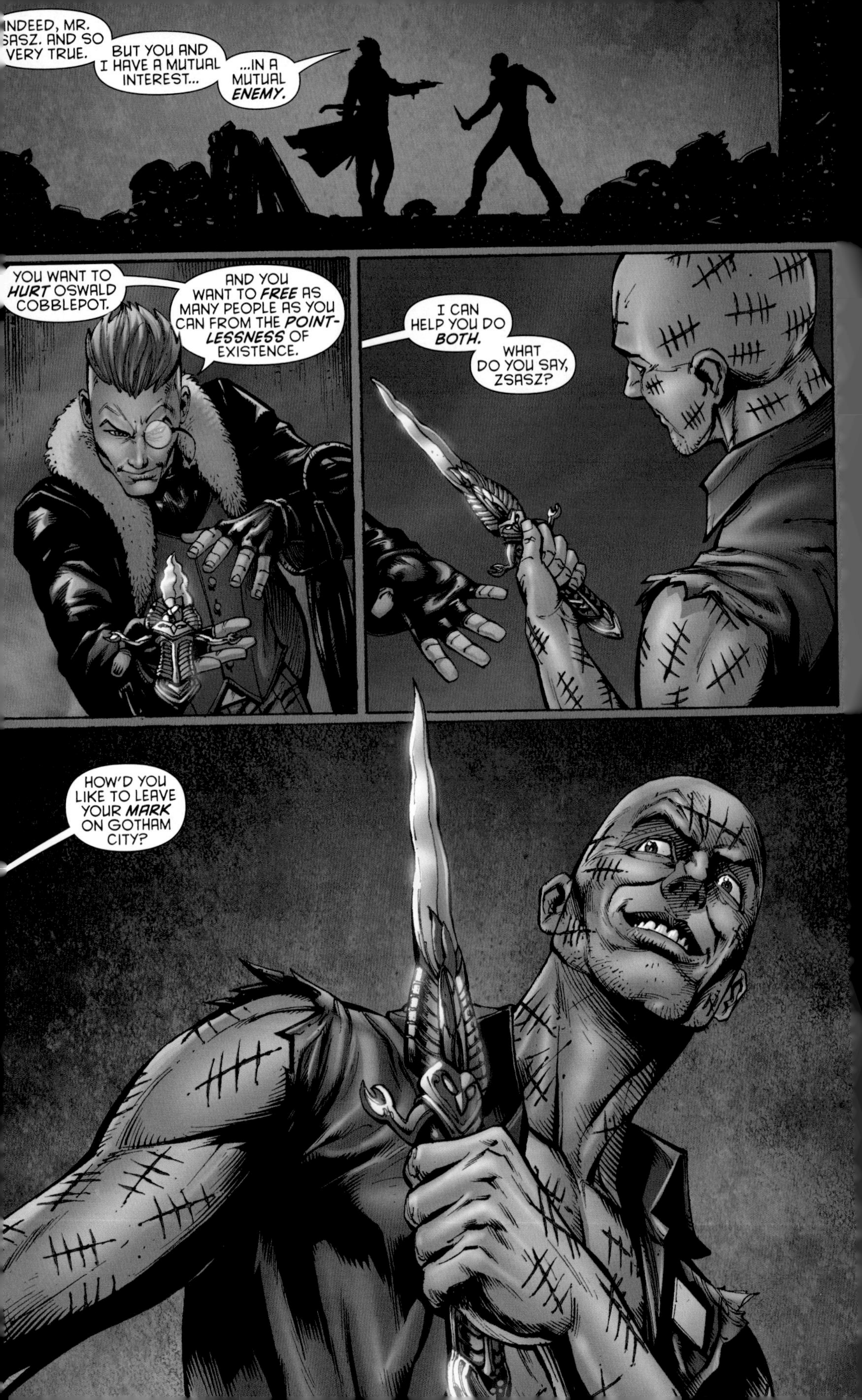
INDEED, MR. ZSASZ. AND SO VERY TRUE.
BUT YOU AND I HAVE A MUTUAL INTEREST...
...IN A MUTUAL ENEMY.
YOU WANT TO HURT OSWALD COBBLEPOT.
AND YOU WANT TO FREE AS MANY PEOPLE AS YOU CAN FROM THE POINTLESSNESS OF EXISTENCE.
I CAN HELP YOU DO BOTH.
WHAT DO YOU SAY, ZSASZ?
HOW'D YOU LIKE TO LEAVE YOUR MARK ON GOTHAM CITY?

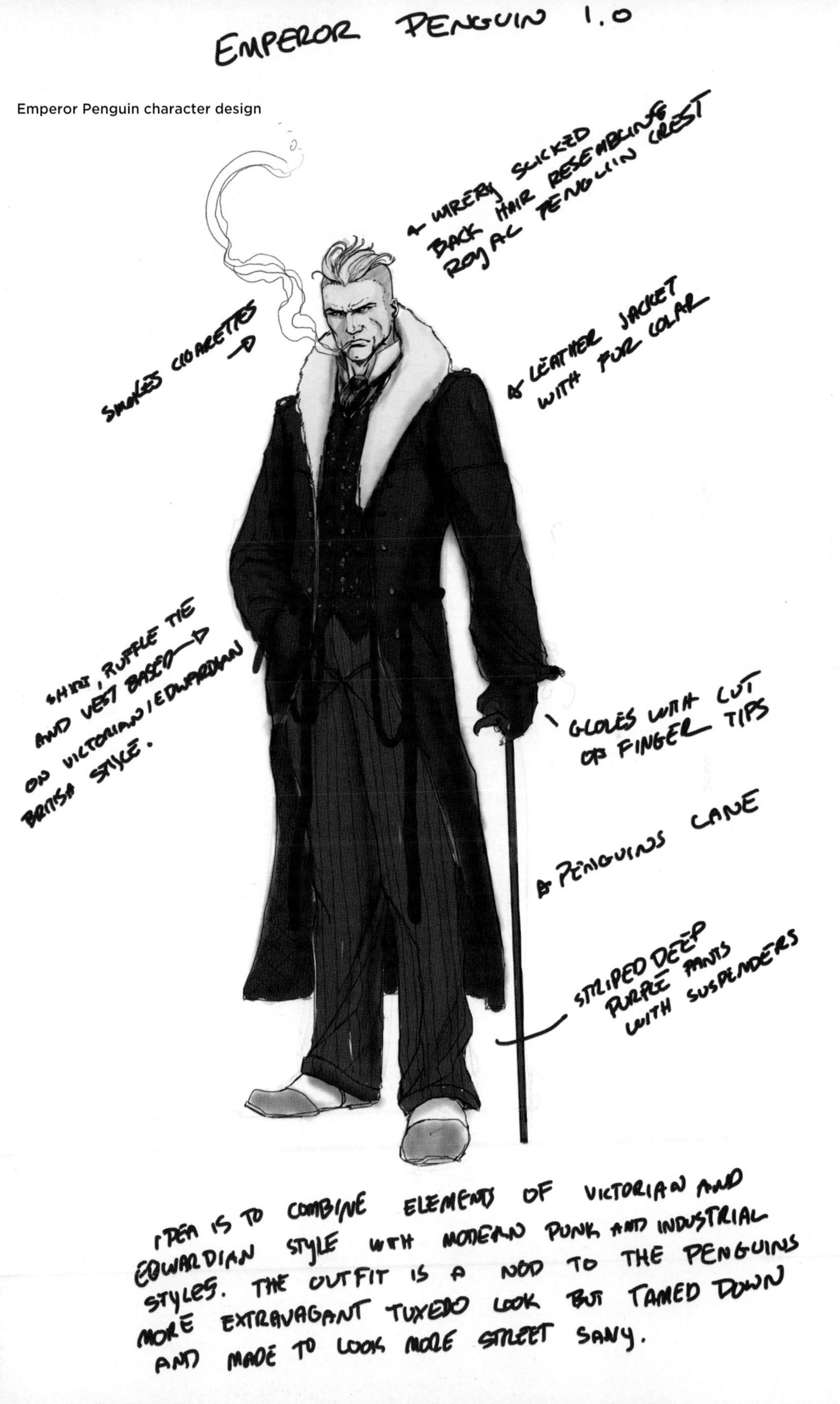
EMPEROR PENGUIN 1.0
A WIRERY SLICKED BACK HAIR RESEMBLING ROYAL PENGUIN CREST
SMOKES CIGARETTES
A LEATHER JACKET WITH FUR COLAR
SHIRT, RUFFLE TIE AND VEST BASED ON VICTORIAN/EDWARDIAN BRITISH STYLE.
GLOVES WITH CUT OF FINGER TIPS
A PENGUINS CANE
STRIPED DEEP PURPLE PANTS WITH SUSPENDERS
IDEA IS TO COMBINE ELEMENTS OF VICTORIAN AND EDWARDIAN STYLE WITH MODERN PUNK AND INDUSTRIAL STYLES. THE OUTFIT IS A NOD TO THE PENGUINS MORE EXTRAVAGANT TUXEDO LOOK BUT TAMED DOWN AND MADE TO LOOK MORE STREET SAVY.

Emperor Penguin character design

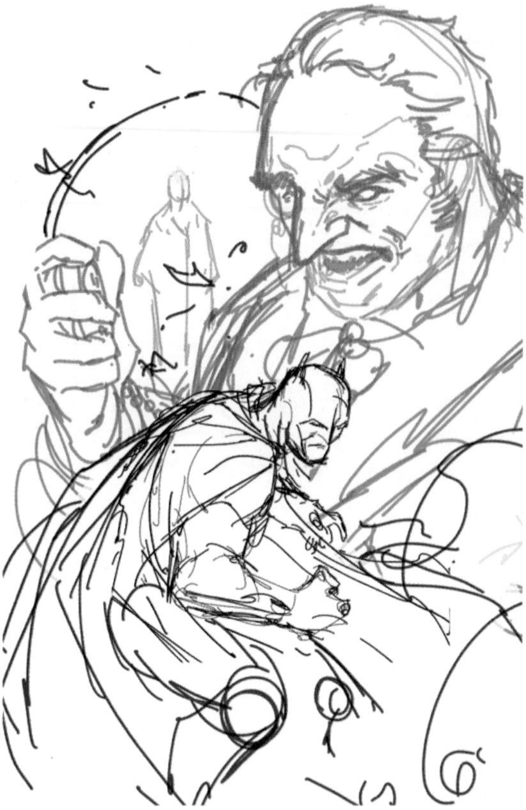

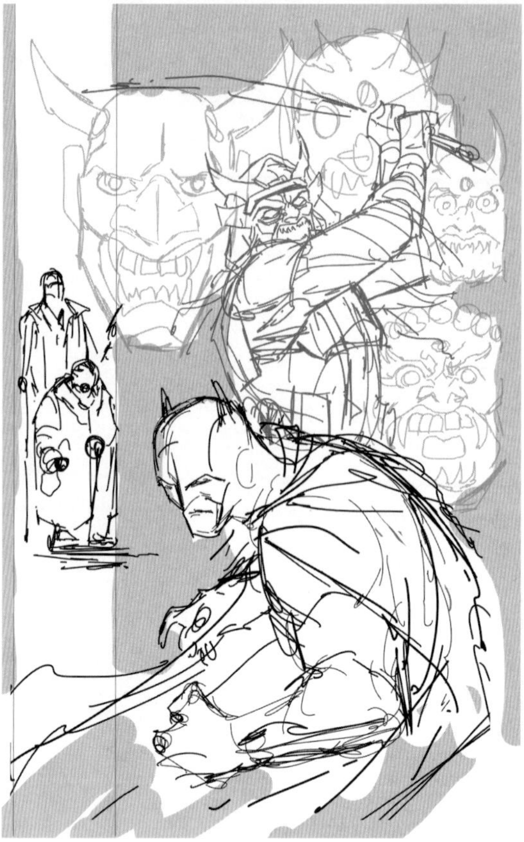

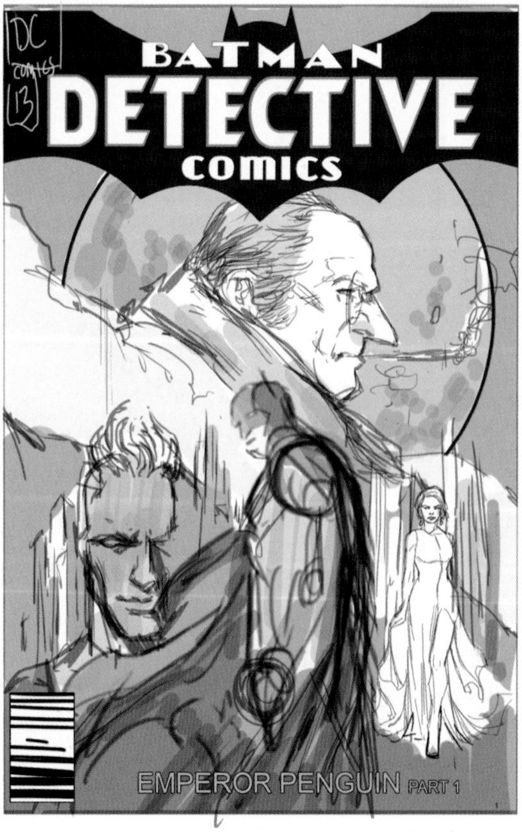
DC COMICS 13
BATMAN
DETECTIVE
COMICS
EMPEROR PENGUIN PART 1

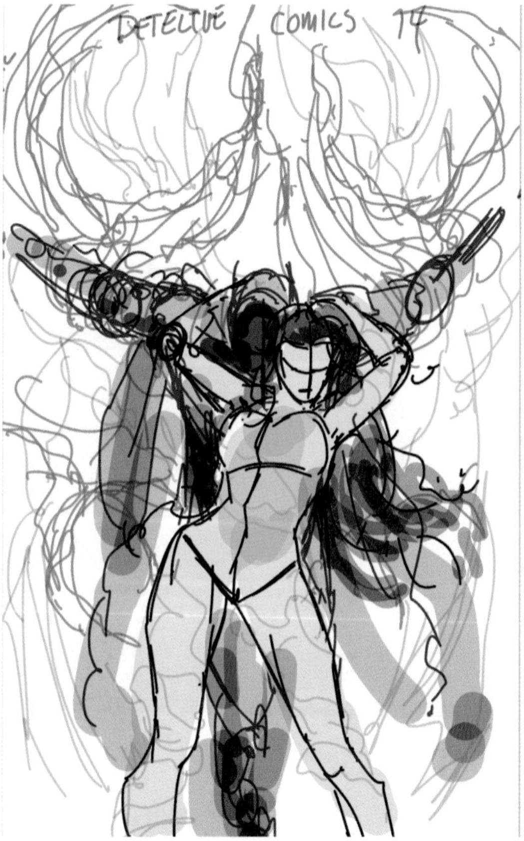
DETECTIVE COMICS 14

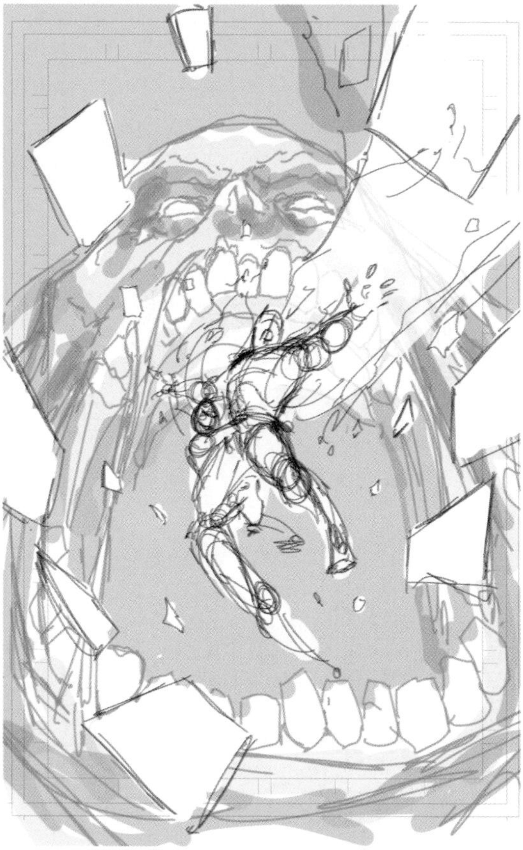
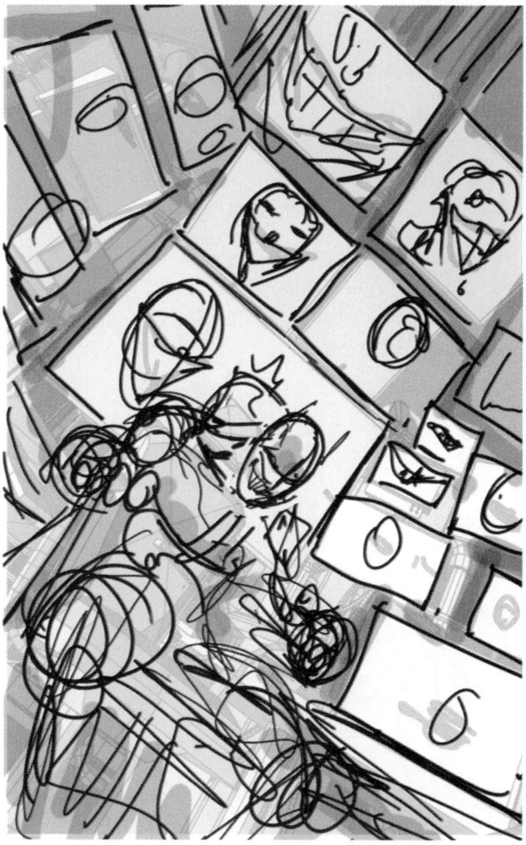
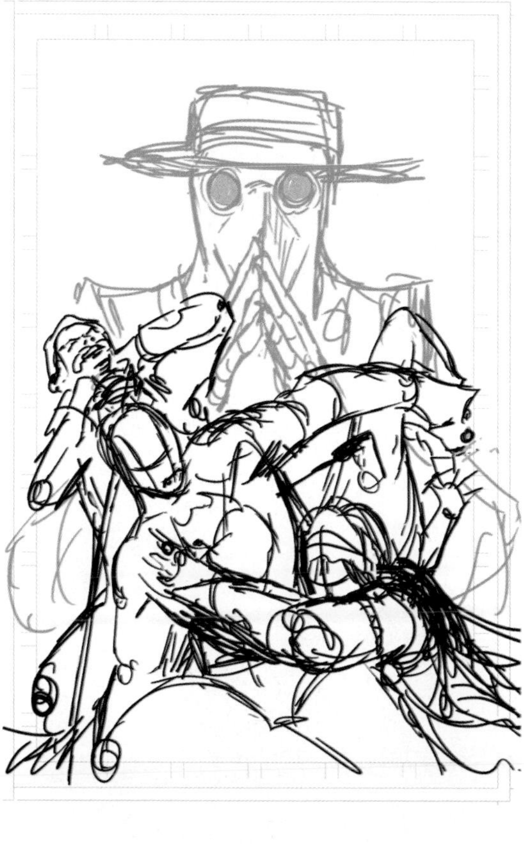
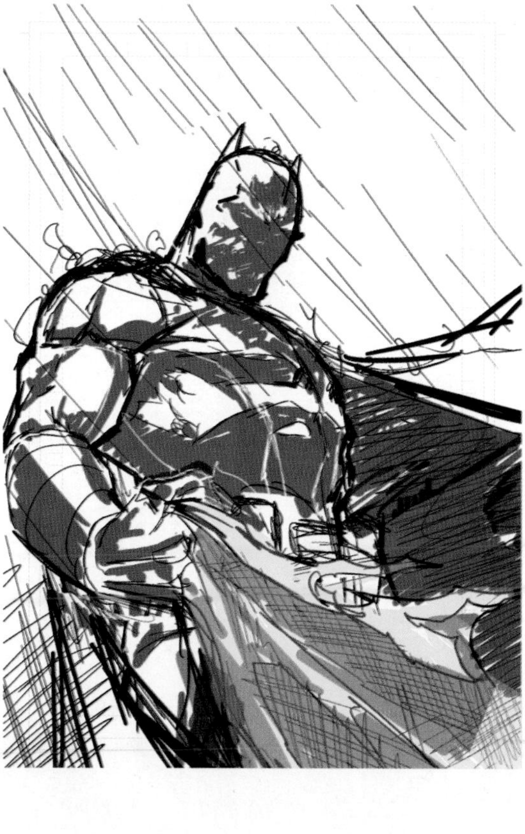

Issue #13 unused cover

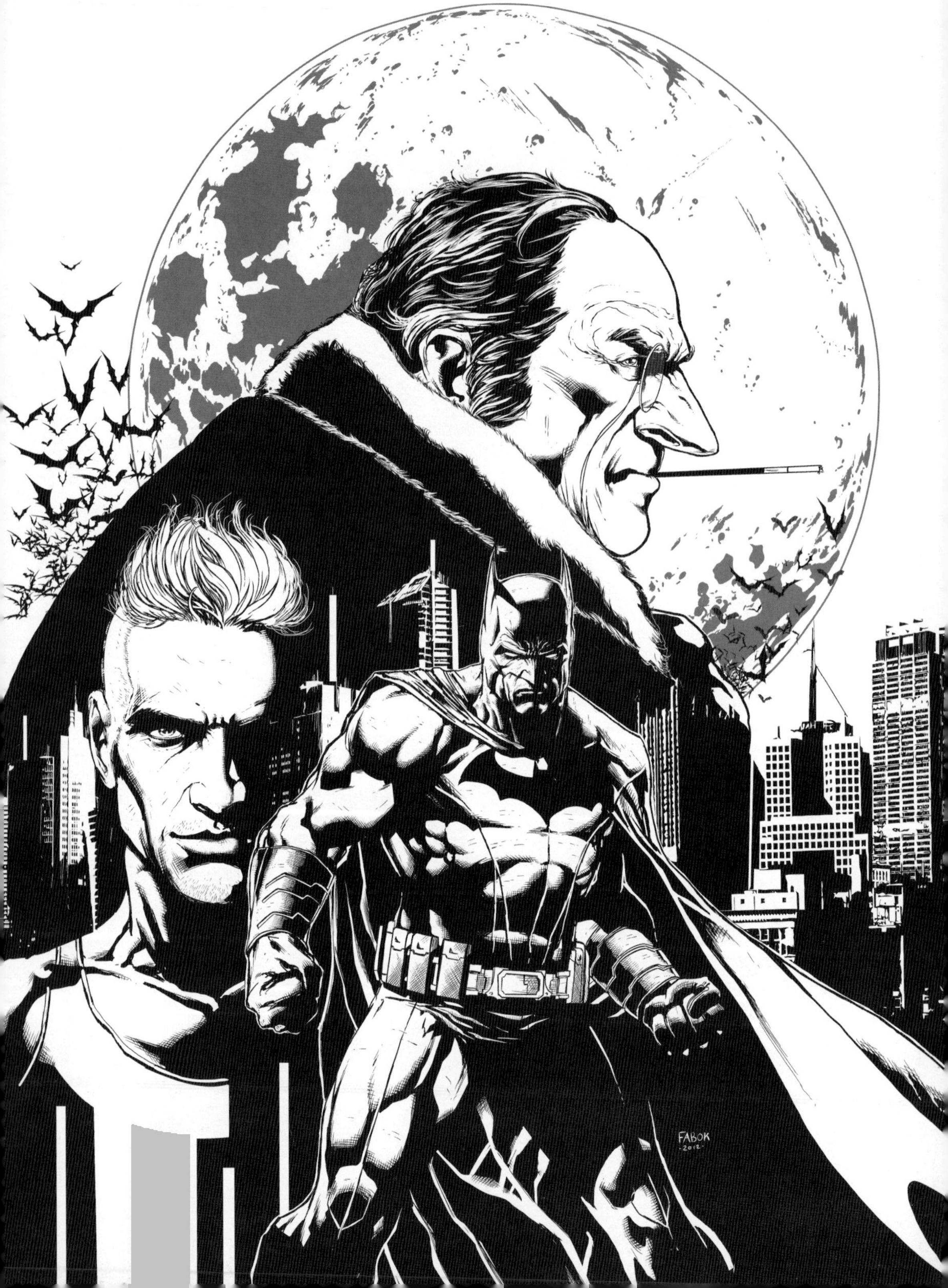
FABOK
·2012·

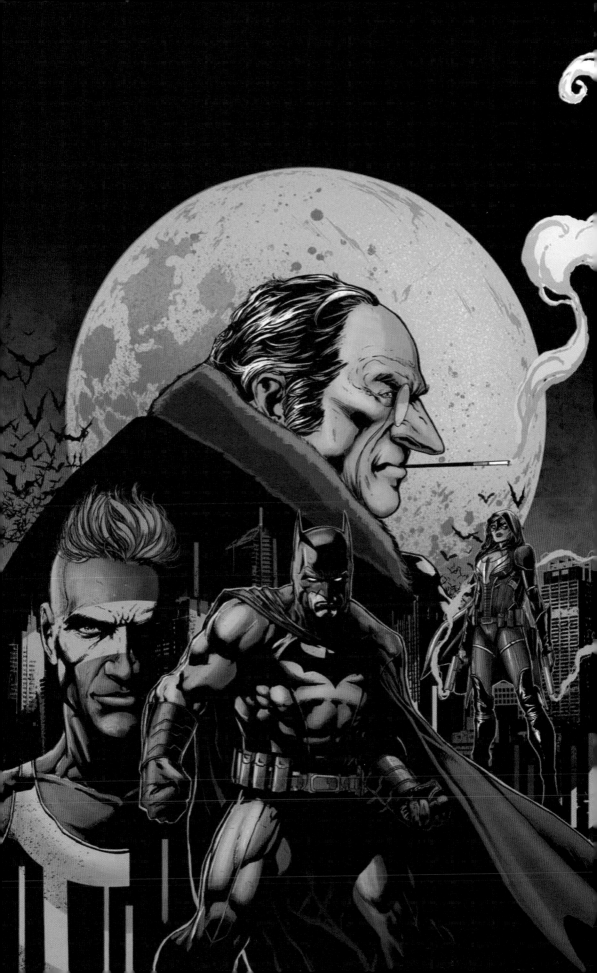

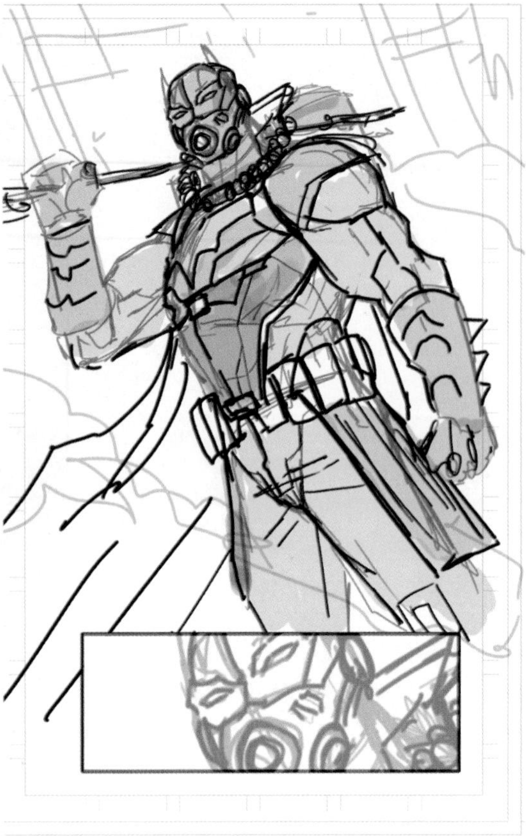

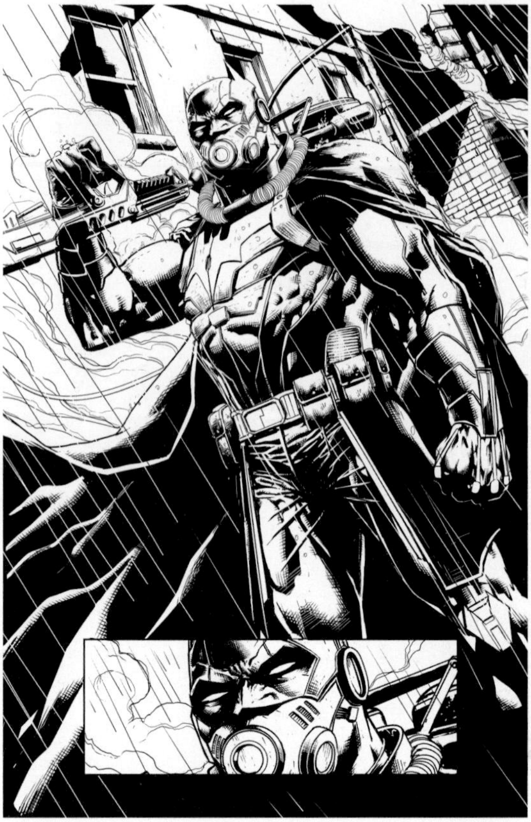

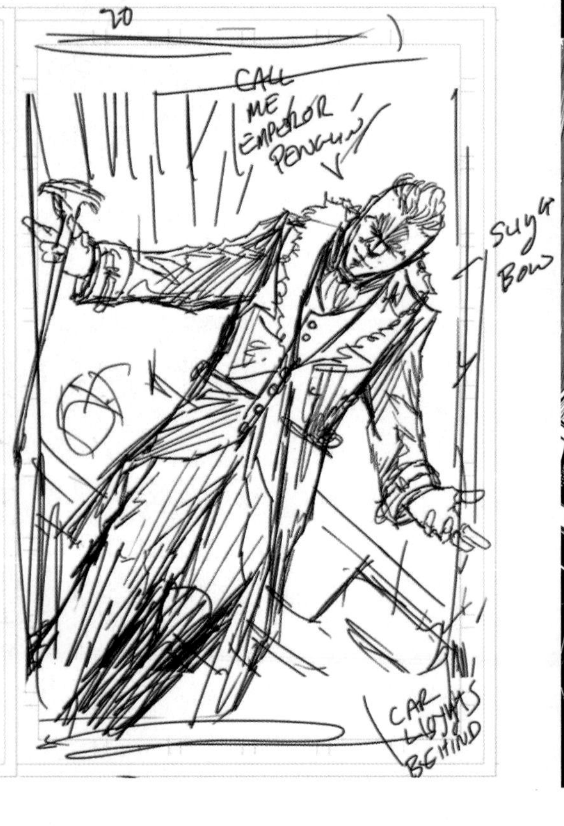

20
CALL ME EMPEROR PENGUIN
SLIGHT BOW
CAR LIGHTS BEHIND

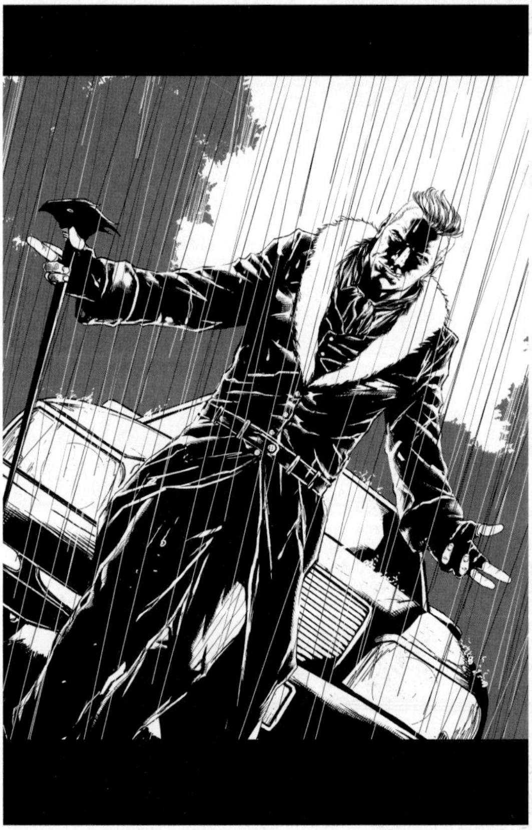

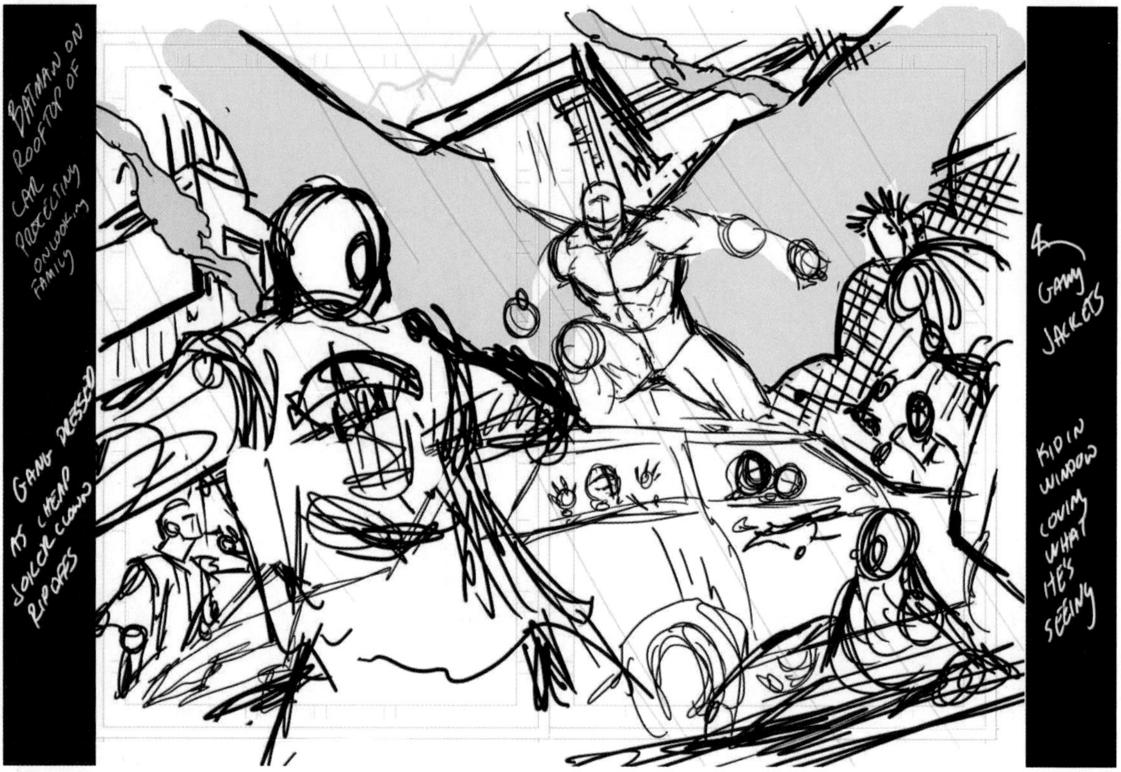
BATMAN ON ROOFTOP OF CAR PROTECTING ONLOOKING FAMILY
GANG DRESSED AS CHEAP JOKER CLOWN RIPOFFS
4 GANG JACKETS
KID IN WINDOW COVING WHAT HE'S SEEING

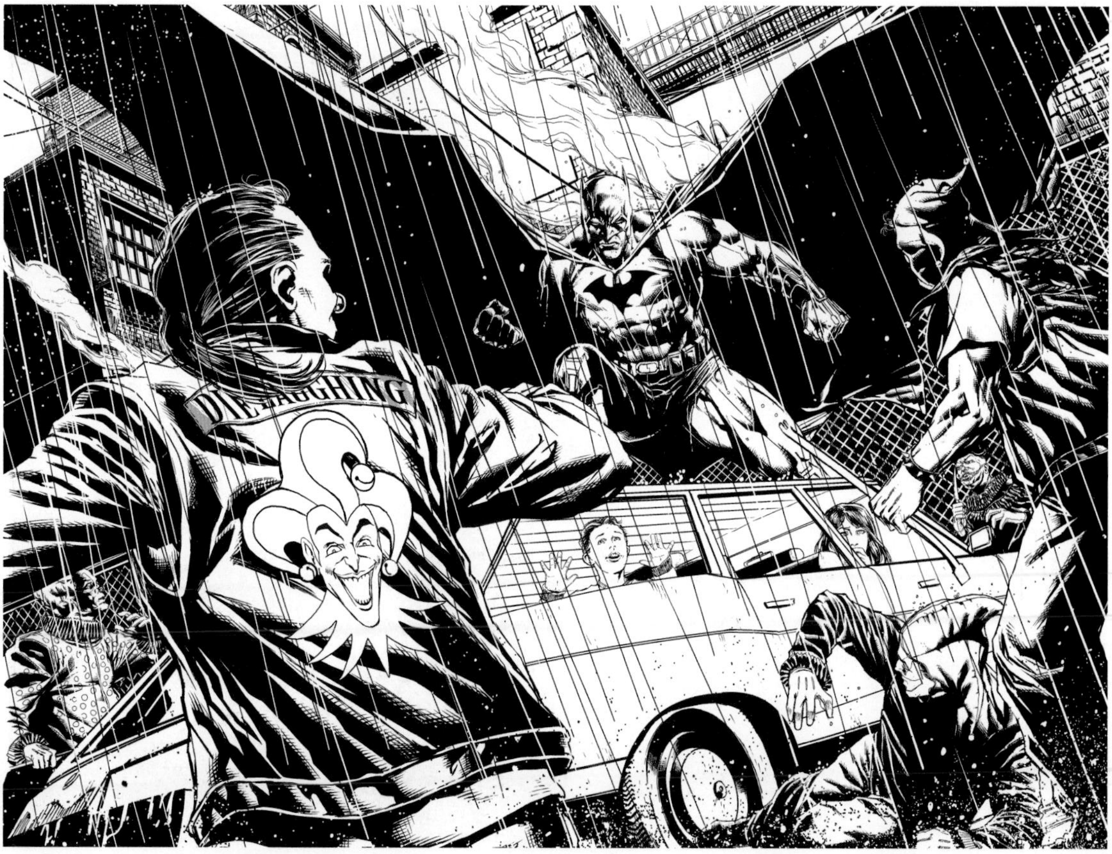
DIE LAUGHING

Joker card designs

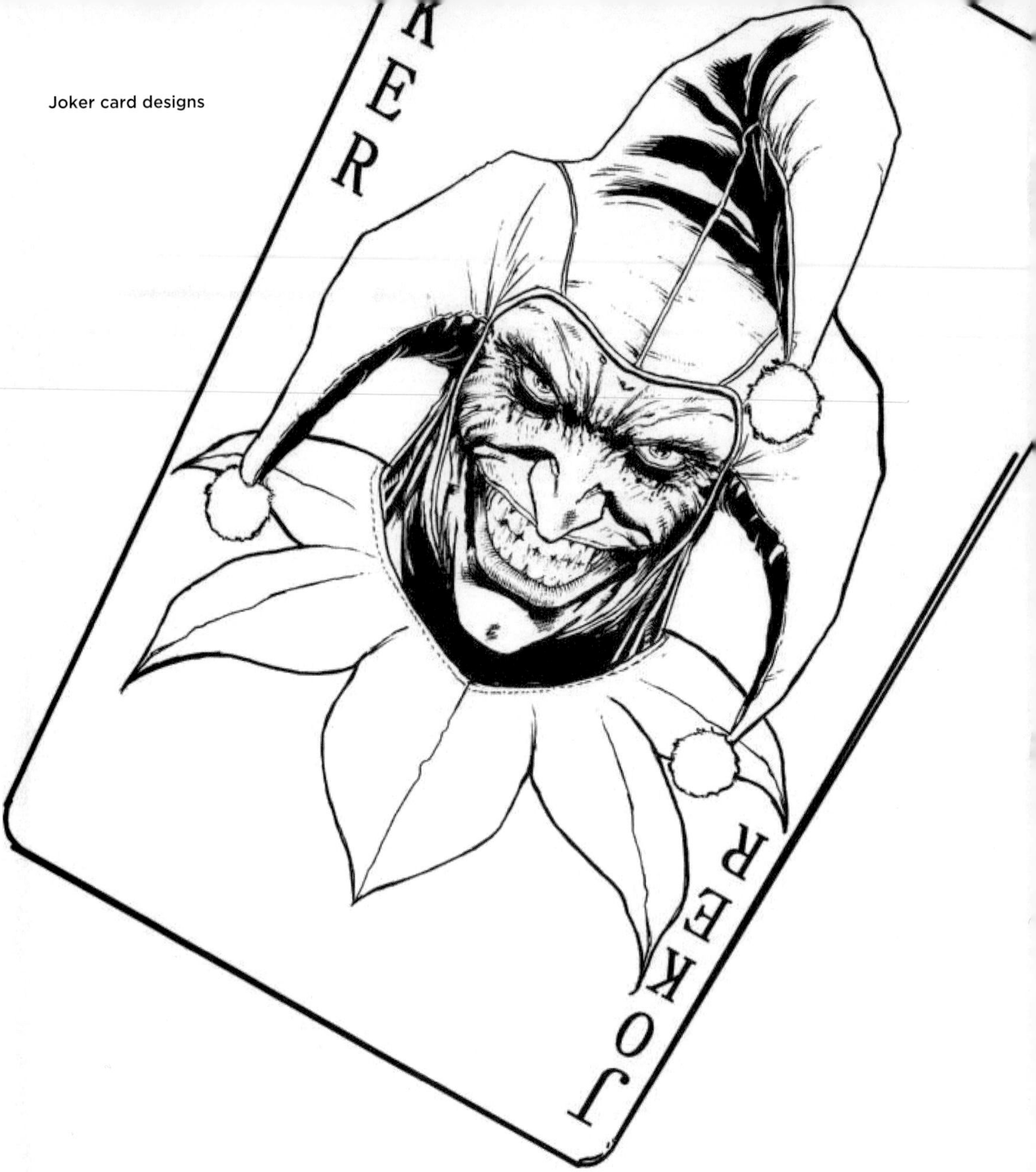
KER
JOKER

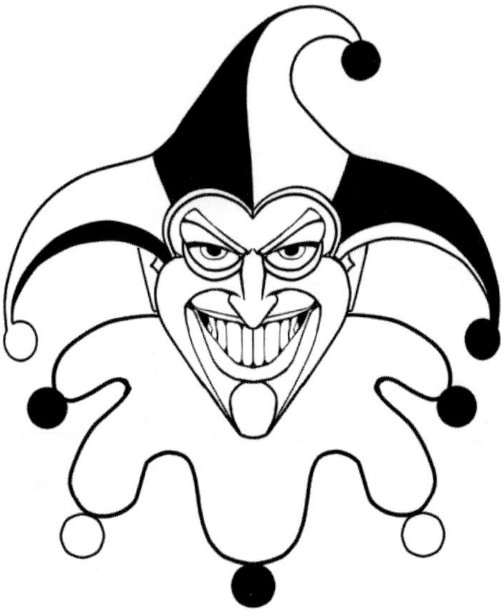